Professional Meeting Management

SIXTH EDITION

Professional Meeting Management

A Guide to Meetings, Conventions, and Events

SIXTH EDITION

EDITOR-IN-CHIEF

Glen C. Ramsborg, PhD, CMP
Professor (Retired)
Kendall College

CO-EXECUTIVE EDITORS

Carol Krugman, MEd, CMP, CMM
Chair & Assistant Professor
Department of Hospitality, Tourism, & Events Management
Metropolitan State University of Denver

Cynthia Vannucci, PhD, CHME, CHSP, CMP, CHE
Professor & Internship Coordinator
Department of Hospitality, Tourism, & Events Management
Metropolitan State University of Denver

EDITORS

Amanda K. Cecil, PhD, CMP
Associate Professor & Program Director
Department of Tourism, Conventions, & Event Management
Indiana University (IUPUI)

Brian L. Miller, EdD
Associate Professor
Department of Hotel, Restaurant, & Institutional Management
University of Delaware

B. J. Reed, EdD, CMP
Professor, Department of Media Studies
Director, Teaching & Learning Center
University of Wisconsin—Platteville

Janet E. Sperstad, CMP
Program Director
Meeting & Event Management
Madison College

B2 BOOKS

AN AGATE IMPRINT
CHICAGO

The Convention Industry Council (CIC) has granted permission to use the Accepted Practices Exchange (APEX) Industry Glossary. Throughout the text, the APEX Key Words are used unless a definition does not exist for the word. Additionally, other references to the contribution of CIC and APEX are noted throughout. All have been used with permission.

Every effort has been made to make attribution to previous contributors and materials in this book. PCMA will be pleased to rectify any omission to the source of information contained within this publication in future editions.

Professional Meeting Management

First Agate B2 printing, January 2015
978-1-93284-197-8 (paperback)
978-1-57284-751-4 (ebook)

Printed in the United States of America
15 16 17 18 19 10 9 8 7 6 5 4 3 2 1

B2 Books is an imprint of Agate Publishing. Agate books are available in bulk at discount prices. For more information, go to agatepublishing.com.

Brief Table of Contents

Table of Contents

List of Figures

Foreword

The Professional Convention Management Association (PCMA) is known as an industry leader committed to delivering superior and innovative education. Educating those in the profession has been the foundation of PCMA since the association's inception in 1957. At the core of our education is *Professional Meeting Management*, a recognized resource for meetings professionals and the academic community for 30 years.

Professional Meeting Management serves as a resource for meeting professionals at all levels: the hospitality student preparing a class paper; the veteran meeting professional designing the next room set or developing the marketing strategy for an event; the convention services manager reviewing an industry standard; and the university or college faculty member preparing curriculum for students. Each of these groups will continue to benefit from the body of knowledge contained in this publication.

Albert Einstein once said, "Learning is not a product of schooling, but the lifelong attempt to acquire it" (Gurteen, frame 1). Lifelong learning is key to staying competitive in our ever-changing world, and that is no different in our industry. While other publications have come and gone, *Professional Meeting Management* has stood the test of time, and is a trusted resource, addressing many of the diverse needs of meeting professionals.

The development of the sixth edition of *Professional Meeting Management* has been an evolution over the past few years. I would like to recognize all of the current and previous contributors and editors, all of whom are experts in the industry. This book would not be possible without their support of PCMA. We have consulted with faculty and professionals alike to develop a new resource that we feel is a current reflection of the industry today.

The world is more digital in nature; nonetheless our research indicates that there remains a significant group interested in studying *Professional Meeting Management* in its traditional format—a printed textbook. As we continue to evolve, we expect this body of knowledge to evolve as well and be available in alternate mediums. Stay up to date with the vast array of resources from PCMA through its website and PCMA365.

I would also like to recognize the PCMA Education Foundation, which supports PCMA through fundraising and grant-giving. Its focus is on education and research that support and encourage the highest levels of professionalism in the meeting industry. As part of the Foundation's mission and through the generosity of its donors, it has helped fund the development and publication of the sixth edition.

PCMA is, and will always be, here to support you throughout your career, and we know this latest edition will become the essential resource for all in the meetings profession.

Deborah Sexton
President & Chief Executive Officer
Professional Convention Management Association
Chicago, Illinois

Preface

When I was writing my dissertation, I stumbled upon a book, *How to Plan a Convention*, published in 1925 and written by P. G. B. Morriss, which states that conventions represent "the most effective means of disseminating information on the progress of any particular industry or field of endeavor" (p. 5). Morriss may have been the first to appreciate the importance of convention management, which he said "has become recognized as a very definite profession, one requiring both natural skill and ability acquired by experience" (p. 35).

In his book, he lists the following as being among the reasons for holding a meeting or convention:

- to impart or exchange business information,
- to foster personal acquaintanceships within an organization, and
- to contribute new ideas for the future betterment of an industry.

He also notes that meetings must be organized around purposes, goals, objectives, and outcomes in order to provide productive interpersonal interactions (Morriss, 1925; Ramsborg & Tinnish, 2008, p. 42).

These characterizations of meetings and conventions should sound familiar: they are not all that different from what industry professionals hope to achieve with today's events. But even though the benefits of conventions have remained consistent over the past century, the ways meeting professionals go about achieving them today are hugely varied.

Thirty years have passed since the Professional Convention Management Association (PCMA) published the first edition of *Professional Meeting Management*. Each edition reflects changes seen in the industry. The sixth edition (commonly referred to as *PMM6*) represents a major change in that it is targeted toward undergraduate and certificate education in the field of meeting management. It also serves novice meeting professionals requiring the basics in preparation to achieve the Certified Meeting Professional (CMP) designation.

The format of *PMM6* is based on curriculum development work of the PCMA Faculty Task Force. Based on faculty feedback after the release of PMM5, this edition is designed to fit into the 16-week-semester curriculum with the chapter organization following the logical planning of a meeting.

Also new with this edition is the inclusion of a sustainability-focused, i.e., environmental, social, or economic, perspective in each chapter. An example of some aspect of sustainability is provided for the purpose of stimulating further discussion in the classroom or exploration in a written assignment or class project.

As the industry has continued to grow, so has *PMM6*. This is my second time serving as the lead editor for this publication, and much has changed in the industry, even since my previous involvement. Greater dependence was placed on the authors, reviewers, editors, and other subject matter experts to ensure the content is completely up-to-date. In this edition, we chose to focus on specific changes in the industry, including how project-management basics are blended with meeting management; how marketing has taken on an even greater significance in the branding of a meeting and its host organization; and the impact technology has on improving the meeting experience—before, during, and after.

It is our hope that the learner will come away from reading and studying this book with a sense that meeting professionals are key contributors in designing and creating a memorable meeting experience. Additionally, we hope that they will apply the principles presented to make a difference in networking, building enthusiasm, and inspiring creativity. Logistics management is the foundation; the focus in *PMM6* is on learning about the full meeting or event experience.

For the love of learning,

Glen C. Ramsborg, PhD, CMP
Editor-in-Chief
Professor (retired)
Kendall College
President
Ramsborg Group Ltd.

"It is essential for educators to love what they are teaching . . . and to love their students even more!"—Sandra Casey Buford, PhD

What's New in *PMM6*?

The PCMA Faculty Task Force and faculty members provided invaluable input for the sixth edition of *Professional Meeting Management.* In addition, the PCMA Educational Foundation funded a research project to help in the development of the content and learning elements of this edition. This new edition incorporates many of the suggestions that came out of this research. It is our hope that the new content and chapter design will guide faculty, students, and meeting professionals in a new and fresh approach.

PMM6 is designed for students in undergraduate and certificate programs and meeting professionals preparing for the CMP Certification Examination. The concepts are presented in such a manner that students can fully understand and assimilate the current knowledge. Each chapter contains common elements in an endeavor to provide students and faculty with a consistent approach to the body of knowledge.

Retained Features

Authorship The authors are recognized leaders in the industry and were selected based on their expertise in the subject matter.

Learner Outcomes Each chapter opens with a list of measureable outcomes for the knowledge and skills that should be attained at the completion of reading and studying the chapter.

Key Words Understanding the industry vocabulary is an important part of learning. The Key Words are bolded in each chapter and listed at the end of the chapter.

Summary Each chapter ends with a brief summary that revisits the most salient points.

Discussion Questions Discussion questions allow the student to apply the information presented in the chapter by providing a scenario or posing a problem and asking for possible solutions.

Glossary The standard glossary for the industry was created by the Accepted Practices Exchange (APEX) initiative sponsored by the Convention Industry Council (CIC). The words listed in italics can be found in the online "APEX Industry Glossary" at http://glossary.conventionindustry.org. Definitions for key words used in the text that are not listed in the "APEX Industry Glossary" are found in the glossary at the end of the book.

References A compilation of references cited in the chapters is found at the end of the book.

New Features to the Sixth Edition

The sixth edition of *PMM* has been rewritten, consolidating a 47-chapter book into a resource ideally suited for a 16-week semester. Thus, significant detail in the form of checklists and other learning resources have been moved to the Instructor Resource Center (IRC) that accompanies adoption of *PMM6*. To access this material, go to http://pmmirc.com.

CMP International Standards *PMM6* is designed to introduce students to the most critical concepts in the world of professional meeting management—it was not developed to address every standard exhaustively. The goal of *PMM6* is to provide instructors with rich content and ample opportunities to teach and build discussion about the standards met in this book in their own classrooms. This edition of *PMM6* is the first student and meeting professionals textbook to align with the new Certified Meeting Professional (CMP) International Standards (CMP-IS) as defined by the CIC. The Standards include 10 domains, 33 skills, and 105 subskills. Each chapter title page identifies the domains, skills, and subskills covered in the chapter. Additionally, this edition includes an overall summary of the CMP-IS contained in *PMM6* so students, faculty, and meeting professionals can develop a clear understanding of the content related to each covered skill and subskill (see Appendix 5, p. 330).

Sustainability in Practice Meetings and events are gatherings of people, many of whom have a desire to give back to society. Likewise, there is a continuing effort by meeting professionals to decrease the carbon imprint left by their meetings. Therefore, we have dedicated a section in each chapter of *PMM6* to corporate social responsibility (CSR) and its application to emphasize its importance.

Key Points These boxes highlight key concepts or terms, allowing students to quickly and easily review content.

Key Questions Meeting professionals ask a lot of questions as a means of learning about a site and venue and to help make decisions. Key Questions boxes provide important questions to ask that are relevant to the chapter content; they are designed to stimulate thought and class discussion as well as to provide guidance on collecting information for decision-making.

Professional Dilemmas Each chapter features a scenario posing a question or situation that requires critical thinking and reflective discussion or writing to resolve the issue. The scenarios put students in a professional quandary, which may have legal or ethical components, and asks them how they would react or respond.

Graphics and photographs Based on faculty research, we have significantly increased the number of figures to visually explain the concepts and enhance learning.

Chapter-by-Chapter Changes

Chapter 1—Overview of Meetings Profession *PMM6* begins with a completely rewritten overview of the current state of the meetings industry. Focus is given to the industry's relationship with all meeting stakeholders.

Chapter 2—Strategic Meetings: Aligning with the Organization Based on the concept of strategic planning, this chapter focuses on aligning strategic meeting design with the priorities of the host organization.

Chapter 3—Blending Project and Meeting Management New to this edition, this chapter provides an overview of project management and the integration and blending of the process with meeting management.

Chapter 4—Designing the Meeting Experience Content from several chapters of the previous edition has been distilled and synthesized into this accessible summation of the many facets essential to developing the meeting experience. Appendices to this chapter provide greater detail and specifications, uses, strengths, and limitations for the various meeting formats, structures, and room sets that are visually presented the chapter.

Chapter 5—Budgeting Basics for Meeting Professionals The level of detail on budgeting has been significantly reduced since research indicates that many programs in meeting management require supplementary coursework in accounting.

Chapter 6—Site and Venue Selection An overview of the site and venue selection process presents various types of facilities and key considerations for selecting a venue.

Chapter 7—Risk Management: Meeting Safety and Security Risk-management coverage now focuses on the safety and security of those attending a meeting or event as opposed to the development of a risk-management plan.

Chapter 8—Negotiations, Contracts, and Liability Readers will receive an overview of five chapters from the previous edition in this chapter. It is a synthesis of salient components of the process that culminates with a signed contract.

Chapter 9—Marketing the Meeting Contemporary technologies have changed the way that meeting professionals market events. Coverage of marketing principles has been updated to address the latest trends in the industry and the world around us.

Chapter 10—Registration and Housing Two parts make up this chapter, highlighting the elements and commonalities of registration and housing. Special focus is given to the care of potential attendees before, during, and after the meeting/event.

Chapter 11—Exhibitions and the Role of Face-to-Face Marketing Material on the planning and function of the exhibition has changed very little from the previous edition. Photos of the various booth/stand types provide visualization of the layout of an exhibit hall.

Chapter 12—Bring Meetings to Life: Event Technology As technology develops, meeting professionals have more and more tools available to engage attendees. The first part of this chapter discusses the array of technological applications meeting professionals can use to design the meeting experience. New technologies from social media to meeting attendee portals to gamification are covered. The second part of the chapter discusses the latest developments to the traditional video, audio, and lighting equipment that bring meetings to life.

Chapter 13—Food and Beverage Fundamentals Food and beverage continue to play a key role in meeting success. This chapter addresses essential considerations related to providing and managing food and beverage at meetings.

Chapter 14—Onsite Management Bringing together all of the elements of arriving to and preparing the site, this chapter covers the essential areas of efficient and effective meeting management, as well as the required meetings with staff, vendors, and volunteers.

Chapter 15—Post-Meeting Follow-Up This chapter is divided into two parts—closing the meeting after the attendees have departed and the evaluation process to obtain pertinent information that becomes part of the needs assessment described in Chapter 4. The use of the information garnered is valuable in terms of improving future meetings/events.

Chapter 16—Career Building in the Meetings Profession New to this edition is a chapter that focuses on ethical behaviors for students and individuals entering the meetings profession. The author proposes 10 areas of awareness that will continue to be issues in the next five years. The chapter also gives the new professional suggestions and tools to learn how to become integrated into the industry.

Contributors

AUTHORS

MaryAnne P. Bobrow, CAE, CMP, CMM, CHE
President
Bobrow Associates, Inc.

Mary E. Boone, MA
President
Boone Associates

Amanda K. Cecil, PhD, CMP
Associate Professor & Program Director
Department of Tourism, Conventions, & Event Management
Indiana University (IUPUI)

Michael J. Dzick, CQIA, CMQ/OE
Conference Manager
American Society for Quality

Rebecca Ferguson
Content Marketer

Tyra Hilliard, PhD, JD, CMP
Speaker, Writer, Multipreneur
Hilliard Associates

Tricia L. Mallett
Event Services Manager
Association of Equipment Manufacturers

Anthony Miller
Chief Marketing Officer
Lanyon

Brian L. Miller, EdD
Associate Professor
Department of Hotel, Restaurant, & Institutional Management
University of Delaware

Godwin-Charles A. Ogbeide, PhD, MBA
Associate Professor
Hospitality Innovation Management
University of Arkansas

Erin R. Peschel, CMP
Events & Project Manager
Hospitality Democracy

Ańdrea S. Peterson, MTA, CMP
Visiting Professor
Department of Hospitality, Tourism, & Events
Metropolitan State University of Denver

Owner & President
ASAP Meetings & Events

Deborah R. Popely
Assistant Professor
School of Hospitality Management
Kendall College

Executive Director
Green Events Source

B. J. Reed, EdD, CMP
Professor, Media Studies
Director, Teaching & Learning Center
University of Wisconsin— Platteville

Lynn R. Reed, MSPM
Project Management Consultant
L. R. Reed & Associates

Richard D. Reid
Vice President, Digital Services
Freeman

Susan A. Sabatke, CMP
Meetings Director
International Dairy-Deli-Bakery Association

Julia W. Smith, CEM, CTA
Senior Vice President, National Sales
Global Experience Specialists (GES)

Rich Tate
Director of Marketing & Creative
Alford Media Services, Inc.

Susan M. Tinnish, PhD
Dean, School of Hospitality Management
Kendall College

Glen C. Ramsborg, PhD, CMP
Professor *(retired)*
Kendall College

President
Ramsborg Group Ltd.

Angela Weller
Event Services Manager
Association of Equipment Manufacturers

Darlene W. Somers, CMP
Senior Meetings Manager
Association Management Center

CONTRIBUTING AUTHORS

Sheila Bartle, PhD
Professor *(retired)*
Kendall College

Donnell G. Bayot, MEd, CPCE, CHE, CFBE
Director of Academic Affairs
The International School of Hospitality

Mary Catherine Sexton, Esq.
Vice President, Human Resources
Evolution Hospitality

Kimberly S. Severt, PhD
Associate Professor
Department of Human Nutrition & Hospitality Management
University of Alabama

Amanda S. Rushing, CMP, Aff. M. ASCE
Director, Conference & Meeting Services
American Society of Civil Engineers

Linda M. Robson, PhD
Assistant Professor
School of Hospitality Management
Endicott College

Patti J. Shock, CPCE, CHT, CGSP
Academic Consultant
The International School of Hospitality

Premila A. Whitney, CMP, CHE
Instructor
Rosen College of Hospitality Management
University of Central Florida

BOOK REVIEWERS

Linda M. Robson, PhD
Assistant Professor
School of Hospitality Management
Endicott College

Beverly A. Bryant, EdD
Professor & Program Director
Hospitality & Tourism Administration
North Carolina Central University

Sandra Casey Buford, PhD
President
Color Media Group
Color MagazineUSA

CHAPTER REVIEWERS

Glenn Baron, MEd
Faculty, Hotel & Restaurant Management
Pima Community College

Sally Bedwell, CMP
Meeting Manager, Meeting & Tradeshows
Produce Marketing Association

Andrew Belton, BA Hons.
Finance Subject Lead, Events, Sport, & Entertainment Faculty
Glion Institute of Higher Education
Switzerland

Vicky Betzig, CMP
Manager, Client Services
Anaheim/Orange County Visitor & Convention Bureau

Sandy Biback, CMP CMM
Instructor
George Brown College
Consultant
Imagination+Meeting Planners Inc.
Canada

Marlene Blas, MTA, CMP
Freelance Meeting & Event Planner
Program Advisor & Instructor
California State University, San Marcos

Ernest Boger, DMgt, CHA, CHE, FMP, MIH
Associate Professor
Chairman, Department of Hospitality & Tourism Management
University of Maryland, Eastern Shore

Mary E. Boone, MA
President
Boone Associates

Sandra Casey Buford, PhD
President
Color Media Group
Color MagazineUSA

Patty Coen, CMM, MBA
Senior Consultant
Great Chicago Events

Janet M. Cooper, CMP
Director, Convention Operations
Meetings Department
Radiological Society of North America

Suzette Eaddy, CMP
Vice President, Conferences, Meetings, & Events
National Minority Supplier Development Council, Inc.

Lisa English, CMP, CMM
SMM Solutions
CWT Meetings & Events

Michael T. McQuade
Director of Sales
Washington State Convention Center

Jeff Jiang, PhD
Professor
Department of Recreation, Hospitality, & Parks Management
California State University, Chico

Joanne H. Joham, CMP, CMM
Regional Director
North America
International Congress and Convention Association

Gert Noordzy, MBA, CAPM, FAIQ
International Hotelier and Hotel Opening Specialist

Godwin-Charles A. Ogbeide, PhD, MBA
Associate Professor
Hospitality Innovation Management
University of Arkansas

Linda M. Robson, PhD
Assistant Professor
School of Hospitality Management
Endicott College

Rebecca Hochradel, PhD, RD
Chair & Associate Professor
Division of Management, Marketing, & Business Administration
Delta State University

Lauren Locke Maguire, MEd
Professor
Hospitality Management
Bunker Hill Community College

Matthew L. Marcial, CMP, DES
Senior Director, Events
Meeting Professionals International

John P. Potterton, MA
University Operations Manager
FMC Technologies, Inc.

Swathi Ravichandran, MBA, PhD
Associate Professor & Program Director
Hospitality Management
Kent State University

Amanda S. Rushing, CMP, Aff. M. ASCE
Director, Conference & Meeting Services
American Society of Civil Engineers

Milena Santoro, CMM, CMP, PIDP
President & CEO
MS Productions Inc.
Canada

Leslie Gail Scamacca, MBA, PhD, CMP
Assistant Professor
LaGuardia Community College

Kimberly S. Severt, PhD
Associate Professor
Department of Human Nutrition & Hospitality Management
University of Alabama

Wayne W. Smith, PhD
Associate Professor
Department of Hospitality & Tourism Management
School of Business
College of Charleston

Victoria J. Stephens, CMP
Green Meetings & Events Consultant

Erinn D. Tucker, PhD, MBA, MS
Assistant Professor
School of Hospitality Administration
Boston University

PCMA STAFF

A special thanks to the PCMA staff for their chapter reviews for alignment and inter-rater reliability with the CMP-IS.

Patrick Crosson, CMP
Events Manager

Jody Egel, CAE, CMP
Director of Events

Thomas Foley, CAE
Senior Director, Member Services & Business Development

Dawn McEvoy, CAE, CMP
Director, Education

Alison Milgram
Senior Events Manager

Sheila Mires, CMP
Director, Member Services

Kelly Peacy, CAE, CMP
Senior Vice President, Education & Events

Dyan Westropp, CMP
Events Manager

Acknowledgments

To maintain coherency, consistency, and style, the manuscripts have gone through multiple levels of editorial review and revision. The chapters as they appear now may include content and views that differ from the original manuscripts originally submitted by the author(s).

Any major project of this nature requires the talents and efforts of a community of professionals to bring it to print. As Editor-in-Chief, I am greatly indebted to each individual who wrote, reviewed, rewrote, and/or edited to produce a manuscript for each topic based on the limited number of words. It is a rare opportunity and a privilege to have been able to serve in this capacity for both the fifth and sixth editions of *Professional Meeting Management*.

Thank you is extended to Drs. Beverly Bryant, Sandra Casey Buford, and Linda Robson who read the manuscripts prior to publication. They provided feedback on the chapters and their work established the inter-rater reliability that determined which CMP-IS skills and subskills are indicated at the start of every chapter.

A special thanks to my colleagues and special group of educators and subject matter experts on the Editorial Team for the contribution to scholarship, insight, and application evident in this edition. Dr. B. J. Reed's knowledge and copy editing skills have been instrumental in bringing this work to publication.

My thanks to Michael McQuade and his staff at the Washington State Convention Center for providing so many of the photographs and to many other individuals who, on short notice, provided photographs to enhance the visual component of each chapter. I am appreciative to the staff at Starbucks, Deer Park, Illinois, for their endless hours of gracious hospitality.

I am deeply indebted to Dr. Susan Tinnish, my colleague and longtime collaborator, for her friendship and wise counsel, which strengthened the content of this edition.

Extra special appreciation goes to David Schlesinger, Editorial Development Manager, who provided oversight of this project. I am so grateful for his contribution, vision, patience, and guidance along with his ability to work with the splendid team of Morgan Krehbiel, Amanda Wilson, Rachel Hinton, Justin Lirot, and Elizabeth Crozier. The leadership team of Agate Publishing provided expert oversight; many thanks to Doug Seibold, Kate DeVivo, and Sarah Wood.

I would be remiss if I did not acknowledge PCMA President & Chief Executive Officer, Deborah Sexton, who believed in me to bring this publication to the marketplace in less than nine months. Special gratitude goes to Thomas Foley, Senior Director of Member Services & Business Development for consistency in communication, encouragement, and support; as well as Sioban Amezcua, Manager, Educational Products and Resources, for her administrative support. Appreciation is extended to PCMA staff members who willingly gave of their time and expertise toward completing this project.

Words cannot fully express my immense thankfulness to my wife, Barbara. With much patience she has endured the many days and hours of work on this project within a very short period of time, as well as my perpetually distracted mind even when not working on this project; and always did so with kindness, grace, and encouragement.

With appreciation and admiration,

Glen C. Ramsborg

About the Editorial Team

Amanda K. Cecil

Dr. Cecil began her academic career in 2002 on the Indiana University's Tourism, Convention, and Event Management faculty. As associate professor, she teaches courses in event management and international tourism. Her research interest involves linking business travel and tourism trends to the convention/meeting market. Additionally, Dr. Cecil has scholarly interests in the development of competency-based curriculum models and the impact of experiential learning. She serves as associate editor for the *Journal of Convention & Event Tourism*. Dr. Cecil has consulting experience in instructional design for educational programs in customer service, business travel management, strategic meeting management, sports travel management, and event management.

Her industry involvement includes 2007–2008 President of the Indiana Chapter of Meeting Professionals International (MPI), the Chair of the 2009–2010 MPI Body of Knowledge Task Force, and the 2008 Chair of the Professional Convention Management Association's (PCMA) Research Task Force. Dr. Cecil was recently designated as a 2012 PCMA Foundation Educator Honoree, and received the 2012 "Member of the Year" RISE Award from MPI, 2011 Indiana Trustees' Teaching Award, 2010 MPI Chairwoman's Award, 2010 MPI Indiana Chapter President's Award, and 2006 PCMA Educator of the Year award. She was named to the Indiana Chapter of MPI's Hall of Fame in 2008.

Carol Krugman

Carol Krugman's career in the global meeting and events industry spans over 30 years. Prior to transitioning into academia, she worked as a corporate marketing manager and an association executive, and was owner/manager of an international meeting-management company. She has lived in France, Mexico, and Brazil and is fluent in French, Spanish, and Portuguese, with a working knowledge of Italian. As a full-time academician since 2009, Ms. Krugman has remained active and involved in the professional associations of the meeting industry. She currently serves on the Education Committee of the Professional Convention Management Association (PCMA) and the Board of Directors of the Convention Industry Council's Certified Meeting Professional (CMP) program, and is Chair of the Meeting Professionals International

(MPI) Student Task Force. A recipient of the MPI Chairwoman's Award in 2010 and PCMA's 2013 Educator of the Year award, her publications include *Global Meetings and Exhibitions*, published by John Wiley & Sons, which is available in English and Mandarin Chinese.

Brian L. Miller

Dr. Miller is an associate professor in the Department of Hotel, Restaurant, and Institutional Management at the University of Delaware. He holds a doctorate degree in Curriculum Development from the University of Massachusetts–Amherst, where his dissertation was "Technology and Learning in the Undergraduate Classroom." His published research includes articles on the use of technology to increase student learning and satisfaction, students' perceptions of the use of simulations in the classroom, building e-loyalty with lodging brand websites, and the effects of tipping on employee organizational and occupational commitment. Dr. Miller's research has been presented at academic and industry conferences in the United States, Europe, the Caribbean, and the Middle East. He has served as the Chair of the Core Competencies Task Force for PCMA. Dr. Miller received PCMA's Educator of the Year award in 2005.

Glen C. Ramsborg

Dr. Ramsborg is president of the Ramsborg Group, Ltd., and retired as a professor in the School of Hospitality Management at Kendall College in Chicago. He holds a doctorate degree from the University of Minnesota in Educational Policy and Administration. He was formerly Senior Director of Education at the Professional Convention Management Association (PCMA) and has been a member for 30 years. He served as lead editor of *Art of the Show*, fourth edition, published by the International Association of Exhibitions and Events™, and executive editor of PCMA's *Professional Meeting Management*, fifth edition. Dr. Ramsborg was a member of the Convention Industry Council's Certified Meeting Professional (CMP) Board of Directors and served as Vice Chair in 2012. He was the 2011 Education Honoree at PCMA Education Foundation Dinner Celebrating Professional Achievement and received the PCMA Educator of the Year award in 2002. Dr. Ramsborg is a certified registered nurse anesthetist and a retired colonel from the United States Air Force.

B. J. Reed

Dr. Reed has held various positions in the meetings industry. She spent several years as an association meeting planner, then moved to the supply side as the executive director for a convention and visitors bureau. Five years later, she moved back to the meeting management arena as an independent planner. Through all of these positions, Dr. Reed was intent on teaching in the industry and completed four degrees in related fields. She joined PCMA in 1987, earned her CMP in 1991, and was recognized as Educator of the Year in 2010 by PCMA. She began teaching full time in 1997. Dr. Reed has self-published

Introduction to Volunteerism, Fundraising, and Grants, and has authored several chapters in texts on meeting management. She served as copy editor for *Professional Meeting Management*, fifth edition; *Art of the Show*, fourth edition; and *Convention Industry Manual*, ninth edition.

Janet E. Sperstad

The professional history of Janet Sperstad reflects her lifelong vocation: driving excellence in meeting and event management and education. She has dedicated her career to defining the competencies and career pathways that articulate meeting planning as a design discipline—requiring skills in the social sciences, executive leadership, and cognitive sciences. In 2002, she founded the Meeting and Event Management associate degree program at Madison College in Madison, Wisconsin. Ms. Sperstad's contributions are global in scope and rooted in over 25 years as a meeting professional and executive leader in the corporate and non-profit sectors, which include high-profile leadership roles that are shaping how the meeting industry defines itself and how competencies impact education and standards development at every institutional level: private sector, academic, national, government, and global. She is currently a member of the Convention Industry Council Certified Meeting Professional (CMP) Board of Directors. Ms. Sperstad was the PCMA Professional Achievement Educator Honoree for 2014 and received the 2007–2008 International Planner of the Year from Meeting Professionals International (MPI). She has been recognized for her excellence in teaching with the Distinguished Teacher of the Year and numerous other awards from Madison College.

Cynthia Vannucci

Dr. Vannucci, a native of Cleveland, Ohio, is a graduate of the University of Nevada–Las Vegas (UNLV) in the Hotel Administration program. With the combined responsibilities of a demanding career in hotel sales and marketing as well as a young family, she followed the encouragement of her UNLV professors to receive her PhD at Penn State with research in the discipline of meeting and events. For the past 15 years, Dr. Vannucci has been at the Metropolitan State University of Denver in the Hospitality, Tourism, and Events Department. Dr. Vannucci holds the Certified Meeting Professional (CMP), Certified Hospitality Educator (CHE), Certified Hospitality Sales Professional (CHSP), and Certified Hospitality Marketing Executive (CHME) designations. She was honored as Educator of the Year in 2008 by PCMA. She received the 2010–2011 Excellence in Teaching Award from MSU Denver, School of Professional Studies; the Meetings Industry Council Leadership Award in 2012; and PCMA's Professional Achievement Award in 2013.

1

Overview of Meetings Profession

B. J. Reed, EdD, CMP
Professor, Media Studies
Director, Teaching & Learning Center
University of Wisconsin–Platteville

Lynn R. Reed, MSPM
Project Management Consultant
L. R. Reed & Associates

Main Topics

- Meetings Placed in Context
- Meetings Managed by Professionals or Volunteers
- Meetings Served by Multiple Entities
- Meetings Guided by Multiple Stakeholders

Learner Outcomes

Upon the completion of this chapter, the student should be able to:

1. Differentiate between the meetings profession and the service and hospitality industries.
2. List common titles and roles associated with the planning side of the meetings profession.
3. Define the types of organizations that host meetings.
4. Describe major entities on the supply side of the meetings profession.
5. Identify multiple stakeholders for a meeting.
6. Explain the value of meetings to a specific audience (attendees), destination, state, and the U.S. economy.

CMP INTERNATIONAL STANDARDS

Domain A. Strategic Planning
Skill 1. Manage Strategic Plan for Meeting or Event
SubSkills. 1.01, 1.02, 1.03
Skill 2. Develop Sustainability Plan for Meeting or Event
SubSkills. 2.01, 2.02
Domain F. Stakeholder Management
Skill 13. Manage Stakeholder Relationships
SubSkills. 13.01, 13.03

Meetings Placed in Context

The meetings and events profession, called the "meetings profession" for simplicity in this overview, is a complex sector in most economies throughout the world. It has a long history, as people have been gathering for centuries to satisfy a common purpose (Batten, 2013), but the profession has been recognized as a significant economic contributor for mere decades.

The Convention Industry Council (CIC), with 33 member organizations connected to the meetings profession, conducted a survey in 2012 to tabulate the economic impact of meetings in the U.S. Their "2012 Economic Significance Study" provided compelling statistics that underscore the impact meetings have not only on attendees, but also on the many people and organizations that work together for meeting success. The direct contributions by the meetings industry were 1.83 million corporate and business meetings, trade shows, conventions, congresses, incentive events, and other meetings taking place in the U.S., resulting in:

- $280 billion in direct spending
- 1.78 million U.S. jobs
- a $115 billion contribution to GDP (gross domestic product)
- $28 billion in federal, state, and local tax revenue
- $66.8 billion in U.S. labor income ("2012 economic significance," 2013, para. 1).

One of the oldest professional development organizations in the meetings profession, the Professional Convention Management Association (PCMA) held its first annual meeting in 1956 ("PCMA History", 2014, para. 1). Since then, the organization has grown significantly in membership and influence. One of its events, the annual Convening Leaders, posted impressive gains: according to PCMA's "2013 Annual Report," "[i]t realized a year-over-year 9 percent increase in professional planner participation with a final attendance of 3,751 and generated over $2.3 million in gross revenues" (p. 4). This meeting is held at different destinations each year and is a coveted piece of business for a destination like Toronto or Boston (see Figure 1.1).

Realizing the economic impact of a profession or industry is significant, but to thoroughly understand and define the meetings profession, a context is necessary.

FIGURE 1.1 A Destination Welcome This sign welcomed the Professional Convention Management Association to the John B. Hynes Veterans Memorial Convention Center, Boston, Massachusetts.

Defining the Meetings Profession

The meetings and events profession includes large gatherings of people for education, business, sports, or entertainment. Meetings may include many types of gatherings, but all meetings share a common characteristic: They are coordinated by an organization or group and bring people together for a common purpose.

The Convention Industry Council's "APEX Industry Glossary," (2011) defines a **meeting** as "An event where the primary activity of the participants is to attend educational sessions, participate in discussions, social functions, or attend other organized meetings." An **event**, on the other hand, is defined by the same source as, "An organized occasion such as a meeting, convention, exhibition, special meeting, gala dinner, etc. An event is often composed of several different yet related functions" ("APEX Industry Glossary," 2011). However, most meeting attendees do not make such complex distinctions between meetings and events—they simply consider meetings to be gatherings for professional purposes and events to be gatherings for social reasons or entertainment.

A coalition of representatives from the meetings profession formed to create the CIC in 1949 ("About CIC," 2014). That council has established the industry-specific glossary mentioned above, templates for common tools, and standards of professional behavior. The critical components of professional knowledge and skill have been articulated in a free online document known as "CMP International Standards" ("CMP International Standards," 2011). These standards are connected to each chapter of this text and guide current professional practice.

Besides tracking economic impact, the profession tracks meetings by size, duration, whether the meeting is open to the public or by invitation only, and where the meeting is held. Many meetings are quite small, with 100 or fewer attendees, while others are so large that they must occur in major metropolitan areas where an adequate number of hospitality providers are located. Generally, small meetings tend to be focused on a local audience, while major meetings, with thousands of attendees, tend to draw from a large geographic area, perhaps worldwide. Small meetings tend to happen within a typical business day, but large meetings often occur over weekends and may be a few to several days in length. These are generalizations, of course, but they demonstrate that meetings are quite varied in type, attendance numbers, duration, purpose, and location.

According to a survey conducted in 2013 by American Express Meetings and Events, "Demand for local meetings once again is expected to gain in popularity [in 2014] in all regions except Asia Pacific. Compliance, cost, and travel time all have been cited by industry experts as reasons for this trend" ("2014 Meetings Forecast," 2014, p. 21). A group was formed in 2009 known as Meetings Mean Business Coalition (MMBC) by the U.S. Travel Association. The coalition's goal is to "showcase the incredible value that business meetings, travel, and events bring to the U.S. economy" ("Meetings Mean Business: About," 2014, para. 1). Efforts like those by the MMBC and American Express strive to elevate the general public's understanding of the importance meetings have for supporting economic structures, conducting business, educating attendees, and fostering achievement of common goals.

Additional information about the economic impact of meetings around the world can be located on the website for Meeting Professionals International (MPI). There, MPI links to the Canadian Economic Impact Studies, the United Kingdom Economic Impact Studies, and additional U.S. studies.

Governments and publics worldwide are interested in the forecast for meetings and events, to plan resource allocations. An area's infrastructure, e.g., roads or docks, has a significant impact on the destination's attractiveness to visitors. Government agencies from the local to federal level look to the hospitality industry's vitality to plan infrastructure improvements. To fund these projects, government agencies and the publics they serve often look to taxes. Taxes may be levied on accommodations and other hospitality services, and through local option sales tax or a value-added tax. Of course, the businesses and publics that require the improvements want to have some influence over how tax revenues are spent. These taxes might support local museums, the arts, and attractions of interest to visitors. They might be spent on community beautification efforts and permanent outdoor signs that direct visitors to key areas throughout the destination.

The individual impact of meetings is often underreported, simply because the meetings industry is so varied and large. PCMA conducts an annual market survey through its monthly magazine *Convene*. In 2014, the 23rd Annual Meetings Market Survey reported a remarkable average of meeting value to the destinations that serve the meetings profession (see Figure 1.2).

Defining the Service Industry

A macro view of the meetings profession will start with a look at an overarching term: the *service industry*. When government agencies attempt to identify economic factors and job growth, they typically provide information about the service industry. This industry can be defined as follows:

> The service industry is a sector of the economy that primarily consists of businesses providing service, rather than tangible products. However, this industry also includes retail, transportation, distribution, food services, health care, and rentable facilities.

To put this business sector into perspective, consider the economic impact of just part of the service industry: retail and food services. According to the U.S. Department of Commerce, "the May 2013 monthly

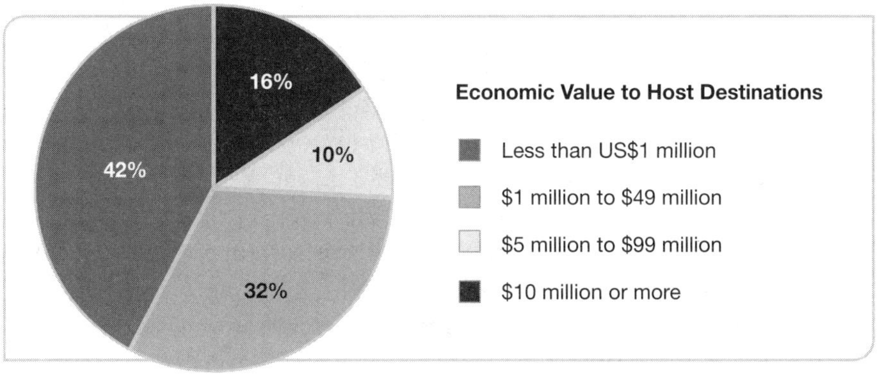

FIGURE 1.2 Economic Value of Meetings to Host Destinations PCMA conducts an annual survey of the meetings industry. In 2014, respondents reported the estimated value of their meetings to their host destinations. This is part of the picture represented by the overall economic impact of the meetings industry (Russell, 2014, p. 51. Reprinted with permission of *Convene*.).

sales for retail and food services were $444 billion" (Economics & Statistics Administration, 2014, para. 1). That was up from the previous month, as well as the same month in the previous year, but still lower than before the economic downturn in 2008.

Defining the Hospitality Industry

The hospitality industry is often considered a part of a greater service industry ("Service-Providing Industries," 2014), and statistics are gathered about the economic impact of that service for a specific economic jurisdiction (a city, county, province, state, or country).

Standard Industrial Classification (SIC) codes in the U.S. include hotels, restaurants, catering, and meeting management as part of the hospitality industry. The *hospitality industry* can be defined as follows:

> The hospitality industry, a sector in the service industry, includes businesses that provide solutions to temporary needs, such as transportation to a distant destination (ground, air, or sea), food provision, venues, and overnight lodging. The hospitality industry includes meetings or events as a sector, because they require all of the services provided by the hospitality industry in a given destination. However, the hospitality industry is typically seen as a provider of service, while the meetings profession utilizes those services.

Identifying the Meeting's Purpose

The economic impact of the meetings profession is part of the macro view. To understand the scope of meetings, a micro view is also helpful. This micro view will focus on what the meeting is for, who organizes the meeting, and who attends the meeting.

Meetings are held for many reasons. One of the more common reasons is professional development. Continuing education, for instance, is mandatory for some service providers, e.g., those in health care. Continuing education credits or units can be earned at professional development meetings. Many meetings are held for discipline-specific certification purposes, such as earning and maintaining the Certified Meeting Professional (CMP) designation, developed by the CIC. When new government regulations are issued to specific industries, meetings are held to offer guidance on compliance. Associations, government agencies, and corporations host such meetings.

When new processes are announced for a large corporation, meetings may be held. Certainly some corporations have hosted meetings that are of great interest to the public; e.g., Apple's product launch events, such as WWDC14. Trade publications and popular media outlets cover these corporate events to share critical news about products and technological advances.

Whether meetings are held to educate or celebrate, the meeting professional will determine the purpose, identify the goals, and specify the objectives for meeting success. The true value of meetings is not captured entirely through economic impact figures. To determine that value, the meeting professional will analyze data from the attendees and many other stakeholders.

Meetings Managed by Professionals or Volunteers

In the organization that hosts a meeting, such as a large multi-national corporation, several people will work for the meetings department. These employees hold various titles, such as meeting coordinator, meeting planner, or meeting manager. They may also have titles that seem unrelated to meetings, such as vice president of marketing or communications director.

key points

Common Titles for Meeting Professionals

- Meeting planner
- Meeting manager
- Meeting coordinator

Regardless of title, their tasks are to handle all arrangements for the meeting—from sending out a **request for proposal** (**RFP**) to selecting menus. Often, though certainly not always, meeting professionals and coordinators have a meeting manager as a supervisor, who sets policy and oversees stakeholder relations. In some organizations, a project manager may also be involved in managing meetings.

Key Positions for Hire

Some organizations contract with another party to manage logistics for their meeting. In this case, the person who plans the meeting may be called an **independent planner** or a third-party contractor.

Outside the U.S., independent planners are often known as **professional congress organizers** (**PCOs**). When an independent planner is tied to a destination in the U.S., the organization is called a **destination management company** (**DMC**). Both PCOs and DMCs are found in large metropolitan areas where meetings are a significant part of the area's hospitality industry. Las Vegas, for instance, has numerous DMCs, while the convention bureau in Paris lists five PCOs for that area. Typically, DMCs and PCOs are corporations with several employees.

The term DMC is often confused with the term **destination marketing organization** (**DMO**), but Figure 1.3 shows how different these organizations are. Some of these organizations call themselves conven-

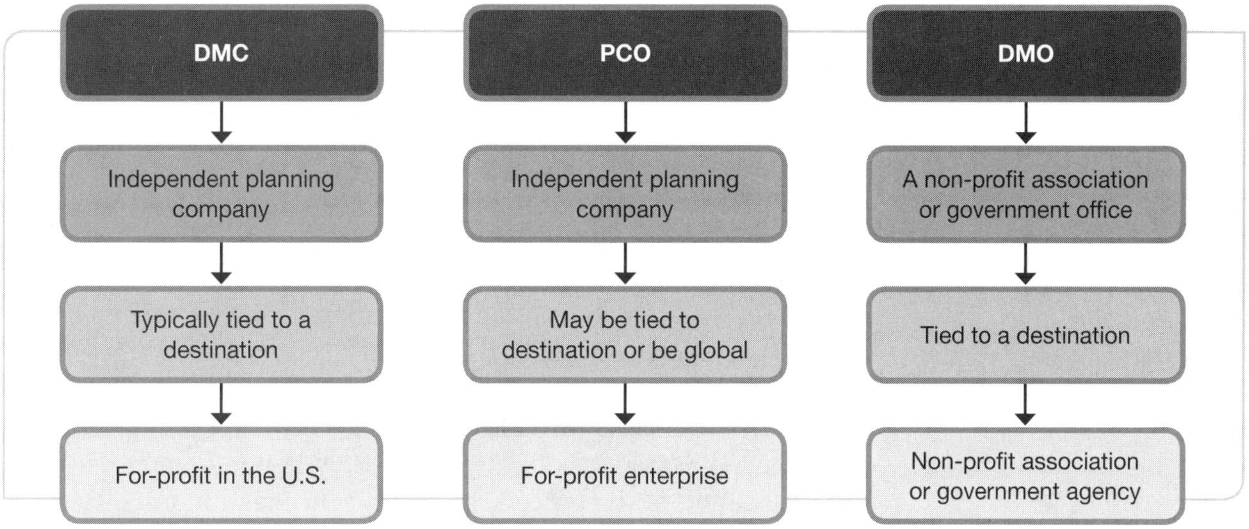

FIGURE 1.3 Understanding DMC, PCO, and DMO The meetings industry has multiple acronyms and terms unique to the industry. To help avoid confusion with these acronyms, this chart shows the key differences between destination management companies, professional congress organizers, and destination marketing organizations.

tion and visitors bureaus (CVBs) instead of DMOs. Large metropolitan areas, counties, or regions that collaborate across county lines usually share one DMO or CVB and it is commonly a non-profit association (or a non-governmental organization [NGO]) that provides marketing and public relations services for the destination's hospitality industry.

Meeting professionals, from volunteers to those who work for DMCs and PCOs, comprise the planning side of the meetings industry. They share one element: Their main interest is a successful meeting from the perspective of the host organization (also known as the "meeting owners"). To accomplish this, they work closely with suppliers. Three types of organizations host meetings that provide the most substantial economic impact for destinations worldwide: associations, corporations, and government agencies.

key points

Most Common Meeting Hosts (or "Owners")

- Associations
- Corporations
- Government agencies

Associations

Associations typically use professional meeting organizers to conduct their meetings and events. However, some associations also utilize the services of volunteers. The structure of associations varies by country across the world. In a 2014 survey of *Convene* readers, PCMA reported that 49 percent of association professionals worked for international associations, while 39 percent worked for national associations (Russell, 2014a, p. 46).

Most associations follow the laws of their state and incorporate to gain federal income tax exemptions on the money they collect through fundraising, grants, and services. Most associations are recognized by a classification determined by the U.S. Internal Revenue Service (IRS), known as "501(c)" associations. Within that IRS classification, more than 30 options exist, but one of the most common types of association is the 501(c)(3) (also known as "charitable organization"). While associations are considered non-profit, that does not mean their meetings are held at a loss to the organization. In fact, for many associations, their annual meeting is also their largest fundraising activity.

Since associations have members, they frequently hold meetings to conduct business and to offer services to those members, who may reside around the globe, throughout a country, or just locally. If the association is a professional trade association—representing members of a specific profession, such as dentistry or car dealerships—those members benefit from networking, training, and sharing new skills, knowledge, and ideas provided at annual meetings. In addition, incorporated U.S. associations are required by law to hold at least one annual meeting of the officers, so many hold that gathering with an annual membership meeting.

Association meetings can be very large and tend to be larger than meetings held by corporations. While 15 percent of association professionals responding to the annual survey by PCMA said their association had fewer than 1,000 members, 20 percent of responders were in associations with 50,000 or more members (Russell, 2014, p. 46). Since a large portion of the membership will attend an annual meeting, very large organizations tend to have very large annual meetings. For example, the Society for Human Resource Management has 250,000 members worldwide. One of their meetings hosts 13,000 human resource professionals and 700 exhibitors (Society for Human Resource Management, 2014). They select large cities to host their annual conference, such as Orlando or Chicago.

Corporations

Organizations that are in business to make a profit are called "for-profit" organizations or corporations. Corporations typically maintain an in-house staff for meeting coordination and travel, but also use independent planners, travel consultants, and other third-party contractors. In some corporations, marketing and public relations professionals plan meetings. In the U.S. and many other countries, these organizations must incorporate following the laws in the country in which they do business. This sector drives the wealth of nations and company owners through the profit made by selling goods and services.

Corporations hold incentive meetings to motivate their employees, conduct product launches, and encourage productivity. They also hold meetings for stockholders, customers, and potential customers. They offer training to staff and other groups, e.g., consumers. Corporation meetings tend to be smaller than association meetings, but corporations tend to have more meetings than associations. The other distinguishing characteristic for corporate

SUSTAINABILITY *in* Practice

Sustainability as a practice is often based on a definition of "sustainable development" put forth by the World Commission on Environment and Development (WCED) in its report *Our Common Future* (1987). According to the WCED, sustainable development is defined as an effort "that meets the needs of the present without compromising the ability of future generations to meet their own needs" (p. 43). Sustainability is further defined as a focus on economic and social development, as well as environmental protection. These three pillars, often called the "triple bottom line," have served as common ground for numerous sustainable business practices (standards, certifications, and "ecolabels").

Organizations of all types are addressing issues of sustainability through a variety of mechanisms including **corporate social responsibility (CSR)** policies, procurement policies, industry-self regulation, marketing strategies, the designation of sustainability directors (or other leadership levels), the creation of alliances or organizations focused on sustainability, sustainability reports, philanthropic activities, and private–public partnerships. Meetings and events have followed suit with a focus on green meetings (environmental sustainability) and more holistic sustainable meetings. Sustainable meetings consider environmental issues like waste, energy use, and water usage; and social issues like fair trade, interruption of normal business, the creation of an environment where residents leave en masse, antagonism of the community; new security/crime threats; the use of local labor; and human trafficking. Meetings and events have both a positive (largely reported) and negative (largely ignored) impact. Meeting professionals must recognize both the positive and negative results of the industry. Only through such awareness can the industry work to mitigate the negative impacts and build upon the positive.

As organizations and the hospitality industry move toward a more sustainable future, it is natural that meeting professionals focus on sustainable meetings, a trend that has been apparent since early 2000. In response to the need for more sustainable meetings, the industry has responded with three meeting/event-specific standards: ISO 20121, the APEX/ASTM suite of standards, and the Global Reporting Initiative (GRI) and the GRI event organizer-specific guidelines. These standards offer a framework for suppliers to provide products and services that aid meeting professionals in creating more sustainable meetings. Organizations of all types are embracing these standards on the path towards sustainability.

—*Susan M. Tinnish, PhD*

meetings is that they tend to have a relatively short planning cycle, in comparison to meetings held by most associations.

Corporate meeting planners tend to be members of MPI, PCMA, or specific organizations for their business focus.

Government Agencies

From the federal government to local jurisdictions, government agencies hold meetings for staff, elected public officials, and the public. These meetings can be held to educate, to discuss political issues, or to encourage community-based giving, volunteering, and participation. Government agencies can include paid public employees and volunteers and they can oversee educational meetings, as well as city festivals. Government agencies include public schools, as well as higher education.

Government meeting professionals have their own unique association, the Society for Government Meeting Professionals (SGMP) headquartered in Alexandria, Virginia. Its annual conference attracts about 1,000 attendees and several exhibitors. The organization is dedicated to the unique needs of these meeting professionals, who are subject to government regulations that go beyond what many associations and corporations experience ("SGMP's History and Future," 2013, para. 2).

Meetings Served by Multiple Entities

Meetings are held in cities, suburbs, and in the wilderness. These locations are called **destinations** in the meetings profession. Destinations often compete for meeting business by developing long-term relations between the destination's representatives, usually staff of the DMO, and meeting professionals. When a destination responds to the RFP from the meeting professional, that destination lists all of the local properties (meeting places, hotels, etc.) that could successfully fulfill the meeting professional's needs. This response is known as a **proposal** and it may be competitive in pricing. The proposal will define facilities, amenities, and other considerations that would lead to a successful meeting at that destination. If the destination is awarded the proposal, the meeting professional still has to select which venues and other suppliers appear to satisfy the selection criteria most effectively.

Meeting Facilities

While the geographic location is called a destination, a specific facility is often called a **venue** (see Figure 1.4).

Venues may or may not have overnight accommodations. Typically, outdoor facilities have very rustic, if any, sleeping spaces. In this case, the meeting professional may anticipate that meeting attendees will supply their own, such as tents, sleeping bags, and/or campers. The Society for Creative Anachronism is an international organization for historical enthusiasts, focused on pre-17th Century Europe. One of their events held each June in Missouri, known as Lillies, hosts thousands of visitors, with hundreds of large tents, over a 10-day period.

Most meetings do occur, though, at venues that are well equipped with technology, food and beverages, and a variety of services to facilitate the meeting. When the venue does not have overnight accommodations, it is usually located adjacent to or very near hotels. The venue may be within easy walking distance or it may be miles away. When the venue and overnight accommodations are not within walking distance, the host organization, venue, or the DMO may provide transportation for meeting attendees.

Besides hotels, many other accommodations exist in the meetings profession. Yachts and cruise liners offer guest rooms, as do bed and breakfast inns, resorts, colleges, and some schools. In some cases, the unique accommodations provide part of the charm and incentive to attend the meeting. However, unique facilities also may require unique solutions to hygiene, food service, waste disposal, and electricity.

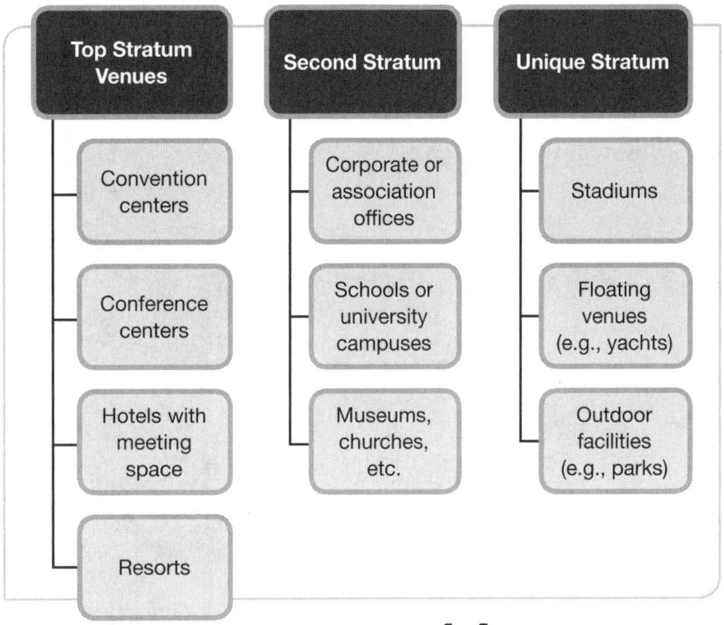

FIGURE 1.4 Meeting Facilities Many different venues and types of meeting facilities are available to meeting professionals to host meetings and events. These facilities are numerous, but some of the more common are shown in this figure and can be adapted to meet the meeting's objectives.

Other Meeting Suppliers

Besides the destination, venues, and sleeping accommodations, a meeting must also be supplied with food and beverage, transportation, and a variety of other services (see Figure 1.5, p. 12).

Food and Beverage Food and beverage (F&B) may be handled by suppliers outside the facilities where the food is served. F&B service is available from restaurants or caterers, who are able to serve food at any open facility, even outdoor venues. The venue decides which caterers are approved to serve food at that facility, but the top stratum of venues typically has its own in-house food service.

Technology Technology services, such as computer systems and projection equipment, are provided by **audiovisual (AV)** technology companies. Some of these companies can provide much more in service and equipment, but one key service is the provision of qualified technicians. When a second party provides AV services, the meeting planner must facilitate communication between that party and the facility to maximize the technology equipment and services provided for the meeting. This requires the meeting professional to have basic AV knowledge.

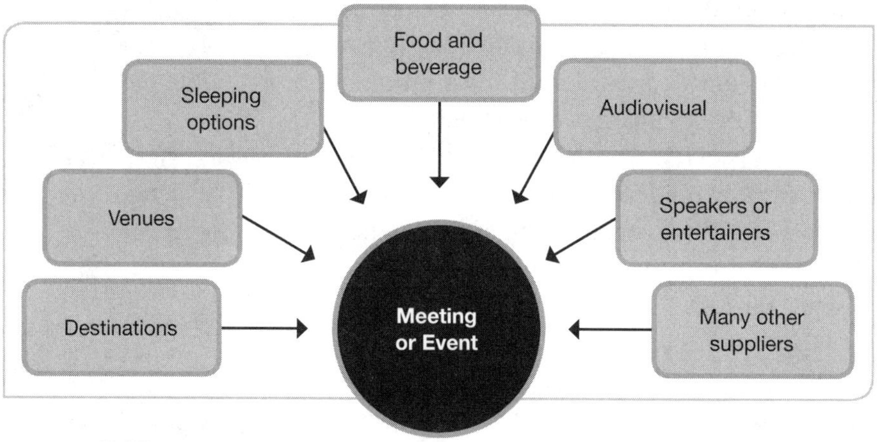

FIGURE 1.5 Meeting Suppliers Many suppliers serve the meetings industry and contribute to the success of meetings and events. These suppliers are numerous, but some of the more common are shown in this figure.

Transportation Another meeting supplier is transportation (ground, air, or water), which may be needed between hotels and the meeting venue, but also between the local airport or train station and hotels, between docks and hotels, and between venues if more than one is utilized for the meeting. Shuttle transportation is closely tied to the number of attendees in hotels, and meeting professionals must attempt to coordinate that transportation with the meeting schedule, needs of attendees, and needs of the transportation provider. Corporations, more often than the other types of host organizations, tend to provide transportation to the destination; associations and government agencies might provide transportation options (often at a negotiated discount), but the attendee makes the final arrangements.

Registration and housing A few suppliers have relatively little contact with attendees, if any, while others are directly involved with attendee satisfaction. One example of this is the registration service provider. Registrations for meetings are most frequently handled online through an application service provider (ASP). These services may be combined with a housing service, where attendees are directed to reserve their sleeping accommodations as soon as they have registered for the meeting. Since the attendee has early contact with the meeting through the registration process, this service can set a tone for the meeting attendees and may heighten the rest of their meeting experience by providing extra amenities—like signing up for individual workshops and receiving a personal itinerary for the meeting.

Other suppliers Many other suppliers are utilized for meetings, including decorators, entertainers, and speakers. These suppliers have direct influence on meeting quality and memorability. Decorators reinforce the meeting's brand, as well as providing ambiance and onsite visual cues for exhibitions, special events, and various functions. Entertainers offer motivation, inspiration, and memorable experiences for meeting attendees. Speakers are the heart of meetings, providing education, provocative viewpoints, issues exploration, and take-away value to the meeting experience. In the meetings profession, these suppliers are essential.

While less directly involved in meeting quality, marketing and public relations service providers have an important role regarding fulfilling basic meeting objectives. One common objective, for instance, is reaching targets set for attendee numbers or tickets sold. Marketing and public relations help spread the word about the meeting, encourage potential attendees to register, and offer incentives to get registered attendees to stay at selected hotels. Marketing and public relations strategies draw attendees to various functions at the meeting, such as product-based exhibitions. Travel decisions are based on information found in marketing materials provided through numerous media, including websites, social media, phone calls, email messages, brochures, advertising, and many other delivery mechanisms.

Security firms, software providers, and companies that provide revenue streams for association meetings (such as event webcasting and video capture companies like Sonic Foundry) are key meeting suppliers. Just as each meeting is unique, so are the service providers. This variety leads to a fundamental process of utilizing RFPs to solicit proposals, followed by proposal review, site selection, and a final selection of suppliers.

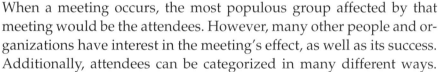

Meetings Guided by Multiple Stakeholders

When a meeting occurs, the most populous group affected by that meeting would be the attendees. However, many other people and organizations have interest in the meeting's effect, as well as its success. Additionally, attendees can be categorized in many different ways. Further, meetings have participants who may not be attendees, but still have a stake in the meeting's outcomes. Generally, while attendees are physically at the meeting, participants are considered key **stakeholders** (because they have a strong interest in the outcome and make strategic decisions that affect the results), but may not be at the meeting. Other stakeholders may be identified, as well.

key points

Attendee Profile Categories

- Public vs. invited attendees
- Voluntary vs. mandatory attendees
- "Paid" vs. "waived-registration-fee" attendees
- Pre-registered vs. registered onsite attendees
- Part of the meeting vs. full meeting attendees
- First-time attendees vs. attendees with meeting history

Attendees

Numerous systems exist to explain why an attendee is at a particular meeting. Some attendees pay a fee, while others are mandated to attend by their employer and attend free. The meeting host will determine the most

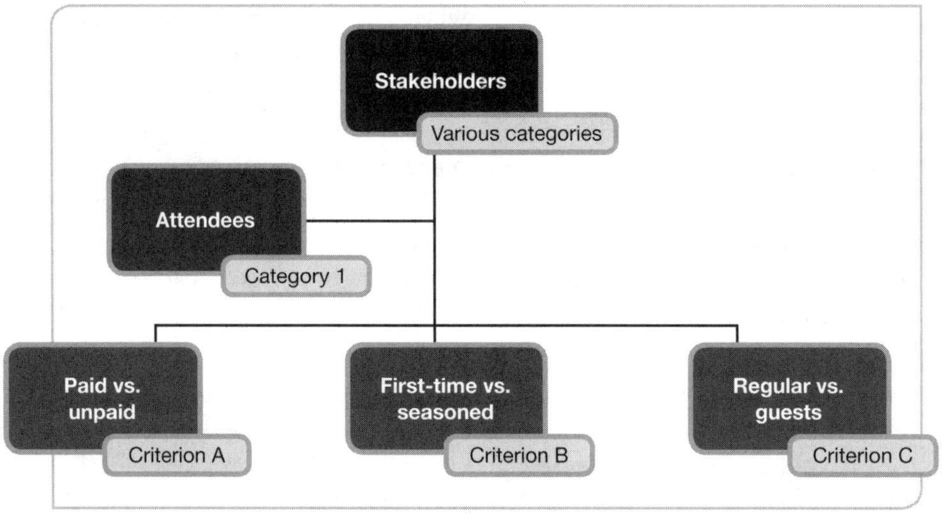

FIGURE 1.6 Stakeholders Described by Categories One of the key categories of meeting stakeholders is attendees, who can be identified further by numerous criteria, such as payment, history with the meeting, or specified types.

appropriate classifications for the meeting's purpose, goals, objectives, and marketing materials.

See Figure 1.6 for a depiction of profiling categories a meeting professional for an association might use to identify attendees. This figure suggests that attendees are stakeholders first, then they are classified by critical factors, such as whether the attendee pays for registration, has a history with the organization, or is a "regular" attendee instead of a guest of another stakeholder.

All of these descriptors, and more, can be used to categorize attendees.

Other Stakeholders

Meeting stakeholders are not necessarily attendees (see Figure 1.7). A stakeholder is someone with a significant interest in the meeting's

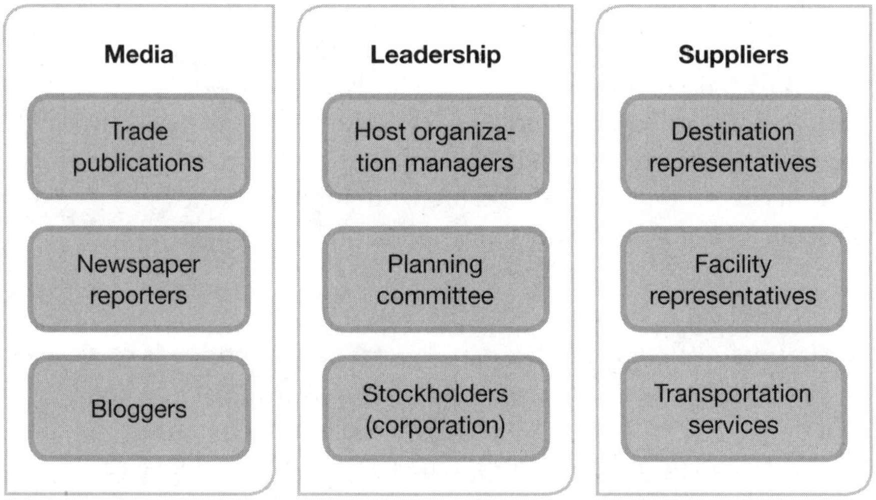

FIGURE 1.7 Meeting Stakeholders The stakeholder groups for a specific meeting are often unique to that meeting and many groups are possible; this is just a partial list of possible stakeholder groups.

PROFESSIONAL DILEMMA

The for-profit organization you work for is planning a large, two-day meeting in Chicago during January. This is an ideal time because January is a slow time of year for the employees. However, you also know that travel in January can be tricky, and even impossible, due to snow, wind, and icy cold weather. Your recommended destination is a place like Albuquerque, New Mexico or Corpus Christi, Texas. You believe the only reason Chicago was selected is because your immediate supervisor has family in Chicago. However, you have family in Albuquerque and Corpus Christi, so you feel awkward suggesting those two destinations. What should/would you do?

success. For example, the host organization may have staff members who remain at headquarters, instead of attending the meeting. In some cases, suppliers may provide their products before the meeting and return to pick up their products after the meeting—such as decorators or local providers of printing or office supplies. They do not attend the entire meeting. Insurance providers have interest, as do transportation providers, yet their attendance at the meeting is unnecessary in most cases. All of these professionals are meeting stakeholders, and they want to know how the meeting was planned, implemented, and assessed.

SUMMARY

The meetings profession relies on suppliers who are part of the service industry and/or the hospitality industry. The meetings profession includes meetings and events of many types and sizes, regardless of duration or location. The service industry includes any organization that provides a service, rather than a product, for the public benefit; this industry incorporates medicine, education, food service, accommodations, transportation, and many other services. The hospitality industry focuses on services for travelers, tourists, social gatherings, and the meeting profession.

Numerous professionals with a variety of titles organize meetings. These professionals tend to work for the top three types of meeting hosts (or "owners"): associations, corporations, or government agencies. Some of these organizations may also utilize volunteers. The host organizations and their employees or volunteers are known collectively as the planning side of the meetings profession.

The supply side of the meetings profession is made up of many entities that provide services and products for meeting hosts. Meeting facilities are one of the largest sectors of the supply side, represented by convention centers, conference centers, and other types of venues. Other meeting suppliers include hotels, transportation providers, caterers, AV providers, decorators, speakers, entertainers, as well as several other categories that make meetings successful.

Besides those suppliers, meetings have multiple stakeholders—from attendees to sponsors, from exhibitors to media representatives. Stakeholders tend to be profiled by categories, such as attendees. Attendees can be categorized in many ways: why they are attending, whether they paid or are given a registration fee waiver, and others. These categories typically relate to the meeting objectives and may drive meeting evaluation. Of course, stakeholders include many people other than attendees. Stakeholders are often described in terms of their interest in the meeting's outcomes and their ability to be involved in the meeting planning or implementation process.

The meetings profession is a complex institution, responsible for significant economic impact on global and local economies, and is made up of many stakeholders with varying perspectives.

KEY WORDS

audiovisual (AV)
corporate social responsibility (CSR)
destination
destination management company (DMC)
destination marketing organization (DMO)
event
independent planner
meeting
professional congress organizer (PCO)
proposal
request for proposal (RFP)
stakeholder
venue

DISCUSSION QUESTIONS

1. You are collecting data about the economic vitality of your local community. How would you define the service, hospitality, and meetings industries in your area? Where will tourism fit into your descriptions?
2. Corporations are run as for-profit organizations and associations are run as non-profit organizations. Which is more likely to have meetings that lose money (i.e., the organization has to subsidize the cost because the meeting makes little or no income to offset those costs)? Why?
3. Government agencies run meetings with special parameters that are not experienced by most corporations or associations. What might those parameters be?
4. Select a meeting of your choice and identify as many categories as you can for attendee types and non-attendee stakeholders.

2

Strategic Meetings: Aligning with the Organization

Mary E. Boone, MA
President
Boone Associates

Susan M. Tinnish, PhD
Dean, School of Hospitality Management
Kendall College

Main Topics

- Strategic Planning Terminology
- Strategic Planning in Organizations
- Strategic Value in Meeting Departments
- Meeting Design for Strategic Meetings
- Stages of Meeting Design
- Measuring Strategic Impact
- Strategic Value and Change Management

Learner Outcomes

Upon the completion of this chapter, the student should be able to:

1. Define the term "strategic planning" and describe the basic steps in a strategic planning process.
2. Explain how and why meeting professionals are involved in strategic planning.
3. Explain how meetings create strategic value.
4. Define the four elements of strategic value for meetings and events.
5. Describe the meeting design process.
6. Explain why the strategic impact of meetings should be measured and how that is accomplished.

CMP INTERNATIONAL STANDARDS

Domain A. Strategic Planning
Skill 1. Manage Strategic Plan for Meeting or Event
SubSkills. 1.01, 1.02, 1.03, 1.05
Skill 2. Develop Sustainability Plan for Meeting or Event
SubSkills. 2.01, 2.02
Skill 3. Develop Business Continuity or Long-Term Viability Plan of Meeting or Event
SubSkill. 3.01

Domain B. Project Management
Skill 4. Plan Meeting or Event Project
SubSkill. 4.07
Domain G. Meeting or Event Design
Skill 14. Develop Program
SubSkills. 14.01, 14.02, 14.03, 14.04

Strategic planning refers to a communication process that captures an organization's aspirations and guides its activities. Strategic planning was formalized as a discipline in the 1960s and it has evolved significantly since that time. As a discipline, strategic planning relates directly to organizations, meeting functions, and the design of individual meetings. A critical skill that is in high demand for meeting professionals is making the connection between organizational **strategy** and meetings by aligning meeting objectives with organizational goals (see Figure 2.1). To master this skill, meeting professionals need to think strategically.

> **key** questions
>
> **Strategic Questions to Ask**
>
> - Does this activity support organizational aspirations?
> - Does it fulfill a definite purpose that creates or unlocks value for the organization?
> - Does this activity take into account the environment, particularly any forces that affect or impede the fulfillment of the strategy?
> - Does it allocate resources accounting for strengths, weaknesses, opportunities, or threats facing the organization?
> - Are there alternatives that better support organizational aspirations?

Strategic thinking involves focusing on what's critical to the organization and its stakeholders. Stakeholders are people both inside and outside the organization who impact or are impacted by, i.e. have some "interest," in an organization's actions.

Many meeting professionals ask why they should understand high-level plans when they are "only involved with the planning" of meetings. The answer to this question can be expressed in one word: alignment. If meeting activities are not aligned with the strategy of the organization, it's unlikely the meeting will deliver results that really make a difference. Without **strategic alignment**, meeting professionals will spend a great deal of time justifying budgets (and sometimes their jobs), and they will be unable to maximize their impact on the organization. Meeting professionals should read their organization's high-level strategic plans and understand the plans of the units or departments involved in specific meetings. Strategic thinking involves asking insightful questions.

Thinking strategically involves understanding the strategic planning process and the contents of the organization's strategic plan. Meeting professionals also need to organize meeting departments to deliver strategic value to the organization and make certain that individual meetings are designed to deliver strategic value.

Meeting design serves as the critical link between an individual meeting and organizational strategy. The concept of "design" for meetings is often associated with the aesthetics of the meeting's location. However, "meeting design" has a deeper meaning, which focuses on support for critical organizational messaging, feedback, information giving, information gathering, and motivational efforts. Meeting design includes the creation of meeting objectives that align with organizational objectives. Specific suggestions and examples related to making individual meetings more strategic are incorporated into the discussion of meeting design.

Strategic Planning Terminology

As a meeting professional, being an expert in strategic planning is not necessary, but understanding the strategic planning concept and

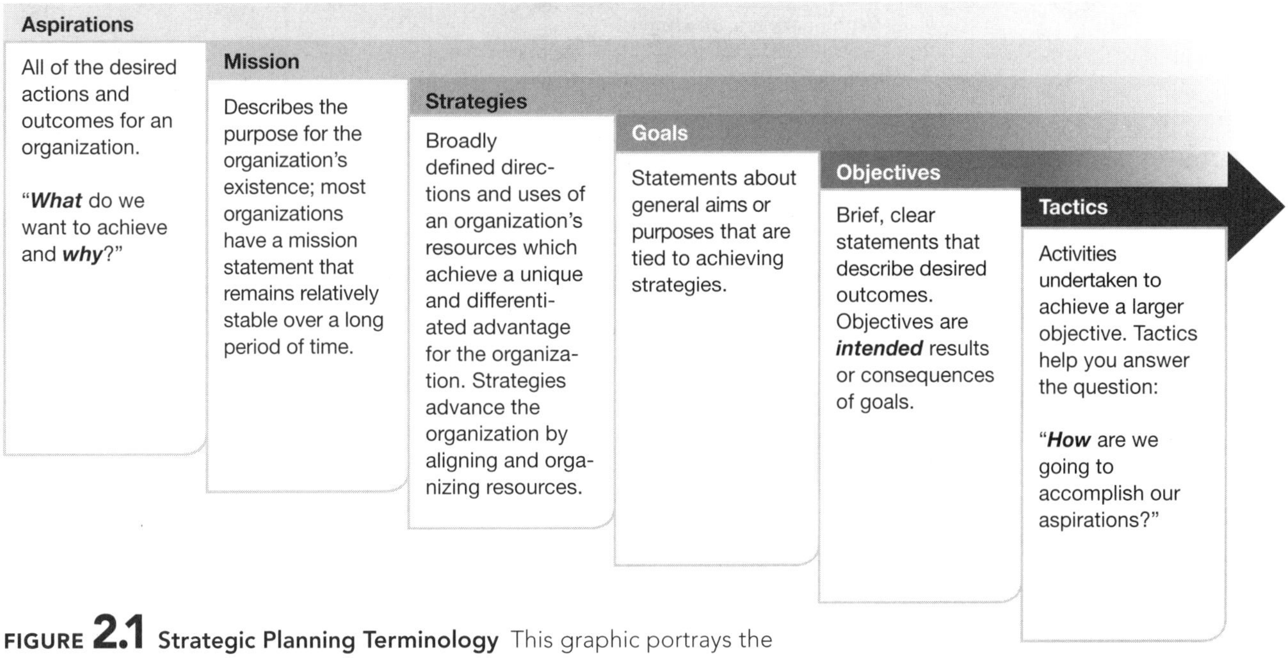

FIGURE 2.1 Strategic Planning Terminology This graphic portrays the vocabulary of strategic planning. It shows the hierarchical relationship between the concepts and provides definitions.

vocabulary is useful. Terms such as "mission," "goals," "objectives," and "outcomes" are often utilized in strategic planning, but a lack of consensus on precise meanings for these terms undermines the process and the impact of strategic planning. Figure 2.1 defines the use and hierarchy of the terms used in this chapter.

In strategic planning, a hierarchy of aspirations and activities is formed. For example, an association might determine that it must grow significantly in order to remain viable in the long term, but membership has been decreasing. Simultaneously, it has learned that global growth potential is considerable. Figure 2.2 (p. 20) portrays an example of how the strategic planning hierarchy for this situation might look. Once the strategies, goals, and objectives are in place, a meeting professional can help deliver on these aspirations by assisting with specific tactics related to meetings.

Strategic Planning in Organizations

Strategic planning is a specific type of planning that addresses the organization's long-term aspirations. Usually based on a three- to five-year time horizon, strategic planning initially involves data collection and data analysis. These steps guide the process of establishing organizational direction by identifying the mission, goals, and objectives. The strategic planning process is also used to plan for the most effective utilization of organizational resources, e.g., time, money, people, equipment, materials, technology, and facilities. The strategic

FIGURE 2.2 Strategic Planning Hierarchy Strategic planning contains four steps: setting organizational strategy, determining the business unit's goals, establishing clear objectives, then planning tactics.

plan communicates the organization's course so that activities can be coordinated (carried out or executed). Organizations of all sizes and types—large and small, corporations and associations—benefit from effective strategic planning.

The quality of an organization's strategic planning process depends on many factors, including the level of employee/stakeholder engagement and inclusiveness, level of effectiveness in communicating the plan, and rigor of the research and analysis done to support assertions and predictions in the plan. For example, an organization might invest in the services of a professional consulting firm to help develop their strategic plan, but employees might not feel ownership of the plan and, therefore, they may not support or embrace the plan.

Execution of the strategy is crucial to the success of a strategic plan, especially when a strategic plan calls for significant organizational change. Organizational change requires specific leadership competencies to design and implement customized change management processes. Organizations often fail to manage the change process effectively, thus undermining the plan.

Steps in the Process

The first step in the strategic planning process is to assess the environment or context in which an overall organization is operating. The environment includes an organization's internal systems (e.g., processes, structures, people, and leadership), larger industry forces (e.g., competition, market conditions) and the broader external environment (e.g., the economy, social changes, and technological changes). Analyzing the external environment involves answering questions such as "Who are the competitors?", "What are they doing?", and "What impact is the global economy likely to have on the industry?"

One very popular planning exercise for understanding context is called a SWOT (strengths, weaknesses, opportunities, and threats) analysis (Humphrey, 2005). Strengths and weaknesses are internal to an organization; opportunities and threats are external to the organization (see Figure 2.3). Another popular planning exercise, STEEPLED, has developed from a model originally labeled PEST or PESTLE. STEEPLED (social, technological, economic, environmental, political, legal, ethical, and demographic) factors are taken into consideration in this planning approach (Morrison, 2007). Note that while these approaches were originally developed for organizational-level strategic planning, meeting professionals also could use these concepts when they develop a plan for an individual meeting or event.

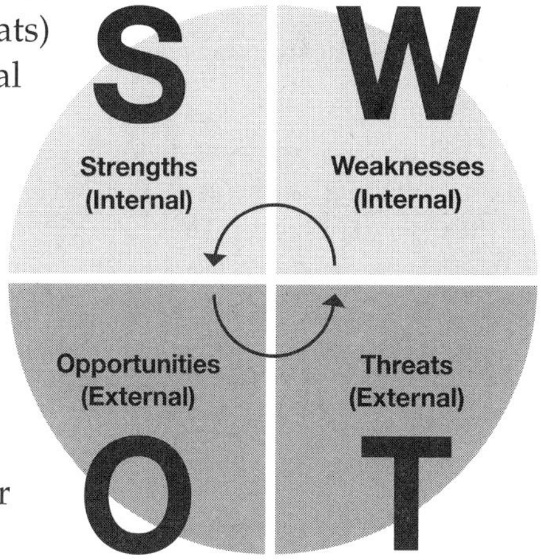

FIGURE 2.3 Elements of SWOT Analysis In a SWOT analysis, the strengths and weakness represent the current situation within an organization while the opportunities and threats are external to the organization.

Part of the upfront strategic planning analysis includes stakeholder identification. Strategic plans are designed and adjusted to meet the needs of a wide range of stakeholders, such as governmental bodies, political groups, trade unions, financiers, suppliers, employees, association members, and/or customers.

In the past 10 years, many organizations have increased their focus on the stakeholder group known as the "community" surrounding the organization. A focus on corporate social responsibility (CSR) by organizations (often) represents a new organizational imperative aimed at meeting the needs of a local or global community. CSR integrates social and environmental issues into the strategic direction, decisions, goals, and operations of an organization. Of course, communities themselves are made up of many stakeholders. CSR stakeholders can include organizations such as political groups and non-governmental organizations (NGOs) as well as individuals.

Once the environment is analyzed and stakeholder needs are identified, strategies, goals, and objectives can be articulated. These aspirations guide what actions the organization will take. Strategies and goals tend to be developed in three- to five-year time frames. Objectives tend to change more frequently because they shift in response to a changing environment.

Resource limitations require that all aspirations and activities be prioritized. Strategic plans also require that the organization have sufficient people, software, time, money, and knowledge to execute the plan. Finally, strategic plans must be written, communicated, and monitored to ensure that plans are understood and used throughout the organization.

Business Continuity

A strategic planning process should include a consideration of business continuity. **Business continuity** ensures that an organization's critical business functions are not compromised when organizations respond to opportunities or threats. Business strategists (Brady, Henson, & Fava, 1999; Esty & Winston, 2009; Figge, Hahn, Schaltegger, & Wagner, 2002; Lubin & Esty, 2010; Porter & Kramer, 2006; Porter & Kramer, 2011) and business practitioners have reframed the idea of "continuity" and the strategic planning process by including a focus on issues such as natural resource supplies, the cost of pollution, sustainable relationships with suppliers, and the economic distress of the communities in which an organization produces and sells products. They argue that long-term business continuity will be achieved through more than just economic measures of success. A sole focus on economics prevents organizations from harnessing their full potential to meet society's broader challenges: social, economic, and environmental. This focus on CSR or the **triple bottom line** is becoming a necessary core element of an organization's strategy (see Figure 2.4).

key points

The Triple Bottom Line

Traditionally in business and accounting, the "bottom line" refers to either the profit or loss recorded at the very "bottom line" on financial statements. The triple bottom line adds two more "bottom lines" or perspectives by including social and environmental concerns. The triple bottom line is a holistic view of sustainability. The triple bottom line is also called the "three P's"—people, planet, and profit (Elkington, 1998).

1. Scan environment and analyze stakeholders—An external and internal analysis provides a clear understanding of the marketplace, the competitive environment, and the organization's true competencies and abilities. Stakeholder analysis determines who will impact (or be impacted by) the plan. Stakeholder input throughout the strategic planning process—especially from employees—can assist with ownership of the plan and can help speed execution of it. CSR considerations should be included in these analyses.

2. Identify strategies at the organizational level—The development of high-level strategies sets the direction of the organization over a specified time period (usually three to five years).

3. Incorporate business unit inputs—Input from business units provides alignment between units and high-level priorities and strategies.

4. Set priorities—At each step in the process, priorities must be identified so that the organization knows where to focus its efforts in order to achieve the goals and objectives.

5. Encourage the development of aligned activities and resource deployment—All of the departments and employees in an organization should align their initiatives, projects, individual activities, and use of resources with the priorities in the plan.

6. Communicate and communicate again—Once the plan is codified, it is critical that people know the final results. Communicate the plan; refer to the plan often when prioritizing projects, initiatives, tasks, and other activities. To ensure the organization is moving in accordance with the strategic plan, frequently review the plan and make appropriate adjustments.

FIGURE 2.4 Strategic Planning Process The steps in this figure briefly summarize the entire strategic planning process.

Strategic Value in Meeting Departments

To align its activities with the strategic plan of the organization, a meeting department must address the four key elements shown in Figure 2.5: portfolio management, measurement, meeting design, and advanced logistics. With these elements in place, the meeting professional will be well positioned to deliver value.

Portfolio Management

Portfolio management is an approach to understanding how all of the meetings and events are performing, in total, in the organization. Consider, for a moment, how a financial planner manages an investment portfolio. To do a good job, the financial planner needs to first understand personal goals such as when a client wants to retire, lifestyle preferences, etc. Then the financial planner determines which investments will best meet those goals. Similarly, when meeting professionals do portfolio management for meetings and events in organizations, they need to use strategic thinking to understand where the organization is going before they determine how specific meetings and events will help the organization achieve those goals.

Each meeting is part of an overall portfolio just like a stock or fund is part of an overall financial portfolio. Portfolio management for meetings helps executives and meeting professionals determine why certain meetings should be held, what the budget for the meeting department should be, and how resources should be allocated to different meetings. Portfolio management should always involve managing both the efficiency (cost savings) and the effectiveness (strategic impact) of all of the meetings that are held by the organization.

One approach to portfolio management is the **Strategic Meetings Management Program (SMMP)**. Most SMMP programs are aimed at reducing costs and improving efficiency of meeting programs through the use of specialized technology to consolidate meeting spending. Relationships are developed with preferred vendors to reduce costs (Boone, 2009).

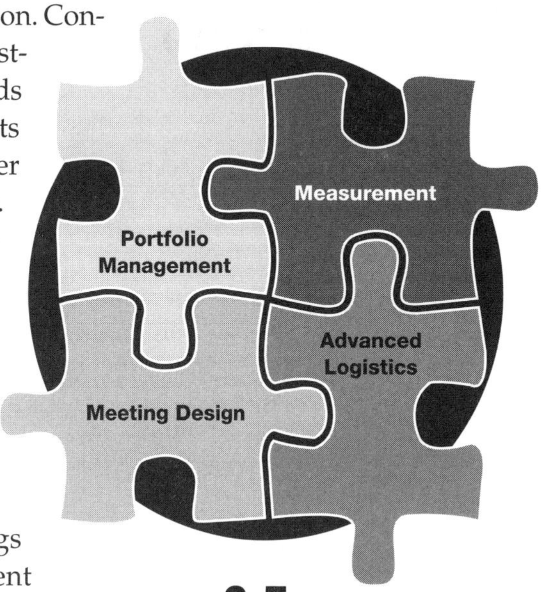

FIGURE 2.5 Elements of Strategic Value for Meetings and Events The four elements represented in this figure provide a framework for the meeting professional to deliver strategic value to the organization (Boone, 2009).

Measurement

Measurement uses a variety of methods to determine the value of an individual meeting (or group of related meetings). In order to conduct portfolio management, the meeting professional must measure the results of individual meetings using any of a variety of methods.

Meeting Design

Meeting design is defined as "the purposeful shaping of the form and content of a meeting to deliver on crucial organizational objectives. Meeting design incorporates methods and technologies that connect, inform, and engage a broad range of relevant stakeholders before, during, and after the meeting. Good design integrates the meeting with other communication activities, maximizes interactivity, and results in a significant return on investment" (Boone, 2012, p. 1). A meeting designer creates experiences that deeply influence the thinking and behavior of the participants and other stakeholders. While some people use the term *design* to refer to the aesthetics

SUSTAINABILITY *in* Practice

Today's meeting professionals must think strategically about how their plans, processes, and purchases support organizational goals, including corporate social responsibility (CSR), environmental issues, and economic policies. As a public activity, meetings are highly visible places to "walk the talk." Sustainable meetings should be designed with the organization's goals, priorities, and stakeholders in mind, and take into account what will happen before, during, and after the meeting. There should be an overall sustainable meeting plan with a vision and goal along with measureable objectives for energy use and carbon emission reduction, waste diversion, water conservation, sustainable procurement, and community impact. Meetings that are wasteful, pollute, or have negative impacts on local communities place the organization's reputation at risk and can undermine stakeholder trust. On the positive side, meetings offer numerous opportunities to reduce environmental and social impacts and to influence the supply chain. Meeting professionals have the "power of the purse" to change the practices of hotels, venues, food and beverage providers, transportation companies, and other suppliers. Well-planned sustainable meetings leave a positive legacy on the communities where they take place. With thousands of businesses and nonprofits issuing CSR and sustainability reports every year, meetings can be a source of positive data and case studies. The environmental and social performance of meetings is finding its way into Global Reporting Initiative (GRI) (2012a, 2012b) reports through a special event organizer sector supplement.

—Deborah R. Popely

or logistics of a meeting, the term *meeting design* is used differently in the four elements framework.

Advanced Logistics

Advanced logistics addresses the *hospitality and environmental* aspects of a meeting, e.g., venues, contracting, sourcing, travel arrangements, food and beverage, lodging, room and furniture arrangement, temperature, technical requirements, and décor. Because the logistics of modern meetings have become so complex, this area of expertise is referred to as *advanced logistics*. Increasingly, meeting professionals also are challenged to include CSR objectives in advanced logistics.

Meeting Design for Strategic Meetings

All four elements of strategic value are essential to the development of a strategic meeting department, but one element in particular is

FIGURE 2.6 Meeting Design Team A meeting design team and a consultant gather to brainstorm for an upcoming event. Industry meetings provide excellent opportunities to gain insight and ideas to include in the design of a specific event.

critical to the connection between strategic planning and strategic meetings, and that element is meeting design. Good meeting design allows meeting professionals to create meetings with organizational impact. Strategic meetings are well designed, and their objectives align with the organizational strategic plan. Thus, they create strategic value.

Fielding a Design Team

Effective meeting design requires a team consisting of the **meeting designer**, the meeting professional, a **creative director**, and the meeting client (see Figure 2.6). The meeting designer focuses on the form and content, the meeting professional concentrates on logistics, and the creative director develops the visual messaging, staging, and artistic elements. A production company, in conjunction with the design team, helps with the execution of the creative aspects of the meeting. The **meeting client** is the person who sponsors or "owns" the meeting and is responsible for organizational results. A meeting client may be internal or external to the organization.

Convincing executives and others of the strategic value of meetings is much easier with the proper design team in place. Influential internal meeting clients can pave the way across change-averse landscapes and marshal the necessary resources when needed. The person in the role of meeting designer is essential to the entire process. This person should be very comfortable with organizational strategy and working with executives. The meeting designer's vision for meetings and how they relate to organizational priorities will be an essential part of convincing executives, participants, and other stakeholders that an investment in a strategic meeting is well worth the effort and expense involved.

Stages of Meeting Design

key points

Stages of Meeting Design

- Discovery
- Development
- Delivery
- Ongoing impact

Meeting design is iterative, not static nor linear. There are four basic stages to meeting design: discovery, development, delivery, and ongoing impact. As the design team works together, it may need to revisit a previous stage if there are changes in the environment.

Discovery Stage

In the **discovery stage**, the design team determines the viability of holding the meeting. The team must ensure that the most optimal vehicle is used to meet the strategic business goals and objectives. The design team also considers alternative types of meetings—face-to-face, online, or hybrid—to determine which would be most appropriate.

The discovery stage of the design process contains activities similar to the "environmental scan" and "stakeholder analysis" described previously for organizational-level strategic planning. In associations, for example, the design team needs to determine the market, i.e., "Are there enough people who would attend the proposed event?", sources of revenue for the event, legislative and regulatory issues, and emerging industry and societal events that might have an impact on the event. In corporations, the design team needs to consider whether other meetings already being held are sufficient to address an issue or whether another communication activity such as a video or slide presentation (in lieu of a meeting) would suffice to address an organizational imperative.

At this stage, the design team also needs to review high-level organizational strategic plans. Occasionally, strategic plans will be non-existent or out of date. When this happens, the design team should seek alternative ways of understanding the direction of the organization. This effort might take the form of an interview or conversation with a savvy executive or a review of memos or other documents that contain information about the organization's plans.

Based on this review of the strategic plan, the design team should ascertain organizational and departmental priorities. Armed with this information, the team will be in a better position to design and deliver a meeting experience that provides real value to the organization.

In addition, the team must balance the differing priorities of various meeting stakeholders. Critical external stakeholders include suppliers, venues, sponsors, convention and visitor bureaus (CVBs), and exhibitors. Critical internal stakeholders include meeting clients, departments that may be affected by an event, senior executives, members, former members, officers, and board members. Participants can be either internal or external stakeholders depending on whether the organization is an association or a corporation. Likewise, speakers can be internal or external stakeholders. The design team needs to satisfy both internal and external stakeholders. Stakeholders will have differing goals, objectives, and perspectives on how the meeting will deliver value to them.

Why consider a wide range of stakeholders in the discovery stage of meeting design? In addition to gaining critical information that will make the meeting valuable to a broad constituency, the design team may also avoid numerous potential problems. For example, CSR stakeholders, i.e., community and government groups and NGOs, have protested at high-profile meetings. Conservative estimates place the crowd who protested the activity surrounding the UNWTO Ministerial Conference in 1999 in Seattle, Washington at over 40,000 people (Seattle Police Department, 2000). The trade negotiations were quickly overshadowed by massive and controversial street protests, which focused on the anti-globalization movement in the United States. The protesters decided that they had a stake in the meeting and wanted to protest a social issue related to trade. Unfortunately for the organizers, they had underestimated the interest from these stakeholders and were unprepared for the protests from a security and risk-management perspective (Oldham, 2009).

The analysis done in the discovery stage can serve two purposes: 1) It serves as the basis for aligning meeting goals and objectives with the strategic priorities of the host organization; and 2) It may reveal whether an organization is on track with its strategic plan. A discovery-stage conversation between the meeting designer and senior executives can renew an organization's commitment to its strategic plan, initiate adjustments to an existing strategic plan, or point out the importance of having a plan if one is lacking.

key questions

Discerning Questions about Priorities

- What are the top three strategies for the association this year?
- What three key goals does the education department need to accomplish?
- What are the membership department's top three goals?

Development Stage

Once the viability of, or need for, the meeting is established, the design team works to develop objectives for the meeting and to determine how these objectives align with the overall goals of the larger organization. This stage of meeting design addresses all the choices related to the form and content of what will happen before, during, and after the meeting, including the selection of different methods and technologies. The **development stage** establishes the overall framework for the meeting and shapes its component parts, i.e., individual sessions or segments. The development of meeting objectives should include momentum toward action, i.e., people should *act* as a result of what takes place at the meetings. For example, in one financial institution, interactive exercises that took place at a leadership meeting of 3,000 executives resulted in the development of project teams during the meeting. Those teams held their first project-team meetings before the leadership meeting concluded.

Designing the meeting objectives correctly ensures desired outcomes. Objectives are *intended* results and outcomes are *achieved* results. The usefulness of meeting objectives is directly related to their level of specificity. Meeting objectives are directly tied to the measurement

PROFESSIONAL DILEMMA

Meeting professionals will face real or imagined conflicts of interest or competing demands for time and resources between stakeholders. How can you, as an astute meeting professional, balance the various demands and make a smart decision?

Consider these situations where various stakeholders have competing interests, resources are limited, and stakeholder needs must be balanced appropriately:

1. A potentially large sponsor has manufacturing operations in a country with human rights violations.
2. Your members have voiced a desire to have a more sustainable meeting, which will require a larger meeting budget, but the meeting client is unwilling to fund this initiative.
3. The meeting design process has recommended use of a technology. However, your meeting attendees are not knowledgeable or comfortable with this technology.

How will you resolve these dilemmas? Please think about these issues in framing your response:

- What data or information do you need?
- Can you find a "win-win" versus a "win-lose" solution?
- How should you balance short- and long-term objectives?
- How should you prioritize stakeholders and stakeholder needs? What issues will you consider (primary or secondary stakeholder status, strategic importance, strategic value)?
- Is any stakeholder suffering from entrenched ways of thinking?

process. In formulating the objectives for a meeting, the design team needs to consider three types of objectives (see Figure 2.7).

Examples of strategic design decisions Meeting objectives guide the development of decisions about specific activities and environmental aspects at the meeting, e.g., room sets or formats. No single formula exists for creating well-designed meetings from a set of meeting objectives; the design team must apply strategy and creativity to develop the "right" design elements to meet the demands of the meeting objectives.

For example, in traditional meetings, the stage is usually populated exclusively with executives and/or experts presenting sequentially in a well-rehearsed fashion while the "audience" listens. Well-designed meetings include much more interaction and action on the part of both speakers and attendees. The strategic design decision might be to have participants sharing the stage, talking with each other, and sharing their opinions in a variety of ways. A simple change in language from the term "audience" to the term "participants" can serve to refocus the design team to develop more impactful design elements. An audience simply listens, but participants get involved.

A host of interactive formats, methods, and technologies can be applied to meetings. Shorter speeches and use of interactive technologies are examples of design decisions.

Shorter speeches Meeting objectives frequently focus on engagement of participants. A desire to increase engagement means the design team must rethink the traditional speech format. In a world of ever-shrinking attention spans, participants will not sit and listen attentively to lengthy monologues.

The TED (Technology, Entertainment, Design) conference is often offered as a model for effective presentations, and one of the key design decisions is related to the length of presentations. Richard Saul Wurman, who originally created the TED conference, had the idea to dramatically shorten the speeches. The current time limit for a TED speech is 18 minutes ("TEDx Speaker Guide," 2014).

Shorter speeches do not have to result in less information being shared. One organization used video "trailers" for speeches prior to the meeting, which contained additional content not presented onstage. They also made small conference rooms available following speeches in order to allow participants to interact with the speaker following the presentation.

Cognitive Objectives: Know
What do you want your participants to know? Participants will be able to list the latest technologies in our industry.
Affective Objectives: Care
What do you want your participants to care about? Participants will leave the meeting with a high level of confidence in the organization's level of technology sophistication.
Behavioral Objectives: Do
What do you want your participants to do? Participants will use at least one of the new technologies that have been demonstrated within the next 90 days.

FIGURE 2.7 Know, Care, and Do: A Model for Developing Meeting Objectives This series of questions allows the meeting professional to design a meeting that addresses the desired cognitive, affective, and behavioral changes that should result from the meeting experience.

Interactive technologies Meetings, especially for associations, frequently include a focus on increasing networking opportunities. After all, one of the main reasons participants choose to attend a conference is for the purpose of networking. Some of the most effective technologies for networking include Twitter™, gamification, and hybrid meetings, which increase networking with remote attendees.

Delivery Stage

The **delivery stage** starts when the actual meeting takes place and involves the meeting execution and any mid-course adjustments that are made during the execution of the design. Design decisions will be made throughout the entire meeting design process; organizational priorities may shift or unforeseen circumstances may arise.

The design team must remain open to the possibility of designing onsite after the meeting has started. For example, design teams frequently discover that adjustments must be made to the timing of activities or sessions. For unforeseen reasons, significant delays may occur that result in the need for adjustments to interactive exercises. Such adjustments could mean significant changes to the original design of a session. The design team must be ready to reconsider the meeting and objectives in the moment and determine how they can be met given the new time constraints.

Ongoing Impact Stage

During the **ongoing impact stage**, the design team works with meeting client(s) to link the meeting to other communication activities so that the meeting itself and the results of the meeting continue to support the overall strategies of the organization on an ongoing basis. The meeting should be designed to deliver value on an ongoing basis, and the design team should ensure that coordination and collaboration issues are addressed in creative ways. For example, if an association's annual meeting session is addressing an important learning initiative for attendees, the activities during that session could be tied to a workshop or webinar on the same topic that is taking place later in the year or being addressed in another part of the organization, such as in its publications.

The overall design process is iterative, not static. The stages outlined above will intertwine and overlap. Currently, many meetings are planned, but in the future, an increasing number of meetings will be both planned and strategically designed. In order for a meeting to deliver strategic value to an organization, it should be both designed and executed with excellence.

Measuring Strategic Impact

The meeting design team should focus on the results of the meeting throughout the design process. If appropriate meeting objectives guide the design process from the outset, measuring the outcomes of the meeting will be easier. In other words, if the design team knows what they want to influence, then they will know where to look to measure results; this is one reason why participation of the meeting client(s) in the design process is so valuable.

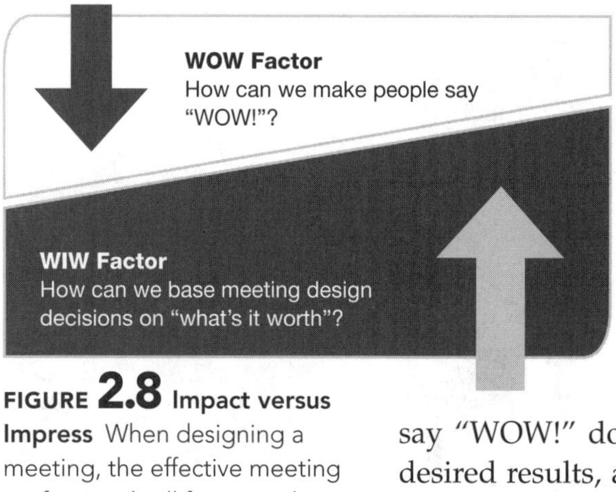
WOW Factor
How can we make people say "WOW!"?
WIW Factor
How can we base meeting design decisions on "what's it worth"?

FIGURE 2.8 Impact versus Impress When designing a meeting, the effective meeting professional will focus on the desired value or impact (the "WIW?" factor) as opposed to focusing on simply trying to impress the participants (the "WOW!" factor).

Throughout the design process, the design team should focus less on the "WOW!" factor of trying to impress participants and more on the "WIW?" (what it's worth) factor. Just because participants say "WOW!" does not mean that the organization will achieve the desired results, as indicated in Figure 2.8. It is more important for a meeting to have a measurable impact than to simply impress people.

Meetings are measured in a variety of ways. The ROI Institute has constructed a five-tier method that expands upon the work of Dr. Donald Kirkpatrick's Learning Evaluation Model (2007). The Phillips ROI Methodology™, which includes return on investment (ROI) measurement, is used extensively in a variety of contexts including both learning environments and meetings. This approach is perhaps one of the most well-known meeting measurement methodologies as well as one of the most rigorous (Phillips, Myhill, & McDonough, 2007). Meeting designers, clients, or meeting professionals can use the methodology to create very convincing business cases for meetings.

Disciplined evaluation can be used to justify the continuation of meetings, expand meetings to other parts of an organization, and build attendance. Both quantitative and qualitative data can enhance understanding and decision making.

Stakeholders who have experience, expertise, and influence within the organization can provide anecdotal data to help reinforce statistical data. For example, the vice president of sales may have access to information that allows a statement to be made, such as, "Conservatively, I feel that this meeting contributed to at least a 10 percent increase in sales." Statistics reinforced with this type of anecdotal evidence, especially when the right person delivers the examples and information, can be very powerful.

Traditionally, organizations measure ROI strictly in terms of economic impact. However, the more recent global business trend toward measuring the triple bottom line (Elkington, 1998) suggests including additional measures. In addition to doing this for altruistic reasons, organizations need to address these issues because of their potential contribution to the efficiency and effectiveness of the meeting, as well as the impact on branding for both for-profit and non-profit entities.

Strategic Value and Change Management

Developing a strategic meetings function and delivering strategic meetings requires innovation and change. Meeting professionals who begin to initiate a more strategic focus may well discover there are barriers to change. For example, executives may or may not initially understand why the meeting professionals want access to strategic plans. The incorporation of new technologies and new methods for a meeting may threaten some people who are more comfortable with the status quo. Instituting new ways of measuring meetings may pose a threat to some people.

In circumstances where change management is called for, meeting professionals should adopt a more stepwise approach to introducing new ideas and new ways of working. The culture of the organization must be taken into account. If the organization has a high tolerance for risk, innovation may be introduced quickly. If, on the other hand, it is more risk-averse, it may be prudent to introduce innovation more slowly by changing a few things at a time.

SUMMARY

Meeting professionals who want to deliver strategic value must understand the organization's strategic plan, structure their functions to deliver organizational objectives, and apply principles of effective meeting design and measurement to individual meetings. There are four elements of value for a strategic meeting function: portfolio management, meeting design, measurement, and advanced logistics. The key role of meeting design is creating strategic meetings. Strategic meetings incorporate interaction and inspire action—before, during, and after the meeting.

Equipped with a clear understanding of an organization's strategic plan and with the knowledge of how a meeting contributes to organizational aspirations, meeting professionals can become major contributors to organizational success.

KEY WORDS

advanced logistics
business continuity
creative director
delivery stage
development stage
discovery stage
measurement
meeting client
meeting design
meeting designer
ongoing impact stage
portfolio management
strategic alignment
strategic planning
Strategic Meetings Management Program (SMMP)
strategic thinking
strategy
triple bottom line

DISCUSSION QUESTIONS

1. Read an organization's strategic plan. List the organization's top three objectives and describe how you would support those objectives with a meeting.
2. Identify an example of a meeting held by an organization. Use the agenda to review the meeting's content. Based upon your review, what meeting goals and objectives do you think the meeting professional had in mind? What business strategies do you think are being addressed by the meeting objectives?
3. Assemble your meeting-design "dream team." Who would be on the team and why would you select those people?

3

Blending Project and Meeting Management

Lynn R. Reed, MSPM
Project Management Consultant
L. R. Reed & Associates

B. J. Reed, EdD, CMP
Professor, Media Studies
Director, Teaching & Learning Center
University of Wisconsin–Platteville

Main Topics

- Personnel Roles in Project Management
- Project Management as a Process
- Project Management Knowledge Areas

Learner Outcomes

Upon the completion of this chapter, the student should be able to:

1. Compare and contrast the major roles in a project management-based organization.
2. Identify the project management process groups and knowledge areas.
3. Differentiate the appropriate responses for a project threat.
4. Differentiate the appropriate responses for a project opportunity.
5. Describe the differences between the meeting planning role, meeting/project manager role, and meeting/program manager role.

CMP INTERNATIONAL STANDARDS

Domain A. Strategic Planning
Skill 1. Manage Strategic Plan for Meeting or Event
  SubSkill. 1.05
Skill 2. Develop Sustainability Plan for Meeting or Event
  SubSkills. 2.01, 2.02
Domain B. Project Management
Skill 4. Plan Meeting or Event Project
  SubSkills. 4.01, 4.02, 4.05
Skill 5. Manage Meeting or Event Project
  SubSkill. 5.01
Domain C. Risk Management
Skill 6. Manage Risk Management Plan
  SubSkills. 6.01, 6.02
Domain F. Stakeholder Management
Skill 13. Manage Stakeholder Relationships
  SubSkill. 13.01

Project management (PM) is a business tool, process, and career path. Based on the systems theory of organizational structure ("The Center," 2014), PM provides a roadmap for collaboration, communication, and action across the organization for successful **project** development, implementation, and evaluation. "Project," in this context, could be an item, a collection of items, an activity, or even an initiative. **Project managers** lead a **project team** and work in health care, manufacturing, government, insurance, higher education, construction, information technology, and many other fields. Virtually any enterprise of sufficient size can utilize the expertise of a project manager.

key points

Important Definitions

- Project—A temporary and unique product, service, or initiative. From the perspective of the meetings industry, a project could be any meeting or event.
- Project management—The process of planning, organizing, directing, and controlling resources for a project.

In comparison to the meetings industry, which has a significant historical presence, PM is relatively new and is used primarily as a tool and formal process to enhance meeting success. Worldwide, the premiere organization for PM is the Project Management Institute (PMI); it has published a text on PM principles, techniques, and tools, known as the *Project Management Body of Knowledge* (*PMBOK® Guide*, 2013). PMI also provides numerous conferences for professional development and certifications for aspiring and current project managers.

In some cases, a meeting professional serves as project manager, but that is not true for all meetings. The meeting professional in an association, for instance, might rely on a volunteer planning committee, i.e., key external stakeholders, for the annual meeting and convention, while the project manager organizes the various department managers, i.e., key internal stakeholders, who have a significant investment in the meeting's success. The purchasing (or procurement), accounting, membership, public relations and/or marketing, human resources, travel, and risk management departments for the association would have a significant investment of time, employees, and other resources.

Personnel Roles in Project Management

Project managers utilize various tools and techniques to accomplish project goals and objectives. A key responsibility is to lead the project team, usually consisting of other department managers who have direct influence on project success. The project manager is responsible for aligning the strategic project outcomes with those set by the various departments, and must ensure those outcomes align with the organization's mission and goals. When the enterprise is large enough, multiple project managers work for a **program manager**, who oversees many activities that fit into a specific domain, e.g., multiple meetings held around the country for regional chapters of an association, or sales meetings held in multiple locations for the large enterprise. The **portfolio manager** is next in this business hierarchy, where a specific manager oversees multiple programs and projects that seem independent, yet are connected by their role in fulfilling an organization's goals.

For example, in a large university, a strategic goal might be to foster inclusiveness, as well as diverse opinions and knowledge. The portfolio could include a project in student affairs that encourages international students to network with their local hosts, a program from the chief diversity officer that helps train professors on inclusiveness techniques, and a review of events across campus that have a variety of participants, e.g., homecoming.

In the meetings industry, PCMA might have a strategic goal of establishing itself as a premier meetings organization in higher education. A project for that goal would be the development of this book. Another project would be the development of partnerships with universities offering meeting-management degree programs. Additionally, the Convening Leaders meeting each January could be added to the portfolio as well as various member services. The portfolio manager evaluates the various initiatives and determines if the initiatives are taking PCMA in the right direction for achieving this strategic goal.

Enterprises are characterized by infinite variety so a strict description of terms like "meeting professional" or "project manager" is difficult. Since the PM discipline evolved from different fields (e.g., engineering) than the meetings industry (the health care field was an early adopter of meeting management principles), the roles and tools that each discipline uses have unique titles but overlap in function. Depending on the size of the organization, a meeting professional could supervise multiple meeting professionals or have a "hands-on" function in the project. In this case, the meeting professional does not hold the same position as a project manager. In other words, a meeting professional could be the equivalent of a portfolio, program, or project manager (see Figure 3.1). On one end of the spectrum, someone is handling logistical planning, e.g., blocking hotel rooms, while another person handles policy development, e.g., creating internal policy that guides purchasing decisions. In the small organization, this could be one person.

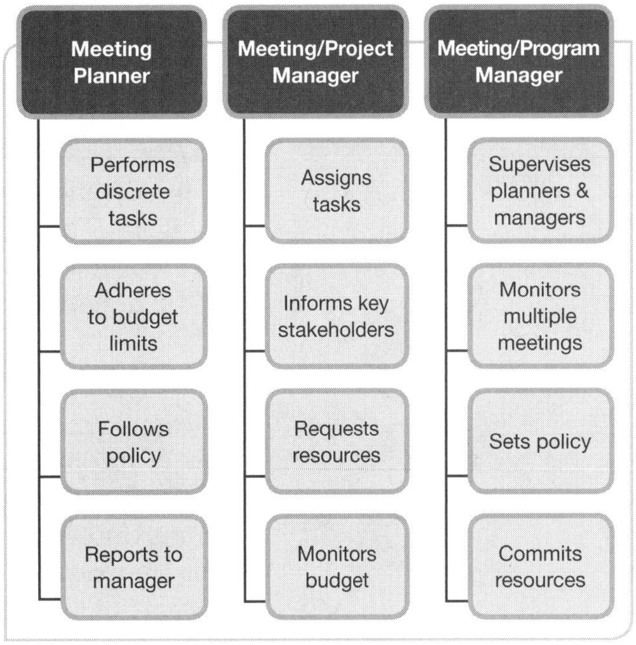

FIGURE 3.1 Meeting Planners, Project Managers, and Program Managers The definitions for some terms in this chapter are not universally accepted, but the definitions do provide one perspective on project management and how it relates to the meetings industry.

Project Management as a Process

When an enterprise uses the principles of PM, the process flows across the project's lifecycle. The basic structure of the lifecycle is: starting, planning, doing, and ending. During all points of the project's lifecycle, the project manager can use tools and techniques from the five process groups: initiating, planning, executing, monitoring/controlling, and closing. These process groups each have predictable

FIGURE 3.2 Project Management as a Process
The Project Management Institute has been instrumental in defining project management terms and suggesting best practices for the industry since 1969 (PMI, 2014).

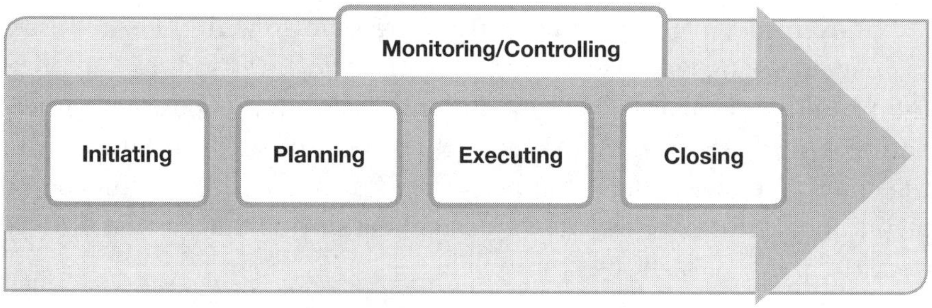

time frames, but do not occur in a clear, consecutive order. PM is an iterative process. Often changes in the project, anticipated or not, cause shifts in tasks, timelines, or budgets. These changes require the project manager to re-evaluate all of the plans and implement new items. The PM process will identify a critical path of necessary tasks for project completion, which guides the project team throughout the project's lifecycle (see Figure 3.2).

Initiating

In the initiating process, the organization must make a decision on the basis of incomplete data. Budget information will be estimated and quite brief. Attendance for the meeting will be estimated, based on either previous meetings that are similar or a needs analysis. PM decisions are made on the basis of facts, but in the initiating phase, those facts are fluid. The key decision made in the initiating phase is whether the meeting will occur. In this phase, the project manager develops the **project charter**, which includes basic information about the project and leads to a decision. A positive decision authorizes the project manager to commit various organizational resources to the project.

Planning

Once a positive decision has been made, the planning process begins. The project manager develops the PM plan in this phase, and defines the project scope. The scope indicates what the project is, as well as what the project is not. This scope definition is imperative when the organization monitors and controls project-associated tasks. To protect valuable resources dedicated to the project, the project manager must avoid **scope creep**. Scope creep occurs when additional tasks are added to a project's plan that would result in unrelated outcomes.

An example will illustrate the concept of scope creep. A non-profit association decides to host a meeting that offers training in new Environmental Protection Agency (EPA) standards for a specific industry. The EPA will provide speakers for this event at no cost to the association. The association, though, relies on memberships to achieve its mission; therefore, the board of directors decides to use the meeting as a membership recruitment forum. Besides some ethical concerns for the EPA, which is not in the habit of endorsing one association over another, the membership drive constitutes scope creep for the project.

Executing

The executing process illustrates a difference of perspective between project and meeting professionals. For the meetings industry, planning occurs constantly from the initiating phase all of the way to holding the meeting, which would be considered the executing phase. However, a project manager would consider the planning phase as strictly preparing to execute. When contracts are signed, tasks are completed (e.g., creating a website to promote the event), and costs are encountered, the project manager is in the executing phase of the project. Differences do exist between the meeting professional's perspective of the project's lifecycle and the project manager's perspective.

Monitoring/Controlling

The project manager and project team are given responsibility for monitoring and controlling resources throughout the life of the project. Monitoring includes the collection of data in order to determine the status of assigned tasks. Controlling includes making decisions and taking steps to meet the project deadline and budget limits, as necessary. Project managers make these decisions based on the facts accumulated, so communication is critical during the monitoring/controlling process. As mentioned previously, actions taken during this phase may result in a re-evaluation of the various plans (scope, time, and risk), updates in the documentation, and new tasks being created and assigned.

Closing

Projects must be concluded, and the closing process is handled with the same attention to detail and data collection used throughout the previous processes. Closing for project managers is similar to the post-convention tasks encountered by meeting professionals, e.g., paying bills, thanking attendees, and conducting evaluations. In this phase, the project manager will find the **post-event report (PER)** provided by the Convention Industry Council (CIC) to be a helpful tool ("APEX Post-Event," 2005). The project manager would include a section known as "lessons learned," which explains unique aspects of the meeting and what the project team recommends for future meetings of this type.

Identifying the Process Group

Since the project lifecycle is both unique to the project and fluid up to a point, members of the project team can find themselves in different phases of the lifecycle at different times (see Figure 3.3, p. 38). If the project team consists of managers from offices such as procurement, travel, risk, and member services, the procurement manager could be working on strategic contract negotiations with an accom-

FIGURE 3.3 Project Management Team in Action
This photo represents a project management team working together while representing various units or departments in the organization.

modation provider, i.e., executing, while the director of member services is determining the appropriate type of speakers, i.e., planning, and the risk manager is waiting for more information so the process of determining response preferences to threats or opportunities can begin, i.e., initiating.

The project lifecycle phases, then, are defined in terms of which tasks occur, not in terms of when a phase begins and ends. The project manager communicates effectively with team members to monitor what tasks are necessary to project success, when they need to be started/concluded, and by whom they need to be done. Because PM has evolved to handle complex projects across many disciplines, the process is robust as well as flexible—the management process must fit the temporary and unique needs associated with a specific project. In this way, project management is a useful approach to organizing a complex meeting.

Project Management Knowledge Areas

PMI has identified knowledge areas for its discipline, just as the meetings industry has done through the CIC's Certified Meeting Professional Standards (CMP-IS), which is used as a guide for the compilation of this text. Some of these knowledge areas overlap between the disciplines (see Figure 3.4). The knowledge areas for PM as defined by PMI are *integration, scope, time, cost, quality, human resource, communication, risk, procurement*, and *stakeholder management* (*PMBOK*®, 2013).

All of these areas have specific inputs (the information and/or resources required to complete tasks or documentation), tools, techniques, and outputs (plans and documentation). Each knowledge area uses basic business skills, as well. Setting objectives and key performance indicators are necessary steps the project team will complete across the knowledge areas.

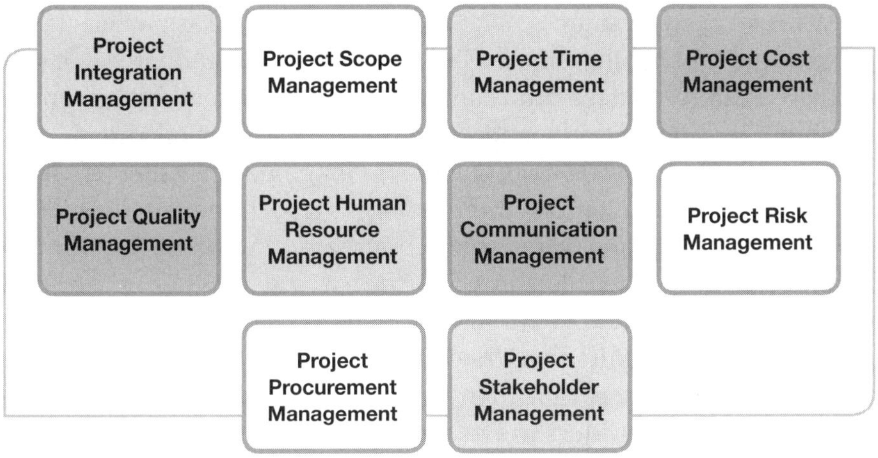

FIGURE 3.4 Project Management Knowledge Areas The project management discipline has identified 10 knowledge areas that define project management practice. This is an evolving discipline, so emerging knowledge areas are anticipated (*PMBOK*®, 2013).

Strategic management principles suggest that the project team will maximize the use of resources and outcomes. In other words, the project team must use critical analysis to determine if this application of resources is appropriate to the organization and preferred project outcomes, or if those same resources could be utilized more productively elsewhere.

Project Integration Management

Typically, a project begins with a project charter. This may be a formal process in some enterprises where a committee or enterprise leader makes a declaration that the project will be undertaken. This project charter authorizes the project manager to start the project and commit enterprise resources to the project. Resource limits may be set at this point, but they are usually preliminary estimates, rather than specific line items for budgeting purposes. The integration of resources across the enterprise is completed through the PM plan, which springs from the project charter.

Project Scope Management

The project manager will be required to define the project scope. This step is critical to successful project completion, because it helps set limits to resource commitment and utilizes project objectives to guide the project lifecycle phases. In the scope management area, the project team will create a **work breakdown structure (WBS)**, which identifies tasks and creates a framework for a timeline or schedule (which is found in Project Time Management) for each of the identified tasks. In addition, the WBS will suggest who will be responsible for task completion and in what order tasks have to be completed.

Project Time Management

The project manager is responsible for developing the project schedule, which can be a complex endeavor. Once all key internal stakeholders have been identified, the project manager must determine when each

key points

Example of Task List for Work Breakdown Structure

- Registration
- Audiovisual
- Exhibition
- Marketing
- Risk management
- Onsite management

department needs resources, who is in charge of each task, which tasks are independent of others, and when tasks are co-dependent. All of this is charted carefully to maximize the application of enterprise resources, to minimize "down" times, and to complete the project on time.

An example illustrates this time management challenge. In a medium-size organization, the meetings department requests that employee travel plans be completed in the first week of July for the annual meeting scheduled in mid-August. The travel department, however, is on a retreat the first week of July. They inform the project manager, who consults the schedule and determines that the travel plans must be made earlier than originally requested. However, the key internal stakeholders are extremely busy during the last week of June and suggest the first week of that month as the target date for travel plans. The travel department concurs; the project manager communicates this information to the budget manager and other members of the project team. The accounting office must make adjustments to their system, since the new target date changes when the cost for travel is encumbered—from the next fiscal year (July through June) to the current fiscal year.

key points

Common Time Management Tools

- Gantt chart
- Program evaluation & review technique (PERT)
- Critical path method (CPM)

Common tools to analyze the schedule and any notable variations include (but are not limited to) the Gantt chart (named after an engineer and management consultant) and program evaluation and review technique (PERT). A website has been devoted to Gantt charts, and it explains that a Gantt chart identifies required tasks, and when they must be started and concluded to meet the project deadline. A simple Gantt chart can be created in Microsoft® Excel, but proprietary software for developing PM charts is available from numerous sources, as well.

The program evaluation and review technique (PERT), created by the US Navy in the 1950s, is used to convey relationships between tasks and how tasks are scheduled. The value of PERT charting is to assist in scheduling tasks when only some of the elements of the task are known. The project manager uses formulas for finding the expected amount of time spent on a task by estimating together the least amount of time, the most amount of time, and the probable amount of time each task will take. A notable event (though certainly not the most recent) to use PERT was the 1968 Winter Olympics in Grenoble, France. PERT was used extensively to plan, implement, and assess that project. Microsoft® provides an application, known as Visio, to create PERT charts with other online apps available for this charting process.

In a digital era, most project managers report to key personnel via an Intranet. When the reporting system contains multiple charts and graphs, the project manager typically creates a **dashboard**. This could be described as an elaborate, interactive table of contents.

The critical path method (CPM) is an essential process utilized by project managers. CPM is often discussed when PERT charts are

SUSTAINABILITY *in* Practice

Sustainability requires the use of high-level project management skills at every stage of event planning, from initiation through implementation, monitoring, and closing. This graphic represents a classic "plan-do-check-act" environmental planning model. This model is applicable to every aspect of the meeting/event planning process, e.g., site selection, housing management, food and beverage, marketing, transportation, and exhibitor coordination. Ideally, sustainability should be integrated into the planning process and not perceived or managed as a separate activity. Meeting professionals should be encouraged to build economic, environmental, or social sustainability requirements into existing processes, e.g., templates and RFPs. Event sustainability also requires careful attention to scope, deadlines, cost, quality control, staff training and accountability, communication, risk management, procurement policies, and stakeholder management. Sustainable event management is increasingly being recognized as a vehicle for greening the supply chain and driving organizational change, as well. Onsite monitoring and post-event data collection and analysis are continuing challenges for individuals and organizations committed to sustainability. Fortunately, meeting professionals can choose from an increasing number of destinations, convention centers, hotels, caterers, and other industry suppliers who are able to provide clients with data on critical issues, e.g., waste diversion, water savings, energy consumption, carbon emissions, local purchasing, and social responsibility program outcomes. In addition, the migration from static documents to online project and event management software is allowing teams to more easily collaborate and be accountable for the necessary follow-up, documentation, and verification of sustainability performance.

—Deborah R. Popely

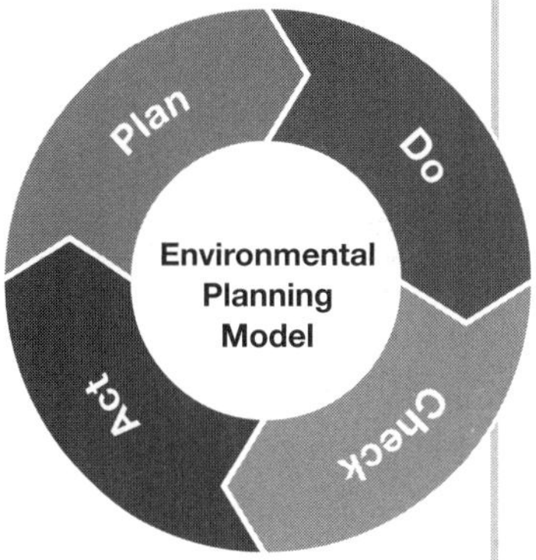

mentioned, although they are also applicable to Gantt charts. The CPM provides a timeline, the tasks, and their relationships, and may evolve as the project lifecycle advances. Tasks, in other words, can be altered, shifted in time, added, or subtracted. Schedule changes, though, should go through a formal process designed to provide documentation as to why, when, and how tasks shift.

Project Cost Management

The concept of cost management goes beyond a simple budget. The project manager must follow contract obligations, accounts payable and receivable, and the timing of cash flow throughout the project's lifecycle. While meeting professionals follow the budget limits, the project manager must monitor costs and revenue across multiple stakeholder groups and keep key internal stakeholders informed of any potential budget adjustments. While a meeting may exceed budget, the project manager would need to provide a sound rationale for this expenditure and items should not be a surprise to the project team.

Project Quality Management

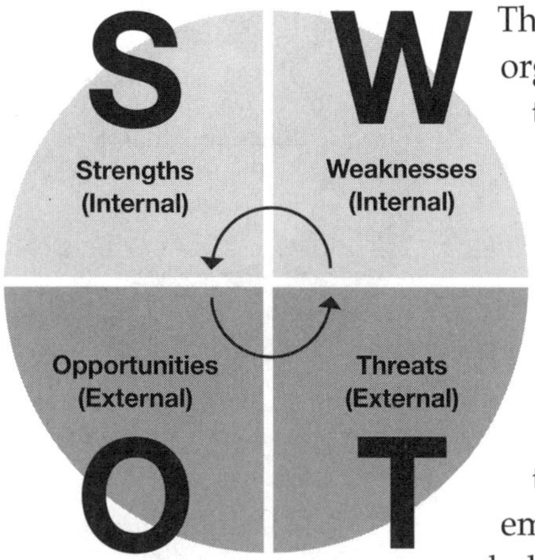

FIGURE 3.5 Elements of SWOT Analysis In a SWOT analysis, the strengths and weakness represent the current situation within an organization while the opportunities and threats are external to the organization.

The American Society of Quality (ASQ) suggests that quality in an organization is based on customer satisfaction (ASQ, 2014); the International Organization for Standardization concurs in its series of publications about quality management (ISO 9000, 2005). Since most project managers oversee a project that is intended for a specific customer, satisfaction with the project outcome is of paramount importance. This parallels meeting management, but the meeting professional has multiple "customers" for a specific meeting. Therefore, meeting professionals and project managers share a focus on quality management as a process. ASQ outlines these elements in the quality management process: customer focus, employee involvement (this could be stated more broadly as "stakeholder involvement"), process orientation, integration of departments across the enterprise, systematic and strategic techniques, continual improvement, fact-based decision making, and critical communication (ASQ, 2014).

Project Human Resource Management

The project manager is focused on a specific area in human resource management—choosing the project team and assigning tasks as needed to complete the project on time. Project managers often request specific people in the organization for the project team, which requires diplomatic skills and talent recognition. Further, the project manager may be called upon to review project team members, and these reviews are shared with the employee as well as the employee's supervisor. The human resources office is responsible for other personnel services, such as benefits and salaries. The project manager, though, is responsible for knowing when an employee is necessary for project success and which employee may be best suited for the assigned tasks.

Project Communication Management

The project manager concentrates on collaboration and excellent communication within the project team and with key stakeholders. This requires numerous communication delivery methods, including email, phone calls, oral presentations, and reports. Project managers rely on numerous tools to convey complex data. Since timing is significant in organizational management, the project manager must quickly communicate costs and tasks, create contracts and schedules, and calculate status as needed throughout the project lifecycle.

Project Risk Management

The concept of risk is associated with negative and positive events that impact the project's critical path or outcome. Threats and opportunities are numerous in PM, and meetings have a unique set of potential risks. For risk management, the project team will identify risks in a SWOT analysis (strengths, weaknesses, opportunities, and threats) by at least three characteristics: probability, potential damage, and resource needs as determined by how the organization responds to the risk (see Figure 3.5). SWOT analysis was developed in the 1960s during analysis of Fortune 500 companies by Albert Humphrey and the Stanford Research Institute; the process focuses on project objectives and risks that may impact the accomplishment of those objectives. It requires objective evaluation of the organization's current situation and identification of predictable events that will, if they occur, utilize organizational resources.

key points

Risk Characteristics

- Probability
- Potential damage
- Resource needs

When a risk is categorized as a project threat, the organization has four possible responses: absorb the risk, mitigate the damage caused, transfer the damage to another party, or avoid the risk. When a risk is categorized as a project opportunity, the organization can exploit, enhance, share, or accept the risk (*PMBOK*®, 2013, pp. 344–346). The project manager is responsible for identifying potential risks, analyzing them, and making recommendations to the organization for possible responses and the potential outcomes (see Figure 3.6).

Threats to meeting success can be man-made or natural. They can be mild or catastrophic. While meetings have numerous potential threats, they also encounter opportunities that, if poorly managed, can be lost. An example will illustrate this point: Exposition A in the information technology (IT) industry hosts hundreds of exhibitors. Exposition B, hosted by a competitor, has been losing attendee numbers over the past five years, so the host cancels future expositions. This is an oppor-

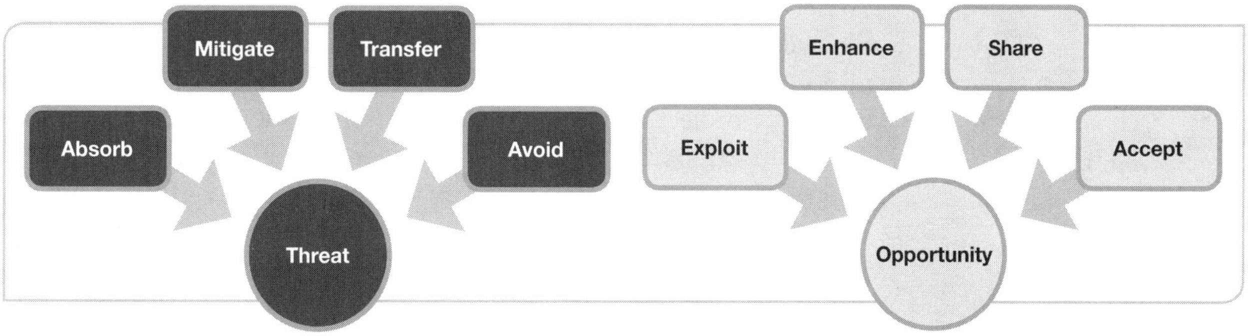

FIGURE 3.6 Possible Responses to Project Threats and Opportunities Risk analysis will identify both threats and opportunities to the project and will make recommendations for organizational response, should these risks actually occur.

tunity for the project team for Exposition A to respond strategically; e.g., contact potential exhibitors for the cancelled exposition with marketing materials for Exposition A, which is still an active project.

Project Procurement Management

Many organizations put procurement (or purchasing) in a specific department that not only manages day-to-day purchases and payments, but also sets policies for employees to follow. The project manager must know the policies. Procurement could set policies for travel, overnight accommodations, food, contract obligations, reimbursement processes and limits, as well as many other meeting-related resources. Part of the difficulty in procurement management is deciding when, how much, and from whom to purchase. The project manager will be responsible not only for following set policy, but also influencing policy development for the organization. Policy requirements can include any of the following and many more:

- Purchase all travel arrangements through an exclusive travel agency.
- Use tax exemption (for a non-profit association) on all allowable purchases. It is important to note that taxation exemptions are determined by local government agencies in some countries. The project manager must know the location taxation requirements as well as organizational policy.
- Provide receipts for all food purchases and provide verification of meals covered by registration fees.
- Use the lowest-priced hotel reserved by the meeting host instead of the most convenient hotel (often the "headquarters" hotel).

Project Stakeholder Management

key points

Classification of Stakeholders

- Internal
- External

Two classifications of stakeholders are important to project managers when the project is a meeting: internal and external. Internal stakeholders are employees, some volunteers, and stockholders (When the company is a publicly held organization, the stockholder is a partial owner of the company). Project managers have various means to profile stakeholders, often based on interest in the project, influence on project success, and communication needs. The essential stakeholder group for project managers is the project team itself and most of the communication from the project manager will be with this group. The project manager will also focus on the organization's leadership, as well as other human resources committed to the project.

External stakeholders are typically of more concern to the meeting professional than the project manager, if these are two separate groups. External stakeholders include exhibitors, suppliers, meeting attendees, potential customers of meeting artifacts (e.g., video recordings of sessions), and many other stakeholders (such as the media).

PROFESSIONAL DILEMMA

You are a freelance project manager who negotiated a favorable contract to work with a government agency that is hosting a major three-day training meeting. In the contract, you agreed to performing "other necessary duties as requested" because a list of every task was not possible. You realized the agency had not planned or hosted large meetings, which is why they wanted a contract with you. Your contract was not based on hours worked but rather a flat fee, which was a concern. The meeting is just months away and you are being asked to perform basic office work that is not typical for a project manager; and now, they want you to be at the meeting. The hours worked are far more than expected. How will you handle your refusal to comply with these "other duties" and what might be the response? What kind of language would you need in future contracts to protect yourself?

The project manager, though, is less likely to be in contact with these stakeholders, unlike the meeting professional, who often knows many of these stakeholders by name. Of course, this is not a universal description of roles; external stakeholder management may be a large part of the project manager's responsibilities.

Expanding Areas of Management

Two significant areas of concern for meeting professionals and project managers are supply chain management and change management.

key points

Areas of Concern

- Supply chain management
- Change management

Supply chain management Supply chain management is the global process of identifying project suppliers and their suppliers to track potential threats and opportunities in the chain. If the food and beverage supplier for a meeting, for instance, is experiencing problems with weather-related shortages for certain foods, adjusting the meeting's menus would be prudent. The meeting professional could wait for the supplier to broach this topic or be proactive and avoid the threat to a successful meeting. At times, knowing what supplies are plentiful in the chain and what supplies might experience delays, shortages, or price hikes can make a significant difference in budget management. According to *Supply Chain Management Review*, changes in recent years in the global economy have led to significant alterations in how companies select suppliers and which suppliers they select: "In order to source from China, an intermediary is hired (in Europe, probably known well, or in China, certainly less well known) who deals with an unknown supplier. The more global the supply chain becomes, and the more intermediaries between your company and the original supplier, the less you know about the quality of that component. Trust is diminished" (Craig & McNamara, 2014, para. 5). Consumer protection laws vary by country, so a thorough investigation of the supply chain and making adjustments as necessary could influence customer satisfaction significantly.

Change management Change management is a process focused on people; it addresses how people will be managed when change is imminent, while change is implemented, and after a change has occurred, but requires reinforcement. Prosci, a company dedicated to helping organizations with change management, identifies senior leadership, managers and supervisors, the project team, and other employees as distinct groups in the organization who will have different reactions to announced change. When a meeting is either the catalyst for change or the outcome of it, change management principles and techniques can make the process more successful and rewarding for the employees involved (Prosci, 2014).

SUMMARY

Project management is often referenced as a business process that plans, implements, monitors, and closes a temporary and unique undertaking. As such, PM is successfully applied to the meetings industry. However, "project manager" and "meeting professional" are not interchangeable terms. The differential element is what, precisely, the project or meeting professional accomplishes for the organization and project success. Many elements commonly assigned to the project manager—from developing the scope to following the critical path—will also serve the meetings industry. Differences between these two approaches to managing a temporary project—like a meeting—do exist. PM, though, is a preferred process in businesses around the globe. Learning PM skills will be an essential professional development focus for the entry-level meeting professional.

KEY WORDS

dashboard
portfolio manager
post-event report (PER)
program manager
project
project charter
project management (PM)
project manager
project team
scope creep
work breakdown structure (WBS)

DISCUSSION QUESTIONS

1. What are the potential advantages when an organization can ask a meeting professional to serve as project manager?
2. What are the potential advantages when an organization has both a meeting professional and a project manager?
3. What is scope creep? Provide an example.
4. What is global supply chain management and how might that impact a meeting for 30,000 attendees held in Europe or the United States?

4

Designing the Meeting Experience

Susan M. Tinnish, PhD
Dean, School of Hospitality Management
Kendall College

Glen C. Ramsborg, PhD, CMP
Professor (retired)
Kendall College

Main Topics

PART ONE NEEDS ASSESSMENT
- Defining Needs
- Elements of the Needs Assessment

PART TWO FROM NEEDS ASSESSMENT TO ACTION
- Strategic Alignment with the Organization
- Learning Objectives and Program Outcomes

PART THREE THE MEETING ENVIRONMENT
- Physical Environment
- Physiological Environment
- Psychological Environment

PART FOUR MEETING-DESIGN DECISIONS
- Meeting Modality
- Meeting Structure
- Program Components
- Formats
- Content
- Sequencing and Pacing the Meeting Flow
- Engaging the Audience
- Emotionally Rich Techniques
- Multi-Sensory Meetings
- Evaluation

PART FIVE THE SPEAKERS
- Finding Speakers
- Speaker Management

Learner Outcomes

Upon the completion of this chapter, the student should be able to:

1. Describe the process of creating a meeting experience.
2. Explain the three responses (physical, physiological, psychological) to a meeting environment.
3. Diagram a minimum of three common room sets.
4. Describe the facets of speaker management for a meeting.
5. Explain the influence of a needs assessment on meeting design decisions.

CMP INTERNATIONAL STANDARDS

Domain A. Strategic Planning
Skill 1. Manage Strategic Plan for Meeting or Event
SubSkills. 1.01, 1.02
Skill 2. Develop Sustainability Plan for Meeting or Event
SubSkills. 2.01, 2.02
Domain B. Project Management
Skill 4. Plan Meeting or Event Project
SubSkill. 4.03
Domain G. Meeting or Event Design
Skill 14. Design Program
SubSkills. 14.01, 14.02, 14.03, 14.04
Skill 15. Engage Speakers and Performers
SubSkill. 15.01, 15.02, 15.03, 15.04
Skill 17. Design Environment
SubSkills. 17.01, 17.02
Domain H. Site Management
Skill 21. Design Site Layout
SubSkill. 21.01

Meetings are a source of inspiration, education, and connection for attendees. Meeting professionals create experiences that inspire the heart, enrich the mind, and rejuvenate the soul for all who attend. This is often described as the **meeting experience**. The meeting experience is an encounter that provides an attendee with an opportunity to engage with others through seeing, hearing, and doing; as a result, higher-level knowledge or skill is achieved.

The meeting professional strives to create a meeting that yields a positive experience for attendees. The meeting experience is designed through the lens of a needs assessment. The process of creating such an experience includes developing the meeting design and logistics, as well as employing strategies that allow attendees to absorb, retain, and apply the main messages of the meeting. The environment, speakers, and other human dynamics define the meeting experience.

PART ONE Needs Assessment

Meeting planning begins with a **needs assessment**. A needs assessment creates the foundation upon which all decisions about the meeting are vetted and considered. Before a meeting professional can design a meeting experience, a needs assessment must be completed.

Defining Needs

The process of a completing a needs assessment is a core business skill for meetings and other projects. Simply stated, a needs assessment helps determine gaps or needs for stakeholders and guides subsequent decision-making. The results of the needs assessment serve as the basis for determining what a project should accomplish. More generically defined, a needs assessment is a process of identifying stakeholder requirements in order to select methods, means, tactics, tools, and approaches to solving problems.

Meeting professionals use a needs assessment to define what a meeting will achieve, or its goals. A needs assessment may be a formal written document, a survey, or a set of information gathered through informal dialogue with stakeholders where the questions "why," "how," "who," "where," and "when" are asked to extract a complete understanding of the meeting's past and its future.

Elements of the Needs Assessment

A needs assessment consists of four elements: the meeting history; stakeholder requirements, objectives, and outcomes; gap analysis; and the target audience profile.

Meeting History

Reviewing the past history of a meeting helps assess its successes and challenges and allows the meeting professional to apply lessons learned from the past to the current meeting. In addition, this historical review allows meeting professionals to extrapolate data to determine future requirements, goals, and objectives. For example, past attendance at an association's annual convention is useful to predict the coming year's attendance. A meeting professional can evaluate the degree to which previous meetings achieved their outcomes (goals). Meeting history provides statistical information, demographic information, and evaluative information. Meeting history may be contained in a post-event report ("APEX Industry Glossary," 2011). When the meeting is a first-time event for the organization, historical data from similar meetings held by the organization can be examined. Additionally, the organization might reach out to other organizations that have experience with a similar meeting.

Stakeholder Requirements, Objectives, and Outcomes

Stakeholder requirements are the reasons, or purposes, for holding the meeting, e.g., to have time for the board of directors to gather on official business. Objectives are action oriented and focus on what the stakeholder is intended to do. An outcome is the result of that action; it is what an organization realizes through the fulfillment of objectives. Organizations measure meeting success through outcomes.

Gap Analysis

Gap analysis builds the bridge between objectives and outcomes and documents what is necessary to span the discrepancy between what exists and what is desired (see Figure 4.1). Another value in the gap analysis is identifying the existing environmental constraints underlying the gap; these may be issues outside the scope of a meeting, i.e., lack of resources or time.

key questions

Defining Meeting Requirements, Objectives, and Outcomes

Requirements
- Are compulsory components in a meeting present?
- Define the necessary conditions for a meeting, e.g., venue, time of year.

Objectives
- Are clear descriptions of intended results stated?
- Amplify goals and translate them into specific aims to achieve within a time frame and with available resources.

Outcomes
- Are achievements that occur as a consequence of the meeting stated?
- Define the end product of successful completion of the meeting's objectives.

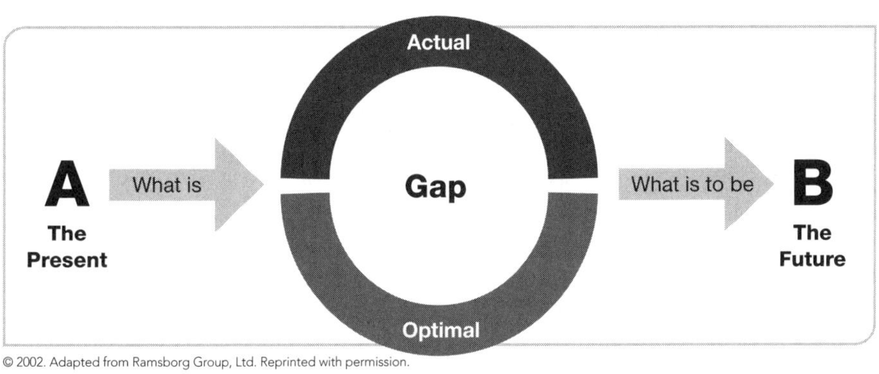

FIGURE 4.1 Gap Analysis Gap analysis is a project-management tool for determining what needs to be accomplished to meet outcomes. Point A is the present situation and Point B is the desired future state. These two points are separated by a gap.

key points

Causes of Gaps

When there is a gap between a current situation and the way a stakeholder group wants something to be, there is usually a cause for that gap. Some common causes of gaps include the following:

- Lack of knowledge
- Lack of skills
- Lack of motivation
- Lack of resources or time

key points

Key Characteristics of the Target Audience

- Audience demographic information
- Audience preferences
- Existing knowledge
- Existing skills
- Current attitudes

A meeting can assist in eliminating the gap or discrepancy in knowledge, attitudes, or skills. This is done by bringing stakeholders together to share knowledge, ideas, and expertise.

Target Audience

Another important element of a needs assessment is defining the audience for a meeting. Audiences can be classified by demographics (e.g., income, age, and location), preferences, existing knowledge and skills, and current attitudes. In addition, this information is useful for designing the meeting and marketing materials.

Fragmentation On occasions, audiences can be fragmented. This happens because either the meeting is serving multiple audiences or the audience profile is quite diverse. To avoid fragmentation, the meeting professional can take various approaches. Three effective considerations are:

Cultural The changing face of U.S. demographics mandates meetings be sensitive to and account for cultural diversity in terms of race, ethnicity, gender, class, religion, and geographic orientation.

Generational It is common to have a variety of generations in an audience. Each generation brings its own values and characteristics, priorities, and definition of success to the meeting. The generational divide manifests itself in changed expectations about work and the workplace and different definitions of success, work ethic, and

Generation	Early Sources of Information
Traditionalists **Born:** 1925–1945	**Radio** where listening is the primary mode of acquiring information and being entertained
Baby Boomers **Born:** 1946–1964	**Television** with black-and-white images, later replaced by color TV, on five channels
Generation X **Born:** 1965–1981	**Standalone personal computers** **Television featuring multiple channels** including programming specifically focused on their generation **Video games**
Millennials or Generation Y **Born:** 1982–2004	**Interconnected personal computers** via the Internet **Customized information and entertainment**, e.g., Netflix or Amazon **Text messaging** with its own vocabulary and rules **Instant messaging** **Instant access** to people and information through cell phones, smartphones, and personal digital assistants

FIGURE 4.2 Early Sources for Learning Across the Generations People's sources and natural modes of learning are affected by their formative learning years. Technology has greatly impacted where and how people access information (Ramsborg & Tinnish, 2008b, p. 48. Reprinted with permission of *Convene*.).

loyalty. These differences often entail younger generations preferring flexibility over structure, valuing participation over hierarchy, and seeing their organizational role in more personal and humane terms rather than serving as an instrument of the organization.

Technological The emergence of new technology often creates further fragmentation. When considering technology, the meeting professional might research how members of the target audience learned information as children. Technologies often represent how audiences "learned to learn" and can dictate comfort levels even years later. While people do adapt to new channels of delivery, contrast how technology affects their early years of absorbing information as depicted in Figure 4.2 (Ramsborg & Tinnish, 2008b).

Media can also lead to fragmentation as consumers demand and receive a very specific type of information targeted to a specific audience, e.g., cable television channels, specialized magazines, and Internet sites (Anderson, 2008). To be effective, the meeting professional needs to satisfy specific audiences while designing a meeting with the power to unite people and help attendees see the ways in which they are alike.

From Needs Assessment to Action

PART TWO

The needs assessment determines what must be accomplished through the meeting. A meeting professional uses organizational information and the needs assessment to predict how a meeting will move the organization in a desired direction. The needs assessment uses organizational strategies, goals, and objectives to plan activities and ensure a meeting is a valuable and strategic use of scarce resources.

Strategic Alignment with the Organization

A meeting must be strategically aligned with the organization's goals and objectives. Creating strategic alignment between a meeting and the organization involves understanding and applying strategic thinking. Primarily, this strategic thinking aims to ensure optimal communication within the meeting, which supports the organization's reputation, brand, and mission.

key questions

Strategic Alignment Questions

- Why is the organization holding this meeting?
- Are there alternatives to a meeting that support the purpose?
- What is the purpose of this meeting?
- How will the meeting align with organizational aspirations?

Learning Objectives and Program Outcomes

The gap analysis identifies current levels of knowledge, skills, and/or attitudes so as to allow an organization to move from the present (Point A) to a more desired, future state (Point B). Based on the requirements, objectives, and outcomes specified in the needs analysis, the meeting professional can develop meeting-specific goals, objectives, and outcomes. In addition, each program component or part of the meeting may include specific objectives and desired outcomes. At the program-component level, these objectives are termed "learning objectives" and "program outcomes."

key points

Concept Application

Objectives and outcomes apply to:

- Entire meeting
- Specific parts of the meeting termed "program components" (see p. 63 for further definition)

The idea of learning might not seem directly related to all meetings; however, all effective meetings include learning. Webster's Dictionary defines "learning" as "gaining knowledge or skill." Learning is a change in the way people think, feel, and/or behave. When this definition is applied, all meetings are about learning. Meetings are held to change what people know, what they do, and/or how they do it. Therefore, all individual program components should include **learning objectives** and **program outcomes**.

Learning objectives (intended attendee actions)

- Focus attention on the specific types of behavior attendees are expected to demonstrate following the meeting.

Program outcomes (results of attendee learning and action)

- Describe precisely what the meeting attendees accomplish or produce as a result of attending the meeting (this may be long after the meeting is concluded).

The purpose of learning objectives for a meeting

- Promote careful thought about what is to be accomplished through the program component.
- Communicate what the program component is about.
- Help attendees make decisions regarding attendance and prioritizing attending specific components.
- Encourage speakers to think carefully about what is important, making presentations more directed and organized.

The purpose of program outcomes for a meeting

- Provide feedback to attendees as objectives are accomplished.
- Define the contract between speaker and audience with explicit expectations.
- Set standards for program evaluation.

Writing Objectives

The effectiveness of objectives is directly related to their level of specificity. Several models exist to guide the important exercise of writing objectives.

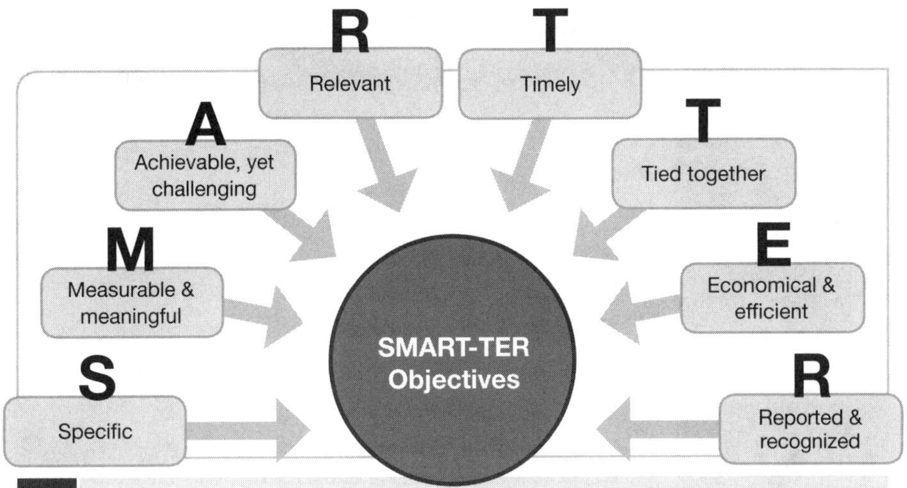

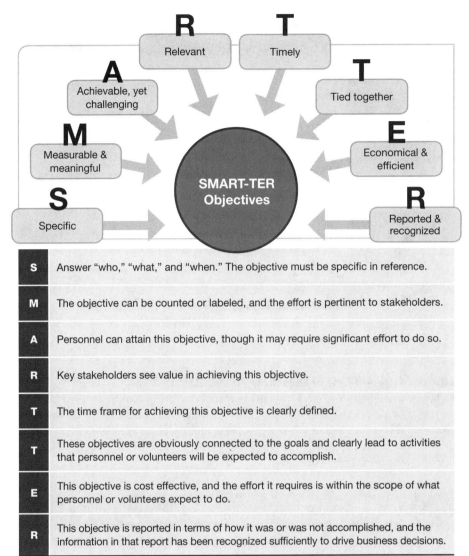

S	Answer "who," "what," and "when." The objective must be specific in reference.
M	The objective can be counted or labeled, and the effort is pertinent to stakeholders.
A	Personnel can attain this objective, though it may require significant effort to do so.
R	Key stakeholders see value in achieving this objective.
T	The time frame for achieving this objective is clearly defined.
T	These objectives are obviously connected to the goals and clearly lead to activities that personnel or volunteers will be expected to accomplish.
E	This objective is cost effective, and the effort it requires is within the scope of what personnel or volunteers expect to do.
R	This objective is reported in terms of how it was or was not accomplished, and the information in that report has been recognized sufficiently to drive business decisions.

FIGURE 4.3 SMART-TER Objectives Use the SMART-TER framework to write objectives that document clearly what will be achieved through a meeting (Reed, 2009. Reprinted with permission.).

SMART-TER Objectives should be SMART-TER, building on the traditional SMART model (Doran, 1981). The expanded and enhanced acronym accounts for various stakeholders' perspectives, i.e., marketing and public relations, human resources, financial management, and other business centers (see Figure 4.3).

A-B-C-D Model Some meeting professionals prefer writing objectives by a specific formula known as the A-B-C-D method (Heinrich, Molenda, Russell, & Smaldino, 1996). "A" is for audience, "B" is for behavior, "C" for conditions, and "D" for degree of mastery needed (see Figure 4.4, p. 54) (Miller & Ramsborg, 2006, p. 294).

In a strong objective, the "B" is represented by an active verb. The action should be observable. When writing learner objectives, it is easy to use words that are not observable or measurable, e.g., know, understand, appreciate, comprehend, learn, enjoy, or believe. However, it is better to use active verbs like those listed in the Key Points box as these behaviors can be observed and measured.

key points

Active Verbs & Observable Behaviors

- Solve
- Develop
- Present
- Apply
- Write
- Publish
- Analyze
- Calculate
- Create
- Evaluate
- Reconcile
- Demonstrate

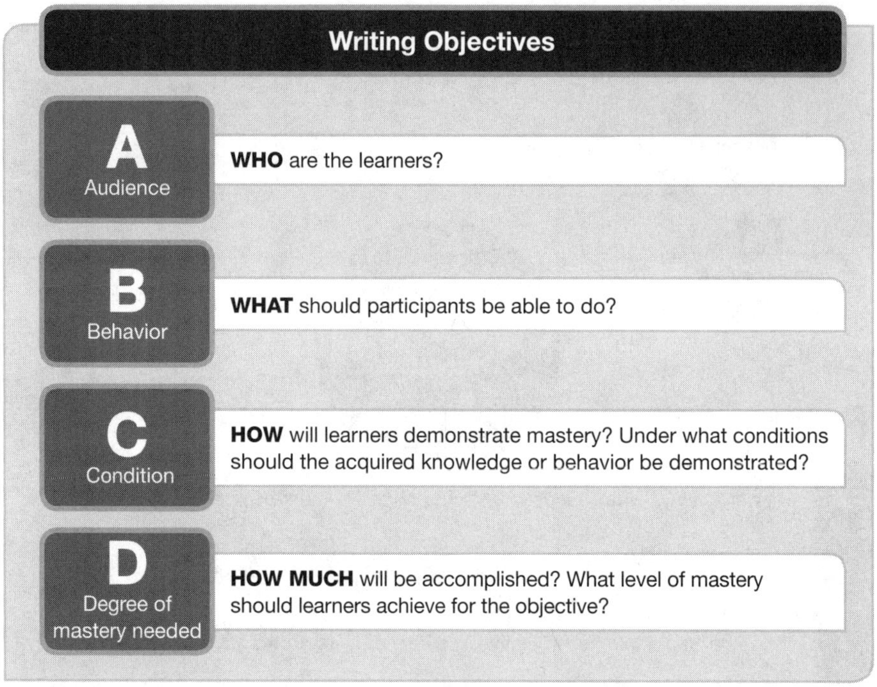

FIGURE 4.4 A-B-C-Ds of Objectives This ABCD formula helps write learning objectives. Although the "A" and "D" are often implicit ("calculate a break-even budget" versus "all attendees will be able to calculate a break-even budget within 10 minutes and with 100 percent accuracy"), complete learning objectives are the underpinning of all program components in a meeting (Tinnish & Ramsborg, 2008c, May, p. 75. Reprinted with permission of *Convene*.).

PART THREE The Meeting Environment

The space where people gather for a meeting is defined as the **meeting environment** and consists of three aspects—physical, physiological, and psychological—as depicted in Figure 4.5.

Finkel (1987) outlines optional spaces that meeting professionals can consider utilizing (see Figure 4.6). The process for creating the meeting experience starts as soon as a site is selected and continues as the program is defined and space within the site is selected and altered.

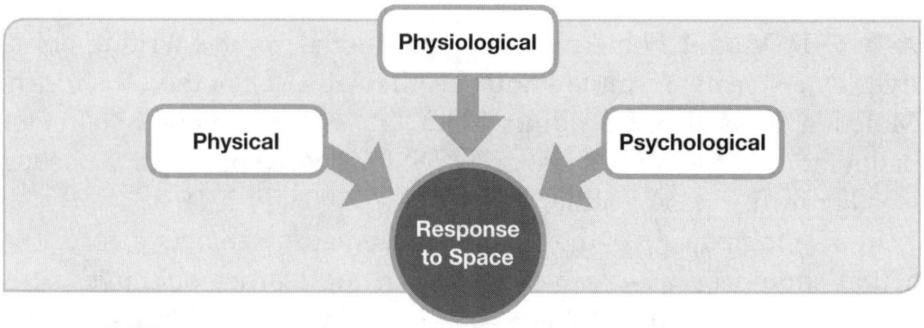

FIGURE 4.5 Participant Responses to Space While people react individually and differently, some base responses are similar. Thus meeting professionals can judiciously use generalized responses to assist in their planning efforts.

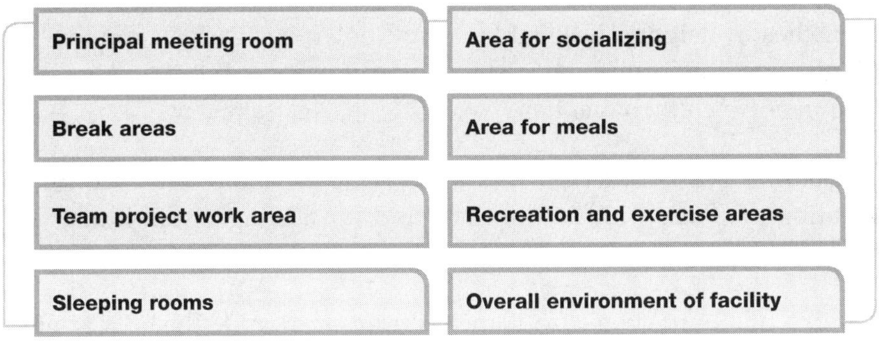

FIGURE 4.6 Physical Gathering Space Each space presents opportunity to create the meeting experience. Informal learning often occurs outside the principal meeting rooms and these alternative areas should not be overlooked as an opportunity to create value (Adapted from Finkel, 1987, p. 22).

Physical Environment

The physical environment is routinely altered for meetings. Meeting professionals consider the environment from both aesthetic and productivity perspectives. Estimates indicate that motivation, meaningfulness, and memory account for approximately 75 percent of learning, while the remaining 25 percent is dependent on the effects of the physical environment (White, 1972; Arieff, 2014; Lippman, 2010; Schweitzer, Gilpin, & Frampton, 2004).

Facility Equipment

At the selected venue, the equipment and available resources can be used to create and prepare the environment. The meeting professional may also need to overcome certain challenges presented by the facility to achieve a specific environmental effect. As part of the planning process, the meeting professional will determine the size of space for each meeting or event and the availability of the necessary equipment to support the format(s) selected. A review of the facility inventory assists in preparing the room set-ups and identifies whether alterations to the proposed configurations are necessary or additional resources need to be secured from an outside source (Beck, 2006).

Tables Most facilities have an inventory of four types of tables: rectangular, round, cabaret, and serpentine.

Rectangular The most common dimensions are 6 to 8 feet in length and standard widths of both 18 and 30 inches. In conference centers, 24-inch-wide tables are common. Commonly called "classroom-style furniture," these tables offer benefits such as increased seating capacity (in comparison to round tables), attendee comfort, and support of learning needs. Rectangular tables are used to create multiple configurations.

Round The 72-inch round table is standard, although some facilities also maintain a supply of 60- and 66-inch tables. Round tables are often referred to as "banquet-style" seating arrangements.

Cabaret These tables vary from 15 to 30 inches in diameter and 36 to 50 inches in height. These tables, also known as "cocktail rounds" or "high boys," are primarily used for cocktail parties and receptions, and within entertainment venues.

Serpentine Also known as "half moons," these tables are used when creating displays and food buffets, and for adding visual interest to the various set-ups (Beck, 2006).

Chairs Standard chairs are 20 inches from the front to the back at their base. Seat widths vary from 17.5 inches to 18.5 inches; however, most chairs in meeting facilities are not as wide as the average person. Tablet chairs, also called writing chairs, can be used when space is at a premium. This style of chair is often found in lecture halls and can be uncomfortable and too small for some attendees (Beck, 2006). Certain conference centers specifically employ ergonomic chairs to increase comfort (IACC, 2012).

Presentation configurations The room set-up would not be complete without accommodation for the front of the room, which most often includes a podium, lectern, and/or head table. A lectern can be either tabletop style or a freestanding floor model and is defined as "a stand upon which a speaker may rest notes or books" ("APEX Industry Glossary," 2011). For example, a panel discussion may require both a lectern and a head table, while a lecture may just require a podium and a small table for the speaker's materials. Lecterns are not podiums. A podium or riser is a raised platform where a speaker stands when presenting ("APEX Industry Glossary," 2011). Another example of a podium is the stand on which Olympic medalists receive their medals.

Risers are frequently used to elevate the head table and lectern, making it easier for speakers to view the audience. They are available

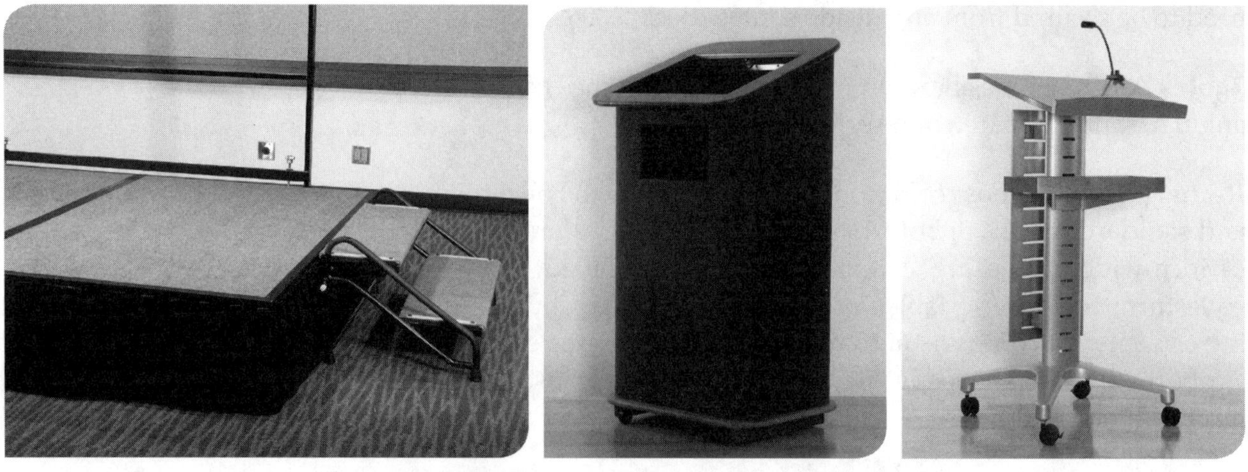

FIGURE 4.7 Examples of a Riser and Lectern Risers generally are 4 feet x 8 feet in size and are configured to create a stage area that will accommodate a lectern, head table, or larger area for entertainment. Risers are available in various heights.

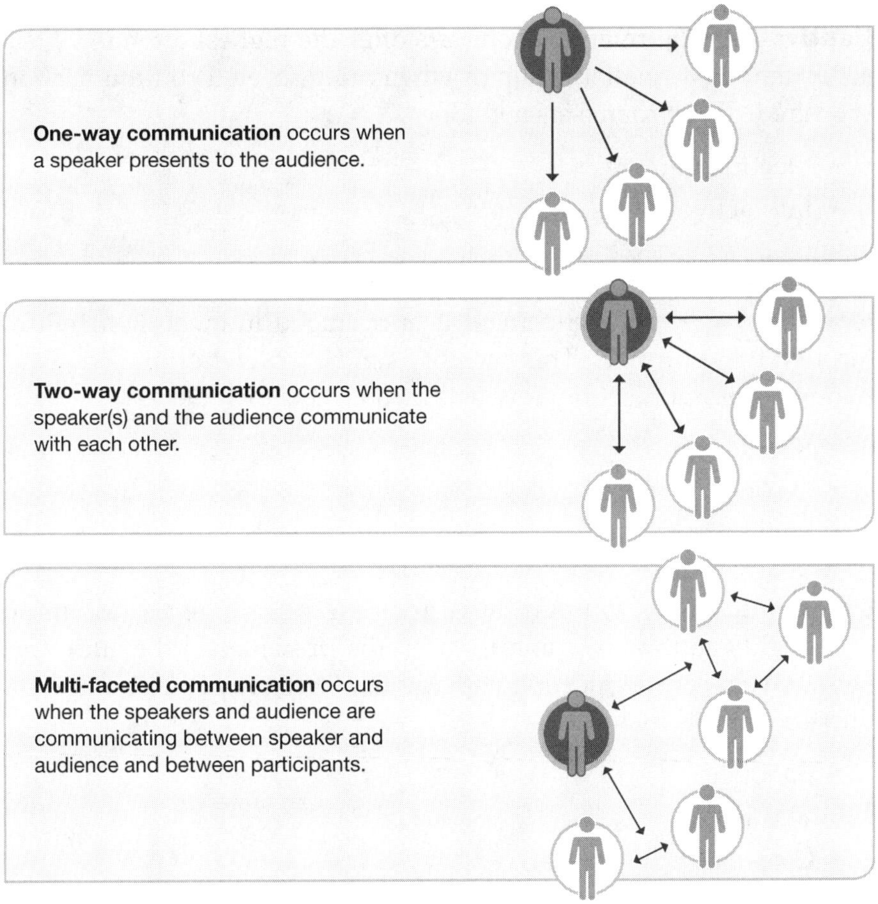

One-way communication occurs when a speaker presents to the audience.
Two-way communication occurs when the speaker(s) and the audience communicate with each other.
Multi-faceted communication occurs when the speakers and audience are communicating between speaker and audience and between participants.

FIGURE 4.8 Direction of Communication More and more meetings design two-way or multi-faceted communication into meetings. The value is in engaging the participants and in gaining their input into the meeting content.

in multiple heights (see Figure 4.7). The amount of rise depends upon the size of the room and number of attendees. Risers elevate the focus of attention by allowing attendees seated in the back of the room visibility (Beck, 2006).

Communication Flow

The **communication flow** describes the way content or information moves between the speaker and the audience. The room sets are directly linked to communication flow, which can be one-way, two-way, or multi-faceted as explained in Figure 4.8.

Overview of Room Sets

The basic layout of the meeting space wields strong influence on the reaction of attendees. **Room sets** are configurations of the tables and chairs and reinforce communication flow.

Choice of room sets requires considerable thought, expertise, and knowledge of what is going to take place in the space and the desired amount of communication. Each option affords different uses and works best under certain conditions. Three categories of room sets are captivating, engaging, and communicative. Appendix 1 (p. 324) describes in greater detail the specifications, applications, advantages, and challenges of the commonly used room sets.

key points

Audience Perceptions

- Ability to see and hear
- Tone, i.e., formal vs. informal
- Level of involvement
- Group dynamics
- Relationship of audience to speaker

Captivating Captivating room sets offer the highest attendee interaction among a smaller group or when multi-faceted communication is desired. These room sets include:

- Meeting pods
- Interactive circles

key questions

Amount of Communication Required

- Is the experience meant to be captivating for a relatively small number of people who closely engage with one another?
- Is the meeting intended to be engaging for the attendees, who interact with one another and/or enjoy two-way communication?
- Is the meeting intended to be primarily communicative so the audience receives one-way communication easily and clearly, but is also able to engage in two-way communication with those nearby?

Engaging Engaging room sets offer a moderate level of attendee interaction. Two-way engagement is encouraged in meeting activities through these formats. This category can be a blend of one-way and two-way communication flow. These room sets include:

- Boardroom
- U-shaped
- Hollow square

Communicative Communicative room sets promote the exchange of thoughts and ideas primarily from the presenter to the audience, i.e., one-way communication with minimal two-way communication. These room sets include:

- Banquet
- Theater
- Classroom

Throughout the chapter, photos of commonly used room sets appear: fixed theater seating (Figure 4.9); theater seating in a meeting room (Figure 4.10); classroom (Figure 4.11); fixed boardroom (Figure 4.12); conference (Figure 4.13); U-shaped (Figure 4.14); banquet seating (Figure 4.15, p. 60); and mod pod (Figure 4.16, p. 61).

FIGURE 4.9 Fixed Theater Seating with Stage Theater-style seating maximizes space; however, theater-style seating is not an ideal set-up for training meetings as attendees cannot easily take notes, enter into discussion with others, or maneuver handouts or training materials.

FIGURE 4.10 Theater Room Set Theater seating in a meeting room is an efficient use of space where seats need to be maximized. This room set can also be used in large spaces to accommodate very large audiences. It is best used when attendees will be passive in learning or being entertained.

FIGURE 4.11 Classroom Room Set A classroom room set is reminiscent of a traditional schoolroom set-up. This configuration is optimal for note-taking and allows all attendees to see the presenter and presentations materials. In this configuration, there are three seats per eight-foot table.

Physiological Environment

Attendees' physiological needs are central to creating a comfortable meeting environment. When basic physiological needs—physical comfort, food, water, room temperature, etc.—are adequately met, attendees are less likely to be distracted and more likely to focus on the content of the meeting.

Food and Beverage

Food and beverage (F&B) is an important physiological requirement. Meeting professionals design menus and plan F&B functions with an eye toward ensuring that the food is appropriate for the group and within the budget guidelines (see Figure 4.15, p. 60).

Food choices also impact an attendee's ability to think and retain information. Andrea Sullivan has been an advocate for improving attendee engagement via brain-friendly foods. Sullivan says, "What we eat greatly influences how we think and how we feel" (as cited in Loomis, 2012, para. 23).

Research is still evolving, but Sullivan notes that neuroscientists can identify the effects of specific foods on brain function: "There are two things I feel are most important for groups and planners to understand," says Sullivan. "The first is the need to keep blood sugar levels stable throughout the day. We do this by serving low-glycemic-index foods while minimizing white flour and sugars—the typical continental breakfast featuring bagels and pastries has got to go. The second is to minimize salt, which has an immediate effect of constricting circulation—within 30 minutes! This leads to decreased oxygen in the brain, harming our ability to think clearly" (as cited in Loomis, 2012, para. 25–26).

key points

Effects of Food on Brain Function

- Level of nerve chemicals in the brain regulating all mental processes
- Development and maintenance of brain cell function and structure
- Speed that nerve cells transmit messages from one neuron to the next
- Level of enzymes and their activity, which enhance brain function
- Amount of oxygen reaching the brain
- Ability of brain cells to transmit electrical messages

FIGURE 4.12 Fixed Boardroom Set Boardrooms feature a rectangular or oval table with chairs around all sides and ends, which is a formal, fixed configuration. This arrangement makes it somewhat more difficult for participants to see each other.

FIGURE 4.13 Conference Room Set A formal arrangement with participants seated around all sides of the table, this room set promotes dialogue between participants. Chairs with wheels enhance the flexibility of this set-up.

FIGURE 4.14 U-Shaped Room Set In this room layout, the meeting attendees can see each other, work in smaller discussion groups with those sitting close by, and see a speaker or audiovisual components at the open part of the U-shaped set-up.

Attendee Comfort

Attendee comfort has a direct effect on concentration and learning. The ambient temperature and lighting in the room impact attention, while noise from surrounding areas causes distraction and decreases attention.

Temperature Temperatures have a profound effect on comfort. Swings in ambient temperatures cause reactions in the brain and the rest of the body. For example, an increase in temperature above the comfort level may cause feelings of tiredness and sleepiness, while a decrease in temperature may cause restlessness and decrease attention span.

What makes for a target or desirable temperature will not be the same for all attendees: some people prefer warmer temperatures and others prefer cooler ones. Achieving the perfect temperature within a meeting space is next to impossible. As a guide, temperature in an empty meeting space should be cooler prior to the meeting start. This is because the temperature increases as the space fills with people. For example, one person emits the equivalent heat of a 100-watt light bulb each hour. Five hundred people in a room cause a considerable increase in the ambient temperature of the room (Ogin, 2014). A warmer space tends to lead to overall irritability and attendees in a cooler space will be less likely to feel sleepy ("Hot Environments," 2014).

key points

Comfort Zone

- Clothed person in winter—
  20–24 degrees (C); 68–75.2 degrees (F)
- Clothed person summer—
  23–26 degrees (C); 73.4–78.8 degrees (F)
- A person's perception of comfort is affected by room temperature, air movement (speed), humidity, clothing, and many other factors. For indoor settings, these temperature ranges are appropriate (University of Tasmania, 2007, pp. 2–4).

Lighting An ideal meeting environment uses natural light; however, this is not always possible. When using artificial light, consider eye

FIGURE 4.15 Banquet Seating Banquet seating is the room set of choice for most meal functions. It is also appropriate for breakout sessions, small committee meetings, or study groups involving group interaction with note taking.

FIGURE 4.16 Mod Pod
A pod room set provides collaborative work groups the capability to brainstorm or complete work projects. They can also return their attention to the facilitator and discuss ideas generated out of each work group.

fatigue or eyestrain. Straining to see in a dimly lit room causes eye fatigue, while lighting that is too bright results in eyestrain.

Lighting also affects presentations displayed on a screen. Direct lighting causes screen wash (hot spots) and decreases contrast. The screen should be positioned away from direct lighting or lighting directly above the screen. Attendee attention decreases significantly when the person has difficulty visualizing images on the screen.

Noise distractions A site inspection is the best opportunity to evaluate potential noise distraction from outside traffic, ventilation equipment, service corridors, kitchens, and audiovisual equipment. This visit is also the time to determine the quality of soundproofing, e.g., "air walls" or wall/curtain configurations, and the potential noise transfer from events on the other side of the wall. For example, a business meeting on one side and a band on the other side of the wall could be very disruptive for the meeting environment.

key points

Positive Psychological Environments

A constructive meeting environment will decrease stress for attendees and promote an affirmative environment where they:

- Learn quickly
- Are curious and creative
- Process complex information in chunks
- Create healthy "noise" while working with others
- Have the necessary personal and work space

Psychological Environment

An attendee's emotional wellbeing is closely linked to his or her ability to think effectively. How attendees feel influences their focus during the meeting. If they are enthusiastic, intrigued, and receptive, then they are psychologically accessible during the meeting.

Meeting-Design Decisions PART FOUR

Meeting professionals face important design decisions when planning meetings. Each design decision affects the meeting experience. Design begins with logistical decisions, but also seeks to unlock the full communication value of meetings. Design decisions should be grounded in the needs assessment, and the strategic alignment between the meeting and organizational strategy. Design decisions should also consider the interpersonal role of the attendees in the meeting. Figure 4.17 identifies some of the critical design decisions.

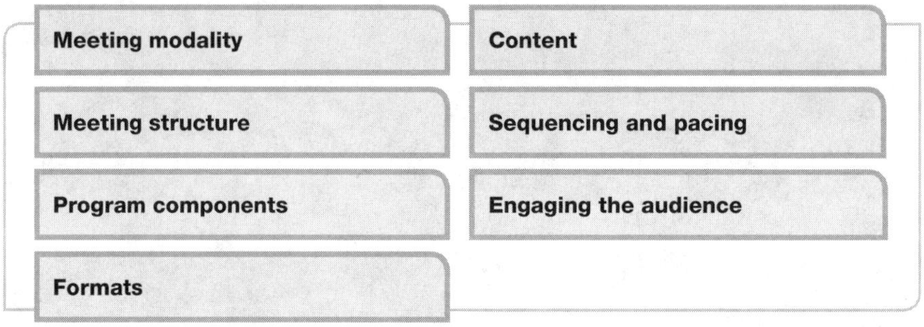

FIGURE 4.17 Design Decisions Impacting Meeting Experience Designing the meeting includes a variety of decisions based upon logistics and human dynamics. These are basic design decisions, which set the stage for the meeting.

Meeting Modality

key points

Reasons for Meetings

- Celebrate
- Create ideas
- Decide on issues
- Enjoy professionally-oriented recreation
- Gain new knowledge
- Maintain relationships
- Persuade, involve, or inspire
- Provide information
- Share work

Face-to-face meetings occur synchronously, i.e., with all members of the meeting gathering at the same time, and with people at the same site. These meetings have unique emotional and psychological advantages including building trust, communicating formally and informally, and supporting organizational culture more efficiently (Arvey, n.d.; Duffy & McEuen, 2010).

Virtual meetings gather groups from separate geographic areas using the Internet. Virtual meetings are also called webinars, collaborative online meetings, video conferences, or web conferences. A primary benefit of virtual meetings is the opportunity to increase participation, as geographic constraints are irrelevant. In addition, virtual meetings further the reach of education and information by archiving content. This content can also serve as a source for future promotion.

Hybrid meetings blend the benefits of face-to-face meetings and virtual meetings. They combine a live in-person component and a virtual online component. Hybrid meetings integrate technology with traditional event practices to create new types of attendee experiences and content delivery tools (Fryatt, Mora, Janssen, John, & Smith, 2012a). Hybrid meetings take four forms: 1) broadcasts of a physical meeting to remote delegates; 2) connections of remote office locations to a main event; 3) meetings that include remote speakers; and 4) meetings that connect multiple sites to a broadcast studio (Fryatt, Mora, Janssen, John, & Smith, 2012b).

Meeting Structure

The **meeting structure** begins with the public name for the meeting, e.g., The Net Impact Conference or The North America Leadership Institute. The name of the meeting offers attendees the first hint of a meeting's nature. Figure 4.18 is a list of common meeting structures. The meeting professional should adhere to common notions about meeting struc-

Exposition
• Large scale
• May be open to public
• Also trade show, trade fair, exhibition
Convention/ Congress
• Large scale
• Recurs regularly
• Several days
• Multiple components
Conference
• Designed for discussion
• Proceedings may be published
Symposium
• Formal
• Specialists present
• May be face-to-face or online
Workshop
• Interactive
• Focused
• Relatively short
• Also institute, seminar

FIGURE 4.18 Typology of Meeting Structures Meetings can be structured (built and marketed) in different ways and support different purposes and intents. Other meeting structures include colloquium, conclave, press conference, product launch, and retreat; as well as many others.

tures to avoid misleading attendees. While the distinctions between meeting structures is arbitrary and two structures can be blended, an event should not be promoted as an "institute" when it is an exposition. (See Appendix 3, p. 328, for additional detailed information.)

Program Components

The meeting content is contained in the individual building blocks within the meeting structure; these **program components** guide the production and management of the meeting. Program components focus on delivering specific outcomes, which result in the creation of the agenda or program structure.

key points

Program Components

- Keynote address
- General session
- Concurrent sessions
- Workshops
- Plenary sessions
- Ancillary activities

Formats

Program components can be produced in a variety of ways called **program formats** (see Figure 4.19, p. 64). Formats are the form, design, or arrangement of a program component. They address the delivery of the individual program components. A variety of formats can be used within a meeting structure.

The distinctions amongst these types of formats are both *critical* and *artificial*. The distinctions are critical because a format decision has immense impact on the meeting. For example, a keynote address could be a lecture or it could be a forum with audience participation. Some keynotes include group discussions or discussion amongst peers to increase engagement and learning. An opening address could be a panel discussion or a single speaker using the lecture format.

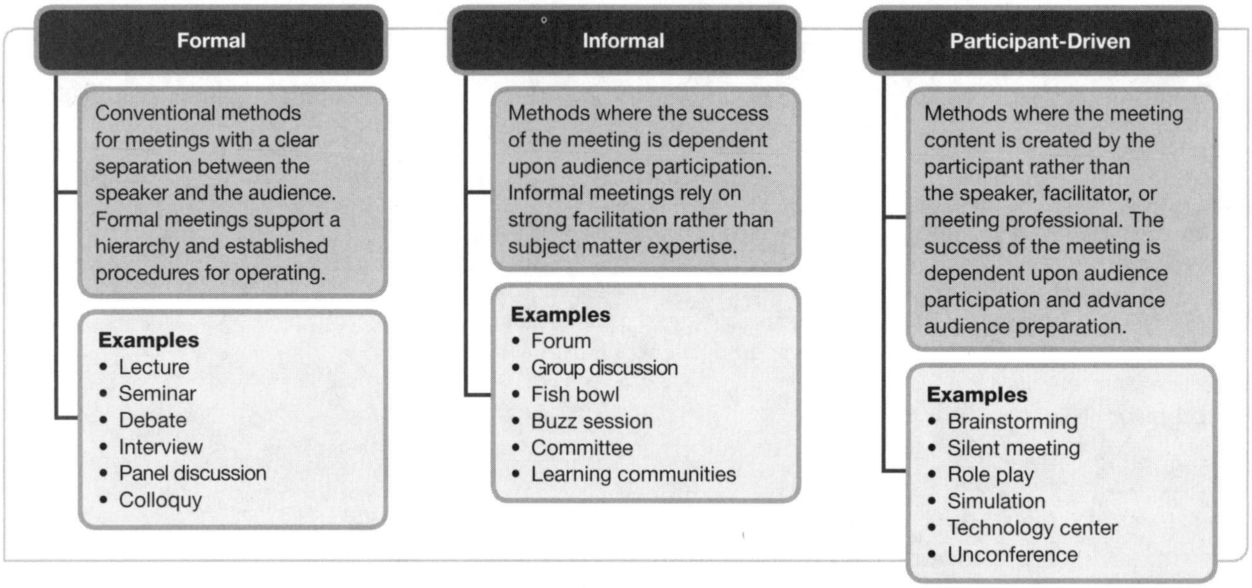
Formal
Conventional methods for meetings with a clear separation between the speaker and the audience. Formal meetings support a hierarchy and established procedures for operating.
Examples
• Lecture
• Seminar
• Debate
• Interview
• Panel discussion
• Colloquy
Informal
Methods where the success of the meeting is dependent upon audience participation. Informal meetings rely on strong facilitation rather than subject matter expertise.
Examples
• Forum
• Group discussion
• Fish bowl
• Buzz session
• Committee
• Learning communities
Participant-Driven
Methods where the meeting content is created by the participant rather than the speaker, facilitator, or meeting professional. The success of the meeting is dependent upon audience participation and advance audience preparation.
Examples
• Brainstorming
• Silent meeting
• Role play
• Simulation
• Technology center
• Unconference

FIGURE 4.19 **Typology of Formats: Formal, Informal, and Participant-Driven**
Formats help set the tone and setting for a meeting. Ranging from the highly controlled lecture by a single presenter to the spontaneous experience of a small, self-selected learning group, format choices affect the meeting experience.

The distinction is artificial because a panel discussion can be a program component as well as a format. For example, a meeting professional can plan an annual conference (meeting structure) with a plenary session (program component) featuring a panel discussion (format). (See Appendix 2, p. 326, for details of program formats.)

Content

Meetings contain an implicit or explicit call to action, which may include activities prior to the start of the meeting (attendee preplanning), during the meeting (deliverables and outcomes), and post meeting (follow-up and reinforcement strategies). While it was once acceptable to plan only content, planning now includes a focus on how content will be delivered during these three time periods, as well as a focus on the content itself.

Content and delivery are closely intermingled, too. Various channels, e.g., live web broadcasts, websites, and networking apps, are used to deliver content and can engage the audience before, during, and after the face-to-face meeting. A meeting professional will determine whether a meeting requires all three types of content.

Increasingly, with social media and technology, the distinction between pre-meeting content and marketing is blurred. Value is added by providing content-rich material before the meeting as both a marketing strategy and an aid in planning the meeting.

During the meeting, relevant, informative, and unique content equates to positive meeting experiences. Content connects speakers to attendees. It is neither simple nor easy to deliver content; it takes a com-

People Planet Profit

SUSTAINABILITY *in* Practice

Another way to look at the meeting experience is to take a sustainable view of the environments, consisting of the natural environment, the enhanced environment, the knowledge environment, and the social environment.

- **Natural environment**—the hotel or setting for a meeting
- **Enhanced environment**—anything provided for the meeting's setting through human activity
- **Knowledge environment**—social practices and technological and physical arrangements intended to facilitate collaborative knowledge building, decision-making, discovery, or self-knowledge
- **Social environment**—norms, the people, and the culture

The first two environments are focused on environmental sustainability, the last two on social sustainability. In the natural environment, use the pre-existing elements of the hotel or site, such as the outdoor space, to encourage people to enjoy the weather, the air, and other elements. When planning an enhanced environment, minimize any building of new materials, from name badges to scenery (rent rather than build from scratch, and reuse rather than discard).

The idea of knowledge environment is less tangible, but no less important. Can the meeting build knowledge in the local community? Can people attending the meeting learn more about the local community—even the challenging aspects? Any corporate social responsibility (CSR) project can focus on adding to the knowledge base of your attendees (e.g., having them learn about literacy efforts by a non-profit) and provide knowledge to the community (e.g., supporting literacy efforts through donation of time or resources).

The social environment, likewise, can be supported through a legacy or CSR project. Think broadly about how meetings can improve the lives of the people in the area without impinging on their culture and norms.

—Susan M. Tinnish, PhD

mitment to meeting the needs of the target market, capitalizing on how adults learn, and determining the best format to deliver that content.

After the meeting, it is generally unrealistic to expect that information, skills, or knowledge transfer 100 percent without reinforcement strategies. When attendees return to work, they return to workloads and pre-existing organizational constraints. This is where reinforcement strategies come into play—to help mold attendee behaviors, skills, or attitudes, thus allowing them to contribute to organizational goals. Reinforcement strategies facilitate transition; reward new learning, attitudes, or behavior; remove obstacles to the desired outcomes; create short-term wins to facilitate feelings of success; and build new norms through rewards, peer pressure, employment contracts, and accountability.

Sequencing and Pacing the Meeting Flow

Meeting professionals are responsible for planning the sequence and pace of the meeting's flow, an intangible but vital design decision. Ideal meetings maintain a varying pace and tempo. Think of how, when listening to music, people quickly tire of too many slow songs in a row; too many energetic songs are equally unappealing. New pieces interspersed with older favorites make a concert memorable.

A meeting must flow seamlessly in a steady and logical manner. Breaks and networking activities can be used to change the tempo of a meeting. They can be a welcome change to the flow. A detailed plan for the meeting with time allotments establishes transitions, crowd control, wayfinding, and active periods contrasted with passive activities.

Engaging the Audience

Engaged attendees are fully absorbed in the meeting, enthusiastic about the content, and moved to positive action following the meeting. Engagement relies upon people perceiving value in the meeting. Employing learning strategies that address a specific target audience helps strengthen engagement.

Marketing Strategies

The notion of marketing is explored more fully in other chapters; however, it is mentioned here as marketing is tied to defining the target audience and creating the meeting experience.

Proper marketing creates awareness and interest within the target market. Compelling marketing triggers the target market to register (e.g., voluntary attendance for association meetings), or be eager to attend (e.g., compulsory attendance at corporate meetings). Marketing entices attendees to "consume" the product by attending. The target market must also be persuaded to "consume" or absorb the main messages of the meeting. Messaging channels such as name badges or signage must be properly designed to convey these core messages. For example, marketing aimed at attracting members of the American Association of Retired Persons may feature larger fonts to accommodate vision changes that occur with age. Appropriate marketing will also encourage the target market to participate. For example, attendees might be asked to wear a special color or a t-shirt with the meeting's logo.

Learning Strategies

When meeting professionals employ learning strategies, they take a conscious approach to how the audiences learn and use information. A learning strategy encourages engagement, comprehension, and retention of meeting content and information. While no audience is completely homogeneous, meetings should provide positive, supportive environments recognizing audience members' emotional, social, and physical needs and recognizing and nurturing individual audience characteristics as much as possible.

The target audiences' prior knowledge about specific subjects and how they might learn dictate learning strategy choices. The study of the science and art of education is called **pedagogy**. While an extensive discussion of pedagogy is beyond the scope of this chapter, this section provides a glimpse into three pedagogical frameworks.

key points

Learning Styles

- Visual—preferred sense is sight/vision.
- Auditory—preferred sense is hearing.
- Kinesthetic—preferred sense is hands-on.

Learning modalities One framework for assessing learning is Fleming's (1995, 2001) Visual Auditory Kinesthetic (VAK) learning styles model. According to this model, most people possess a preferred learning style.

Multiple intelligences Figure 4.20 explores another theoretical framework based on Howard Gardner's concept of multiple intelligences. Gardner (2011) identified that people are "intelligent" in eight ways. By considering how context influences intelligence, meeting content can be adapted to the target audience. For example, people from the Institute of Biological Engineering are likely to possess logical-mathematical intelligence. Different approaches would be used for planning networking for this group than for the National Association of Social Workers, who would tend to have high interpersonal intelligence.

Adult learners It has been widely recognized that adults' motivation to learn differs from that of children. Knowles has studied adult learning and characterizes an adult learner as being self-directing, dependent upon a repertoire of experience and skills, and internally motivated to learn material that can be applied immediately

Linguistic—sensitivity to spoken and written language, e.g., writers

Logical-mathematical—capacity to analyze problems logically, carry out mathematical operations, and investigate issues scientifically, e.g., economists

Musical—skill in the performance, composition, and appreciation of musical patterns, e.g., composers

Bodily-kinesthetic—potential of using one's whole body or parts of the body to solve problems, e.g., surgeons, athletes

Spatial—potential to recognize and use the patterns of wide space and more confined areas, e.g., architects

Interpersonal—capacity to understand the intentions, motivations, and desires of other people, e.g., social workers

Intrapersonal—capacity to understand oneself, to appreciate one's feelings, fears, and motivations, e.g., psychologists

Naturalist—capacity to discriminate among living things (plants, animals) as well as sensitivity to other features of the natural world (clouds, rock configurations), e.g., botanists

FIGURE 4.20 Eight Ways Meeting Participants Can Be Intelligent Every person's intelligence is contextual. The most educated, logical-mathematical person may be at a disadvantage when in the Australian bush, compared to an Aborigine woman who possesses naturalist intelligence (Gardner, 2011).

Organization & Target Audience	Age	Interests	Attitudes / Preferences / Skills	Learning Style
AARP (American Association of Retired Persons) Americans	50+ Could be new to retirement and issues of aging	Retirement Travel	***Preferences:*** Larger fonts on printed or projected information	***VAK:*** Visual or reading
Music Teachers National Association Music Teachers	Varies from 24–65 Ranges from high to low depending upon years teaching	Teaching Music	***Skills:*** Musical ***Preferences:*** Meetings do not conflict with school calendars	***VAK:*** Auditory or listening ***Gardner:*** Musical intelligence
Royal National Institute of Blind People (RNIB) British citizens who are blind or partially sighted	All	Practical and emotional support	***Skills:*** Reading Braille; managing seeing-eye dog; use of white cane or blind stick	***VAK:*** Auditory or listening ***Gardner:*** Bodily-kinesthetic intelligence through the use of Braille or spatial intelligence by mapping out things visually in the brain to remember
Young Republican National Federation Republicans	Under 40	Grassroots support for candidates and conservative issues Future Republican candidates and leadership	***Attitude:*** Politically conservative	***Gardner:*** Interpersonal intelligence, as they relate to people and care about solving large societal issues

FIGURE 4.21 Target Audience and Learning Strategies By their nature, association members share commonalities and can be characterized by their interests, attitudes, preferences, skills, and learning styles. Using a learning strategy appropriate to the target audience elevates the meeting's strategic value.

(Knowles, Holton, & Sawnson, 2011). According to Knowles' work, adults relish opportunities to:

- learn relevant and applicable information;
- be involved and interactive in their learning;
- be challenged and challenge others; and
- build upon their own knowledge and experiences.

Applying the concepts of target audience characteristics, age, interests, attitudes, skills, preferences, and learning style allows a meeting professional to develop a learning strategy, i.e., an approach to encourage engagement, comprehension, and retention of meeting content and information (see Figure 4.21). For individual program components, applying a learning strategy consists of providing an environment that supports the selected content and communication strategies, as well as communicating the program's objectives and outcomes to attendees and conveying information to speakers.

Emotionally Rich Techniques

A rich appeal to the attendee's emotions can be very effective as a motivational tool. An attendee forms better connections and "owns" the message more if the information is presented in an emotionally appealing way. Also, decision-making is both a cognitive (logical) and emotional process. Offering information using emotionally rich techniques is more persuasive than delivering information in a completely objective style.

key points

Techniques with Emotional Richness

- Stories
- Metaphors
- Themes
- Visual imagery/visualization
- Symbols
- Music
- Icons
- Social interaction

Multi-Sensory Meetings

Creating a successful meeting experience depends on using all physical senses and immersing attendees in various complex, interactive experiences. A highly sensory experience produces a meaningful and memorable message, creates an emotional connection and richer experience, and appeals to a wider range of learning styles. Lighting, color, and music, for example, affect the attendees' experience and learning.

Lighting

Lighting impacts attentiveness, creates a mood, and supports branding or messaging. It helps to create a mood by drawing positive attention or causing disengagement. "Up lighting" of a speaker helps create positive attention; the use of gobos and other lighting effects enable branding and customizing the meeting.

Color

Color affects mood (psychological) and creates bodily changes (physiological). Use color strategically to create interest. People's eyes are naturally drawn to light. Draw their attention to a poster or other visual image mounted on a wall by using a cool, dark color for the background color (the wall) so the attendees' eyes are immediately focused on the image without the distraction of seeing a light-colored wall background. Facilitate quick understanding for attendees with highly recognizable patterns and colors, e.g., always indicating water with blue on a map.

Music

Music involves multiple brain functions for musicians and their audience. Music possesses surprising benefits for improving memory, focusing attention, and physical coordination (Brewer, 1995). Not all types of music have positive effects. Music can be distracting if it is too loud or too jarring. It can enrich the meeting experience by building memory, connecting with emotion, affecting the listener's physical state, and providing networking support.

Building memory Researchers find music stimulates brain regions responsible for memory, motor control timing, and language.

Connecting with emotion Music utilizes multiple parts of the brain. Some music connects with the brain's emotional centers; it allows the brain to connect multiple neural pathways in the brain. The theory is that connections help build stronger memory by strengthening synapses.

Affecting the listener's physical state Music influences the heart rate (blood flow) and immune system (stress levels). Music can trigger the neurotransmitter serotonin (i.e., influencing attention, learning, and mood), and the hormone epinephrine, which controls the "fight or flight" response.

Networking support Music builds camaraderie; it is an experience the entire audience shares (Glynn, 2013).

Evaluation

Meetings, and often the individual program components, warrant evaluation, which serves as the basis for learning and improvement. The original needs assessment sets the stage to create evaluation instruments and report on outcomes. Learner objectives and program outcomes form the basis for writing questions for the evaluation instrument. Two levels of evaluation can be conducted:

- Attendee reaction—How did attendees react to the meeting? Did they enjoy the experience? How do they value what they learned? How relevant was the content to their needs and expectations?
- Attendee learning—How well did attendees learn? Will they be able to transfer the meeting message to actual performance? Do they plan to change based upon attending the meeting and what they learned (Tinnish, 2007a)?

The results from the evaluation process become the basis for future needs assessments. The quantitative data (numerical data) and qualitative data (stories, anecdotal evidence) from previous evaluations and stakeholder observations (including those of the meeting professional) are critical to being able to conduct a comprehensive needs assessment.

PART FIVE The Speakers

Selection of speakers dramatically influences the entire meeting experience as well as attendance. Speakers affect knowledge gained, mood, credibility of the meeting, and meeting results through the content they deliver; they impart knowledge and convey deep and substantive expertise, capturing attention and keeping the audience engaged.

While speakers bring expertise to the meeting, they require input from meeting professionals to be successful. All speakers need audience demographics, as well as organizational and meeting goals and objectives from their specific part of the meeting. Regardless of the speaker's background, a speaker-management process and clear speaker guidelines increase speaker effectiveness.

key points

Type of Speakers

- Subject matter experts (SMEs)
- Facilitators
- Entertainers
- Professional speakers
- Celebrities

Finding Speakers

Meeting professionals expend time and energy finding the perfect speakers because speakers provide critical content and are the conduit for gaining new knowledge, skills, or awareness. Speakers are identified and secured through a variety of methods.

Speakers' Bureaus

A speakers' bureau maintains relationships with numerous professional speakers who present on a variety of topics within a range of fees, thus providing access to multiple speakers with just one contact. Bureaus continually add and evaluate speakers, and are able to recommend the best speaker in their bureau for a specific meeting, objectives, or topic.

Speaker Showcases

Speaker showcases, often sponsored by speakers' bureaus, are short (one- or two-day) events designed to preview speakers and entertainers (see Figure 4.22). Showcases feature short snippets from speakers covering a variety of topics. Speakers are available for one-on-one consults about specific needs.

key points

Speaker Sources

- Recommendations
- Personal experience
- Internet listing or speaker directory
- Speakers' bureaus, i.e., for professional speakers
- Speaker showcases, i.e., for professional speakers
- Call for presentations/proposals, i.e., for subject matter experts or industry experts

FIGURE 4.22 Speaker Showcase An array of speakers attend and provide a short presentation, similar to an audition. Meeting professionals can more easily make decisions regarding speaker selection at this type of event.

FIGURE 4.23 Viewing a Potential Speaker in a Live Presentation Experiencing a speaker presentation firsthand is an ideal way to determine the feasibility of extending an invitation to present at your meeting. Attending industry meetings is an efficient way to "scout" for potential speakers.

Call for Presentations/Call for Proposals

A call for presentations/call for proposals is a formal invitation for industry experts and subject matter experts (SMEs) to speak on topics at upcoming meetings. Typically, these "calls" include the invitation, topics of interest for the meeting, guidelines for speaking, and a request for a formal proposal. Calls for proposals, posters, abstracts, and papers follow a similar format. Online submission systems for speakers help to manage the submission of presentations or proposals. The proposal in response to the call will include an abstract of the presentation, title and description, important dates, and speaker contact information. The speaker's expertise on the topic, experience, and other persuasive information will be included.

After identifying potential speakers, meeting professionals, in conjunction with their meeting stakeholders, choose the "right" speakers for the meeting. Viewing a speaker live is the optimal way to vet candidates (see Figure 4.23); viewing a videotape is second best, with the caveat that an entire presentation, not just a brief clip, should be vetted. The meeting professional will also review references, testimonials, a biography and credentials, any awards and certifications, e.g., Certified Speaking Professional (CSP), and articles or books the speaker has written. A popular review tool is YouTube®. Another consideration is checking the speaker's affiliations with professional organizations, e.g., the National Speakers Association.

Speaker Management

key points

Speaker Communication

- Affirm
- Confirm
- Reaffirm
- Thank (Palmer & Jenkins, 2006, p. 309)

Speaker management establishes two-way communication between the speaker and the hiring organization. At a minimum, a meeting professional will issue speaker contracts on behalf of the organization. The contract sets expectations of the speaker and contains typical legal information, i.e., signatures, cancellation and failure to perform clauses, and special riders. Speakers are often paid or provided some form of compensation, e.g., complimentary registration, travel, and/or hotel accommodations. The contract may also contain additional speaker

key points

Information Contained in Speaker Contracts

- Title of speaker
- Date, day, time, and duration of presentation
- Format of session
- Level of audience, i.e., basic, intermediate, or advanced
- Preferred room set
- Compensation, i.e., fees, travel arrangements, and registration
- Important dates for submitting presentation materials
- Important dates for submitting marketing information, e.g., photograph and biography
- Audiovisual requirements
- Copyright and intellectual property provisions
- Recording permission release
- Information for an administrative or other speaker contact person

information like speaker registration and emergency contact information. Some organizations may include the information in the Key Points boxes on this page in the contract and/or speaker guidelines (TEDx Speaker Guide, n.d.).

Speaker Guidelines

Speakers and the people hiring them desire positive evaluations from the audience. Positive evaluations of speakers reflect well on the speaker, the organization, and the planner. One way to help prepare speakers, especially SMEs who may have limited experience presenting, is through speaker guidelines. Speaker guidelines provide information about effective public speaking practices. In addition, guidelines help speakers provide compelling, relevant, substantive, and useful content to the audience.

Speaker Care

Speakers are fundamental to a meeting's success and they warrant appropriate attention. Accessibility issues, dietary restrictions, and

key points

Information Contained in Speaker Guidelines

- Title of presentation
- Organization's history and mission
- Date, day, time, and duration of presentation
- Appropriate attire
- Appropriate and/or inappropriate language
- Level of formality at the meeting
- Audience profile
- Meeting purpose, goals, and objectives
- Room set-up
- Timing of elements needed from the speaker, e.g., presentation description, AV requirements, etc.
- Expectation for speaker arrival and departure
- Any other services, e.g., book signings
- Limitations on selling products
- Introduction script
- Special accommodations, e.g., ramp to platform, dietary provisions, etc.

special considerations routinely pop up for speakers. They may merit VIP status, a hosted experience, complimentary registration, special introductions, and a **speaker preparation/ready room**. Increasingly, a speaker's social media presence can enhance the meeting's promotion efforts.

PROFESSIONAL DILEMMA

Speaker guidelines serve to prepare speakers for the meeting, and that may impact the evaluation of the speaker and presentation. Often meeting professionals express concern that they do not have control over content, as the educational component is the primary responsibility of the education department. However, the organization has a very specific set of defined expectations and guidelines that include length of presentations, learning resources to capture the attention of all types of learning styles, and a process to guide speakers in preparation for the target audience of the meeting. Should meeting professionals be responsible for preparing speakers? If not, then who should have this responsibility? What level of information should meeting professionals provide?

SUMMARY

The needs assessment reveals requirements, which drive all logistical and group dynamics decisions. It sets the framework to align the meeting with organizational goals and to define meeting modality. It sets the stage for decisions about the meeting structure, where the organization identifies the fundamental meeting purpose and the meeting professional (or a meeting-planning team) determines program components. Out of a needs assessment comes ideas about content and format for each program component.

Content can be delivered before, during, and after the meeting with specific objectives and outcomes. The needs assessment suggests strategies to engage the audience and establishes how to market to the target audience and how to communicate with them before, during, and after the meeting. It recognizes the impact of the environment (see Figure 4.24) and drives decisions about sequencing and pacing the meeting's flow.

Using the needs assessment allows a meeting professional to design a meeting experience that will support the objectives and outcomes of the meeting. Some potential outcomes are shown in Figure 4.25.

Strategic and logistical decision-making allows meeting professionals to provide positive, productive results that help propel the organization forward. Through the careful planning of the meeting format, room sets, speakers, and learning strategy, meeting professionals are able to engage and involve attendees and create a multisensory environment that is memorable and impactful. Selecting the correct program components, room set, speakers and technology

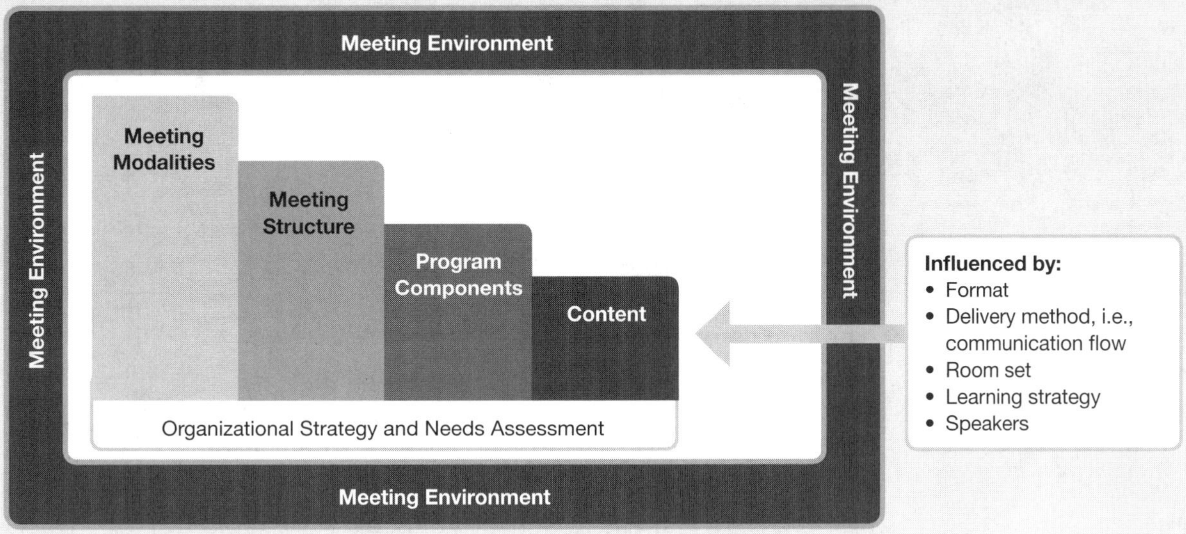

FIGURE 4.24 Building a Meeting Experience Decisions about designing the meeting experience, while interrelated and iterative, can be segmented into the components noted in this figure. The meeting experience involves the interplay of logistics with interpersonal dynamics.

support allows for an open, inquiring environment, which enables attendees to absorb, learn, discuss, and reflect on the content. In designing such a meeting experience, a meeting professional delivers inspiration, education, and connection for attendees and a meeting that helps the organization move toward the future.

Limitations

A meeting occurs in the larger context of the organization and stakeholders should be realistic about what it can accomplish. Thus what can be solved or delivered in one meeting is constrained by culture, organizational support, ability and desire to change, values and beliefs, support for innovation, and resources. Generally, skills and knowledge will not transfer 100 percent without reinforcement strategies following the learning experience, nor can attitudes be changed overnight.

Social interaction and exchange

Engagement and involvement in the meeting

An open, inquiring environment that allows for information to be absorbed and made relevant, with time to discuss and reflect on learning

Supportive technology and tools

A positive, productive result

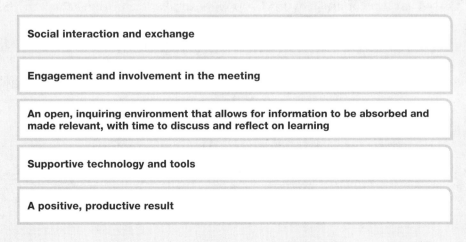

FIGURE 4.25 Outcomes from a Positive Meeting Experience Meeting professionals leverage the information contained in a needs assessment to make design decisions that result in these outcomes. Logistics and design decisions support human interaction and human relationships to achieve desired organizational outcomes.

CONTRIBUTING AUTHOR

Sheila Bartle, PhD
Professor (retired)
Kendall College

KEY WORDS

communication flow
face-to-face meeting
gap analysis
hybrid meeting
learning objective
meeting environment
meeting experience
meeting structure
needs assessment
pedagogy
program component
program format
program outcome
room set
speaker preparation/ready room
virtual meeting

DISCUSSION QUESTIONS

1. Using the A-B-C-D tool, write a learning outcome from the following description of a course: Conflict Resolution—Attend this workshop to learn seven principles of empathetic communication for conflict resolution.
2. Identify a meeting and its agenda. Classify the meeting according to the typology presented in this chapter. What is the modality? What is the meeting structure? What are the program components? What type of room set(s) would likely be used? Describe the content using the vocabulary of the chapter.
3. Using the meeting identified above, what recommendations would you make to improve the meeting experience?
4. Research the physiological and psychological impacts of color or music and apply your findings to a meeting. For example, what impact does the use of the color red have on meeting attendees? What type of music would you want to play prior to the start of an opening session and why?

5

Budgeting Basics for Meeting Professionals

Godwin-Charles A. Ogbeide, PhD, MBA
Associate Professor
Hospitality Innovation Management
University of Arkansas

Main Topics

- Importance of Budgeting
- Budgets and Financial Goals
- Types of Budgets
- Budget Elements
- Budget Development
- Fund Management
- Post-Meeting Financial Analysis

Learner Outcomes

Upon the completion of this chapter, the student should be able to:

1. Explain the importance of developing budgets for meetings.
2. Describe how a meeting's budget relates to the financial goals of the organization.
3. Compare and contrast incremental and zero-based budgeting techniques.
4. Identify revenue streams common to meetings.
5. Calculate a meeting's net income.

CMP INTERNATIONAL STANDARDS

Domain A. Strategic Planning
Skill 1. Manage Strategic Plan for Meeting or Event
SubSkills. 1.01, 1.02, 1.03, 1.04, 1.05
Skill 2. Develop Sustainability Plan for Meeting or Event
SubSkills. 2.01, 2.02
Domain D. Financial Management
Skill 7. Manage Event Funding and Financial Resources
SubSkills. 7.01, 7.03, 7.04, 7.05
Skill 8. Manage Budget
SubSkills. 8.01, 8.02, 8.03, 8.04
Skill 9. Manage Monetary Transactions
SubSkills. 9.01, 9.02
Domain I. Marketing
Skill 26. Manage Meeting or Event Merchandise
SubSkill. 26.02

The **budget** is "a statement of estimated revenues and expenditures for a specified period of time; divided into subject categories and arranged by principal areas of revenue and expense" ("APEX Industry Glossary," 2011). In regards to meetings, **budgeting** is the process of planning and preparing estimated revenues and expenditures in order to achieve the meeting's financial goal. The budgeting process provides a plan, in numerical terms, for effective production of a meeting. The importance of budgeting and the relationship of budgets to financial goals cannot be overemphasized.

Importance of Budgeting

Can a meeting's financial goal be achieved? What is the minimum amount of money needed to produce the meeting? Are sufficient resources to produce the meeting available? These are important questions meeting professionals contemplate when planning meetings. In order to answer these questions, a basic level of effective budgeting skills is required. Budgets must be accurate and should align with the organization's financial goals for the meeting (also known as the **budget philosophy**). The budget is based on the meeting's expenses and the income (revenue) needed to offset those expenses. Then the budget is monitored and modified as needed throughout the planning process. A well-developed budget allows effective and strategic management of resources for numerous reasons, as listed below.

- Making plans for achieving the meeting's budget philosophy.
- Anticipating plans for an effective meeting production.
- Clarifying the areas of responsibility for achievement of budget targets.
- Promoting efficient planning and production of meetings.
- Providing a basis for the meeting's financial performance appraisal, by comparing and contrasting the actual financial performance results against the budget.
- Facilitating the allocation of resources during meeting planning.

Budgets and Financial Goals

In the beginning of the planning phase, meeting professionals need to be cognizant of the organization's financial goals for the meeting before developing the budget. There are three common financial goals for meetings.

- **Profit** (net income) goal: Revenue exceeds expenses
- **Break-even** goal: Revenue equals expenses
- **Deficit** (subsidized) goal: Expenses exceed revenue (host or organization provides funding to meet expenses)

Examples of meetings that create a deficit include committee meetings, training meetings, and board meetings. Although these meetings do not generate revenue to offset the expenses, they are justified as investments for the future development of the organization. On the contrary, some meetings are designed to make a profit or break even. Association meetings are often organized to make a profit, which the organization dedicates to its mission. Government agencies often hold meetings that must break even. The agency is not prepared to subsidize a deficit, but cannot justify to stakeholders the goal of making a profit on meetings. Regardless of the financial expectations, meeting professionals are expected to develop and execute meeting plans to achieve the meeting's financial goal. As most meeting professionals are not financial experts or accountants, budgeting can be a challenging task.

A well-developed budget indicates the amount of revenue needed to offset the total expenses of the meeting. However, the meeting professional must be diligent in estimating the appropriate sources of revenue, and must honestly assess whether the host is willing and able to subsidize the event if revenues fall below the level of expenses.

However, some organizations set a financial goal to produce meetings that are fiscally successful. Answers to the key questions listed on this page serve as a guide during planning to help determine the potential levels of revenue and control expenses rationally.

key questions

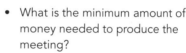

- What is the minimum amount of money needed to produce the meeting?
- Do we have enough resources or money to produce the meeting?
- With the level of revenue and expenses calculated, does the meeting generate an appropriate level of return on investment?

Types of Budgets

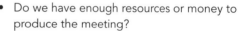

There are two major ways to create budgets, depending on the context and purpose. If there is an existing budget for a meeting, the next year's fiscal budget can be created, starting with the existing budget, then adjusting as needed. This type of budgeting is called **incremental budgeting**. However, if a budget is created without using an existing or previous year's budget, this type of budgeting is called **zero-based budgeting**.

key points

Types of Budgets

- Incremental
- Zero-based

Incremental Budget

Incremental budgeting is a process of creating a budget by using past budget or actual performance as a foundation and then making changes as necessary for the new budget period. Under incremental budgeting, the change to each variable, i.e., line item, is calculated by considering the impact of inflation and other changes to the variable, such as volume or the amount needed. Increments are then subtracted or added to the projected revenue or expenses to show a budget

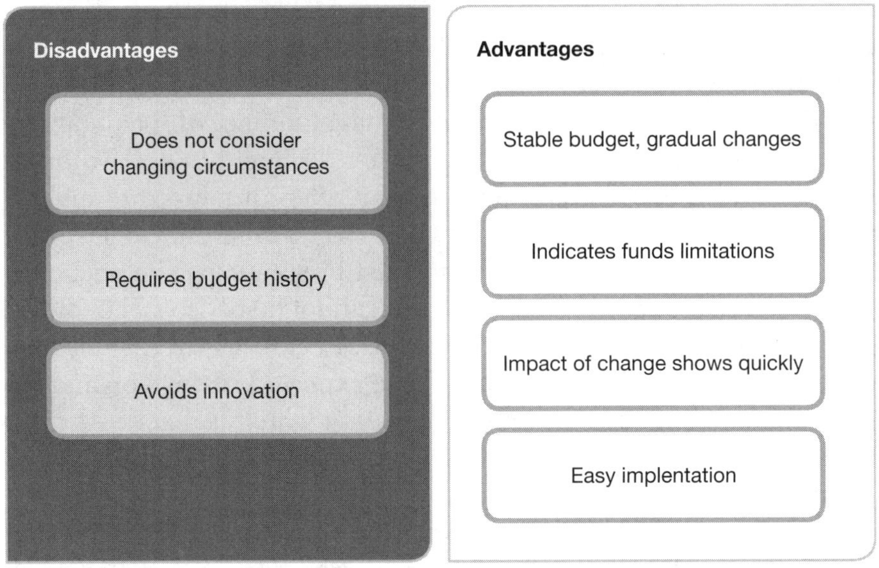

FIGURE 5.1 Disadvantages and Advantages of Incremental Budgeting The advantages and disadvantages of incremental budgeting are represented in this figure, allowing for the variables that will impact the total budget based on economic and other factors.

decrease or increase in the next budget. Some of the advantages and disadvantages of incremental budgeting are shown in Figure 5.1.

In the incremental budget (see Figure 5.2), increments are subtracted or added to the projected revenue or expenses of the previous year's budget, e.g., 2014 budget, to show a budget decrease or increase for the following year, e.g., 2015 budget. Meeting professionals must consider the economic conditions now and in the predictable future, and be very precise and rational about the potential expenses and revenue when making alterations for the new budget. The meeting professional must evaluate and consider the differences between the previous year's budget and actual performance as a benchmark for generating the following year's budget.

ZERO-BASED BUDGET

Zero-based budgeting is a process of creating a budget without the benefit of a previous year's budget or past performance. This type of budgeting depends on very good forecasting of the organization's potential meeting revenue and expenses. Under zero-based budgeting, each variable, i.e., line item, must be justified and reviewed prior to implementation. Several questions should be considered in preparing a zero-based budget review.

The purpose of the questions is to maximize the organization's return on investment by rationally eliminating unnecessary expenditures, i.e., costs that exceed their benefits. Figure 5.3 (p. 82) lists the disadvantages and advantages of a zero-based budgeting process. An example of a zero-based budget is found in Figure 5.4 (p. 83).

key questions

Zero-Based Budget Questions to Ask

- Should this product or service be part of this meeting?
- What will happen if the product or service is not included in this meeting?
- What quality of the product or service should be considered?
- What amount of the product or service should be provided?
- Should an alternative product or service be considered?

Godwin Destination Management Company, Inc.						
	2014 Budget			2015 Budget		
Revenue	**Budget**	**Actual**	**Variance**	**Budget**	**Actual**	**Variance**
Registration	$ 1,969,000	$ 1,870,550	$ −98,450	$ 1,969,000		
Exhibit Sales	$ 195,000	$ 185,250	$ −9,750	$ 215,500		
Sponsorships	$ 225,000	$ 213,750	$ −11,250	$ 225,000		
Advertising	$ 32,000	$ 30,400	$ −1,600	$ 35,500		
Merchandise Sales	$ 105,000	$ 99,750	$ −5,250	$ 115,500		
Total Revenue	**$ 2,526,000**	**$ 2,399,700**	**$ −126,300**	**$ 2,560,500**		
Expenses	**Budget**	**Actual**	**Variance**	**Budget**	**Actual**	**Variance**
Salary and Related Expenses	$ 368,000	$ 368,000	$ 0	$ 368,000		
Marketing	$ 140,000	$ 190,000	$ 50,000	$ 200,000		
Programming	$ 230,000	$ 230,000	$ 0	$ 230,000		
Registration Costs	$ 112,800	$ 120,800	$ 8,000	$ 121,000		
Freight/Transportation	$ 11,000	$ 15,000	$ 4,000	$ 15,000		
Exhibits Contractors	$ 57,500	$ 65,500	$ 8,000	$ 66,000		
Facility Rental	$ 30,300	$ 30,300	$ 0	$ 30,300		
Food & Beverage	$ 1,040,000	$ 1,040,000	$ 0	$ 1,040,000		
Awards and Recognition	$ 227,000	$ 227,000	$ 0	$ 227,000		
Miscellaneous	$ 31,400	$ 80,400	$ 49,000	$ 50,000		
Total Expenses	**$ 2,248,000**	**$ 2,367,000**	**$ 119,000**	**$ 2,347,300**		
Net Income	**$ 278,000**	**$ 32,700**	**$ −245,300**	**$ 213,200**		

FIGURE 5.2 Example of an Incremental Budget This example demonstrates the variance of budget line items from the 2014 budget and the actual amounts for revenue and expenses, with revisions for the 2015 budget. The accounting office might use (U) for unfavorable or (F) for favorable to indicate the variance, or a minus sign to indicate the unfavorable variance. A negative indicator in expenses is favorable, whereas a negative indicator in revenue is unfavorable.

Budget Elements

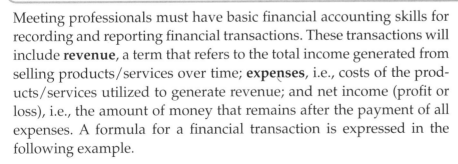

Meeting professionals must have basic financial accounting skills for recording and reporting financial transactions. These transactions will include **revenue,** a term that refers to the total income generated from selling products/services over time; **expenses,** i.e., costs of the products/services utilized to generate revenue; and net income (profit or loss), i.e., the amount of money that remains after the payment of all expenses. A formula for a financial transaction is expressed in the following example.

Revenue – Expenses = Net Income (profit/loss)

$125,000 (revenue) – $105,000 (expenses) = $20,000 (profit)

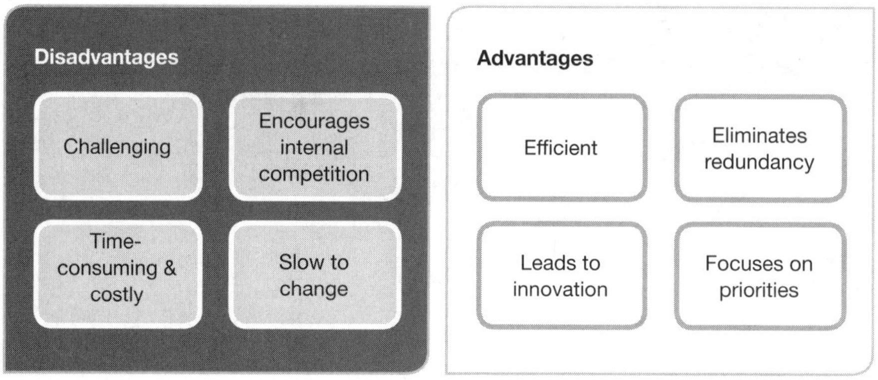

FIGURE 5.3 Disadvantages and Advantages of Zero-Based Budgeting The disadvantages and advantages of zero-based budgeting are graphically portrayed in this figure.

With the financial transaction formula, a budget can be created for each meeting. For example, a list of all the expenses can be inserted into the financial transaction formula to determine the revenue required to meet the financial goal. If the desired profit is $20,000 and the expenses are $105,000, then the revenue required to realize the profit would need to be $125,000.

Revenue

In regard to meetings, revenue refers to the total income generated from registration fees, exhibit sales, vendor fees, sponsorships, advertisements, and merchandise sales. However, meeting professionals should carefully identify total expenses before planning the revenue portion of the budget to ensure that the projected revenue will be able to cover the total expenses.

key points

Major Sources of Revenue

- Registration fees
- Exhibit sales
- Vendor fees
- Sponsorships
- Advertising
- Merchandise sales

Registration fees Registration fees are defined as the "amount payable for attendance at a conference; and may vary according to the level of participation or type of membership" ("APEX Industry Glossary," 2011). When determining the registration fees, the projection must be rational and deliberate to ensure that a sufficient amount is charged to satisfy the meeting's financial goal. In some cases, members of an association will be charged less than non-members. Similarly, students and guests are usually charged less than members or non-members. How much less is determined by careful predictions for expenses and the meeting's financial goal. Additionally, price breaks are often considered as a motivator for behaviors, e.g., early registration. An effective pricing strategy should be developed to maximize revenue generated from each of the meeting's registration categories.

Exhibit sales The revenue from exhibits varies from one meeting to another. If the event is primarily an exhibition, exhibit sales usually constitute the largest portion of the total revenue. Exhibition revenue is generally based on the size and location of booths on the exhibition show floor, but another consideration is the value of contact with the audience. If the audience is made up of buyers, a single buyer

Godwin Destination Management Company, Inc.			
2015 Budget			
Revenue	**Budget**	**Actual**	**Variance**
Registration	$ 1,870,550		
Exhibit Sales	$ 185,250		
Sponsorships	$ 213,750		
Advertising	$ 30,400		
Merchandise Sales	$ 99,750		
Total Revenue	**$ 2,399,700**		
Expenses	**Budget**	**Actual**	**Variance**
Salary and Related Expenses	$ 368,000		
Marketing	$ 200,000		
Programming	$ 230,000		
Registration Costs	$ 120,800		
Freight/Transportation	$ 15,000		
Exhibits Contractors	$ 65,500		
Facility Rental	$ 30,300		
Food & Beverage	$ 1,040,000		
Awards & Recognition	$ 227,000		
Miscellaneous	$ 103,000		
Total Expenses	**$ 2,399,600**		
Net Income	**$ 100**		

FIGURE **5.4** **Example of a Zero-Based Budget** Using other budgeting resources for a meeting similar to that shown in Figure 5.2, this example demonstrates the use of a zero-based budget, predicting the organization's potential revenue and expenses for fiscal year 2015.

constitutes a significant sales transaction for the exhibitor, and if hundreds, if not thousands, of buyers will be attending the meeting, the meeting host can charge a correspondingly high fee for booths. Further, different types of booth options exist, e.g., island booths and peninsula booths. These types of booths may command different fees than the typical in-line or standard booth space in the exhibit hall. The rates charged for each booth will vary according to the size, placement, and date of the contract confirmation, e.g., "early-bird" or onsite.

key points

Customers & Consumers

- Customers *purchase* a product or service
- Consumers *use* the product or service
- Example: The host organization is the *customer* purchasing food and beverage service, but the attendees are the *consumers*.

Vendor fees In some meetings and events, such as festivals, vendor fees are a major source of revenue. Vendor fees are similar to exhibit sales in that each vendor's rate depends on the size of the space allotted to the vendor. The larger the space allotted, the higher the fee. At some events, vendors also pay a percentage of sales to the host organization.

Sponsorships According to the "APEX Industry Glossary" (2011), sponsorships are "donated financial or material support, usually in exchange for recognition" or a "paid opportunity for an entity or exhibitor to increase its visibility at the meeting." Sponsorships can be a major part of revenue generation if a robust program exists for soliciting suitable sponsorships. In many cases, sponsorships are a leading source of revenue. Thus, the sponsorship package, or asset, must provide value and essential benefits to engage the potential sponsor. The greater the sales effort and the more attractive the sponsorship benefits, the better the chance of acquiring increased revenue and participation in the program.

key points

Benefits of Sponsorship

- Increased awareness
- Greater revenue
- Image enhancement
- Networking with potential customers or consumers

Advertising Another source of revenue is advertising. A well-planned marketing strategy helps to promote the meeting, resulting in increased attendance. Part of that strategy should include soliciting associated firms or products to advertise in the meeting's promotional materials and throughout the event. As attendance grows, the acquisition of advertisers increases, as does advertising revenue.

Merchandise An often-untapped source of revenue is the sale of tickets for various activities that occur during a meeting, e.g., fund-raising parties, golf tournaments, or charitable events. Additionally, meeting related items, e.g., caps, t-shirts, or bags with a sponsor's logo, can be offered for sale to generate additional revenue through ancillary merchandise.

Expenses

A delineation of expenses associated with the meeting is essential prior to forecasting revenue. There are different types of expense categories that need to be considered in preparing the budget, mainly **fixed costs (FC)** and **variable costs (VC)**.

key points

Overnight Accommodations

Overnight accommodations are considered a consumable product because the hotel room is available to one customer on a specific date—it cannot be "sold" to two customers at the same time. As a consumable product, overnight accommodations are VCs for the meeting host, as the cost of overnight accommodations for staff and VIPs will change according to the number of rooms occupied.

Fixed cost An FC is "the day-to-day cost of doing business that is pre-committed, such as salaries, insurance, lease expenses, utilities, and so forth" ("APEX Industry Glossary," 2011). FCs usually remain the same, regardless of the changes in attendance or revenue volume. FC is also known as non-controllable cost, since it will remain the same regardless of changes to other factors associated with the meeting.

For example, the rental of audiovisual (AV) equipment, a convention facility, meeting space within a hotel, or security in the exhibition hall are FCs. The cost of AV in a meeting room is the same whether 50 or 100 people are present. Likewise, the cost of contracted meeting space will remain the same regardless of attendance or number of exhibition booths sold. Similarly, salaries of the organization's staff are an FC, regardless of attendance or other factors.

Variable cost VCs are the "expenses that vary based upon various factors, such as the number of attendees" ("APEX Industry Glossary," 2011). VCs are controllable costs and can be changed in the short term with increases or decreases in attendance. As a general rule, food and beverage, specialty items, overnight accommodations, and other consumables are VCs.

Total cost The **total cost (TC)** of a meeting is described as the total expenses needed to produce a meeting. It is made up of VCs plus the FCs and can be expressed in the following formula.

$$FC + VC = TC$$

The relationship of TC to the number of attendees is important to understand for meeting professionals. In the example presented in Figure 5.5, the VC for the meeting is $50 per attendee, so that the VC for 10 attendees is $500 (10 × $50). If the number of attendees increases to 60, then VC is $3,000 (60 × $50). Unlike VC, the FC of a meeting remains the same regardless of the number of attendees. If the FC for 10 attendees is $500, the FC will still be $500 for 60 attendees. Therefore, with increases in attendees, the TC of the meeting will increase, but the TC per attendee will be reduced as attendance increases.

Net Income

Net income is the difference between the total revenue and expenses. Depending on the accounting system, federal taxes, value-added tax (VAT), sales tax, and/or tax on goods and services may have to be

Number of Attendees	Variable Cost Per Attendee	Variable Cost	Fixed Cost	Total Cost	Total Cost Per Attendee
10	$ 50	$ 500	$ 1,000	$ 1,500	$ 150.00
20	$ 50	$ 1,000	$ 1,000	$ 2,000	$ 100.00
30	$ 50	$ 1,500	$ 1,000	$ 2,500	$ 83.33
40	$ 50	$ 2,000	$ 1,000	$ 3,000	$ 75.00
50	$ 50	$ 2,500	$ 1,000	$ 3,500	$ 70.00
60	$ 50	$ 3,000	$ 1,000	$ 4,000	$ 66.67

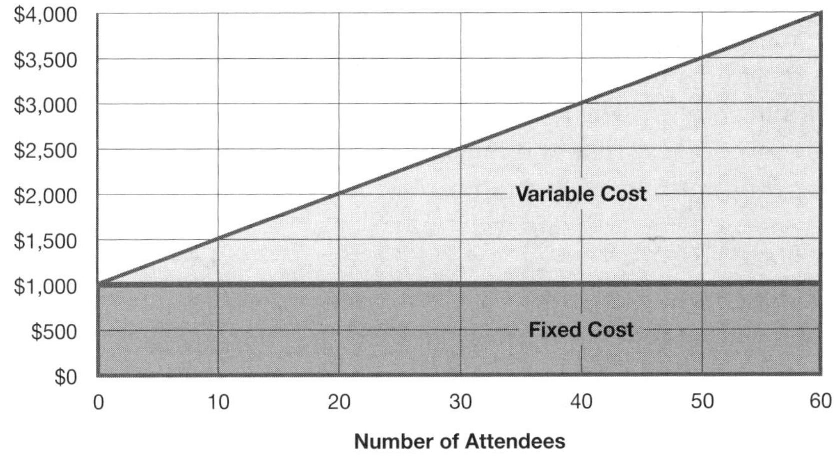

FIGURE 5.5 Illustration of Total Cost This figure details the changes in variable costs in relationship to fixed costs, using both a table and graphic format.

PROFESSIONAL DILEMMA

A membership-based association has held an annual meeting for more than 100 years. The meeting has a reputation for being a reasonable expense for public officials who must be diligent in watching expenses and accounting for return on investment. In fact, the annual meeting has operated at a loss each year, which the organization has subsidized as needed. However, financial conditions are compelling the organization to increase its revenue stream from the meeting to generate a profit. The planning committee has examined the budget and determined that revenues can be increased, with broad changes to how the organization promotes assets available to sponsors, exhibits, and registrations for the meeting. Sponsor relations are very delicate. Should the organization increase registration fees to attendees and the costs of booth space for exhibitors to avoid increasing what it asks sponsors to cover for the assets they receive? Would the organization be more transparent to raise sponsorship requests to cover the undervalued assets, and let sponsors bear a "fair" share of increases in revenue? What is your rationale for these decisions?

deducted from the revenue prior to the calculation of the net income. Tax rates depend on governmental policies and regulations in different parts of the world. Hence, meeting professionals must be informed of the tax system in the location of the meeting venue when preparing a budget. The projected net income is a measure of how well a meeting is expected to perform from a budgeting perspective. Determining the net income is expressed in the following formula.

Revenue – Expenses = Net Income

In a meeting budget, net income is determined by subtracting revenue generated from expenses incurred. In the budget presented in Figure 5.6, the budgeted net income for the meeting planned for the Godwin Destination Management Company, Inc. is $278,000.

Budget Development

When budgeting, the purpose of the meeting and the expected net income must be transparent to key stakeholders. As previously stated, the meeting's financial goal can be to break even, make a profit, or result in a deficit. The following will present a simplified way to generate meeting expense and revenue budgets without overlooking the budget philosophy of a meeting.

Expense Budget

The first step in generating a meeting's budget is to establish the meeting expenses. When doing so, all the necessary expenses should be listed under the appropriate category in the expense budget. This makes any modification of the expenses easy to accomplish. In this

Godwin Destination Management Company, Inc.			
2015 Budget			
Revenue	**Budget**	**Actual**	**Variance**
Registration	$ 1,969,000		
Exhibit Sales	$ 195,000		
Sponsorships	$ 225,000		
Advertising	$ 32,000		
Merchandise Sales	$ 105,000		
Total Revenue	**$ 2,526,000**		
Expenses	**Budget**	**Actual**	**Variance**
Salary and Related Expenses	$ 368,000		
Marketing and Promotion	$ 140,000		
Programming	$ 230,000		
Registration Costs	$ 112,800		
Freight/Transportation	$ 11,000		
Exhibits Contractors	$ 57,500		
Facility Rental	$ 30,300		
Food & Beverage	$ 1,040,000		
Awards & Recognition	$ 227,000		
Miscellaneous	$ 31,400		
Total Expenses	**$ 2,248,000**		
Net Income	**$ 278,000**		

FIGURE **5.6** **Calculating Net Income** The budget depicted in this example demonstrates revenue, less expenses, with the result in projected net income.

process, reasonable estimates of expenses should be obtained from all suppliers that will be involved with the meeting. Each line item expense must be estimated, if the precise cost is not available. Otherwise, the meeting professional could use the previous costs (from an earlier meeting) plus potential inflation. For example, if the cost of advertising is $5,000 in the previous year's budget and the rate of inflation is 2 percent, the estimate for advertising for the next fiscal budget will be $5,100 ($5,000 + [$5,000 × 2 percent]).

Additionally, historical data can be used to estimate line items. By comparing the last two or three years' expenses with consideration for current economic conditions, line item estimates should be fairly accurate. The goal of budgeting is to prepare an accurate budget, thus the meeting professional should take care not to underestimate the expenses, especially if the budget philosophy of the meeting is to make a profit. When preparing the budget, a record should be developed to show the expense categories, quantity, cost, and the calculation for each line item. A precise and detailed record of the expense budget will make budgeting for future years or meetings a lot easier. Once the budget has been developed precisely, detailed records of all line item expenses should be kept as they are incurred. Figure 5.7 illustrates the 2014 expenses of Godwin Destination Management Company, Inc. The expense budget shows the following:

- Expense categories
- Line items in each category
- Quantity of each line item
- Cost associated with each item
- Estimated budget of each line item

For example, one of the expense categories in Figure 5.7 is "administration." The example below describes the calculations of these line items.

- Salary, benefits, and tax for 9 employees (quantity), at an average cost of \$39,000. This calculates to \$351,000 (9 employees × \$39,000).
- Insurance cost at an estimated budgeted amount of \$12,500.
- Travel for 9 employees (quantity), at an average cost of \$500, which made the estimated budget for travel \$4,500 (9 × \$500).

The subtotal for administration is the addition of all the estimated line items, which is \$368,000 (\$351,000 + \$12,500 + \$4,500). The rest of the expense budget categories, e.g., marketing and promotion, programming, registration costs, freight/transportation, and facility rental, can be computed the same way. Another option would be to include the calculations in the budget spreadsheet.

Revenue Budget

Several critical steps must be followed when projecting the meeting's revenue in order to meet the meeting's financial goals.

key points

Revenue Projection Steps

1. Estimate the expense budget
2. Set a financial goal
3. Forecast a realistic number of attendees
4. Set a rational goal for revenue sources
5. Compute the registration fees

Step 1. Estimate the expense budget. The expense budget is estimated at \$2,248,000.

Step 2. Set a financial goal. The financial goal of the meeting budget example resulted in a profit (net income) of \$278,000. Using the financial formula shown below, the total revenue required to generate a net income of \$278,000 can be calculated.

Revenue – Expenses = Profit (Net Income)

Using the above formula, the total revenue required to accomplish the financial goal of this meeting is \$2,526,000 (\$2,248,000 + \$278,000). The required revenue has been established; a realistic forecast of attendees' fees must then be completed to meet the projected revenue.

Godwin Destination Management Company, Inc. 2015 Budget			
Budget Category / Line Items	**Quantity**	**Cost**	**Budget**
Administration			
Salary, Benefits, & Tax	9	$ 39,000	$ 351,000
Insurance	1	$ 12,500	$ 12,500
Travel	9	$ 500	$ 4,500
Subtotal			*$ 368,000*
Marketing and Promotion			
Advertising	1	$ 20,000	$ 20,000
Printing	1	$ 60,000	$ 60,000
Promotions	1	$ 60,000	$ 60,000
Subtotal			*$ 140,000*
Programming			
Speakers Honoraria	25	$ 500	$ 12,500
Speakers Accommodation/Travel	75	$ 1,500	$ 112,500
Program Technology System	1	$ 12,500	$ 12,500
Audiovisual	1	$ 50,000	$ 50,000
Printing/Copying	1	$ 25,000	$ 25,000
Program Committee Charges	7	$ 2,500	$ 17,500
Subtotal			*$ 230,000*
Registration Costs			
Registration Staff	1	$ 20,000	$ 20,000
Onsite Hardware	1	$ 7,000	$ 7,000
Materials/Supplies	3,900	$ 10	$ 39,000
Online System	3,900	$ 12	$ 46,800
Subtotal			*$ 112,800*
Freight/Transportation			
Deliveries/Shipping	1	$ 10,000	$ 10,000
Vehicle Rental	1	$ 1,000	$ 1,000
Subtotal			*$ 11,000*
Facility Rental			
Staff Accommodation/Rooms	9	$ 1,200	$ 10,800
Meeting Space/Rooms	1	$ 19,500	$ 19,500
Subtotal			*$ 30,300*
Exhibits			
Exhibit Service Contract	1	$ 32,000	$ 32,000
Security Contract	1	$ 10,000	$ 10,000
Poster Boards	50	$ 70	$ 3,500
Signage Contract	1	$ 12,000	$ 12,000
Subtotal			*$ 57,500*
Awards and Recognition			
Scholarships	100	$ 1,500	$ 150,000
Achievement Awards	20	$ 100	$ 2,000
Recognition Reception	1,500	$ 50	$ 75,000
Subtotal			*$ 227,000*
Food and Beverage			
Opening Reception	3,900	$ 100	$ 390,000
Continental Breakfast	2	$ 20,000	$ 40,000
Breaks	6	$ 20,000	$ 120,000
Luncheons	2	$ 140,000	$ 280,000
Closing Banquet	3,500	$ 60	$ 210,000
Subtotal			*$ 1,040,000*
Miscellaneous			*$ 31,400*
Total Expenses			**$ 2,248,000**

FIGURE 5.7 Projected Expense Budget The expense budget includes the categories and line items for a meeting, representing the quantity of each line item, cost per unit, and the total.

SUSTAINABILITY *in* Practice

There is a common misconception that it costs more to produce a sustainable meeting. While some sustainable items can cost more, many practices actually save money. For example, elimination of bottled water; reductions in paper use and printing; reuse of banners, signage, badge holders, and lanyards; and shipping less often can save thousands of dollars. By reducing the overall amount of waste generated by a meeting, the meeting professional may reduce waste disposal costs, too. Depending on the location, the meeting professional may be able to negotiate the use of china, silverware, and linens instead of disposables for no extra cost. Compostable service items, such as cups, utensils, and napkins, can cost more, but prices are coming down as demand goes up. Local and organic foods and beverages typically cost more than traditional menu items, but restaurants and caterers have developed many creative ways to include them in event menus. For instance, adjusting portion sizes, featuring in-season fruits or vegetables, or including items from the property's garden can make an impact at little or no additional cost. Keeping close track of meal attendance can keep costs down by eliminating waste. Keeping track of both savings and expenses produced by your sustainability initiative can help you stay within your budget and achieve your organization's sustainability and financial goals.

—Deborah R. Popely

Step 3. Forecast a realistic number. This step can be described as the ability to use historical data to estimate the future number of attendees. In order to develop a realistic **forecast**, a meeting professional will consider the following:

- Inputs from past meetings or market research
- Economic conditions
- Scope of other meetings
- Consumers' income and interest in the meetings
- Organization's marketing plan

For the purpose of this example, the realistic forecast of attendees has been established and a projection of revenue for each type of attendee category can be calculated.

- Members = 2,400
- Non-members = 1,200
- Students = 220
- Guests = 100

Step 4. Set a rational goal for revenue sources. A rational goal for each revenue source requires careful consideration. The tendency to overestimate must be avoided, as overestimating revenue can be a serious obstacle to meeting success. An example of revenue projections will include all sources that 1) have been accounted for in the expense budget, 2) justify the effort that needs to be expended to realize their estimated revenue, and 3) are in keeping with the organization's policies and goals. For example, revenue cannot be realized through the sale of printed t-shirts unless the t-shirts are purchased, or if wearing printed t-shirts is prohibited by organizational policy. Sufficient resources must be allocated to marketing and promotion in the expense budget, in order to meet the budget goal for each revenue source. The projected revenue rates for this example are:

- $1,969,000 from registration fees
- $195,000 from exhibit/vendor fees
- $225,000 from sponsorships
- $32,000 from advertising
- $105,000 from merchandise sales

Step 5. Compute the registration fees. Meeting professionals should consider the following factors when setting registration fees.

- Economic condition, e.g., impact of fees on the likelihood of attendance.
- Research on similar meetings' fees.
- Length of meeting, i.e., if the meeting is more than one day, allowing fees per day of attendance.
- Attendee categories, e.g., member and non-member fees; fee structure for students.
- Policies and procedures needed to ensure that each attendee participates only on the day for which the attendee is registered.
- Earlier registration, e.g., offering early, advanced, and onsite registration rates for each category of attendee.
- Potential discount for more than one registration from the same organization.

For the purpose of this topic, using the realistic forecast for attendees described above, the meeting professional can calculate how many attendees in each category, with the established rates for each, will yield.

Attendee Category	Fee	Projected Number of Attendees	Projected Revenue*
Members	$495	2,400	$ 1,188,000
Non-members	$595	1,200	$ 714,000
Students	$225	220	$ 49,500
Guests	$175	100	$ 17,500

*Projected Revenue = Fee × Projected Number of Attendees

The total registration fees add up to $1,969,000 ($1,188,000 + $714,000 + $49,000 + $17,500). After establishing the rate per attendee and computing the projected revenue from registration fees (see Figure 5.8), the meeting professional must ensure the combination of all revenue sources will add up to the at least the total revenue required to accomplish the financial goal of the meeting.

$1,969,000	+	**$195,000**	+	**$225,000**	+	**$32,000**	+	**$105,000**	=	**$2,526,000**
Registration Fees		Exhibit Fees		Sponsorships		Advertising		Merchandise		Total Revenue

Fund Management

Depending on the amount of income anticipated and when it is expected, the meeting professional may need to open special bank or investment accounts well in advance of the meeting. If large amounts of income will be received months in advance of the meeting, investment income could be realized by investing the funds in short-term, interest-paying accounts.

Otherwise, setting up a separate bank account for the meeting's income is recommended. This allows all income directly related to the meeting to be deposited into one account. Doing this is especially important when using online registration, as the technology allows attendees and exhibitors to register and pay online. Depositing these funds into a separate bank account allows easier tracking of income and fees, e.g., credit card fees. This is especially helpful when international attendees register and pay with bank transfers.

Tax-Exempt Status

Instituting tax-exempt status (if applicable) well in advance with vendors is important. Most facilities and other vendors require credit applications and tax-exempt verification when contracting for services. However, some organizations are tax-exempt only in certain locations. If the organization has tax-exempt status, tax laws should be investigated at the meeting's destination. Saving taxes on payments to the facility and other vendor charges, if applicable, can result in a substantial decrease in expenses.

Collecting Cash Onsite

A determination should be made regarding the amount of cash that is anticipated to be collected onsite at the meeting. If a large amount of cash is expected, a bank account at the meeting location may be warranted. Deposits should be made locally each day and then transferred to the organization's main bank account at the end of the meeting. This way, funds can begin to draw interest immediately upon deposit. If onsite revenue is not expected to be great, consider depositing all cash receipts with the host facility as an advance

Godwin Destination Management Company, Inc.			
2015 Budget			
Budget Category / Line Items	**Quantity**	**Cost**	**Budget**
Registration Fees			
Members	2,400	$ 495	$ 1,188,000
Non-Member	1,200	$ 595	$ 714,000
Students	220	$ 225	$ 49,500
Guests	100	$ 175	$ 17,500
Subtotal			*$ 1,969,000*
Exhibit/Vendor Fees			
Commercial	106	$ 1,500	$ 159,000
Non-profit	36	$ 1,000	$ 36,000
Subtotal			*$ 195,000*
Sponsorships			
Sessions	3	$ 10,000	$ 30,000
Breaks	6	$ 5,000	$ 30,000
Lunches	2	$ 20,000	$ 40,000
Award Dinner	1	$ 25,000	$ 25,000
Receptions	2	$ 45,000	$ 90,000
Tote Bags	2	$ 5,000	$ 10,000
Subtotal			*$ 225,000*
Advertising			
Commercial literature displays	36	$ 750	$ 27,000
Nonprofit literature displays	10	$ 500	$ 5,000
Subtotal			*$ 32,000*
Merchandise			
Memorabilia	4,000	$ 10	$ 40,000
Collectables	2,000	$ 20	$ 40,000
Souvenirs	1,000	$ 25	$ 25,000
Subtotal			*$ 105,000*
Total Revenue			**$ 2,526,000**

FIGURE 5.8 Projected Revenue Budget The revenue budget includes the categories and line items for a meeting representing the quantity of each line item, cost per unit, and the total.

payment against charges to the **master account**. This provides an effective security measure, by avoiding transporting cash, and may result in a cash-in-advance discount from the facility. Registration staff who are also handling funds should be bonded. Additionally, clear and well-defined policies regarding cash handling are prudent. Place tight controls on the receipt and disbursement of funds and keep the number of personnel handling funds to a minimum.

Post-Meeting Financial Analysis

While performing continual financial analysis is important to identify potential challenges, make changes/corrections, and better inform facilities and vendors of the meeting's status in advance of the program, another important step in the financial management process takes place after the meeting has ended. Reviewing actual revenue and expenses as compared to the budget once the meeting is over allows for an analysis to identify any variance for each line item of the budget and the reasons for that variance (see Figure 5.9).

Master Account

Master account review is a key element of financial management for meetings. A master account is an arrangement for credit between the host organization and the venue to be paid directly by the host organization. Charges to master accounts should be reviewed daily and as part of the post-meeting follow-up. Making changes while onsite, when information is fresh for the facility's representative and the meeting professional, is much easier than attempting to negotiate changes when an invoice is received 30 days after the meeting.

When contracting for meetings, the meeting professional should include language indicating that the master account will not be paid until all post-meeting reports are provided by the facility. The required reports should be negotiated in the contracting stage. An additional provision is that all undisputed charges will be paid within 30 days of receipt of the final invoice, while the balance, i.e., disputed charges, will be paid within 30 days of successful reconciliation of disputed charges. Many of these potential issues can be avoided by reconciling the master account onsite, both on a daily basis and at the post-event meeting at the venue.

All onsite suppliers should be encouraged to produce invoices by the end of the meeting as well. Again, all charges should be reviewed either daily or prior to the end of the meeting to ensure charges are in agreement with contractual arrangements. Completing this task onsite will alleviate any later misunderstandings. Negotiating disputed charges onsite is better than after the fact.

Analysis of Variance

Analysis of **variance** is conducted to determine the extent that the budgeted revenues, expenses, and profits matched the actual performance. The formula for calculating the variance dollar amount is by subtracting each line item's actual amount by the budgeted amount.

If the result is a positive number, then more revenue, expenses, or profits will be realized. If the result is negative, then less revenue, expenses, or profit will be realized.

Actual Line Item – Budget Line Item = Variance

Additional analysis of variance should be calculated for the percentage of change. The formula for the percentage of change is to subtract the income statement line's actual from the income statement budgeted line, then divide the result by the income statement budgeted line. Regardless of whether an incremental or zero-based budget is used, an analysis of variance between the actual performance compared to the budgeted performance should be completed.

$$\frac{\textbf{Actual Line Item – Budget Line Item}}{\textbf{Budget Line Item}} = \textbf{Percent of Variance}$$

Undertaking this step will improve understanding as to why actual financial performance differed from what was budgeted. This understanding may drive new policies for everything from site selection and contract negotiation to speaker guidelines and future pricing. At the conclusion of the meeting, the emphasis should be placed on analyzing the overall financial records to confirm or change financial philosophies based on actual performance in the future.

FIGURE 5.9 Budgeting Process Complete Once the budgeting process is complete, the documents and reports are monitored frequently to determine if adjustments are necessary, based on activity for each line item in revenue and expenses. The prudent meeting professional carefully manages the many reports and compares the forecast with actual amounts.

SUMMARY

Meeting the financial goals of an organization is extremely important to the success of a meeting. Today's meeting professionals need to understand how to draft and manage the meeting's budget. The ability to budget competently will lead to effective meeting production, provide for appropriate financial performance review, and facilitate the efficient allocation of resources as well as other positive outcomes.

The three common outcomes associated with meetings are making a profit, breaking even, or incurring a deficit. Effective management of budgets can ameliorate the outcome of losing money when producing meetings. Understanding the mechanics of developing budgets for revenues and expenses enables the meeting's financial outcomes to align with the financial goals of the host organization. Successful meeting professionals will use budgets to develop marketing strategies that drive revenues and reduce expenses. Finally, understanding the relationship of variable and fixed costs in conjunction with meeting participation will lead to financially sound outcomes for meetings.

KEY WORDS

break-even
budget
budgeting
budget philosophy
deficit
expenses
fixed cost (FC)
forecast
incremental budget
master account
profit (net income)
revenue
total cost (TC)
variable cost (VC)
variance
zero-based budget

DISCUSSION QUESTIONS

1. Describe the three common financial goals, i.e., budget philosophy, of meetings.
2. Explain the importance of budgeting to the success of meetings.
3. Explain the advantages and disadvantages of zero-based budgeting.
4. Explain the advantages and disadvantages of incremental budgeting.
5. What is the formula to calculate the variance for a budget's line items?
6. A meeting organizer estimated (budgeted) programming expenses for a meeting to be $255,000. If $265,000 was actually spent, what is the variance for the meeting?
7. List the major sources of revenue common for meetings.

6

Site and Venue Selection

Amanda K. Cecil, PhD, CMP
Associate Professor & Program Director
Department of Tourism, Conventions & Event Management
Indiana University (IUPUI)

Main Topics

- Types of Venues
- Sourcing Destinations and Venues
- Site Visit
- Other Considerations in Selecting Venues
- Key Professionals at the Venue

Learner Outcomes

Upon the completion of this chapter, the student should be able to:

1. Differentiate between the various types and locations of meeting venues.
2. Detail the process of sourcing a meeting venue.
3. Define the roles of key professionals at the meeting venue.
4. Identify important considerations when selecting a meeting facility.

CMP INTERNATIONAL STANDARDS

Domain A. Strategic Planning
Skill 2. Develop Sustainability Plan for Meeting or Event
SubSkills. 2.01, 2.02
Domain B. Project Management
Skill 4. Plan Meeting or Event Project
SubSkill. 4.04
Domain H. Site Management
Skill 20. Select Site
SubSkills. 20.01, 20.02

Meeting professionals have a variety of **venues**, defined as sites or facilities, to choose from when organizing small or large meetings or special events. Selecting a destination and site is a strategic decision that involves many factors.

This chapter describes each type of meeting venue, and details the advantages and disadvantages of hosting a meeting in that facility. The choice of venue should closely link to the facilities' services, layout, and management. Additionally, the process of selecting a meeting site is detailed and key roles of personnel at the destination and venue are discussed.

Types of Venues

Meeting venues can range from convention or congress centers and hotels or conference centers to non-traditional facilities such as cruise ships, art galleries, and movie theaters. Choosing a meeting facility involves consideration of key factors including venue availability, dates and seasonality, and attendee preferences. The meeting professional will carefully investigate the availability of and access to transportation providers, the venue's sustainability practices, and attendee accessibility.

Convention or Congress Center

A **convention** or **congress center** is a multi-purpose facility that hosts meetings, public and industry trade shows, and large events. The function space is large and diverse to accommodate multiple shows,

FIGURE 6.1 Orange County Convention Center, Orlando, Florida The second-largest convention center in the U.S. has facilities equipped to accommodate meetings, trade shows, conventions, special functions, or the performing arts. Approximately 7,000 hotel guest rooms are within walking distance of the center.

FIGURE 6.2 McCormick Place, Chicago, Illinois The McCormick Place complex offers meeting and exhibition space for large to mega-large conventions, featuring the attached Hyatt McCormick Place hotel with 1,250 guest rooms and additional meeting space.

meetings, or events at the same time. Most facilities are defined by the available square footage, type of space available—finished versus unfinished—and the suite of services and amenities. The facility can also feature large lobby space for registration, receptions, exhibits, open space meetings, and other events.

Convention centers host local, state, regional, national, and international meetings, exhibitions, and events. They are typically located in a metropolitan, or downtown, area that has a number of hotels, restaurants, and attractions for attendees traveling to the destination. Convention centers do not have sleeping rooms in the facility, but may be connected to hotels that provide overnight accommodations.

This type of meeting facility offers **in-house** and **exclusive services** to the meeting professional, including food and beverage, audiovisual, technology, production, security, and other offerings. The convention center's union (or right-to-work) policies, city and state ordinances, and federal laws governing the property may differ greatly.

Before inspecting or contracting with a convention center, the meeting professional should note who owns and manages the facility. Convention or congress centers are typically owned by a government, community, or public entity, but may be managed by a private firm or quasi-public corporation.

According to an article titled "Top 10 U.S. Convention Centers" in *Business Review USA*, Orlando, Chicago, and Las Vegas have the largest and most profitable convention centers (Cruz, 2012). Orange County Convention Center (OCCC) in Orlando, Florida, offers meeting professionals 2.1 million square feet (195,096 square meters) of exhibit space in its 7-million-square-foot (650,321-square-meter) complex (see Figure 6.1, p. 98). The OCCC provides Central Florida with a remarkable amount of economic benefits at no cost to the county's citizens, and activity in the center yields an annual estimated tax savings of $117.20 per Orange County household (Fishkind & Associates, 2014).

Chicago's McCormick Place (see Figure 6.2, p. 99) has the distinction of being the largest convention center in the U.S. Its four interconnected buildings located on and near the shores of Lake Michigan are all noteworthy, but special accolades must be given to the West Building, which has 250,000 square feet (23,226 square meters) of meeting space, including 61 meeting rooms and a 100,00-square-foot (9,290-square-meter) ballroom ("Facility Overview," 2014).

key points

IACC Quality Standards

- Priority of the business
- Conference room design
- Conference and business services
- Food and beverage
- Technology
- Guest services

Conference Center

Conference centers are designed to provide the optimal learning environment and are dedicated to educational and training meetings. In order to be members of the International Association of Conference Centers (IACC), facilities must demonstrate a commitment to its professional quality standards, including priority of the business, conference room design, conference and business services, food and beverage, technology, and guest services (see Figure 6.3). These venues are focused on the comfort of the guest and provide a high level of service to meeting professionals.

The most notable differences between a conference center and a venue not specifically designed for training meetings are its meeting facility design and packaging of services. The meeting space is designed to minimize distractions and focus on productivity. Many conference centers offer a **complete meeting package (CMP)**, which is an inclusive per person/per day package including guest rooms, meals,

FIGURE 6.3 Conference Room in a Conference Center Châteauform' La Borghesiana conference center is located in Rome, Italy, and has a total of 55 guest rooms available. The conference room in this photo accommodates 60 participants.

FIGURE 6.4 The Hilton Chicago, a Convention Hotel The Hilton Chicago is a full-service convention hotel that provides over 1,500 guest rooms; 234,000 square feet (21,739 square meters) of event space with 50 meeting rooms, three ballrooms, and four exhibit halls; and many other amenities.

continuous refreshment breaks, technology, meeting space, service charges, and gratuities.

There are six different types of conference centers:

- **Residential**—full-service facilities (includes meeting and sleeping rooms) located in major metropolitan areas or suburban locations
- **Non-residential**—facilities that are full service, but have no sleeping rooms. They may be connected or close to a hotel.
- **Ancillary**—facilities that are part of a larger complex. They may be floors or wings of a conference center, hotel, or resort.
- **Corporate**—facilities owned and operated by a corporation for internal training
- **Resort**—full-service facilities (includes meeting and sleeping rooms) that also have significant amenities such as golf, fitness, and spa
- **University**—full-service facilities (may or may not have sleeping rooms) located on college campuses for university and outside groups (Bolman, 2006, p. 217)

Convention Hotel

Meetings and events can also be held at convention hotels. These properties are located near or connected to the convention center. Hotels can be categorized as full service, limited service, resort, or airport. The hotel may be able to accommodate the entire meeting or, for larger meetings, may be one of many properties used.

A full-service convention hotel offers hundreds of sleeping rooms and flexible space for general sessions, educational breakouts, small meetings, and exhibits. In addition, most have exclusive or in-house vendors for food and beverage, audiovisual, business center, and other amenities (valet service, room service, fitness area, spa, etc.). These types of hotels are located in the downtown area typically and service both the business and leisure markets. They tend to be more expensive and parking can be a challenge (see Figure 6.4, p. 101).

Limited-Service Hotel

Limited-service hotels are located either downtown or in the suburbs. These properties tend to attract regional visitors looking for a lower-cost stay. Most have 50 to 200 rooms to reserve (see Figure 6.5).

FIGURE 6.5 Residence Inn Portland Pearl District This limited-service property offers meeting and ballroom space as well as extended-stay accommodations. Small meetings and board meetings nicely fit into the new surroundings of this property.

FIGURE 6.6 An Outdoor Beach Reception A resort property generally has unique outdoor event options. The Aulani, a Disney Resort and Spa, is perfectly positioned on the beautiful beaches of Ko Olina, which is on the leeward coast (away from the ocean breezes) of O'ahu and nestled between lush green mountains and serene ocean waters. An outdoor setting for relaxation and networking is inviting after a day of learning and meetings. It is important to have an alternate space reserved for the event in case of inclement weather, regardless of the location.

Unlike the full-service property, most limited-service properties have no food and beverage service, very few meeting rooms, and no staffing for valet, room service, or other customer services. Some services may be contracted to an outside vendor if requested, e.g., audiovisual or catering. However, this type of property tends to offer free and accessible parking and nice rooms. Some offer free breakfast or refreshment hour.

Resort Property

Resort properties are often outside of the metropolitan area and in secluded areas. Like other properties, resorts have a number of guest rooms or suites, meeting space, and other necessary services. Notably, this type of property offers upscale recreational **amenities**, e.g., golf, tennis, spa, skiing, and fitness services (see Figure 6.6). Meeting professionals selecting resort properties should carefully consider the program to allow time to enjoy the resort and its amenities. Additionally, most resorts will require additional travel time from the airport and these properties tend to be the most expensive.

Airport Property

Airport properties are attached or located near major airports. Most large airports have both full-service and limited-service properties within a few minutes driving time. These properties serve mostly

FIGURE 6.7 The Westin Hotel Detroit Metropolitan Airport Holding a meeting at an airport location provides easy access to transportation, while having the convenience of spacious meeting facilities and full-service food and beverage opportunities. These venues are perfect for short "in-and-out" meetings and smaller events.

business transient travelers, staying for a few nights in the area. At airport hotels, meeting professionals can host large or small meetings utilizing food and beverage, audiovisual, and other services (see Figure 6.7). These properties also tend to offer complimentary shuttle service to and from the airport.

Non-Traditional Venues

Meeting professionals use many non-traditional types of venues, such as cruise ships, museums, zoos, movie theaters, libraries, restaurants, and universities, to host unique meetings and events. Selecting a non-traditional venue can be both interesting and challenging.

Cruise lines Cruise lines are considered a major competitor to land-based meeting destinations, as meeting professionals give shipboard meetings consideration. Most new ships are adding conference and meeting facilities and shortening their itineraries to attract this exciting market. The major advantage to selecting a cruise line for a meeting destination is the all-inclusive, up-front package pricing.

The cruise package includes accommodations, meals, entertainment, meeting space, and a number of attractive amenities, e.g., spa, formal dining, movies, golf courses, ice skating rinks, fitness areas and classes, stateroom upgrades, and room gifts. Selecting the right ship with an itinerary that meets the group's programming needs can be difficult. Many meeting professionals look for ships that offer multiple days "at sea" so educational opportunities can be offered (see Figure 6.8). In addition, attendees who bring a spouse or family can pose additional needs such as children's programs, recreational activities, childcare services, and unique dining requests.

Other attractions Attractions, e.g., museums, zoos, art galleries, amusement parks, restaurants, and public libraries, often have a large area or theater space, and small rooms can be utilized for a variety of meetings and events (see Figure 6.9). Many of these venues offer standard meeting services and event packages. Meeting professionals can negotiate good deals with attractions during off-season or non-peak days or seasons. These options can be very attractive to attendees, but may bring different challenges to the meeting professional. If the venue is also open to the public, noise and other distractions may hinder the meeting's success.

FIGURE 6.8 Island Cruise Stop Cruises offer a variety of meeting venues onboard with dedicated meeting space, fully equipped theaters, and other venues that offer a creative alternative for educational programs, corporate meetings, incentive programs, and a wide array of entertainment options. Disney Cruise Line offers the added benefit of Castaway Cay, its own private island where groups can host team-building and other private events.

University facilities Universities are a great setting for meetings and educational events. The atmosphere lends itself to encouraging learning and high-level engagement. Some universities have a full-service conference center facility on campus. Other universities only have classroom space and minimal ancillary services available. Many universities rent space to the public when classes are in recess or space is not being utilized. This venue option presents obstacles, such as a lack of variety of food service, inability to rearrange rooms, and limited parking and housing. The range and cost of services can vary considerably depending on the university's location and menu of services.

FIGURE 6.9 SeaWorld, Orlando, Florida An outside event at a local attraction adds to the meeting experience, providing meeting participants with a change from formal programming and an opportunity to network with peers. This experience blends imagination with nature and enables participants to celebrate and care for the natural world.

Sourcing Destinations and Venues

Sourcing the meeting destination and venue(s) can be a long and overwhelming process for a meeting professional. There are several important considerations that a meeting professional must evaluate before entering into the contract stage. Understanding and appraising these factors can reduce meeting costs and increase the value of the business to a venue. In addition, researching the property's physical space, service offerings, and amenities can save the meeting professional time and effort if the property does not meet the basic space requirements or minimum expectations of the group.

Meeting Goals and Objectives

Meeting professionals should not lose focus on the meeting's goals and objectives. The meeting professional must ask: "What is to be accomplished as a result of this meeting?" Meeting stakeholders should identify the purpose of the meeting before considering the meeting's destination or venue(s). The organization's culture may determine this process.

In addition to reviewing the meeting's goals and objectives, meeting professionals should consider any market research available, the meeting budget, and the outline of the meeting program. Selecting a meeting destination and venue should be a strategic decision and careful consideration should be given before contracting.

Meeting Value and Profile

The meeting professional must calculate the value of the meeting before sourcing a meeting destination and venue(s). Gathering and analyzing financial data and historical information on the meeting are valuable exercises. Some categories of sources include: room block, meeting space, audiovisual, food and beverage, transportation, spend, and the influence and profile of the attendees. Hotels and facilities typically require three years of history. If the event is being conducted for the first time, historical data from previous similar meetings conducted by the group should be gathered.

Request for Proposal

key points

Phases of RFP Process

- Creation
- Solicitation
- Evaluation

A request for proposal (RFP) is an invitation to bid on a specific meeting's business. An RFP is the written meeting specifications document prepared for facilities to assist them in evaluating the appropriateness of their property for the group. The RFP describes the meeting objectives, historical data, physical requirements, and attendee interests and expectations. It also identifies the general area and type of facility desired. There are three phases in the RFP process: 1) creation of the RFP, 2) solicitation of proposals through the RFP, and 3) evaluation of the returned proposals.

Preparing the RFP requires careful thought and articulation of the group's needs. The professionally prepared document facilitates consistent communication to all suppliers. As part of the RFP, establish the due date, define who will review the proposal, and identify the decision date for the selection (Lewis, 2006).

When preparing an RFP, the meeting professional should provide as much historical detail about the event as possible. Sleeping room usage, i.e., block and pickup, daily meeting space allocations, food and beverage requirements, i.e., numbers served, and exhibit space needs are just a few of the items that should be documented within the RFP. The master schedule or group résumé from a previous event can provide a facility with a comprehensive overview of the meeting. Through the Convention Industry Council, the Accepted Practices Exchange (APEX) provides sample RFP documents for meeting professionals to use when creating the RFP for the venue.

key points

Request for Proposal Considerations

- Key information about the group or organization holding the event
- Purpose of the event
- Information about the meeting attendees
- Preferred dates and optional dates, if available
- Number and type of guest rooms required each day
- Number, size, and usage of meeting rooms, along with estimated times they are needed
- Range of acceptable rates
- Number and types of food and beverage events, including dates and estimated attendance
- Food and beverage expenditures per event, i.e., exclusive of service charges and taxes
- Exhibits and any other special events or activities
- Any related information, such as complimentary requirements
- History of the meeting including guest room pick-up and food and beverage expenditures

Role of the Destination Management Organization

Destination marketing organizations (DMOs), also referred to as convention and visitors bureaus (CVBs), assist meeting professionals with the venue sourcing process. The DMO's primary goal is to market and promote the destination and its hospitality offerings and attractions. The result of these efforts is positive economic impact. The DMO has three primary areas of responsibility: sales, marketing, and service. These roles are outlined in Figure 6.10, p. 108.

One of the benefits of using a DMO is the amount of time and money saved by the meeting organization during the **sourcing** process. Meeting professionals can submit the meeting's RFP to the DMO sales representative and he/she collects proposals from the destination's venues. Those proposals are shared with the meeting host. Once the meeting host reviews the proposals, specific venues are selected for further review. The DMO sales team can assist with scheduling a site visit at the venues the meeting professional would like to experience and evaluate.

Site Visit

Before considering a meeting venue, the meeting professional should conduct a site visit to thoroughly evaluate the venue's meeting space, food and beverage options, and sleeping rooms, if needed. Another

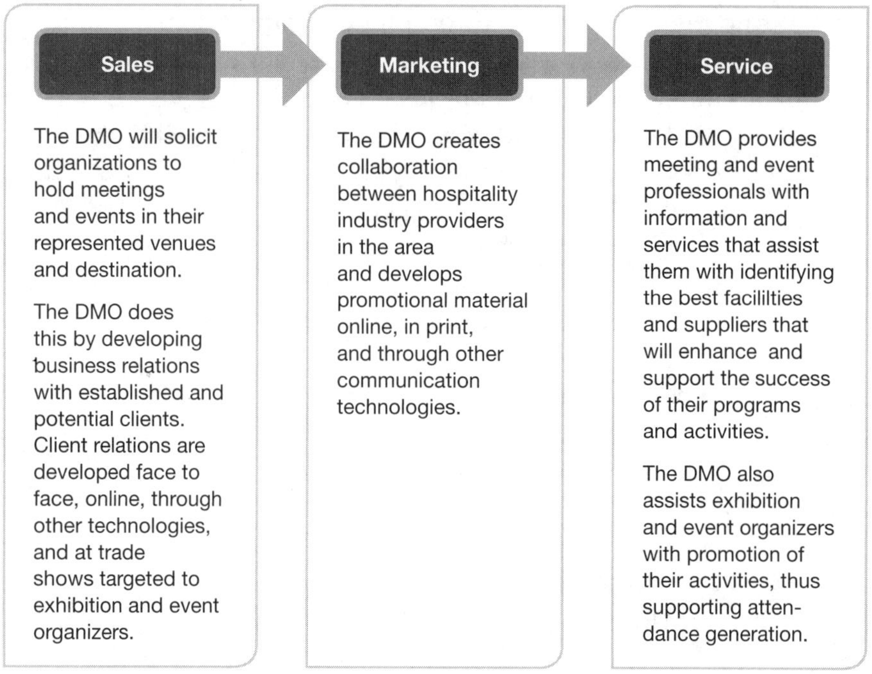

Sales
The DMO will solicit organizations to hold meetings and events in their represented venues and destination.
The DMO does this by developing business relations with established and potential clients. Client relations are developed face to face, online, through other technologies, and at trade shows targeted to exhibition and event organizers.
Marketing
The DMO creates collaboration between hospitality industry providers in the area and develops promotional material online, in print, and through other communication technologies.
Service
The DMO provides meeting and event professionals with information and services that assist them with identifying the best facililties and suppliers that will enhance and support the success of their programs and activities.
The DMO also assists exhibition and event organizers with promotion of their activities, thus supporting atten-dance generation.

FIGURE 6.10 Destination Marketing Organization (DMO) Responsibilities The DMO offers a significant amount of local expertise and assistance during the meeting-management process and is a valuable resource of the services provided by its member organizations. The DMO helps build attendance to increase the ROI (DuBois & Gonzales, 2013, p. 124. Reprinted with permission.).

task is to compare the property's offerings to the physical specifications for the meeting (usually indicated in the RFP). For example, when a meeting requires 150 sleeping rooms, a large ballroom for a general session, 12 breakout rooms, and specific food selections to accommodate attendees' needs, the meeting professional will examine each of these specifications during the site visit.

key points

Site Visit Areas of Interest

- Sleeping rooms
- Meeting space
- Exhibit space
- Ancillary space
- Food and beverage
- Amenities

The hotel environment must also match the attendees' expectations and style. It is important for the attendees of the meeting to feel comfortable and safe at the selected hotel venue. Meeting professionals will also ensure the service level of the venue's personnel meet the group's standards. The standard could be different based on the nature of the meeting and its attendees. For example, a meeting attracting business leaders will have higher service standards compared to a conference hosting high school students. Political and economic stability, any safety and security concerns, and local organizational support should be discussed during this visit.

Sleeping Rooms

The number of sleeping rooms at a hotel property is only one factor to consider when selecting a venue. The meeting professional will also seek information about the types and availability of rooms, based on the group's booking history. Most hotels have a combination of single rooms, double rooms, and suites to offer. Additionally, hotel rooms can vary in square footage and amenities offered. During the site visit, all types of sleeping rooms should be evaluated.

key questions

What the Hotel Sales Staff will Ask

- What will be the total number of sleeping rooms needed each night, from the earliest arrival through the last departure?
- What is the percentage of single versus double room occupancy?
- What has been the average room rate for this meeting? The highest? The lowest?
- Are room rates important to the group? (Lewis, 2006, p. 145–146)

Meeting, Exhibit, and Ancillary Space

Meeting space in venues can be configured in a number of ways. The meeting professional must articulate, to the DMO and facility representatives, the meeting's space requirements, based on projected attendance, room-set, and program schedule. The program may require theater, banquet, classroom, boardroom, and/or open space configurations during the meeting.

key questions

What the Venue Sales Staff will Ask

- How many meeting rooms will be required on a daily basis?
- Are rooms to be set up theater-, classroom-, conference-, or banquet-style?
- How will the AV plan impact requirements for meeting rooms?
- What is the facility's flexibility concerning the tentative agenda (increases or decreases in meeting space)? (Lewis, 2006, p. 146).

Exhibitions

If the meeting also includes an exhibition, the venue will need to provide space for exhibition booths, loading dock access, and headquarters space for an official services contractor (OSC). Most large trade shows are held at a convention center or in large ballrooms. For smaller shows, a hotel lobby or other large open space may be used. The number and size of the exhibits, exhibition space requirements, and service needs should be disclosed to the venue when sourcing the property.

key questions

What to Discuss with the Venue Sales Staff for an Exhibition

- Are there exhibits in conjunction with the meeting? If so, what is the gross and/or net square footage required?
- Will exhibits and aisle signage require high ceilings and/or column-free space?
- How much time is needed for move-in and move-out of displays?
- Are the exhibits suitable for the facility, i.e., hotel versus convention center? (Lewis, 2006, p. 147)

Ancillary Space

Ancillary space needs include space for the registration area, staff offices, storage, technology kiosks, and other special requests such as a speaker-ready room or a media office. The minimum requirement for a meeting venue is to provide adequate space for all programmed functions; ideally, the space will also include ancillary function space that is not necessarily part of the meeting program, e.g., areas for coat check. To ensure meeting success, the venue will meet all basic requirements and provide appropriate services, as well.

key questions

What to Discuss with Venue Sales Staff for Ancillary Space

- How large an area is needed for registration purposes?
- Are adequate utilities available, including wireless high-speed Internet, electrical outlets, and ample lighting?
- How many rooms are required for headquarter offices and press offices? What size must each be? Is storage space needed? (Lewis, 2006, p. 147)

Food and Beverage

Most venues have onsite catering services, employing a full-time chef and culinary staff. For venues that do not have onsite kitchen facilities, many have exclusive or preferred contacts with local or regional catering companies. If the attendees of the group have specific dietary needs, it will be important to disclose that information to the catering department at the venue. Meal plans may or may not be offered by the venue. These can include a Full American Plan, Modified American Plan, European Plan, or voucher system.

Additionally, the meeting professional should review the service and staffing levels provided for each function. There are several service styles that may be requested. The most popular for meetings are the American-style, buffet, or family-style service. For smaller, intimate meals at meetings, Russian or French-style may be appropriate.

key questions

What to Discuss with Venue or Catering Staff

- How many food and beverage events will be held, and when? What types—casual, formal, or themed?
- What kinds of food and beverage events will be held, i.e., breakfast, lunch, dinner, refreshment breaks?
- What is the estimated attendance at each event? What has been the attendance at previous functions?
- Are there any indoor or outdoor events planned? (Lewis, 2006, p. 146)

Amenities

Meeting venues can offer meeting professionals several amenities based on the size and spend of the group. Amenities can include

PROFESSIONAL DILEMMA

Hotel A is modern, well set up for the technology demanded by most meetings, and also quite expensive. The facility has an institutional look and feel, with little personality or attractive decor. The property is located downtown. Half of your planning committee members think the facility is adequate. Hotel B, on the other hand, is on the National Register of Historic Places, has gorgeous wood walls and solid oak doors, fantastic ambiance, and character. This hotel is 15 miles from the city center. Half of your planning committee is convinced this facility is perfect. The facility does have lower costs for your identified needs.

Make a list of the pros and cons for each property. You have the deciding vote for Hotel A or Hotel B. What is your choice and why? Would your answer change if you knew that Hotel A was part of a chain, so you might be able to negotiate better rates in the future at a different location for the next meeting you plan? Why or why not?

WiFi, upgrades on guest rooms, complimentary transportation, fitness centers, concierge service, and many more. The level and offering of amenities will be determined by the overall package that the meeting professional and venue negotiate.

Other Considerations in Selecting Venues

The meeting professional has several other important factors to consider when selecting an appropriate meeting venue. Physical space and services are critical, but planners must additionally acknowledge and understand attendee preferences, meeting patterns, and destination best practices. In venue selection and contract negotiation, these elements become increasingly important for making final destination and venue decisions.

Dates, Rates, and Availability

Meeting professionals must know and understand the event market, conditions of the economy, the destination and venue's seasonality, and the event's preferred dates and patterns. If the venue is in need of booking business during a certain period of time, then the meeting professional can expect to get a better deal. The converse is also true. If the venue is in demand, there is little incentive to offer discounts or amenities for free.

Most venues have **high** and **low seasons** and a **shoulder season**. The venue typically experiences high occupancy rates during the high season and lower rates during the low season. The shoulder season is in the middle. Meeting professionals have negotiation power during the low and shoulder season and venues will compete aggressively for the meeting business. If forced to book during high season at a property, meeting professionals should not expect reduced rates, significant concessions, or commissions.

key questions

What to Discuss with DMO Sales Staff

- Is the meeting limited to a specific set of dates or time period?
- Does the meeting have date/pattern flexibility?
- Is there a need to avoid certain religious, ethnic, state, or federal holidays? If the meeting is in another country, are there local holidays that must be considered? (Lewis, 2006, p. 145)

SUSTAINABILITY *in* Practice

The meeting site is one of the most important factors in sustainable meeting planning. The site's facilities, setting, amenities, practices, and policies, along with the proximity of lodging, transportation systems, and other resources in the destination, have a major impact on what can be achieved. Communication and teamwork between the meeting professional and site are needed to ensure that sustainability requirements are understood and supported before, during, and after the meeting. At minimum, a sustainable meeting site should have documented energy efficiency, recycling, waste reduction, water conservation, and sustainable purchasing programs.

Meeting professionals are increasingly using the RFP process to determine whether destinations and sites can work with them to meet sustainability goals. Others are pre-screening sites based on practice information and metrics published on websites or destination and site-search platforms. Others are relying on green certifications for guidance, e.g., LEED®, Green Seal®, Green Key, Green Globe, or TripAdvisor's GreenLeaders. While these shortcuts provide assurance of a basic level of sustainable operations, they may not cover the full range of meeting professionals' sustainability needs. At this time, destinations, convention centers, and other suppliers that have achieved APEX/ASTM certification are better positioned to provide comprehensive sustainable meeting services. A registry of certified suppliers can be found on the website of the Green Meeting Industry Council.

—Deborah R. Popely

key questions

What the DMO Sales Staff will Ask

- What is the anticipated attendance for the meeting?
- What has been the attendance at the past five years' previous meetings of this type?
- What are the demographics of the group?
- Will attendees want to bring family members?
- Are recreational or leisure activities important to attendees? (Lewis, 2006, p. 145)

For example, if an organization wants to host a meeting in Orlando during March or April, the entire city may be experiencing high occupancy during the spring break travel season. On the other hand, venues in the Midwest are seeking business in November or December and may offer great deals to book close to the holidays. The meeting's dates and patterns are extremely important factors. If the organization is flexible on the month, days of the week, and arrival/departure schedules, the group can negotiate the space and rates.

Attendee Preferences

Estimated attendance and attendees' preferences in meeting destination and venue types should not be ignored. The meeting professional will inquire about where attendees would like to see the meeting hosted, what time of year works best, and what types of properties the group prefers. If the group has specific needs during the suggested travel time, destination and venue must be able to meet the expectations.

Accessibility

The **Americans with Disabilities Act of 1990 (ADA)** is a law enforceable only in the U.S. It requires public buildings, e.g., hotels and restaurants, to make adjustments or accommodations to meet minimum standards that make the facilities accessible to individuals with physical disabilities. The ADA was amended in 2012 to encompass even more accommodations, many of which pertain to the needs of meeting attendees.

While most public facilities in the U.S. are now built or adapted to be in compliance with ADA requirements, some "historic" venues and buildings that cannot be adapted reasonably are exempt from some ADA requirements. Depending on the attendee profile, the number of participants with special needs, and the particular accommodations required, meeting professionals should weigh the pros and cons of booking a venue that is not ADA compliant.

Meeting professionals working outside the U.S. should be familiar with the national laws and local regulations concerning accommodation for persons with disabilities at the particular destination. Even though ADA regulations do not apply in other countries, meeting organizers have a professional responsibility to provide accommodations for this group of individuals whenever and wherever possible.

Transportation

Air and ground transportation to/from the destination should be key considerations. Attendees need easy access to and from the airport (or other destination access system) and venues, as well as transportation throughout the destination. Meeting professionals have a variety of options when considering ground transport for attendees, including public and private transportation options. Shuttle bus service, train, taxi service, rental cars, chauffeured cars, and other forms of ground transportation may be required, based on the needs of the attendees. Depending on the nature and travel patterns of the group and the selected destination, discounted airline and/or charter air service should be explored.

Key Professionals at the Venue

The meeting professional will work with a number of people at the meeting venue(s) during selection, contract negotiation, promotion, planning, execution, and evaluation of the event.

General Manager

The general manager or venue owner is the senior staff member at the property and is ultimately responsible for the overall success of the sales and service of the venue. Depending on the size of the venue, the general manager may only play a role in the initial site visit to

FIGURE 6.11 Hotel Leadership Welcoming the Meeting Professional As a customary practice, the hotel representatives of the headquarter hotel welcome the meeting professional upon arrival. This act of hospitality epitomizes the value the facility places on the business relationship.

assist with serving the group when onsite. Most general managers are very eager to welcome and the interact with meeting professionals (see Figure 6.11).

Once a meeting professional shows interest in booking a venue, the facility's sales team will become the lead venue contact. The sales department may have different divisions for staff that focus on certain markets; e.g., corporate, association, sports, social, or leisure sales. Another way to divide a sales team is by region. In the U.S., the regions may be divided by sections of the country, e.g., Northeast, Northwest, Midwest, or South. The division of the sales team will depend on the size and scope of the property. Regardless of the sales representative assigned to the meeting professional, he/she will arrange the site visit, initiate the first draft of the contract, and negotiate the agreement with the meeting professional.

key points

Key Professionals at the Venue

- General manager
- Director of marketing
- Service manager

Director of Marketing

The director of marketing at a meeting venue is responsible for assisting the meeting professional in promoting the property and the destination to its attendees. Depending on the value of the group's business, services can include attendance building, information and resources to promote the destination and venue, and other shared promotional opportunities.

Service Manager

Once the contract is finalized, the meeting professional will be assigned to a member of the convention service team. Most venues assign the meeting professional to a specific **convention service manager (CSM)** or **event manager (EM)**. This individual coordinates all of the meeting professional's needs before, during, and after the meeting. The service manager may be introduced to the meeting professional in the negotiation cycle to ensure an easy transition from the sales to the service team. If the group is hosting a large meeting at the convention center and using multiple hotels, the meeting professional may have a CSM/EM at the convention center and at each hotel. Again, it depends on the size and scope of the meeting.

The CSM is responsible for communicating and coordinating catering, hotel front desk, meeting room set-up, housekeeping, security, audiovisual, and the official services contractor (OSC) within the venue. If the meeting is hosted at a large property, the meeting professional may also be working with a catering director for food and beverage service.

The CSM will start by gathering all of the meeting's information and organizing that into **function sheets** or **meeting event orders (MEOs)**. Each function sheet or MEO will detail the specific requirements of each individual function and the requirement of each department in the venue. These documents are reviewed at the **pre-convention meeting** that all key event personnel attend. If catering is separate, meeting professionals may also need to review and approve the **banquet event orders (BEOs)**. These forms detail the type and amount of food, staffing requirements, location, set-up and tear-down instructions, and any additional unique needs for food service. These detailed worksheets are put into an **event specifications guide (ESG)** to be used by the meeting professional and venue team to ensure each function is set up and carried out correctly.

The CSM/EM will compile all of the group's invoices and finalize the billing. This professional is responsible for hosting a **post-convention meeting** to evaluate all elements—both positive and negative—of the meeting. The general manager and the sales team representative often attend this meeting to review the meeting contract and talk about future business.

SUMMARY

Selecting the destination and the meeting venue(s) are strategic decisions made by the host organization. Destinations have very different meeting venues and attractions for meeting professionals to consider. The process of sourcing and selecting meeting sites is a complex one with many factors to consider. Meeting professionals must know the organization and event's requirements and evaluate the site's ability to meet these requirements. Meeting professionals must have a firm grasp of the meeting's objectives, physical requirements, and attendee expectations before conducting a site inspection.

A wide variety of facilities from which to choose are available when deciding where to hold a meeting. The meeting professional might consider the logistics of meeting in a metropolitan area, suburban area, airport area, resort, conference center, or convention center. The suitability of each will depend on the needs of the meeting being planned. Numerous important details need attention during the site inspection. The key questions included in this chapter provide a good starting point.

The meeting's success will be based on the meeting professional's ability to match these factors and the offerings of the destination and venue(s), while working with the key stakeholders and partners in the planning process.

CONTRIBUTING AUTHOR

Premila A. Whitney, CMP, CHE
Instructor
Rosen College of Hospitality Management
University of Central Florida

KEY WORDS

amenity
Americans with Disabilities Act (ADA)
banquet event order (BEO)
complete meeting package (CMP)
conference center
congress center
convention center
convention service(s) manager (CSM)
event manager (EM)
event specifications guide (ESG)
exclusive service
function sheet
high season
in-house service
low season
meeting event order (MEO)
post-convention meeting
pre-convention meeting
shoulder season
sourcing
venue

DISCUSSION QUESTIONS

1. List the benefits and drawbacks of using a convention center vs. conference center.
2. What are the key differentiators between metropolitan, suburban, resort, and airport hotel properties?
3. Describe how a meeting's date and pattern can affect the venue's ability to offer discounted rates, concessions, and commissions.
4. Explain how to calculate the business value of a meeting.
5. Detail the role of a DMO in the venue sourcing process.
6. What is the responsibility of the sales vs. service staff at a meeting venue?

7

Risk Management: Meeting Safety and Security

Tyra Hilliard, PhD, JD, CMP
Speaker, Writer, Multipreneur
Hilliard Associates

Main Topics

- Safeguarding Meeting Elements
- Meeting Threats
- Prioritizing Potential Risks
- Risk-Management Plans

Learner Outcomes

Upon the completion of this chapter, the student should be able to:

1. Identify six meeting assets that require protection.
2. Explain the difference between risk, emergency, crisis, and disaster, specifically as they relate to meetings.
3. Describe three categories of threats/hazards to meetings that require risk management.
4. List four strategies for dealing with meeting and security risks.
5. Identify six types of security personnel that may be part of an emergency response team.

CMP INTERNATIONAL STANDARDS

Domain A. Strategic Planning
Skill 2. Develop Sustainability Plan for Meeting or Event
SubSkills. 2.01, 2.02
Skill 3. Develop Business Continuity or Long-Term Viability Plan of Meeting or Event
SubSkill. 3.04
Domain C. Risk Management
Skill 6. Manage Risk Management Plan
SubSkills. 6.01, 6.02, 6.03, 6.04, 6.05
Domain I. Marketing
Skill 28. Contribute to Public Relations Activities
SubSkill. 28.05

Meeting safety and security are the responsibilities of everyone involved in the meeting. While safety and security are certainly significant responsibilities for the venue, meeting professionals also have a significant role when the safety of meeting attendees is threatened, the meeting host is facing potential liability, and when the security of meeting accessories is in jeopardy. Even when protective measures are already in place, the meeting professional should also be making appropriate decisions about meeting safety and security, sharing the plans with the venue, and developing the plans with selected meeting suppliers as needed.

Although hotels, convention centers, venues, and other facilities typically have security on staff, that security is there to protect the venue—not necessarily the meeting organizer or the meeting participants. Using a venue that has onsite security is a wise choice; however, the savvy meeting organizer understands limitations inherent in this choice and must be prepared to supplement the gaps.

Safeguarding Meeting Elements

Risk management is a process designed to safeguard the various elements of a meeting by minimizing the amount or severity of harmful events that may occur. Protecting the health and wellbeing of people is always the paramount concern, followed by the prevention of loss or damage to property, breach or theft of proprietary information, loss of the financial investment made in the meeting, and even damage to the public image of the organizing entity (see Figure 7.1).

Understanding Safety and Security

Managing meeting safety and security is not just a best practice; it is a legal and ethical obligation. When a crisis, disaster, or emergency occurs onsite at a meeting or event, the risk of a lawsuit increases. The ethical issues that arise from failure to prepare and respond appropriately to risks can adversely affect both the meeting professional and the sponsoring organization for years.

Legal requirements To effectively manage risk and reduce potential damages, many organizations rely on the legal concept of **due diligence**. This means the meeting professional must do what a reasonable, prudent colleague would do in the same circumstances. Due diligence suggests the organization will commit enough resources and effort to projects, daily operations, and major initiatives to avoid or **mitigate** risks that are predicted to have potential impact on the organization. If the meeting professional is **negligent**, i.e., does not meet a reasonable expectation or does something that should not be done, then that person, as well as the sponsoring organization, may be found liable for injury or damage caused by this negligence.

Meeting Elements Requiring Protection	Examples
People	• Attendees • Speakers • Exhibitors • Vendors • Sponsors • Event staff
Information	• Corporate trade secrets • Credit card information • Contact information • Medical information
Property	• Computer equipment • Audiovisual equipment • Communication equipment • Exhibits • Prototypes • Copyrighted materials • Trademarks
Financial investment	• Meeting organizer's budget • Attendee expenditures • Exhibitors' booth fees and other expenses • Speaker honoraria
Organization image	• Public image of meeting organizer, facilities, or others involved in the meeting
Professional reputation	• Reputation of the meeting organizer, the venue, the destination, or third-party/independent planner

FIGURE 7.1 Examples of Protected Items This figure provides examples of areas and individuals that need consideration when developing a risk-management plan (Adapted from Krugman, 2010).

Contracts between the meeting organizer and the venue or other involved parties may specify legal requirements related to meeting safety and security, e.g., the requirement to hire security personnel, carry insurance coverage, or adhere to fire codes. The meeting professional must read contracts carefully to ensure that all requirements are addressed and fulfilled.

Ethical issues Even if a meeting safety and security issue does not rise to the level of being illegal, failure to address safety or security may still be categorized as unethical or unprofessional. In the meetings industry, a reputation for thoroughness and professionalism is one of a meeting professional's most valuable assets. A reputation for being careless or unethical, e.g., cutting corners on security measures, can adversely affect an individual's entire career.

Meeting Threats

Meetings require detailed coordination of multiple components and, even with the most careful planning, every potential risk cannot be eliminated (see Figure 7.2, p. 120). In order to plan for safety and security issues, the meeting professional must be aware of where the **hazards** (also known as **threats**) might originate. Additionally, some risks come in the guise of opportunities. If an opportunity arises and

FIGURE 7.2 Safety Hazards During Exhibit Hall Set-Up Controlling the entrance of non-essential personnel during the exhibit hall set-up is of paramount importance for the safety of exhibitors and labor. Security at the entrances should be monitored. Heavy machinery, freight, and activity by those involved can make for dangerous situations for those unaccustomed to an exhibit hall.

the organization is not posed to respond to this opportunity appropriately, the risk can have a negative impact on the organization.

Hazards can generally be grouped into three different areas: naturally occurring, technological, and human-caused (see Figure 7.3). Additionally, hazards in each category may manifest themselves before, during, or even after the meeting.

Threat Response Strategies

Once recognized, risks can be accepted, reduced/mitigated/managed, transferred or shared, or avoided altogether. Depending on the particular circumstances of the meeting, one or a combination of these options may be implemented.

key points

Threat Response Strategies

- Accepting risk
- Reducing/mitigating/managing risk
- Transferring risk
- Avoiding risk

Accepting risk Some risks are worth accepting, either because they are so unlikely to happen that planning for them is not an efficient use of time (low probability of occurring) or because, even if they do happen, they are unlikely to result in much harm, i.e., they are low impact. For example, no matter what the meeting or event and no matter where it is held, a possibility exists that someone will fall and be injured. Planning for first-aid assistance onsite (see Figure 7.4), providing precautionary information about hazardous locations, and being able to quickly access emergency medical staff are all examples of accepting risk.

Reducing/mitigating/managing risk Numerous labels have been used for the response that minimizes the likelihood a risk will occur

Category	Sub-Category	Examples
Naturally occurring	Geological	• Earthquake • Volcano • Mudslide
	Meteorological	• Flood • Forest fire • Snow/ice
	Biological	• Disease affecting humans, animals, or plants (e.g., **pandemic**) • Insect infestation
Technological	Computer	• Data loss • Computer crash • Equipment loss
	Ancillary support	• Failure of essential audiovisual equipment • Equipment failure • Lack of service
	Telecommunications	• Telephone service failure • Cell tower overloaded or reserved for emergency responders
	Energy/power/utility	• Power outage • Water shortage or contamination
Human-caused	Accidental	• Hazardous material spill • Transportation accident • Explosion
	Intentional	• Terrorism • Labor dispute • Violence

FIGURE 7.3 Hazard Categories and Examples Awareness of the hazards or threats is important in developing a risk-management plan. Each category provides examples to further focus on specific situations that may develop during the course of the meeting or event (Adapted from NFPA 1600, 2007).

and/or minimizes the potential damage a predicted risk might cause—reducing, mitigating, or managing risk are common labels.

Many methods to reduce the risk of safety and security issues are available to meeting professionals, depending on the nature of the risk. Hiring outside security personnel may be the best method of reducing the risks associated with loss of property and equipment, as well as assuring the safety of attendees. For example, requiring trained bar staff can reduce the risk of over-serving alcohol that may lead to possible illness or injury (see Figure 7.5, p. 122).

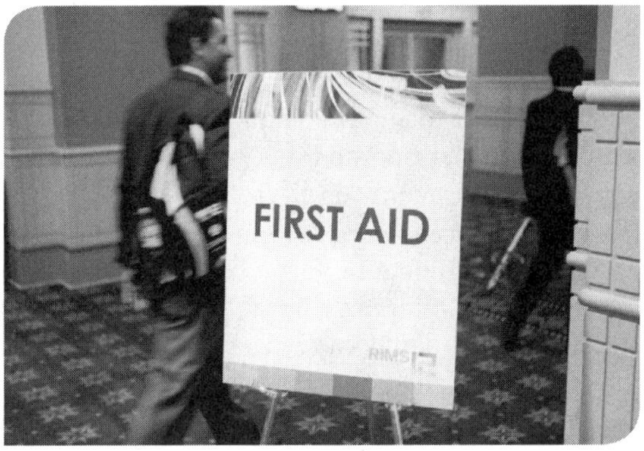

FIGURE 7.4 First Aid Station A well-marked area onsite where medical assistance is available is a requirement in many facilities and a prudent component of every risk-management plan.

The severity of the consequences, if the risk is realized, can also be reduced. For example, medical staff onsite at a meeting may help to reduce the severity of an injury or illness by eliminating the need to transport an attendee to a hospital and providing immediate medical attention. Sometimes risk mitigation is as simple as doing a thorough site inspection of a potential destination or venue, or checking references for any vendors that will be contracted. Doing everything reasonably possible to

Risk	Reduction Strategy for Meetings
Over-consumption of alcohol	• Trained and certified bartenders • Drink tickets
Equipment stolen from exhibit floor	• Security personnel • Locked door with limited distribution of keys
Heatstroke or sickness	• Provided transportation • Tents • Fans
Terrorism	• Crisis management plan • Back-up destination
Injury	• Taped-down wires • Floor kept clear and dry

FIGURE **7.5**
Risk-Reduction Strategies for Meetings Examples of reduction strategies for common safety and security concerns are outlined in this figure.

identify potential hazards and to foresee potential negative consequences is a key component of risk mitigation.

Transferring risk Although the meeting professional assumes the overall responsibility for safety and security, some risks are outside the professional's expertise (see Figure 7.6). In such cases, the meeting professional would be prudent to transfer these risks to others who are more qualified or positioned to absorb them. The most common ways to transfer risks are purchasing insurance policies and negotiating contracts.

Many types of insurance may be needed, and are available, for a meeting. The specific types vary depending on the nature and size of the meeting and whether the facility, the meeting organizer, or both purchase insurance.

Generally, facilities will have different types of policies and may specify the types of coverage and policies required of the meeting organizer. One of the most common policies is comprehensive **general liability insurance** (CGLI), which protects the insured in case of injury on the property or at the meeting and damage to property. For example, the meeting organizer with a CGLI policy transfers, to the insurance company, the financial risk of having to pay for an injured person's medical care or wrongful death lawsuit. In exchange for receiving the insurance premium, i.e., the cost of the insurance policy, the insurance company accepts the risk that someone will be injured onsite at the meeting. Since serious injury at the meeting is unlikely, the insurance

FIGURE **7.6** **Community Service Day** Many organizations host a workday preceding a meeting to give back to the community. Each community has needs that can be made easier with many people working together. In this photo, members of Risk and Insurance Management Society (RIMS) are demolishing a run-down garage in Denver, Colorado. With construction and other activities, individuals are sometimes injured when they are unaccustomed to the work. This type of liability exposure needs to be covered in the risk-management plan with adequate insurance.

PROFESSIONAL DILEMMA

Many meeting professionals are often challenged by the reluctance of their senior management (or clients) to include funding for risk management and/or contingency planning in the meeting budget. People and organizations that have never experienced an adverse event tend not to think about it or are reluctant to allocate money to something that might not even occur.

One company, whose products were insurance programs for large corporate clients, refused to approve funding for cancellation and interruption insurance for a major incentive to South America. The total budget for the program was over $3 million, including $1.5 million for a full-ship charter of a six-star luxury cruise ship. The meeting professional recommended hiring security specialists, who were asking for $200,000 to develop and implement a comprehensive risk-management plan. In addition, the meeting professional wanted to include a line item for 1 percent of the total budget for cancellation/interruption insurance and contingency funds in case of any unexpected emergency or disaster. The management refused, preferring to allocate that money to the food and beverage and entertainment components of the program. Six weeks before the 300 incentive winners and guests were scheduled to fly to Buenos Aires to begin the program, the bottom dropped out of the Argentine economy, causing enough political unrest and uncertainty to scare the sponsoring company into cancelling the first three days of the program in Argentina and reorganizing everything to take place in Santiago, Chile, before boarding the ship. The cancellation charges in Buenos Aires and additional charges in Santiago were over $250,000. The last-minute extra security service hired to calm the nervous participants cost another $250,000. The final program cost came in at half a million dollars over budget. The meeting professional never had difficulty contracting for security or obtaining approval for cancellation/interruption insurance again.

How might a meeting professional who experiences resistance in the organization to hire security services and obtain appropriate insurance coverage overcome that resistance? What skills and knowledge must the meeting professional cultivate to handle this professional dilemma?

company is willing to take the chance that it will not have to pay out a claim more expensive than the premium it collected.

Apportioning risk among the involved parties is an important reason for the existence of contracts. While a contract is just a piece of paper, it could secure the future of a company or organization by identifying who is liable and who is not legally responsible if a loss, damage, or injury occurs. It may also define what types of insurance are required by each party as well as other liability and risk-management issues—the reason contract negotiations are so important. A meeting professional and legal counsel should read every word in a contract and proactively negotiate the clauses that may lead to liability or risk assignment.

Avoiding risk There are few risks that can truly be avoided. To avoid a risk, one must be able to control it. Think about some of the major risks mentioned already in this chapter that are unavoidable, such as

FIGURE 7.7 Warning Sign Outside Exhibit Hall during Set-Up This sign cautions individuals entering the exhibit hall during set-up that there are forklifts in use and alerts them to the dangers of entering the area.

key points

Unavoidable Risks

- Natural disaster
- Citywide power outage
- Some fires
- Disgruntled worker with a weapon

Avoidable Risks

- Serving undercooked meat
- Allowing unsafe exhibit décor
- Failing to provide security measures for heavy equipment

a natural disaster, citywide power outage, fire, or even a disgruntled worker with a weapon. The meeting professional can neither control nor avoid these types of risk. For example, the only way to avoid a risk like a hurricane is to avoid coastal regions during hurricane season. Even then, a hurricane may strike a major airline hub and the travel of attendees with connecting flights may be disrupted, making it impossible to get to the meeting. So, it cannot truly be avoided completely.

On the other hand, some risks are avoidable if they are recognized and appropriate steps are taken to change the circumstances that might lead up to the risk's occurrence. The meeting professional can hire security personnel and work with the venue to make sure appropriate safety measures are in place throughout the property (see Figure 7.7). The key step, though, is to develop a comprehensive risk-management plan with the help of key stakeholders, communicate the plan, and update the plan as appropriate.

Prioritizing Potential Risks

There is no one-size-fits-all risk-management plan because each meeting is different. So risks must first be identified and then analyzed as part of the process to develop a comprehensive risk-management plan.

Identifying Risks

While there are some common categories of risk, the particular risks associated with a meeting will vary widely based on specific characteristics such as meeting type, time of year, location, duration, number and profile of attendees, and possible budget constraints.

Risk assessment is the identification of possible risks, which can be difficult when working at an unfamiliar destination or venue. Supplier partners can be an invaluable source of information and assistance when identifying and prioritizing potential risks. When developing the risk-management plan, the meeting professional will probably work with the local destination marketing organization (DMO), destination management company (DMC), hotel and/or convention center, and other service providers.

Analyzing Risks

Since the meeting professional cannot avoid every potential risk, the meeting professional should estimate which risks have the highest probability (or likelihood) of occurring and which risks have the most severe consequences (or impact) if they do occur. These risk are the ones upon which the meeting professional will focus attention.

An easy tool for analyzing risk is to create a table and allocate each risk a number (where 1 is low and 5 is high) for both probability and severity, using information provided by local supplier partners, municipal agencies, and other data sources. Those potential risks with the highest sums should be addressed first (see Figure 7.8).

Planning for Risks

Once the probability and consequences for specific risks for a meeting have been determined (identifying risks) and which ones have been deemed the most likely and/or potentially damaging (analyzing risks), a risk-management plan is developed. To be effective, a risk-management plan must be prepared in advance of the meeting,

Potential Risk	Category (N, H, T)*	Probability 1 (low) to 5 (high)	Consequences 1 (low) to 5 (high)	Total
Sound system malfunction	T	1	3	**4**
Terrorism	H	1	5	**6**
Violence (assault, fight)	H	4	4	**8**
Tornado	N	2	5	**7**
Power outage	T	1	3	**4**
***N = naturally occurring, H = human-caused, T = technology**				

FIGURE 7.8 Risk Analysis Model This figure illustrates an analysis model that will assist the meeting professional in developing a risk-management plan that can easily be implemented and updated for future meetings in order to keep the information current and up-to-date.

written down so it can be shared with the appropriate personnel, implemented when necessary, and reviewed, evaluated, and revised if necessary after each meeting.

Risk-Management Plans

Basic elements of a meeting risk-management plan include a chain of command that defines the members of the **crisis response team** and the responsibilities of each team member, a crisis communication plan naming specific spokesperson(s), contingency plans for high-probability disruptions, and a description of when and how the onsite response to disruption should be implemented (see Figure 7.9).

Response Team
• Name, title, organization
• Contact information
Responsibilities
• Tasks
• Response team leader
Risks (Threats and Opportunities)
• Occurrence, analysis process, and results
• Response strategy and results data collection
• Monitoring situation, reporting process

FIGURE 7.9 Response Plan Content This information, adapted from the Centers for Disease Control project risk management plan template (2006), is general in nature and can be used for each meeting held. However, depending on the composition of the onsite team, some elements will require customization for each meeting.

Working Together

In the event of a crisis, disaster, or emergency, the meeting organizer must work closely with supplier partners, including the facility, the destination, and key stakeholders. The plan should be formulated collaboratively so that all are able to work together as an effective crisis response team.

There may be times when a meeting organizer requires additional security, either because of contractual requirement by the facility, special circumstances, or people involved in the meeting. In these situations, a **security contractor** or a **security service** is hired to perform security functions beyond what can be provided by the planning organization, venue, or destination.

Selecting Security Personnel

Hiring additional security personnel is an excellent means of mitigating risk. Some of the factors that influence the type of security obtained include the type of event or meeting, the attendee profile, the various threats identified in the risk assessment, and the budget (see Figure 7.10).

Meetings often use multiple types of security for different purposes. Security personnel or volunteers working for the meeting organizer coordinate with the proprietary security personnel within a meeting facility who are most familiar with the venue and its security policies. The meeting professional must designate who supervises who in an emergency, crisis, or disaster, to avoid confusion, promote an effective response, and minimize response time.

Contracted security professionals These professionals are hired from a security firm for a specific meeting or event. The security firm should be responsible for any licenses, uniforms, or equipment needed by the

Type of Security	Example
Contracted	• Security guards hired through a security company
Law enforcement	• If meeting is on a university campus, campus police have jurisdiction • City police officers • County police officers • State patrol officers • Federal investigators
Peer	• Bouncers (such as at a bar) • Concert security
Personal	• Bodyguard • Secret Service (federal)
Proprietary	• Hotel security
Volunteer	• Badge checkers at an exhibition • Volunteers at a convention who stand outside the ballroom doors until it is time for a program to start

FIGURE 7.10 Types of Security Issues and Responders This figure represents six common categories of meeting security along with examples of responders with more detailed information about each category that follows (Adapted from Silvers, 2008).

security personnel (see Figure 7.11, p. 129). A contract between the meeting organizer and the security firm specifies details such as the number of personnel to sufficiently cover the meeting or event, date(s), time, and location for each individual, and the total cost for coverage (Silvers, 2008).

Law enforcement The meeting or event may require a higher level of security. This refers basically to the police, whether federal, state, county, or city. Additionally, when meetings are held on a university campus, the university may have its own police force with jurisdiction on university property. Often, these are the only type of security personnel who may carry weapons at an event. Their first priority is generally to the public, not necessarily to the event attendees. In fact, their role may be to ensure control or containment of the event attendees so the attendees do not disrupt the public with noise, belligerent behavior, or property damage (Silvers, 2008).

Peer security A blend of security personnel that are approximately the same age and appearance of the attendees is often a first-line type of security. At times, these individuals may wear t-shirts that say "Security" so that there is an awareness of a security presence. While security personnel are often authoritative in demeanor and even physically menacing, peer security personnel must be able to keep calm and thoughtful in tense situations. It is their job to identify

SUSTAINABILITY *in* Practice

Risk management is essentially the process organizations use to identify and manage risks that may impact their ability to profit or operate. A focus on sustainability, whether driven by regulatory, political, financial, or stakeholder changes, has shifted the risk-management and decision-making process. This has given rise to the topic of sustainability risk management. According to Peter Graf, executive vice president and chief sustainability officer for SAP, "Sustainability today is about managing risk" (Tweed, 2010, para. 2). Sustainability risks arise when organizational behavior or the actions of others in an operating environment, e.g., suppliers, media, and government, create vulnerabilities that may result in financial, operational, or reputational losses in value.

The overlay of sustainability adds a new dimension to risk management. Meeting professionals must view their meetings from a risk, safety, and security perspective that includes sustainability considerations.

- **Strategic risk** A meeting professional must view the meeting from the perspective of a number of strategic sustainability issues including marketing position, changing member preferences/consumer demand, stakeholder communications, and sponsors. Reputation management is paramount in this arena.
- **Operational risk** Extreme weather events, such as earthquakes and hurricanes, have always presented operational risks for meeting professionals. Mitigating operational risks for meetings should also include addressing supply-chain risks or creating a safe, non-toxic environment.
- **Compliance risk** Many companies face new and expanding compliance requirements resulting from an increasing number of international, national, and regional programs. Organizations, especially corporations, have to comply with government regulations. They are often compelled to comply with the best practices established by other companies. As organizations focus on sustainability at an organizational level, meeting professionals must ensure that their meetings support organizational commitments, compliance, and governance issues.

For example, the American Public Transportation Association has a commitment to sustainability. A meeting held by this association or one of its members without regard to sustainability may be a strategic and compliance risk.

Meeting professionals must position their risk-management plans to account for any loss of reputation, operation, or compliance. Meetings, as a visible, public vehicle, should support resource management, effective use of financial resources, strong partner relationships, maintenance and creation of knowledge, and innovation management. Meeting organizers should not put themselves in a position where denial is the defense.

—Susan M. Tinnish, PhD

FIGURE 7.11 Contracted Security Personnel Security personnel are often contracted through a security firm to assist in controlling entrance to certain areas of a convention center and, in general, are cognizant of the activities and traffic in and out of the building. They also may be first responders in the case of an emergency.

problems and defuse situations before they rise to the level of needing higher-level security action.

Personal security These individuals are often tasked with protecting one or more people who are at high risk, e.g., a celebrity or a president or prime minister of a country. Especially with international travel and meetings, certain countries pose kidnapping or other threats to high-profile figures.

Proprietary security These individuals are employees of the organization or facility that is hosting the meeting or event. The types of security in the meetings industry that work in a hotel or convention center are considered proprietary security. That is, they are proprietary to those facilities and in some cases, proprietary security are independent contractors or sub-contractors rather than employees of the host facility.

Volunteers Volunteers may be used for certain security functions, but volunteers generally should not be considered security personnel. They often are untrained or trained only briefly. Volunteers can be used for things like checking badges as meeting attendees enter an exhibit hall, providing directions, or maintaining order when a crowd is entering a keynote session. Volunteers should be informed about the limitations of their authority and should also be well aware of whom to contact in case a different type of security is required, e.g., breaking up a fight, injury to an attendee, or the activation of an alarm.

A meeting or event may use multiple types of security for different purposes. As long as each security provider understands the limits of his or her responsibilities and is coordinated by a clear hierarchy, this is an excellent way to balance safety, security, and customer service. All security personnel and volunteers working for the meeting organizer must coordinate with proprietary security within a meeting facility. A clear delineation of responsibilities regarding who directs decisions and actions in an emergency, crisis, or disaster is of great importance and an essential distinction to make before the meeting begins. Having different security personnel vying to be in charge during an emergency, crisis, or disaster will only slow the response time, cause confusion, and potentially make the situation worse.

key points

Planning for Safety & Security

- Planning a program
- Choosing speakers or entertainers
- Choosing a destination or venue
- Identifying function space
- Choosing a menu for meal or social functions
- Hiring vendors

People-First Focus

When in doubt, the meeting professional should do what is best for people first. This means considering safety and security at every stage of planning, managing, hosting, and servicing meetings. Risk management is not another task to be accomplished; rather, it is a professional way of managing quality meetings (see Figure 7.12).

A reasonable meeting professional will focus on risk management, safety, and security to provide the best possible experience for all stakeholders. Although risk management can seem daunting, anything a meeting professional does to protect meeting attendees, staff, and the organization are small steps in the right direction.

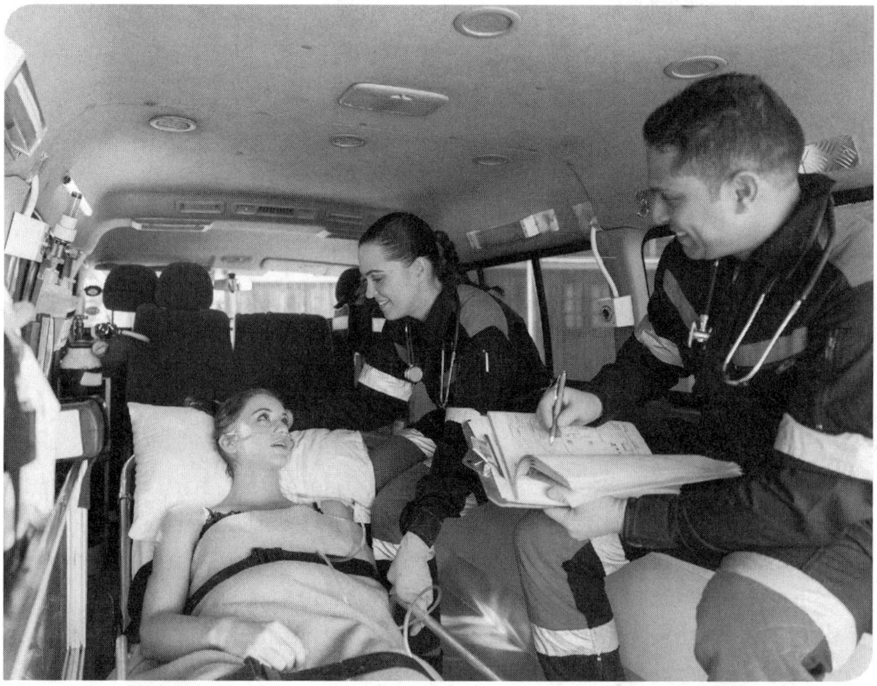

FIGURE **7.12** **Caring for People First** First-aid assistance should always be available onsite to ensure the safety and security of attendees, suppliers, and staff. It is essential that an emergency-response process be considered in advance and activated should someone need medical attention beyond the scope of care offered onsite. All key personnel should know how to activate the process when more advanced medical care is needed and immediate transport to a fixed medical facility is required.

SUMMARY

The meeting professional is responsible for the logistics of a meeting, as well as its strategic, legal, and ethical components. Identification, analysis, and management of potential threats are critical meeting planning skills that help to ensure the safety and security of attendees and staff. The meeting professional cannot identify or plan for every potential threat to a meeting and its participants. However, the meeting professional might be able to anticipate the most probable threats or potential disruptions. If a risk can be anticipated, it often can be prevented. If it cannot be prevented, the severity of the negative effect may be diminished.

The highest-value component of a meeting is the people—attendees, staff, exhibitors, guests, facility personnel, and anyone else involved. Planning for the safety and security of these people, and executing effective risk management and emergency responses when required, are fundamental job requirements for a professional meeting organizer.

KEY WORDS

crisis response team
due diligence
general liability insurance
hazard
mitigate (mitigation)
negligent (negligence)
pandemic
risk assessment
risk management
security contractor (security service)
threat

DISCUSSION QUESTIONS

1. In August 2005, a suicide bomber exploded a bomb in the lobby of the Grand Hyatt Hotel in Amman, Jordan. Although thousands of miles away, this emergency resulted in a lawsuit filed in Los Angeles, California, where one of the victims had lived. His widow filed a lawsuit against Global Hyatt Corporation and Hyatt International Corporation, alleging that the hotel was negligent in protecting guests from foreseeable violence (Hotel Online, 2007).
    - In your opinion, was this lawsuit justified?
    - If the victim had been part of a meeting group at the hotel, could the meeting professional and sponsoring organization have been sued for negligence as well?
    - What risk-management techniques should be implemented by both facilities and meeting professionals in locations that are known to be prone to increased violence and/or terrorism?

2. In April 2010, the Eyjafjallajökull volcano in Iceland erupted (see Figure 7.13). Although it did not cover any meeting venues with lava, it did affect many meetings, especially those in certain areas of Europe at, or around the time of, the eruption. The extensive ash cloud caused by the eruption grounded airplanes for several days. Hundreds of flights were cancelled because they could neither fly into nor out of many major European meeting destinations. Thus, meeting attendees were stranded in European cities or were unable to get to those cities to attend meetings that started after the eruption. To make matters worse, for those attendees staying in European hotels, guests who were able to drive to their destinations were demanding rooms, but attendees who could not get out had nowhere to go (Hatch & Kovaleski, 2010).
   - If you had been the meeting professional of a group detained in a destination for several extra days, what would you have done to assure the wellbeing of your attendees?
   - If you had been the meeting professional of a meeting whose destination was unreachable because of the effects of the volcano, what contingency plan would you have implemented to minimize both financial loss to your organization and inconvenience to your attendees?
   - What specific risk-management techniques protect both meeting professionals and facilities against financial loss in the event of this type of natural disaster?

FIGURE 7.13 Planning for the Unexpected The eruptions of the Eyjafjallajökull volcano closed much of European airspace and caused the largest air-traffic shut-down since World War II. An analysis of the impact concluded "that some 107,000 flights were canceled during an 8-day period, representing 48 percent of the total air traffic. Certain days as much as 80 percent of total flights were canceled. Around 10 million passengers were affected by the Eyjafjallajökull ash cloud" (Bye, 2011, para. 7).

8

Negotiations, Contracts, and Liability

MaryAnne P. Bobrow, CAE, CMP, CMM, CHE
President
Bobrow Associates, Inc.

Main Topics

- Request for Proposal
- Negotiation Process
- Contracts and Requirements
- Contract Performance
- Contract Elements and Clauses
- Liability and Insurance
- Other Supplier Contracts
- Sponsors and Sponsorship Agreements

Learner Outcomes

Upon the completion of this chapter, the student should be able to:

1. Identify the requirements for a contract.
2. Explain the relationship between an RFP, a proposal, and a contract for a meeting.
3. Give examples of legal issues that could arise in connection with a meeting.
4. List the basic elements of a hotel contract for a meeting.
5. Explain key facility contract clauses.

CMP INTERNATIONAL STANDARDS

Domain A. Strategic Planning
Skill 2. Develop Sustainability Plan for Meeting or Event
SubSkills. 2.01, 2.02
Domain B. Project Management
Skill 5. Manage Meeting or Event Project
SubSkill. 5.02
Domain G. Meeting or Event Design
Skill 15. Engage Speakers and Performers
SubSkill. 15.04

The meeting professional will work through contracts with a variety of suppliers, including hotels, convention centers, and other venues, as well as general service contractors, audiovisual technology providers, speakers, and other service providers. Contracts develop as a result of a specific process that begins with a request for proposal (RFP), proceeds through negotiations between the involved parties, and ends with the execution of the contract by authorized signers.

Request for Proposal

Generated by the meeting professional, the RFP provides a supplier with details about the scope and potential value of the meeting to the supplier and the local community. The RFP is the initial outreach by the meeting professional to providers of facilities, lodging, food and beverage, technology, speakers, transportation, and a variety of other meeting-related services. The Convention Industry Council, through its APEX Initiative, provides the "APEX RFP Workbook" (2012) to assist meeting professionals in preparing the RFP.

In addition to the "APEX RFP Workbook," other meeting-related sites offer RFP samples, as do many suppliers, including hotels and facilities. Whatever the source, a well-written RFP is a roadmap for the meeting organizer and supplier hoping to develop a contractual relationship. The RFP outlines the various logistical elements of the

FIGURE 8.1 Dynamics of Negotiations The meeting professional and the vendor or supplier enter into discussion regarding the needs and wants for the meeting. Through the process of negotiation, agreement is either reached or a decision is made to look elsewhere.

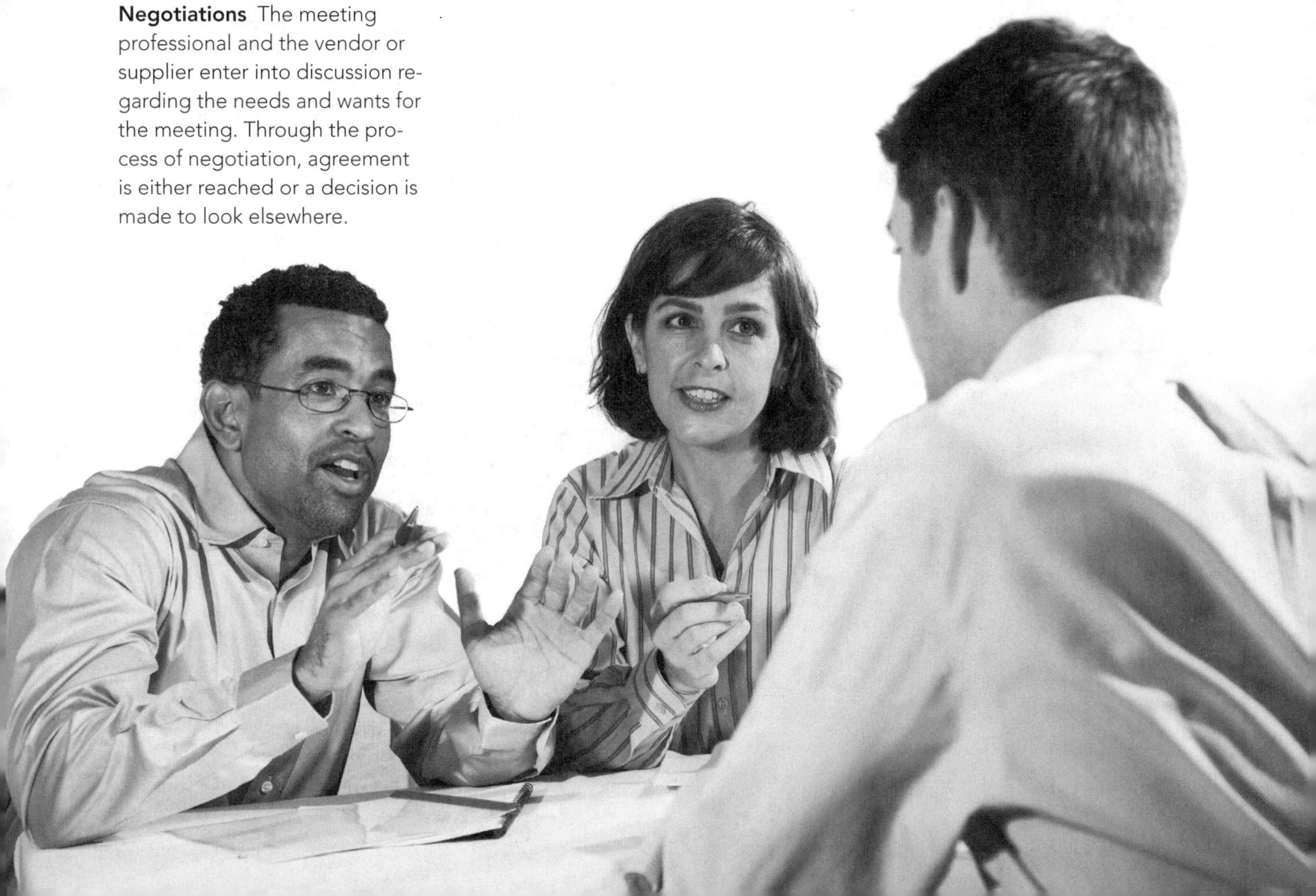

meeting and indicates which priorities of the meeting sponsor must be included in the final contract. Budgetary information may also be provided to assist the supplier in developing a realistic response ("Guidelines for Developing," 2003).

Sourcing meetings through the **e-RFP** (electronic RFP) is popular with meeting professionals, since an online request can instantly be sent to multiple suppliers. However, as a result, many suppliers can become inundated with requests and have difficulty responding quickly. Effective and professional use of e-RFP's includes sending requests only to those who may be able to meet the specifications detailed by the meeting organizer.

The response to an RFP is the beginning point for negotiation. Discussions concerning the items contained in the RFP response are a prelude to contract formation. In preparation for these discussions, establish clear objectives to be achieved during the process and be prepared with definitive information and data that will help to arrive at a solution that is fair and equitable to both parties.

Negotiation Process

Negotiation is a process in which people with shared interests, yet different goals, engage in an exchange of promises intended to achieve each party's goals in the form of an agreement which is acceptable to all those involved (see Figure 8.1). Reaching agreement on the essential terms will move the process forward to creating and executing a final contract. Negotiations with hotels or convention centers can be most challenging for the meeting professional, since the goal of the facility, which is to earn as much revenue as possible, conflicts with the goal of the meeting organizer, which is to keep the meeting expenses as low as possible. A successful negotiation results in a compromise in which each party secures enough of its priority requests to move forward with the project.

The first step in successful negotiation is to establish goals and prioritize needs prior to meeting with the other party. Without a clear idea of what must be obtained at the end of the process, the parties risk giving up too much, or possibly too little, to reach a satisfactory conclusion. Beginning with a complete outline of the meeting requirements, the organizer should prioritize the importance of each component as it relates to overall meeting success. While many methods of prioritizing exist, a simple list of requirements divided into three groups—"must have," "nice to have," and "can manage without"—is one easy method. For example, a guest-room rate no higher than a certain amount per night may be a "must have" to accommodate budget parameters. Complimentary or reduced parking fees for local attendees may be a "nice to have," while additional housekeeping service in the evenings for all meeting attendees may not be important and falls into the "can manage without" category.

key points

Prioritizing Needs

- Must have
- Nice to have
- Can manage without

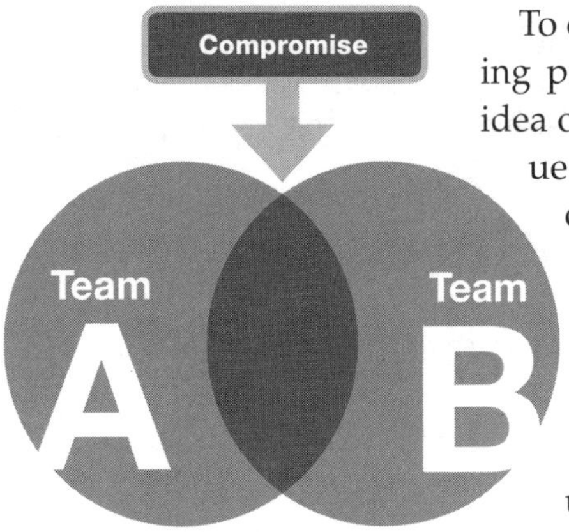

FIGURE 8.2
The Negotiation Process Ending in Compromise
Through discussion between both parties, agreement is reached following the evaluation of the compromise—a win/win situation.

To obtain as much as possible from the "must have" list, the meeting professional should enter the negotiation process with a firm idea of the value of the meeting under discussion, as well as the value of any future business to the property that may come from the organizing group. Perhaps the meeting sponsor is a company with other divisions or departments that will be organizing future meetings. Perhaps the meeting under negotiation is an annual event that has regularly provided significant revenue to the facility. Providing the history of annual or similar meetings might increase the perceived value of the business under negotiation.

Analysis, planning, and preparation are the foundation of any successful negotiation (see Figure 8.2). The meeting professional should enter negotiations with a thorough understanding of the other party's priorities. For example, if achieving a certain amount of revenue from a particular sleeping-room rate is a "must have" for a hotel, the meeting professional should identify and request other areas for cost reduction. If a property needs to fill space over a certain set of dates, a meeting organizer may be able to secure more favorable room rates over that period, if the original meeting dates can be changed.

Rates, Dates, and Space

Negotiations between meeting professionals and facility sales personnel begin with the three most important items for both of them, specifically, the dates available for the meeting, the availability of the required number of sleeping rooms and function space over those dates, and how much the facility will charge. In a perfect world for meeting organizers, all space needs would be available during the exact time period requested, at just the right cost to meet budget parameters. In a perfect world for venue sales personnel, all space requested would be available over a time period in which there was no other group business interested in the same space, at a rate that would meet or exceed revenue and profit projections.

Neither of these perfect worlds exists, so rates, dates, and space are the first major areas of negotiation. Meeting professionals who are able to obtain everything required in all three areas often feel like lottery winners, as the industry saying "dates, rates, and space—you can rarely get all three" most often applies. The meeting dates may be flexible, but the amount of space required or room rate allocated in the budget are not. The organization might have some flexibility in how much can be paid for sleeping rooms and function space, but the dates and space requirements cannot be changed. Once these essential terms have been agreed to, the parties will move forward and discuss other key contract provisions.

key points

Hotel Areas of Negotiation

- Rates
- Dates
- Space

- Guest-room rate
- Guest-room upgrades
- Meeting dates
- Meeting- and function-room rates
- Complimentary or discounted meeting-room or function space
- Food and beverage costs
- Staff-to-guest service ratio for food and beverage functions
- Registration assistance
- VIP amenities and services
- Commission for third-party agents
- Transportation services

FIGURE 8.3 Common Negotiable Items for Meeting Facility Contracts The meeting professional generally has a list of items needed for the meeting that are negotiated during the contracting discussions. Based on the value of the business to the facility, the contract is written to include those items that are deemed acceptable within the value proposition.

Negotiating Concessions

Once the dates, rates, and space have been agreed upon, the other meeting components outlined in the RFP are open for negotiation. **Concessions** are items in a contractual agreement where one party provides something of value to the other party in exchange for something else. Knowledge of the priorities of the other party is a valuable asset when negotiating for concessions, as well as knowing the "hard" vs. "soft" costs at a particular property. Hard costs relate to items or services that generate actual revenue collected by the property, e.g., guest-room rates, food and beverage costs, meeting-room rental. Soft costs are generally those which can be absorbed by a property without incurring undue additional expense, e.g., upgrades to a higher category of guest rooms that would remain unsold over the meeting dates, or a reduced rate for a certain number of staff rooms. Figure 8.3 lists RFP items that are routinely negotiated prior to the contract phase.

Contracts and Requirements

The "APEX Industry Glossary" (2011) defines a **contract** as an "agreement between two or more parties that creates in each party a duty to do or not do something and a right to performance of the other's duty, or a remedy for the breach if the other party fails to perform its duty." More simply stated, a contract is an agreement between two or more parties. If one party fails to satisfy the contract obligations, the other party has a legal right seek a remedy. Remedies vary depending on the situation and the terms of the contract.

A meeting contract spells out all of the details of the product or service to be provided, to minimize misunderstandings between the meeting organizer and the supplier. Contracts are a means of ensuring that both parties have the same expectations and providing a written record of the details discussed. When contracts are well written and

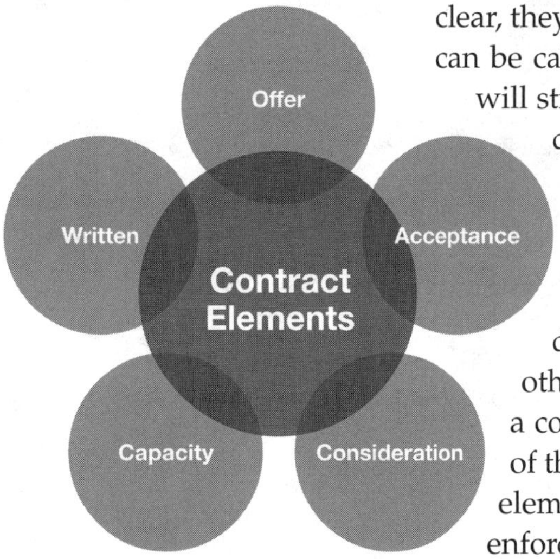

FIGURE 8.4
Contract Elements A legally enforceable contract requires an offer, acceptance, consideration for the offer, and capacity to sign on behalf of the obligated parties, and it should be in writing.

clear, they can deter (though not always eliminate) disputes. A contract can be called by other names, e.g., a **letter of agreement (LOA)**, and will still be binding if the document contains all of the elements required by law. Regardless of the term used, this document is legally enforceable and binding upon both parties as long as certain requirements are met.

In the U.S., the five legal elements required in a contract are an offer, acceptance, consideration, capacity, and a written document signed by the involved parties (see Figure 8.4). In other countries or regions, similar requirements exist. Wherever a contract is negotiated and written, it should clearly include all of the specifics intended by both parties and contain the required elements. In some instances, a contract for goods or services can be enforced even when it has not been set in writing.

Offer

An **offer** is a promise, proposal, or other expression of willingness to deliver specific obligations under proposed terms with another party. A space and rent proposal from a facility is an offer. It may be in the form of a completed contract form, license, space use agreement, or part of the proposal. However, the offer must be specific, addressing all essential elements, dates, and rates. Rates quoted in the future should specify a formula or other method for setting those rates. A proposal or offer lacking specific determinable pricing is unenforceable, as a key element of the contract would be missing from that offer.

Acceptance

When an offer is made, **acceptance** is indicated when the party receiving the offer signs the contract. If the recipient makes any changes to the offer before signing, this constitutes a counter offer, not acceptance. Once a counter offer is made, the original offer is voided and the counter offer, if accepted by both parties, becomes the contract. If further revisions are made, the process of counter offer continues until all parties reach agreement. This negotiation process remains ongoing until terms are agreed to or one party or the other withdraws the last offers or counter offers.

Consideration

The legal definition of **consideration** has nothing to do with being nice to someone. Rather, it refers to exchanging something of value between the parties, i.e., it is the price paid for the offer. The "price" may be monetary or a promise to do or not do something. Consideration is an essential element to forming a valid contract. Without consideration being exchanged, the agreement is not legally binding. For contracts between venues and meeting organizers, the venue makes the

PROFESSIONAL DILEMMA

An independent meeting professional wins the bid for a major conference from a large, multi-national corporation. The time frame for planning is very short and by the time the rather lengthy and complicated contract for service works its way through the corporate legal department, the first deposit is due to the hotel and various other deposits will be due to other suppliers. The meeting professional is unable to obtain any advance funding to pay these deposits until the contract with the facility has been signed and the official meeting budget has been approved. The hotel calls with the news that another company is requesting the same space over the same dates and is ready to pay a deposit immediately. Will the planner's client release the space or will the deposit be forthcoming in the next 48 hours, after which the option on the space will expire? What suggestions can be offered to the meeting professional to ensure that the space will be held for the client?

offer of space and/or sleeping rooms on specific dates, in exchange for the consideration of paying specific rates. Numerous concessions are possible in this contract. For contracts with other providers, a product or service is the offer and a similar consideration, usually money, is provided. Both parties to the contract must get something of value for the element of consideration to be reflected in the contract.

Written

Under the Statute of Frauds in the U.S., certain contracts must be in writing to be enforceable. This generally includes contracts involving meetings and events. While the Statute of Frauds varies from jurisdiction to jurisdiction, the performance and sale of goods clauses are similar regardless of dollar value. Outside of these requirements, an oral contract is enforceable, but the terms of oral contracts are difficult to verify. Prudent practice is to require all contracts in writing. The process of discussing terms during negotiations allows the parties to provide clear expectations and avoid future conflict. The more discussion that takes place in advance of the contract being executed, the more likely the parties are to be clear as to the cost and definition of services or goods being exchanged.

Capacity

Capacity is defined as the legal qualification, competency, power, or fitness to enter into a contractual agreement, i.e., the person signing the contract is legally authorized to sign contracts that bind the party employing the signee. Persons below the legal age of majority (minors) may not enter into contracts. The legal age is eighteen in the U.S., but may vary in other countries. Persons under the influence of alcohol or drugs, as well as persons with mental disabilities, may not enter into contracts. Some organizations may designate in writing which employees are legally allowed to sign contracts on

FIGURE 8.5 Seek a Legal Counsel Review Prior to signing a contract, the meeting professional should seek a review of the contract by legal counsel to ensure it is written to the benefit of both parties and reflects the outcome of the negotiation process.

behalf of the employer and which employees are forbidden from signing contracts.

Any person signing a contract must have legal **authority** to do so by the employing organization as indicated by the phrase "actual authority." In both the U.S. and the United Kingdom, contracts signed by persons believed to have apparent authority may be enforceable. In this case, a reasonable person would conclude the person signing the contract is acting in good faith and is allowed to sign the contract (often called "implied authority" based on how the person has behaved during negotiations). An example might be a sales representative signing a contract on behalf of the management of a hotel. To avoid any confusion or uncertainty, signees should provide documentation regarding their authority to bind the organization and might add a clause attesting to their authority to sign the contract. Legal counsel should review all contracts prior to signing (see Figure 8.5).

Contract Performance

Generally, parties to a contract are expected to meet the obligations to which they have agreed. If one contracting party fails to perform under the contract, a material breach of contract occurs. Breaches specifically occur when one party fails to perform, impedes the ability of the other party to perform, or asserts the intent not to perform.

Failure to perform, or **non-performance**, is defined as neglect or failure to carry out an agreement ("APEX Industry Glossary," 2011). The failure or neglect to render performance specified in a contract holds the non-performer liable for damages. When a party sues for breach of contract, the court may mandate several different remedies. It may award damages, order the breaching party to perform the work, cancel the contract, or rewrite the contract.

1. Preamble: includes names of sponsoring organization and hotel
2. Official dates of the meeting
3. Number and types of rooms and cut-off date for reservations
4. Rates/commissions
5. Arrival/departure pattern
6. Meeting space and release date, e.g., when unused space can be released back to the hotel
7. Complimentary and reduced-rate rooms
8. Working space, offices, and media room
9. Exhibit space
10. Food functions
11. Refreshment breaks
12. Liquor
13. Gratuities and service charges
14. Audiovisual equipment
15. Union regulations
16. Master account and credit procedures
17. Method of payment
18. Termination/cancellation clauses
19. Damage clause (liquidated or mitigated damages)
20. Attrition clause—guest room, food and beverage, meeting rooms
21. Arbitration/dispute resolution
22. Warranty of authority
23. Insurance requirements and indemnification clause
24. Other contract matters/addenda

FIGURE 8.6 Standard Elements of a Meeting Contract While the list of required elements in a basic contract is relatively short, the elements common to a meeting contract are much more numerous. The elements will vary with the type of supplier involved.

Types of Damages

There are two common types of damages—**actual damages** (sometimes referred to as compensatory damages) and **liquidated damages**.

Actual damages compensate for actual injuries or loss. Liquidated damages are a reasonable estimation of actual damages to be recovered by one party if the other party breaches the contract. An example might be the amount owed to a hotel as compensation for the cancellation of a meeting. In order for actual damages to be awarded, the injured party must take steps to mitigate, i.e., diminish or make less harmful, the adverse impact of any damages, injury, or costs.

key points

Types of Damages

- Actual damages
- Liquidated damages

Contract Elements and Clauses

Contracts generally contain standard elements as listed in Figure 8.6. Additionally, there are more and more clauses included in meeting contracts (listed in the Key Points box on the following page), which may meet the specific needs of the meeting organizer. Key contract clauses covered in this section and in greater detail are attrition, cancellation, and *force majeure*.

Attrition

Attrition is the "difference between the actual number of sleeping rooms occupied (or food and beverage covers or revenue projections) and the number or formulas agreed to in the terms of the facility's contract" ("APEX Industry Glossary," 2011). Facilities agree to price the rooms and space based on the value of the business. In order to avoid the attempt to get a better price or additional concessions by overpromising, contracts have evolved to the point where attrition clauses are standard. If a group does not meet its minimum room block and/or food and beverage commitments, this clause details the compensation due to the facility.

Damages may be calculated according an estimated amount of lost revenue or lost profit, according to what has been negotiated in the contract (Foster, 2006). Damages agreed to in any contract clause must be reasonably related to the actual harm caused by the failure to fully perform, in order to be enforceable. The courts will not enforce excessive payments, which constitute a penalty. When writing attrition clauses, the parties take into consideration how easy it would be to mitigate the losses. In other words, the amount of damages may be lower if the party that cannot meet its obligations notifies the other party early in the period covered by the contract. While omitting the attrition clause might seem like a tempting way to avoid possible damages, the result could be just the opposite. In the case of cancellation, and in the absence of a clear formula in the contract for calculating attrition charges, the facility could demand 100 percent of the amount due for the room block (Tesdahl, 2012).

With regard to food and beverage attrition, a simple solution to avoid damages is to order food and beverage consistent with the monetary value stated in the contract. Even if the overall number of attendees drops, the meeting professional would benefit from an upgrade in menu selections if necessary to spend the committed funds on food and drink, rather than to spend it on attrition fees.

key points

Common Contact Clauses

- Acceleration
- Americans with Disabilities Act (ADA)
- Ancillary fees, taxes, surcharges
- Audit
- Change in ownership of hotel
- **Condition of premises**/deterioration in quality
- Concessions
- Construction or renovation
- Contingency
- Credit arrangements, master account
- Liquor liability
- Competing groups
- Pre- and post-event pickup reports
- Quiet enjoyment
- **Relocation/walk**
- Resale
- Third-party agents and commissions
- Unavailability of facility
- **Waiver**

Cancellation

A **cancellation clause** is a contract provision that outlines the damages to be paid to the non-canceling party in the event of a breach of contract by the other party. Cancellation of all or part of the agreed to contract, space, room block, or food and beverage can result in a partial cancellation fee coming due, depending on how the clause is written. A cancellation of the whole meeting would constitute a full cancellation. A typical cancellation clause in a hotel contract will include the timing of the notice of cancellation and the liquidated damages to be assessed, as illustrated in Figure 8.7 (see p. 144).

Note that the closer the cancellation is to the meeting date, the greater the amount of liquidated damages. This is because after holding the room block off the market for months, it may be difficult for the hotel to find another group on short notice. Nevertheless, the meeting professional should be sure to include refund of any cancellation fees in the contract in the event that the property is able to resell the cancelled sleeping rooms and function space.

SUSTAINABILITY *in* Practice

The earlier you include sustainability requirements in the RFP and contracting process, the easier it is to find vendors who can partner on sustainability initiatives. Sustainable event policies or requirements should be incorporated into destination and site RFPs. If sustainability is a particularly high priority, direct the RFP to green destinations and/or venues with recognized green certifications, assuming these sites align with space, travel, and room-rate requirements. The Green Meeting Industry Council maintains a registry of destinations and convention centers that have earned APEX-ASTM certification and are therefore fully equipped to support sustainable meetings. Although a particular vendor may not be able to fulfill all requirements within budget, the site should be willing to work with the meeting professional to find creative ways to keep costs down. Include tracking, documentation, and data requirements in the final contracts, e.g., waste diversion data and donation documentation. Some meeting professionals tie final payment to receipt of post-event performance data.

—Deborah R. Popely

Force Majeure

The ***force majeure*** clause in meeting contracts applies to any disruptive occurrence that cannot be anticipated or avoided, relieving the parties of their obligation to perform the contract.

Events that fall within *force majeure* include civil war, rebellion, revolution, insurrection, terrorist activities, embargo, labor dispute, strike, lockout, and extreme weather. Another common term for *force majeure* is **act of God**, i.e., something so unexpected and overwhelming that it is out of the control of any person or entity. For example, a heavy snowfall in a major airline hub has ripple effects throughout the entire world. Access to airports and air travel are prevented in the area selected for the meeting. Attendees will be unable to reach their destination until runways and roads are cleared, airplanes repositioned, and public and private transportation resumed. A weather-related event may paralyze the meeting location, while in other parts of the country it may be a non-event. Figure 8.8 (see p. 145) shows the impact of a major snowfall and resulting cancellation of air travel. Whether it is grounds for relief under your cancellation provision will be determined based on facts. What percentage of the attendees actually are unable to travel to the venue? Look at the percentage spelled out in your cancellation provision. Is the city as a whole shut down or just the airport? Has a state of emergency been declared at the location? All of these factors help to evaluate the seriousness of the event. Snowfalls of large amounts are

Notice of Cancellation Received	Liquidated Damages
More than 180 days prior to arrival	40% of anticipated room revenue
90–179 days prior to arrival	50% of anticipated room revenue
30–89 days prior to arrival	60% of anticipated room revenue
Less than 30 days prior to arrival	75% of anticipated room revenue

FIGURE 8.7 Cancellation Schedule of Charges An example explains the calculation formula on a sliding scale of revenue to compensate the group for liquidated damages based on the timing of the cancellation.

common in certain areas and the airport and city services are prepared for and handle them. In these locations, a snowfall is probably not going to be an event that causes a cancellation. In parts of the Southwest, a couple of inches can paralyze a city for days.

After the terrorist attacks of 2001 in the U.S., meeting professionals began to include contract language with not only "impossibility," but also "inadvisability" for holding the meeting. Not surprisingly, lawsuits followed, as groups attempted to extend the definition of inadvisability to include "travel fears." This excuse for non-performance was struck down by the courts, which ruled that unwillingness to fly to a destination did not constitute a *force majeure* situation, since it was both possible and practicable for attendees to access the meeting venue. Planes were flying, making the decision to not travel to the meeting venue personal and discretionary, rather than the result of some overwhelming catastrophe.

Similarly, some meeting professionals and their meeting attendees in the U.S., who were uneasy with any terrorist attack anywhere in the world, attempted to cancel programs and claim *force majeure* even when an incident occurred in another country. As a result, meeting cancellation insurance policies since 2001 include exclusionary language regarding the proximity of a *force majeure* event (25 miles) and the time period of the event in relation to the meeting (30 days). The U.S. courts have not viewed the following as legitimate reasons for invoking *force majeure*: economic conditions, lower event participation, or withdrawal of commitments by sponsors, exhibitors, and/or attendees.

Meeting professionals should seek legal counsel when drafting a *force majeure* clause to ensure protection for the meeting organizer. A well-drafted clause may also work to relieve the meeting organizer from paying damages (sometimes referred to as "partial *force majeure*") if only a portion of the contract cannot be performed. For example, a meeting is scheduled to take place in the Pacific Northwest. Advance teams arrive at the meeting site days before, and attendees arrive for pre-event meetings. The night before the official commencement of the meeting, unusually high winds and strong

FIGURE 8.8 Paralyzing Snowfall—Act of God Weather forecasts often set off a chain of reactions that include implementing a crisis response plan for DMOs, facilities, and event planners. While the forecast is a scientific prediction, the weather often makes sudden changes. The meeting professional must be flexible and quick to respond appropriately.

storms across the U.S. and Canada force cancellation of flights and closure of airports. The event goes on as scheduled; however, there are fewer attendees. A well-defined *force majeure* clause could obviate damages for the extreme weather even though the event proceeded as scheduled.

Liability and Insurance

Liability is associated with legal responsibility. There are numerous potential liabilities for meeting professionals and their organizations, some of which they can control, and others of which may be out of their control completely. Similarly, a hotel property may get sued for something that was the fault of the client. This is why a reciprocal indemnification clause is standard in most meeting contracts.

Indemnification

In an **indemnification clause**, also known as a hold harmless clause, one party agrees to pay damages or claims that the other party may be required to pay to another. For example, if a hotel is sued by a attendee who is injured at an event due to the fault of the group, an indemnification clause might require the group to reimburse the hotel. Similarly, if a hotel light fixture falls on the head of a meeting attendee, the attendee may sue the group. The hotel would have to indemnify the group from and against all liability, because the light fixture (and how it was hung) was within the control of the hotel.

Contract parties should agree to indemnify each other (also known as holding each other harmless) in meeting contracts. Sometimes, a hotel contract will be written without a mutual indemnification clause and inexperienced or novice meeting professionals will miss this—

key points

Common Types of Insurance

- General liability
- Professional liability
- Cancellation/interruption

yet another reason to be sure to have all contracts reviewed by legal counsel. The goal in writing an indemnity clause should be to make each party responsible for any costs related to property damages or personal injuries caused by their own actions.

Insurance is tied to indemnification and is a crucial component of risk management. The three most common types of business insurance in the meetings industry are comprehensive **general liability insurance**, **professional liability insurance** (also known as errors and omissions insurance) and **cancellation/interruption insurance**.

General and Professional Liability Insurance

General liability and professional liability are standard insurance coverage for most businesses. If a party is required to indemnify your organization against costs related to damages of property or injury to persons, asking for evidence of insurance is a way to be certain that party has the ability to pay. Carrying sufficient comprehensive general liability insurance (CGLI) against these types of liabilities is a standard business practice. There are times when an organization should request that the other party name the organization on its CGLI policy as an additional insured. The risk of being sued for an accident that is not caused by the organization's actions increases with the number of service providers and vendors providing services or goods at the event. The meeting professional should be certain to allocate risk in each contract clearly. Additionally, each party the organization has contracted with should produce documentation to indicate it has sufficient financial assets in the event some type of accident occurs. Insurance policies may be that documentation. Companies should carry enough insurance to pay for the defense and a judgment of a claim. Minimum coverage varies, but should generally be at least $2 million, given the cost of litigation throughout the U.S. Seek advice from qualified counsel at the destination when hosting a meeting outside the U.S.

FIGURE 8.9
Insurance Coverage Reminder Appropriate and adequate insurance is an essential consideration for the meeting organizer. Various types of insurance should be considered based on the type of meeting/event and advice of legal counsel.

The meeting professional should also require any party who is using its own employees at a U.S. meeting to provide evidence of workers compensation insurance, in case one of its employees is hurt while working at or for the meeting (see Figure 8.9).

Cancellation/Interruption Insurance

Cancellation/interruption insurance is purchased for a specific meeting, depending on its size and the potential financial loss if something occurs that either interferes with the orderly execution of the meeting or prevents the meeting altogether.

Other Supplier Contracts

In addition to venue contracts, the meeting professional may be required to negotiate agreements with a variety of additional suppliers, including a destination management company (DMC); audiovisual, transportation, information technology, and/or communications companies; speakers; entertainers; and, if the meeting also includes an exhibition, an official services contractor (OSC) and exhibitors. While the details of the contracts with each of these suppliers may differ, the core principals of negotiation still apply and many of the basic contract components and clauses found in facility contracts are applicable.

Sponsors and Sponsorship Agreements

Sponsors are an essential component of meetings and events, particularly those held by non-profit organizations. Sponsors act as strategic partners to the meeting organizer and may provide additional revenue to support the meeting's goals. A sponsorship agreement should be formalized in writing because the sponsorship details are often complex and vary from sponsor to sponsor and meeting to meeting. In addition, the professionals who negotiated the sponsorship deal may leave their organization by the time the event occurs; those who replace the negotiators are not obligated to adhere to any prior agreements that were not legally executed in writing.

Sponsorship agreements require the same five elements that make a contract valid and should include other protections for both parties to ensure fulfillment of the contract. In addition, sponsorship agreements should describe sponsorship benefits and delivery in detail. At a minimum, the contract should include the components listed in Figure 8.10.

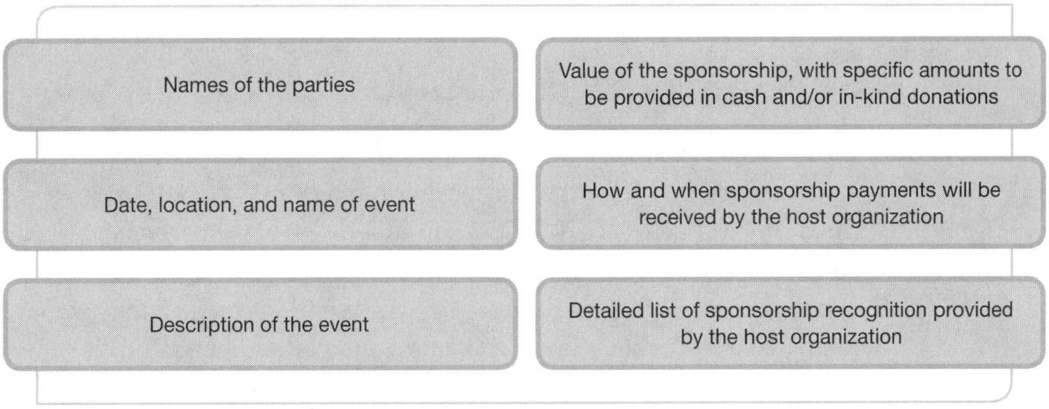

Names of the parties
Value of the sponsorship, with specific amounts to be provided in cash and/or in-kind donations
Date, location, and name of event
How and when sponsorship payments will be received by the host organization
Description of the event
Detailed list of sponsorship recognition provided by the host organization

FIGURE 8.10 Basic Components of a Sponsorship Contract Sponsorship is an increasingly important aspect of meetings. A formal agreement should be reached and committed to a written contract prior to entering into a partnership with a sponsor.

SUMMARY

A meeting professional must acquire sufficient knowledge to adequately prepare RFPs, conduct negotiations, enter into contracts, and ensure benefit to sponsors for underwriting meeting components. While that meeting professional does not need to be an attorney, he or she should understand what legal terms apply to meeting contracts, why basic meeting contracts clauses are needed, what to include in the contract given the meeting's unique circumstances, and when to consult legal counsel for advice.

CONTRIBUTING AUTHOR

Mary Catherine Sexton, Esq.
Vice President, Human Resources
Evolution Hospitality

KEY WORDS

acceptance
act of God
actual damages
attrition
authority
cancellation clause
cancellation/interruption insurance
capacity
concessions
condition of premises
consideration
contract
e-RFP
force majeure
general liability insurance
indemnification clause
letter of agreement (LOA)
liability
liquidated damages
negotiation
non-performance
offer
professional liability insurance
relocation/walk clause
waiver clause

DISCUSSION QUESTIONS

1. What are some of the challenges with regard to attrition and cancellation that meeting professionals in non-profit organizations often confront? Do corporate meeting organizers have similar issues?
2. What are some of the ways in which the meeting professional and the facility can protect themselves and each other from potential lawsuits related to over-consumption of alcohol at meetings?
3. Of the three major types of insurance, which is most important for an independent meeting professional with a small planning company?

9 Marketing the Meeting

Andrea S. Peterson, MTA, CMP
Visiting Professor
Department of Hospitality, Tourism & Events Management
Metropolitan State University of Denver

Owner & President
ASAP Meetings & Events

Main Topics

- Traditional P's of Marketing
- Marketing Research
- Marketing Plan Management
- Marketing Distribution Channels

Learner Outcomes

Upon the completion of this chapter, the student should be able to:

1. Identify the traditional P's of marketing.
2. Distinguish target audiences and relevant demographics/psychographics.
3. Create a comprehensive meeting marketing plan.
4. Recognize the pros and cons of meeting marketing distribution channels.
5. Craft a multi-prong marketing strategy.
6. Utilize traditional and cutting-edge marketing mediums and technology.

CMP INTERNATIONAL STANDARDS

Domain A. Strategic Planning
Skill 2. Develop Sustainability Plan for Meeting or Event
SubSkills. 2.01, 2.02
Domain I. Marketing
Skill 24. Manage Marketing Plan
SubSkills. 24.01, 24.02, 24.03, 24.04
Skill 25. Manage Marketing Materials
SubSkills. 25.01, 25.02, 25.04
Skill 26. Manage Meeting or Event Merchandise
SubSkills. 26.01, 26.02
Skill 27. Promote Meeting or Event
SubSkills. 27.01, 27.02, 27.03
Skill 28. Contribute to Public Relations Activities
SubSkills. 28.01, 28.02, 28.03, 28.04

An important function for any meeting professional is the appropriate preparation and management of **marketing**. For meeting professionals, this applies specifically to how the meeting's messaging is communicated using the four traditional P's of marketing. How the **marketing mix** is approached and brought together will determine the overall marketing strategy for the meeting. Most often the **integrated marketing** approach is used for ultimate success. Proper due diligence in the form of surveying stakeholders' needs, reviewing any existing meeting profiles, conducting appropriate market research, and understanding the competition should take place prior to undertaking marketing planning.

Once meeting background research has been conducted, focus can be placed on creating a strong **marketing plan** using traditional, tried-and-true practices and leading-edge technologies, including many web-based platforms. Savvy meeting professionals understand the importance of crafting a winning plan, including all relevant marketing mediums, and managing the various components for ultimate success.

Traditional P's of Marketing

Marketing is a process through which customer needs are identified and a demand is developed for particular products or services. This process is based on coordinating four elements known as the *product*, *place*, *price*, and *promotion*.

Product

The product is the meeting. Accurate communication of product value to potential consumers is paramount. Convincing them that dynamic value exists through attendance creates demand. In the book *The Experience Economy*, Pine and Gilmore (2011) point out, "Indeed, in a world saturated with largely undifferentiated goods and services, the greatest opportunity for value creation resides in staging experiences" (p. IX).

Place

The location of the meeting forms the place. Just as in real estate, location is a key consumer motivator. Meeting professionals accurately communicating the benefits of a meeting's location, including special ancillary activities and attractions, provide potential participants with clear incentive to attend. Showcasing all a location has to offer often involves partnerships with local destination marketing organizations (DMOs) or convention and visitors bureaus (CVBs).

Price

The concept of perceived value is often tied to the price of the meeting. In planning a meeting, both registration fees (if any) and all related housing and travel costs make up the price attached to attendance. Meeting organizers use standard financial philosophies for pricing meetings, computing meeting production costs, and adding required profit margins or desired retained earnings. Other factors include considering the price of competitors' events and the prevalent economic conditions.

Promotion

Creating adequate awareness and intrinsic benefits of attending are the cornerstones of promotion. With a plethora of messages competing for consumer attention, focused communication that resonates with prospective participants is key. Popular promotions for meetings today consist of multiple distribution channels, including traditional printed products and web-based campaigns.

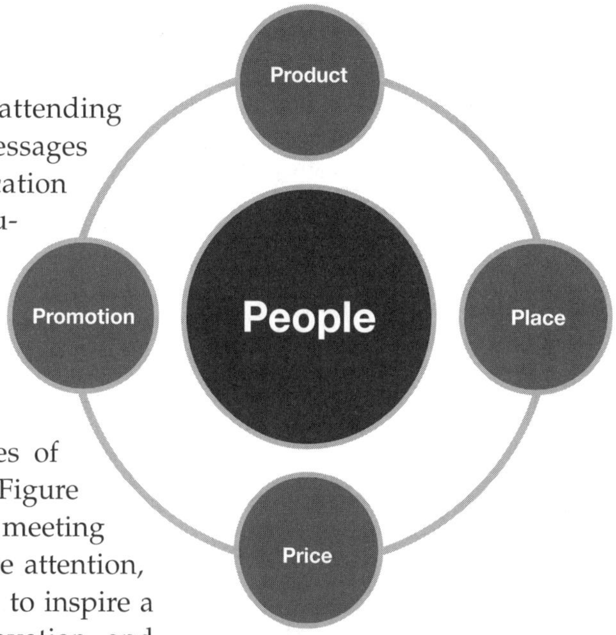

FIGURE 9.1 The Five P's of Marketing The diagram of the five P's of marketing includes four traditional representations, along with a fifth element—*people*—which is the center of marketing.

People

The target audience or actual registrants and attendees of meetings are now often recognized as the "fifth P" (see Figure 9.1). According to McEun and Duffy (2010), organized meeting planning brings people together primarily "1) to capture attention, particularly for initiating something new or different; 2) to inspire a positive emotional climate, fostering collaboration, innovation, and performance; and 3) to build human networking relationships" (p. 1). Of course, the people who provide the product and other stakeholders are also part of the people in the five P's of marketing.

Integrated Marketing

Jantsch (2009) indicates that an integrated marketing approach is not simply a strategy, but instead is the tactical delivery of said marketing strategy, further contending that the most strategic way to gain competitive advantage over the competition is "the intentional blending of online [web-based] and offline [traditional] tools and tactics around a single marketing strategy" (para. 7). The goal of integrated marketing is "to make all aspects of marketing communications (such as advertising, sales promotion, public relations, and direct marketing) work together as a unified force, rather than permitting each to work in isolation" (Munford, 2012, para. 1). This leads to a seamless experience for the customer when communication materials are created with a similar tone and style, reinforcing core branding of the meeting itself and the hosting organization.

With multi-faceted marketing channels spanning print, outdoor, digital, and other platforms, meeting professionals must identify and understand the **demographics** of their target audience and craft an appropriate strategy to reach that audience.

key points

Association Marketing Plan Strategies

- **Focus group** feasibility study with the local association chapter
- Print postcard "save-the-date" mailed to membership and prior attendees
- Dedicated annual meeting website
- Printed invitation brochure—including registration details, meeting website address, and designated meeting **hashtag**—mailed to membership, potential members, and prior meeting attendees
- Video blogs posted on association website, creating buzz around topics and guest speakers
- Written blog posts on meeting website and guest posts on related industry sites
- Meeting logo creation and placement on host city DMO website and association website, linking to meeting-specific website
- Facebook® page
- **Press kit** creation and distribution to relevant channels
- Targeted email campaign, with multiple sends
- Regular posts via Twitter® utilizing identified meeting hashtag
- Regular updates on association's Facebook® and LinkedIn® profiles, highlighting activities and speakers included in meeting
- Discounts or promotions for early registrants
- Video advertisement sent to chapters for sharing at local meetings
- **Quick-Response (QR) Code** creation to promote meeting website in printed materials
- Advertising campaign creation for industry publications

Marketing Research

Conducting appropriate research serves as the cornerstone of marketing efforts. Understanding what is being marketed and to whom provides the framework for developing key messages and identifying their placements. Additionally, the marketing planning team will consider the organization's overall goals and objectives, as well as the meeting-specific goals and objectives, before drafting the marketing plan. This preliminary work sets the foundation for an effective marketing effort (see Figure 9.2).

The goals and objectives for specific data mining can be customized for each meeting. Generally, however, meeting research seeks to identify the various **market segments** based on categories such as demographics, e.g., geography and/or buying power, and **psychographics**. Through market research and segmentation exercises, significant sub-groups may be discovered, leading to untapped niche markets for growing meetings in new and creative ways.

Astute meeting marketing will include and highlight vital learner outcomes and benefits. Regardless of whether an organization pays for an employee's attendance or an individual association member covers the bill, return on investment (ROI) is imperative for expense justification across all economies (Toups, 2006).

Target Markets

The consumers to whom a host organization wants to sell its products and services make up the **target market**. Identifying these groups and

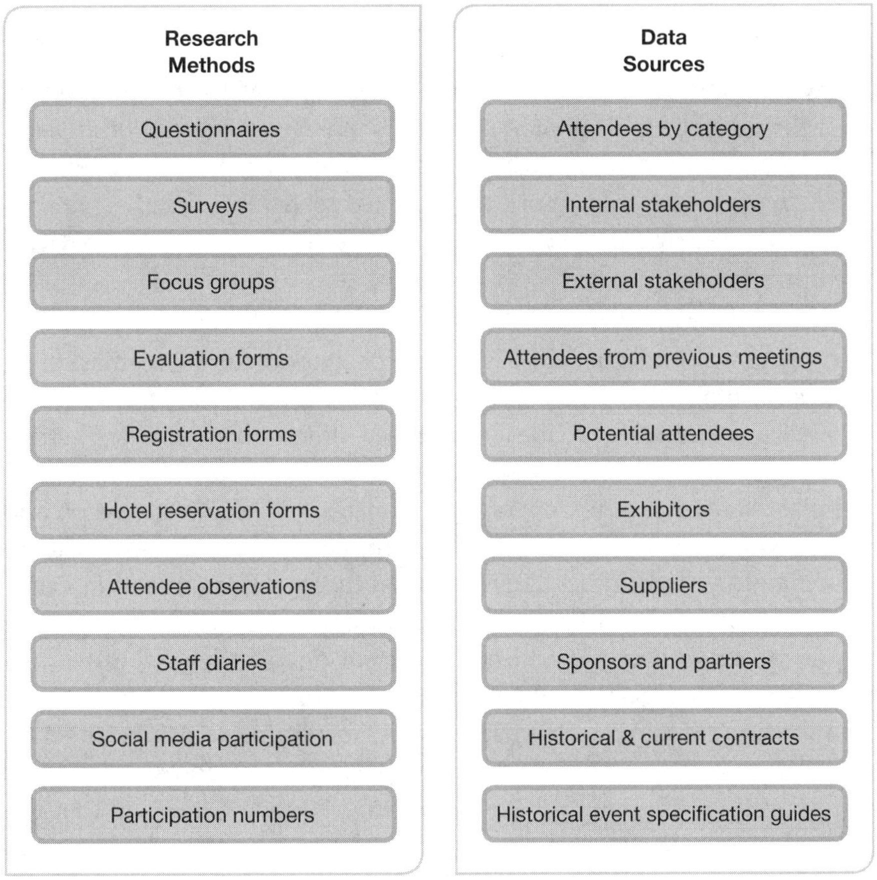

FIGURE 9.2 Common Data Collection Methods and Sources Data for marketing research can be collected through numerous methods and from various sources, as this list outlines.

their unique qualities is essential in the development of a marketing plan. No hard-and-fast rules exist for determining a meeting's market segments, as numerous associations and authorities choose varying divisions. Meetings serve the diverse needs of multiple audiences and stakeholders, including attendees, exhibitors, suppliers, volunteers, sponsors, management, speakers, and more. Understanding what each group achieves through attendance and participation leads to creating focused marketing messages.

Meeting Profile

The event specifications guide (ESG) serves as the source for some of the most important research information for a meeting professional to obtain in the strategic planning phase of meeting marketing. Access to data and specific statistics on former or similar events provides a distinct advantage through which a planner can readily determine the specific types of marketing used in the past, success rates, and areas for improvement. This type of information is vital to development of an effective marketing plan.

Marketing Plan Management

Many components come together to make up the effective marketing plan for a meeting. This plan can be a separate document or an individual section of the organization's complete marketing plan. Regardless, the same key areas work together to create a solid, cohesive, and functional document.

Mission and Vision

According to Lundquist (2011), "The expected outcome of a marketing plan is results" (p. 2). Thus, a well-written marketing plan for the meeting will serve as a clear roadmap for the host organization as they strive for strategically planned outcomes.

Full statement and review of the organization's existing mission and vision ensure planning reflects the company, product, and audience appropriately (Lundquist, 2011). In most cases, the organization's mission statement as written is sufficient for planning. However, some larger meetings take the additional step of developing a specific mission statement relevant to the meeting.

As vision statements are aspirational in nature, the large meeting planning committee might also develop a specific vision statement for the meeting. This might be more appropriate for a meeting that is a significant milestone for the organization and has the likelihood of being repeated several times in the future.

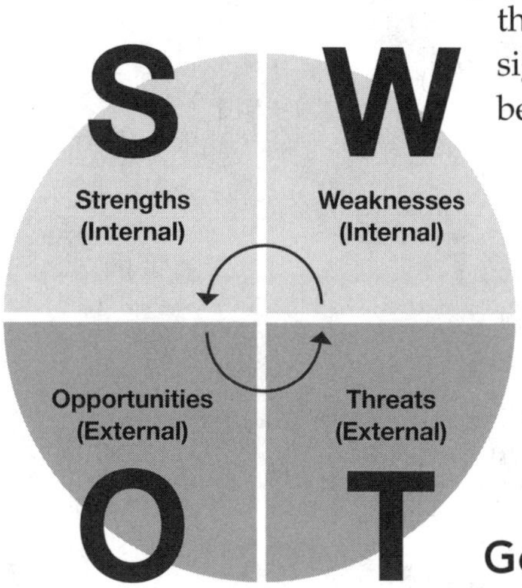

SWOT Analysis

A SWOT analysis is generally included in a meeting marketing plan in order to incorporate the majority of market research conducted. This section will include details of the target audiences and related segmentation, market size and share, competitors, and stakeholder needs and how this data fits within the strengths, weaknesses, opportunities, and threats of the meeting.

Goals and Objectives

According to Lundquist (2011), "In a marketing plan...the goal is the big picture" (p. 12). In business terms, goals are achievable through the use of related viable objectives for completion. As described in Chapter 4, SMART-TER objectives create a specific strategy for realizing the meeting's goals. The marketing plan's goals for a specific meeting should be the encapsulating statement(s) crafted to provide the visionary framework for marketing the meeting, while clearly stipulating defined outcomes or objectives that will be evaluated for success.

Strategy and Budget

Identifying goals with measurable objectives allows the meeting professional to develop a more specific marketing strategy and

SUSTAINABILITY *in* Practice

Meetings are communication tools able to deliver key messages for different stakeholders. Meetings utilize branding, theming, and messaging to communicate and contain supportive marketing elements. Meeting professionals market using placement or distribution through typical messaging channels including signage, name badges, graphics, PowerPoint® presentations, handouts, materials, save-the-date promotions, invitations, promotional products, banners, newsletters, and daily trade-show papers.

Sustainable marketing contributes strategically to an organization in three important ways: 1) embedding sustainability in the meeting planning process; 2) embedding sustainability into the marketing materials; and 3) embedding sustainability in the message in order to drive behavioral change. Consider three ways meeting professionals can operationalize sustainability in a meeting:

- **Materials** Using more sustainable media throughout the meeting will improve sustainable practice. For example, print material onsite to reduce shipping/transportation emissions, make use of electronic marketing to reduce paper consumption, and use recyclable products whenever possible.
- **Inclusion and accessibility** Inclusion safeguards that every person regardless of ability or background can meaningfully participate in the meeting. Also, inclusion ensures that marketing materials have information and images of various members, reflecting diversity of age and gender and including people with disabilities. Accessibility deals with issues ranging from how a specific marketing medium, e.g., paper and website, works for people with disabilities to how an organization's marketing reaches across the digital divide. By dispelling myths and reducing real and attitudinal barriers around inclusion and accessibility, meeting professionals can educate all participants.
- **Messaging** Marketing in meetings also persuades participants to consume the main meeting messages. Meetings will carry a primary message—the main purpose for the event. However, meetings can incorporate a second-level message where information is shared about sustainability. (Tinnish & Mangal, 2012)

—*Susan M. Tinnish, PhD*

related budget, explaining precisely how intentions will be reached and at what cost. For example, most organizations hope to grow their attendance year over year. This would readily be considered a typical goal. Determining the method to actually grow attendance involves developing specific objectives that may, for example, result in contracting a high-profile keynote speaker to reach a specified percentage growth, while also delivering superior industry education. While the expectation is that the prominent speaker will draw additional attendees, specific and potentially costly marketing and promotion initiatives will need to be employed to spread the word about the speaker's participation, thus adding to the meeting marketing budget's bottom line.

Competition Strategic market research demands knowledge and awareness of a meeting's competition. **Direct competition** exists in the form of similar meetings, including those occurring in various forms. Obvious competitors to a typical association conference include those executed by competing industry associations and even the host organization's local chapter meetings. In today's electronic age, webinars and online training can also be potential competitors. **Indirect competition** exists in the form of certification programs, self-study programs, and university courses.

Differentiating a meeting from both the competition and the customers' needs through strategic marketing efforts serves as a key driver in securing desired **market share**. It is imperative the meeting delivers on promised components and messaging. Misrepresentation of key pieces and attributes, e.g., keynote speakers, program content, and learner outcomes, affects the reputation of the meeting as a whole, with negative ramifications for the host organization and potential future sponsors (Toups, 2006, p. 65).

Ashe-Edmunds (n.d.) wrote extensively about the marketing budget and stated, "[Some] businesses make the mistake of limiting their marketing budget to marketing communications costs such as advertising, public relations, direct mail, and promotions. A true marketing plan includes the upfront planning, communications expenditures, and ongoing monitoring and tracking of your marketing efforts. Include all three components of a marketing strategy in your budget plan to spend your dollars with maximum efficiency" (para. 1). Upfront planning includes market research and tracking includes related post-event evaluations. Thus, careful consideration must be given to completing a comprehensive budget for all costs involved. Organized budget planning should take on the form of specific categories and line items for each area, including estimates for all specific tools needed, costs for professional services (such as creative/design, public relations, and advertising agencies), and all related expenses for media personnel attendance.

Timelines The timelines included in the marketing plan map chronologically the tactics tied to each strategy. Marketing timelines must be carefully constructed with specific details identifying to whom the task has been assigned, specific task(s), and relevant deadlines. Gantt charts are a tangible method for preparing this type of marketing tool.

Evaluation and Measurement

The final piece of an effective marketing plan outlines the methodology to be used for evaluating and communicating return on investment (ROI), as well as the effectiveness of the marketing plan and strategy. Lundquist (2011) commented, "Measurement is the ultimate deciding factor in the success of the event, and, as such, accurate measurement is key. Successful event producers prove their results by using pre-determined measurement techniques and reporting the results as facts: good, bad, or indifferent" (p. 23).

Further, Lundquist (2011), suggested, "Scheduling measurement is equally as important as deciding what to measure" (p. 27). Thus, successful meeting organizers identify in advance what needs to be measured and how and when the measurement will take place in order to adequately evaluate and report on the meeting's results. This leads to successful scheduling of data collection opportunities such as pre- and post-event surveys and questionnaires, as well as data-collection opportunities during the meeting, e.g., focus groups, radio-frequency identification (RFID) chips in name badges, and social media hashtag usage and related comments.

Marketing Distribution Channels

The successful strategy outlined in a meeting's integrated marketing plan incorporates the wealth of marketing mediums available. An appropriate marketing mix is based on research results. It combines advertising, public relations, media coverage, direct mail, and electronic marketing to ensure the target audience is suitably exposed to the marketing message.

Advertising

Specific messages crafted and communicated via mass media regarding a product are known as advertising. Advertising serves to inform, attract, influence, remind, and retain potential targeted audiences. Due to the high costs, traditional advertising (print, broadcast, outdoor) is less often a preferred choice in marketing meetings. More specialized and targeted media are available and used with excellent results.

While digital platforms and email campaigns are popular options for today's meeting advertising, based on the target market, some meeting professionals opt for traditional advertising outlets (see Figure 9.3 & Figure 9.4).

Placement Marketing research influences the important science of where and when to advertise. Careful attention must also be given to the purpose of advertising and the means that will most effectively communicate its message. Successful advertising campaigns incorporate the common components of reach, frequency, consistency, and timing in planning to whom and how often messages are distributed.

Agencies As with many other areas in marketing, hiring talented and capable professionals is money well spent. The area of advertising is no exception. Toups (2006) advocated, "Utilizing the talent in an advertising agency can be very cost-effective in the particular area as most agencies receive a commission for placements" (p. 72). While many ad agencies specialize in marketing, when it comes to the promotion of meetings, an agency with experience in the industry should receive due consideration.

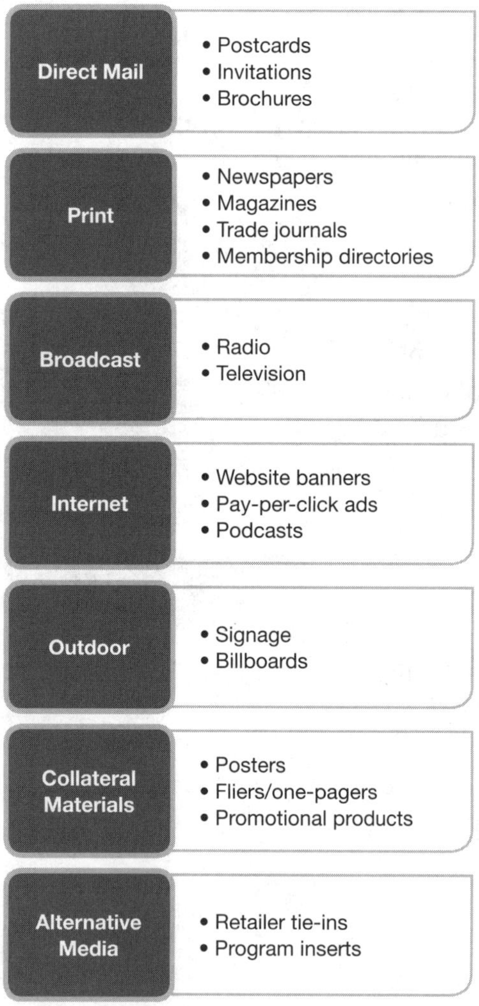

FIGURE 9.3 Popular Advertising Media This figure lists many popular advertising options that can be included in the marketing mix, each of which should be developed using the AIDA formula explained in Figure 9.4.

Public Relations and Media

Like advertising, public relations serves to inform, attract, influence, remind, and retain potential targeted audiences in execution of the marketing plan. However, the placement of targeted marketing messages is accomplished through third-party placement in the media, rather than by direct payment to an information outlet.

Public relations Public relations (PR) is currently defined and publicly accepted as "a strategic communication process that builds mutually beneficial relationships between organizations and their publics" ("What Is Public Relations?," 2011/12, para. 3). The great American philanthropist and businessman John D. Rockefeller once stated, "Next to doing the right thing, the most important thing is to let people know you're doing the right thing" (Goodman, 2007, p. 175), summarizing the heart of PR.

Taken a step further, with online access to opinions and thoughts, how the public perceives an organization's meeting must be carefully monitored. Public relations efforts must focus on the primary goal that the public recognizes, accurately, the mission, vision, goals, and objectives of the meeting and the organization overall.

Previously accomplished through creation of traditional press kits, the public relations campaign has changed dramatically in format, target audience, and delivery method. Rather than using tangible, professionally produced kits, organizations now utilize online media rooms

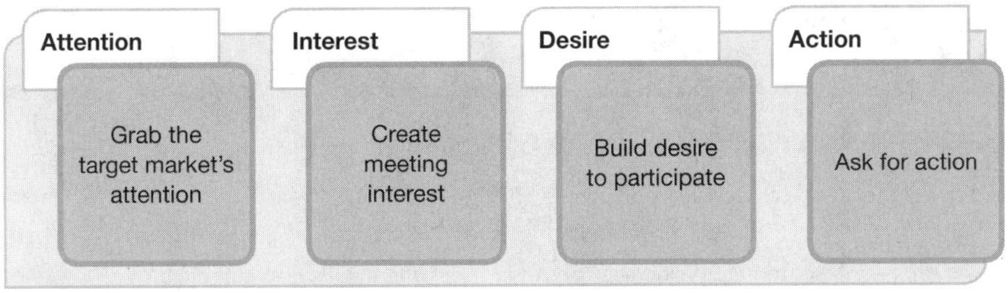

FIGURE 9.4 AIDA Formula Regardless of delivery mode, successful meeting advertising is best designed using the AIDA-formula outlined in this graphic.

that house readily accessible electronic versions of press releases, public service announcements, spokesperson contact information, photos, videos, and even trendy **infographics**.

Press release Today's savvy communicators write **press releases** with key words in mind, understanding this leads to prominent search engines picking up words in online searches. Additionally, with shrinking media staffs at press outlets, writing documents that read as articles, and including video or pictures, provides today's media staff with a needed advantage.

Bloggers A robust point of contact for publicizing meetings is through **blogs.** Numerous industry-specific blogs provide ample avenues for meeting promotion. Introductions to reporters and bloggers are best made via email, providing an electronic link to the established online media room. Proper press release distribution etiquette recommends never sending attachments in emails, as unfamiliar recipients are reluctant to open for fear of potential computer viruses.

Press conference Gaining publicity requires attracting the attention of suitable media. At times it is appropriate to hold a **press conference**. The attendance of a prominent keynote speaker with political or celebrity status, a vendor's launch of a new product, or even an initial technology demonstration at the meeting could provide the newsworthy angle for a press conference.

Pressroom Another key responsibility of a meeting professional involves planning an effective and comfortable **pressroom** with amenities, on location and in close proximity to the action.

Timelines As part of the overall marketing promotions plan, successful meeting organizers will pre-determine a publicity timeline for a successful promotions campaign: "The timing of press releases and press conferences is a key factor in determining whether the meeting will receive favorable and timely publicity" (Toups, 2006, p. 71). Meeting professionals must be familiar with production schedules for

key points

Pressroom Amenities

- Strong and fast Internet access, usually in the form of Wireless-Fidelity (Wi-Fi)
- Computers and printers, as well as charging stations for electronic devices and even traditional phone lines
- Areas for holding meetings or taking personal calls
- Full-time staff member to serve as a receptionist in the room for check-in, credentials distribution, and overall hospitality
- Hosted or sponsored food and beverage
- Comfortable furniture

Advance Timing from Meeting	Activity
40 weeks (10 months)	• Distribute *first press release*: general meeting information and branding. • Launch meeting website with basic information. • Create relevant social media event pages and designate hashtags.
26 weeks (6.5 months)	• Distribute *second press release*: more detailed sessions, speakers, and events information. • Submit keynote speakers' articles to industry publications. • Publish keynote speakers' and prominent workshop leaders' articles in association publications.
20 weeks (5 months)	• Begin participating in industry-related online magazines and blogs. • Recruit speakers to participate as guests on blogs. • Distribute *third press release*: press-worthy aspects of meeting.
16–12 weeks (4–3 months)	• Send personal invitations to media representatives to attend meeting at no charge. • Follow up via phone to personally discuss the key ideas that will be covered at the conference.
12 weeks (3 months)	• Create cover story for distribution to various publications. • Submit second round of keynote speakers' articles to industry publications. • Publish keynote speakers' and prominent workshop leaders' article(s) in association publications.
6 weeks (1.5 months)	• Send *fourth press release*: feature stories and complete details regarding the meeting.
3 weeks	• Send personal reminders to press. • Arrange for press conference or interviews with interested parties.
1 week	• Follow up media invitations with phone calls.

FIGURE 9.5 Publicity Timeline Managing publicity in an effective and efficient manner requires a timeline to keep the process on target and on time (Toups, 2006, p. 71. Reprinted with permission.).

targeted publications and ensure proposed content is delivered in a timely fashion, and in the format required, to warrant the publicity anticipated (see Figure 9.5).

Public relations management Due to the popularity of social media websites, monitoring posts and comments specific to a meeting stands as an integral part of public relations management. It only takes one or two disgruntled former participants or potential attendees to launch a negative campaign, wreaking havoc on an upcoming meeting. Many electronic tools exist to assist PR management in monitoring online chatter, including careful watch of any affiliated celebrities and speakers. Since participation in social media platforms is all about interacting with the public and specific target audiences, opportunities for criticism are as real as applause. Disputing or discrediting sources of negative information is never a good idea. A better tactic would be engagement with dissenters, working to clarify misperceptions, rectifying the spread of misinformation, and addressing issues whenever possible.

Direct Mail Marketing

Numerous forms of print marketing are available in today's multi-dimensional marketplace. Traditionally postcard **teasers**, invitations, brochures, letters, flyers, posters, and other promotional materials have been used in tangible printed form and distributed via either direct mailings or special deliveries. Spam filters and negative issues affiliated with electronic marketing mean printed items continue to maintain a prominent presence. In fact, Schiff (2012) wrote, "Despite the perception in the marketing industry that direct mail and telemarketing are less effective than digital channels, the Direct Marketing Association (DMA) has found that direct mail boasts a 4.4 percent rate, compared to email's average response rate of 0.12 percent" (para. 1).

Copyright Astute meeting professionals will work diligently to ensure that all **copyright** laws are strictly followed in marketing materials. With easy and widespread digital access, a particular area of concern involves photography usage. **JPEG (or .jpg)** files are easily copied and downloaded from the Internet. However, laws stringently protect photos as the **intellectual property** of the owner, i.e., the person(s) having legal ownership of the work, not just possession or creator status. Thus, appropriate permission(s) must be secured and any required copyright information included for images, graphics, and photographs used in marketing materials.

Signage Some meeting organizers concerned with consistent branding across all marketing platforms will include signage in their print production budget. This notion points to signage as marketing the meeting effectively onsite to the attendee customer. Often economies of scale, i.e., savings realized when more units of a good or service can be produced on a larger scale, are achieved in total costs with a printer when signage is included in the overall contracted print needs for a meeting. However, many facilities are incorporating electronic signage options onsite to manage sign quality, convenience, rapid and relatively easy changes, and costs.

Professional printing Very few meetings are able to handle printing needs through desktop publishing capabilities alone. Most tangible printing needs are outsourced to a professional print house. Traditionally, bidding processes for print requirements involve gathering three or more bids and comparing and contrasting the offerings for the best price relevant to quality and reputation.

Electronic Marketing

The Internet has rapidly become the primary source of information regarding a meeting through use of advertising, social media, and web pages. Indeed, the amount of data and interaction occurring on a daily basis across digital platforms is simply staggering.

Websites With 2.1 billion people making up the global Internet population (James, 2012), statistics suggest a robust website promotes a meeting well. Maximum attention to and appropriate budgeting for a dedicated meeting website is vital. Preston and Hoyle (2012) suggest, "You want your website to have charisma, that certain something that invites attention and involvement, and which grabs the browser into wanting to stay on the site and navigate around" (p. 119). Additionally, meeting websites must work properly on smartphones. According to recent reporting by emarketer.com (2014), smartphone users currently make up the majority of mobile phone users in 10 of 22 countries. The site further reports, "mobile phone usage is close to ubiquitous in Western Europe, North America, and Central and Eastern Europe" ("Worldwide Mobile Phone," para. 4). Thus, following technical standards and design protocols for mobile computing with multiple platforms, systems, and devices is in demand.

Through communication via print and direct mailings, social media activities, and email marketing, the web address for a meeting can be clearly disseminated to target audiences. However, today's technology-savvy Internet users often opt to use search engines for locating information. To that end, meeting professionals should understand **search engine optimization** (**SEO**), which is the use of repetitive words and phrases to promote visibility in online searches, and use this knowledge to full advantage, factoring any associated costs into the budget. While the algorithms used to conduct a search are closely guarded trade secrets, SEO is a skill worth developing. It is based on estimations, as well as trial and error, but the effort to optimize the website's opportunity for being located by a popular search engine is worth the meeting professional's time.

Web analytics Due to the popularity of the Internet and websites, numerous analytical tools have been developed for assessing website effectiveness. One area of huge growth, led by the powerhouse company Google, is in the area of free website analytics. By simply adding the services, website owners are capable of gleaning a wealth of data regarding website operations. Items such as hits, click-through rates, and other important elements are readily measured for evaluation, allowing meeting marketers to make necessary adjustments to effect real-time changes throughout the marketing campaign. These facts and figures are also highly valuable data for inclusion in the marketing team's final report to management.

Blogs A trendy and popular version of content marketing involves the creation and regular maintenance of one or several active blogs surrounding a meeting. Readily incorporated into the meeting or host organization's existing website, blogs are a simple yet effective method for invoking attention to the upcoming meeting and all it has to offer. Meeting organizers can include blog participation in speaker

PROFESSIONAL DILEMMA

During the process of marketing a meeting, a professional will quickly discover the necessity of working closely with other departments, key individuals, and/or external stakeholders to reach decisions regarding vital components of the event. Thus, fostering great relationships becomes a primary concern. Key items, such as the event venue and date, must be confirmed before the meeting professional can extend invitations and create appropriate marketing materials. Situations often arise during the planning process that can compromise these fundamental decisions. During the author's employment as a corporate planner working for a large, international company, a situation arose when the desire was expressed that all marketing materials exhibit cohesive branding. The design of the materials was seriously delayed by upper management's slow approval of the event's theme. Since the marketing director did not want to launch the custom registration and website without the branding completed, this delay seriously affected the timeliness of marketing materials. A savvy meeting professional will consider all factors when developing a viable project management schedule for the successful marketing, clearly communicating the deadlines to all relevant parties.

contracts, requiring new posts on a scheduled basis. Other industry experts can also be approached to share thoughts and ideas throughout pre- and post-event messaging. Fees or honoraria paid to bloggers should be included in the budget. Blogs provide interactive opportunities for registered and potential attendees to share in a discussion, ask questions, and contribute ideas and information.

Webcasting Content-rich information can be accessible to registrants and targeted audiences alike through **streaming media** from a meeting website. Meeting organizers who provide retrievable webcast segments leading up to, during, and following meetings enjoy multiple visits to the meeting website, offering strong messaging opportunities. Some of today's time-stretched employees are simply unable travel to attend the marketed meetings in person. Savvy planners providing streamed content during the actual live meetings, or on-demand following the event, realize an obvious edge in customer engagement and satisfaction. This technology allows the user to consume the information on a more flexible timetable, while still reaping the advantages and benefits. The costs associated with the planning and execution of webcasts should be incorporated into the budget.

Email Since the onset of regular personal email accounts and usage in the mid-1990s, organizations have recognized email marketing as yet another method of communicating messages to target audiences. Certainly the benefits of instant delivery and extremely low cost to the sender yield a prominent position for this type of marketing in today's economy. Despite low response rates, noted as 0.12 percent by the Direct Marketing Association in 2012, "email is more cost-effective than direct mail or telemarketing," yielding the highest ROI (Schiff, 2012, para. 1 & 7). Studies and success rates substantiate the validity of email marketing. Rottman (2013) highlighted the golden rule for successful email marketing: Maintain a consistent branded look for every email message sent, yielding the targeted progression in actions (see Figure 9.6).

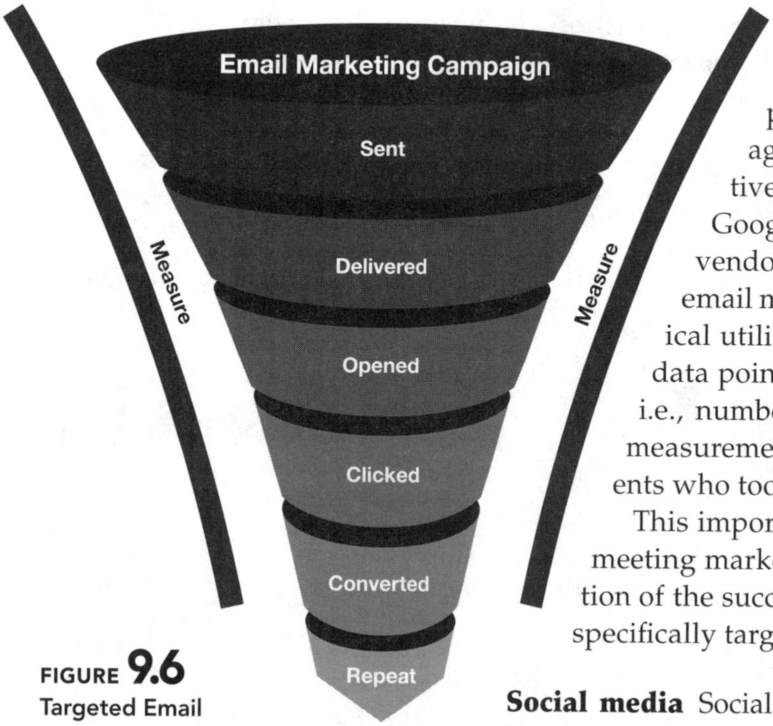

FIGURE 9.6 Targeted Email Marketing Action The success of an email marketing campaign depends on the statistical data generated at various stages by the response of the target audience. Careful attention to the responses at each step will guide campaign effectiveness.

As established previously, every component of the meeting marketing plan should be consistently evaluated against the marketing goals and objectives. Thanks to free platforms, such as Google® Analytics, and the tools built into vendor email services, this is easily done for email marketing. Figure 9.7 outlines the analytical utilities primarily used to measure five key data points, starting with the easiest to measure, i.e., number of emails sent, and ending with the measurement of success, and the number of recipients who took preferred action.

This important mined data is incredibly useful for meeting marketers as it allows for thoughtful evaluation of the success and failure of email campaigns and specifically targeted email messages.

Social media Social media marketing has been dubbed the "word of mouth" marketing of the digital age. Social marketing was first introduced as a discipline in the 1970s when members of the Kellogg School of Management at Northwestern University used the term "to describe the application of commercial marketing principles to health, social, and quality of life issues. Social marketing was defined as 'seeking to influence social behaviors not to benefit the marketer, but to benefit the target audience and the general society'" (Patterson, 2009, para. 5).

This form of marketing incorporates unique and creative usage of social networking platforms and activities as depicted in a word cloud in Figure 9.8, delivering a "two-way communication link between the consumer/customer and the brand" (Patterson, 2009, para. 5). During the research phase of marketing planning, effective meeting organizers will determine the preferences for and usage of social networking platforms by their target markets. This information provides the

FIGURE 9.7 Data Points From Low to High Significance A thorough understanding of the data analytics will assist in making alterations to an email campaign and guide future endeavors.

1. **Number of emails sent**—during a specified period of time
2. **Open rates**—how many emails sent that were actually opened
3. **Click-through rates**—measures actual performance since open rates can be skewed by emails read in preview panes
4. **Unsubscribe rate**—number of recipients unsubscribing following the communication
5. **Conversion rates**—number of recipients who took a preferred action

FIGURE 9.8
Social Media Word Cloud
Social media is another effective means of reaching the target audience. This graphic represents the myriad meanings for the contemporary use of the phrase "social media cloud" (Nijjar, 2012).

opportunity to interact specifically and purposefully with various potential attendees and registrants where they are already spending time. Preston and Hoyle (2012) wrote, "The social media marketer is required to tap into an existing flow of information and seed positive communications between individuals and groups in virtual social networks" (p. 115).

Technology tools Since 2008, growth in creation of a new breed of dynamic and elongated graphics has risen exponentially: "Between the years of 2011 and 2013, an average of 110 new infographics were created and published for the world to see everyday" (DeMers, 2013, frame 3). Seen as a perfect opportunity to communicate large amounts of data, statistics, and other information in graphic, eye-catching form, infographics serve as an easy and rapidly deployed tool for viral distribution of meeting concepts, as showcased in Figure 9.9 (p. 166). Additionally, Quick-Response (QR) Codes are easy to create and readily customizable for inclusion in advertisements, promotions, and infographics.

Distribution Timelines

Disseminating the marketing message in a timely manner is as important as the message itself. Developing a strategic timeline to release the information facilitates this process.

Touchpoint Meeting marketing pieces are meant to grab attention, explain benefits of attendance, clearly and concisely communicate critical content, and provide a strong call to action (Toups, 2006, p. 68). Most

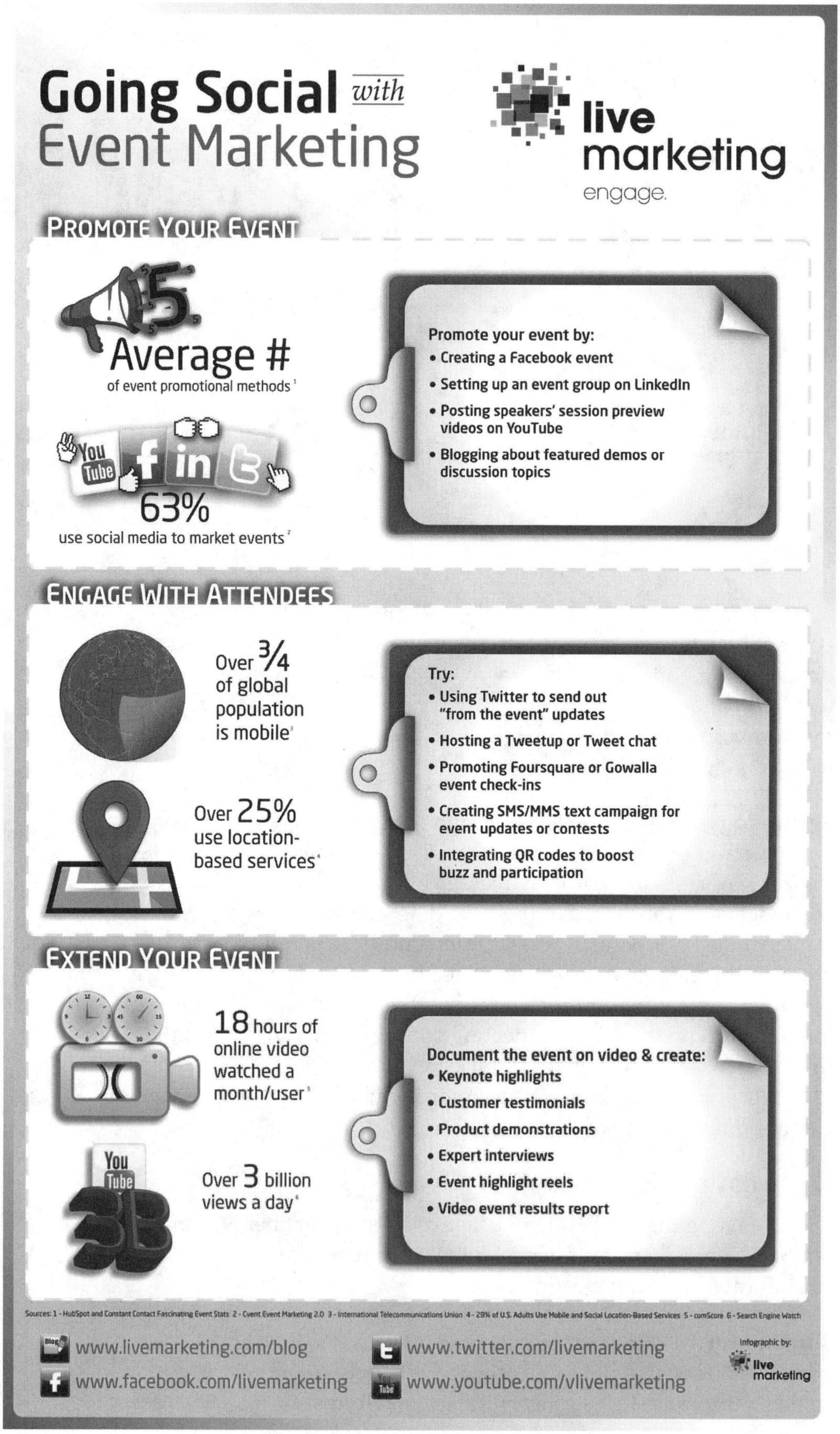
Going Social with
Event Marketing
live
marketing
engage.
PROMOTE YOUR EVENT
5
Average #
of event promotional methods [1]
You Tube
63%
use social media to market events [2]
Promote your event by:
• Creating a Facebook event
• Setting up an event group on LinkedIn
• Posting speakers' session preview videos on YouTube
• Blogging about featured demos or discussion topics
ENGAGE WITH ATTENDEES
Over 3/4 of global population is mobile [3]
Over 25% use location-based services [4]
Try:
• Using Twitter to send out "from the event" updates
• Hosting a Tweetup or Tweet chat
• Promoting Foursquare or Gowalla event check-ins
• Creating SMS/MMS text campaign for event updates or contests
• Integrating QR codes to boost buzz and participation
EXTEND YOUR EVENT
18 hours of online video watched a month/user [5]
You Tube
Over 3 billion views a day [6]
Document the event on video & create:
• Keynote highlights
• Customer testimonials
• Product demonstrations
• Expert interviews
• Event highlight reels
• Video event results report
Sources: 1 - HubSpot and Constant Contact Fascinating Event Stats 2 - Cvent Event Marketing 2.0 3 - International Telecommunications Union 4 - 28% of U.S. Adults Use Mobile and Social Location-Based Services 5 - comScore 6 - Search Engine Watch
www.livemarketing.com/blog
www.twitter.com/livemarketing
www.facebook.com/livemarketing
www.youtube.com/vlivemarketing
Infographic by:
live marketing

FIGURE 9.9 Infographic: Social Media Event Marketing This infographic is a technology tool that depicts the viral use of graphics to send a message to the target audience (Veach, 2011).

Advance Timing from Meeting	Activity
52 weeks (12 months)	• Announce date and location of an annual meeting at current meeting. • Include dates, location, theme, tagline, and other teaser copy in materials distributed at current meeting. • Devote page(s) in current meeting's onsite program for promotion of next year's meeting.
40 weeks (10 months)	• Order and/or cultivate/prepare direct mail lists for all audiences. • Begin monthly postcard campaign. • Craft social media strategy and posting timeline.
24 weeks (6 months)	• Send first preliminary electronic brochures to various target audiences via email. • Begin scheduled social media postings.
16 weeks (4 months)	• Mail second/complete brochures to all target audiences; measure response rates. • Send emails linking to electronic brochure on the website. • Monitor number of downloads of the brochure. • Continue social media postings, seeking interaction.
8 weeks (2 months)	• Mail complete brochure a second time. • Begin sending special event and other invitations. • Send last reminder postcard to those not yet registered, directing to website. • Continue social media postings, seeking interaction.
6–8 weeks (1.5–2 months)	• Send personalized letters to key members of target audiences, encouraging their participation and assistance in promoting meeting. • Fully engage in social media postings and interaction, conducting pre-meeting contests as relevant.

FIGURE **9.10** **Distribution Timeline for Marketing Materials** A timeline for the distribution of marketing materials is the most efficient manner to manage the distribution process (Toups, 2006, p. 69. Reprinted with permission.).

experts say it takes seven to twelve contacts, or **touchpoints**, before customers are ready to buy (Krotz, 2011, para. 2). Thus, to make a sale, a series of messages must be developed and delivered over time, with each one clearly communicating a reason for a customer to purchase a product (see Figure 9.10).

SPONSORSHIP

In marketing for meetings, **sponsorships** are a strategic relationship between meeting organizers/hosts and commercial or non-profit entities, translating into a mutually beneficial affiliation. **Sponsors** provide financial and **in-kind donations** to the meeting organizer's overall needs in exchange for exposure and access to attendees. Sponsors are not chosen at random, but with much forethought and planning, as they are an integral element in the marketing mix.

Sponsor relations Sponsorship considerations begin with meeting organizers conducting an asset analysis of the areas where sponsorship dollars are preferred for their particular meeting. For example, organizers might desire an expanded meet-and-greet for attendees arriving from varying international locations. This creates an opportunity for a sponsor by financial or in-kind donation, while the sponsor garners goodwill and exposure with attendees.

According to Goldblatt (2005), "Sponsorship becomes more valuable if the event organization is able to offer precise targeting that matches the marketing objectives of the prospective sponsor" (p. 287). Therefore, qualifying potential sponsors before approaching them with the opportunity is paramount. This process involves much research and forethought and should begin at a minimum of 18 months prior to the meeting. Goldblatt also stated, "Perhaps one of the more important reasons event organizers align themselves with commercial sponsors is the opportunity to achieve greater credibility for the event" (p. 289). Thus, well-established sponsorships become strong, mutually beneficial relationships for both parties.

Once the official sponsorship is established via a written, contractual agreement, meeting organizers must activate the relationship. This involves regular and ongoing communication with the sponsor, focus of dedicated meeting personnel, and a consistent plan of service to ensure the details of the sponsorship agreement are met. All hospitality services and perks promised must be handled accurately. In a world where corporate social responsibility (CSR) is a current topic, many meeting organizers are choosing to include these important activities in their schedule. CSR provides an opportunity for including sponsors who have aligned themselves with similar causes.

In-kind donations Sponsor participation can take the form of nonfinancial contributions. Business entities are given the opportunity to showcase their products and services to a wider audience by providing meetings with needed décor, equipment, and food and beverage products. Specialty items might also be provided, e.g., printed t-shirts, carry bags, and other serviceable items.

Partnerships/Cross-Promotions

Successful pre-marketing research often reveals opportunities for strategic relationships with industry partners in cross-promotional forms. Like-minded organizations are often open to co-locating meetings to share expenses and tap into similar target markets. Savvy meeting professionals will consider this opportunity as another form of cost savings to their meeting, producing stellar results and long-term strategic relationships.

SUMMARY

Successfully marketing a meeting involves understanding and utilizing the traditional four P's: product, place, price, and promotion, and the fifth dynamic of people. Proper market research must be conducted to identify appropriate target audiences for focused, results-driven marketing messages. Creation of a thorough and dynamic written marketing plan—including mission and vision statement(s), SWOT analysis, goals and objectives, strategy, budget, and evaluation options—is paramount to marketing a meeting successfully.

Today's marketplace offers a wealth of media systems, including traditional advertising, public relations, and direct mail campaigns, as well as electronic media opportunities. The growth of social media communications and relationships continues to change the marketing atmosphere, requiring focused management of content and postings. The saturation of messages bombarding today's consumer requires seven to twelve actual marketing touchpoints before action is taken, meaning a focused and rigorous timeline is vital to marketing a meeting.

Sponsorships serve as a viable opportunity for additional marketing relationships for all parties involved, providing financial and in-kind donations to the meeting host. Strategic partnerships provide meeting professionals with opportunities to reach a broader potential audience.

KEY WORDS

blog
copyright
demographic
direct competition
focus group
hashtag
indirect competition
infographic
in-kind donation
integrated marketing
intellectual property
JPEG (or .jpg)
marketing
marketing mix
marketing plan
market segment
market share
press conference
press kit
press release
pressroom
psychographic
Quick-Response (QR) Code
search engine optimization (SEO)
sponsor
sponsorship
streaming media
target market
teaser
touchpoint

DISCUSSION QUESTIONS

1. Outline comprehensive steps to be taken to conduct appropriate market research for an upcoming annual conference of the Risk Management Society (RIMS; www.rims.org), including identification of perceived competitors.
2. Describe tactics for including a prominent keynote speaker in a large annual association meeting's marketing. (Hint: Consider additional promotional opportunities for the meeting the speaker can provide prior to the event, particularly through social media.)
3. Write three fully developed, SMART-TER marketing plan objectives for PCMA's annual Convening Leaders (conveningleaders.pcma.org) convention based on the following goals in relation to the prior year's meeting:
    - Increase attendance by 15 percent
    - Achieve 25 percent higher social media engagement via hashtags
    - Realize greater positive reaction to marketing campaign
4. Review the meeting websites (pages) for the following annual industry meetings and compare and contrast common and distinguishing features noting advantages and disadvantages.
    - ISES's "The Special Event"
    - MPI's World Education Congress
    - NACE's Annual Conference and Expo
    - PCMA's Convening Leaders

The author would like to acknowledge the valuable contribution to this chapter by Carole Shifman, Principal, New Shoes Communications, on the topic of social media promotion and timelines.

10

Registration and Housing

Tricia L. Mallett
Event Services Manager
Association of Equipment Manufacturers

Angela Weller
Event Services Manager
Association of Equipment Manufacturers

Main Topics

PART ONE REGISTRATION

- Registration Processes
- Pre-Meeting Phase
- Onsite Phase
- Reporting & Analyzing Registration Data

PART TWO HOUSING

- Building the Room Block
- Contracting the Hotel
- Maintaining the Room Block
- Housing Reports

Learner Outcomes

Upon the completion of this chapter, the student should be able to:

1. Identify the various options for registration.
2. Define the steps necessary to manage financial information, demographics, and policies associated with the registration process.
3. Implement effective onsite registration procedures, including temporary staff training and crowd management.
4. Identify the procedures for determining rooming needs.
5. Describe the process of contracting with hotels for room blocks.
6. Describe the process for monitoring and maintaining the room block.
7. Summarize post-meeting findings and reports that will lead to future successful events.

CMP INTERNATIONAL STANDARDS

Domain A. Strategic Planning
Skill 2. Develop Sustainability Plan for Meeting or Event
SubSkills. 2.01, 2.02
Domain B. Project Management
Skill 4. Plan Meeting or Event Project
SubSkill. 4.07
Domain D. Financial Management
Skill 7. Manage Event Funding and Financial Resources
SubSkill. 7.03
Domain E. Human Resources
Skill 10. Acquire Staff and Volunteers
SubSkills. 10.01, 10.02
Skill 11. Train Staff and Volunteers
SubSkill. 11.01
Skill 12. Manage Workforce Relations
SubSkills. 12.01, 12.02
Domain G. Meeting or Event Design
Skill 19. Develop Plan for Managing Movement of Attendees
SubSkills. 19.01, 19.02, 19.03

Registration and housing are two critical aspects of the meeting-planning process, as they are the first impression of the event for most attendees. Since registration is often the first time attendees will interact with an event, the ease of locating information and registering will help determine confidence in the meeting's value. Available accommodations can also present an image of the meeting's quality. For example, if luxury hotels are being used, attendees may perceive the event as exclusive and high quality; however, if the hotel's price is too high for potential attendees, they may decide the meeting has little appeal since it is unlikely to offer a high return on investment (ROI), given the price. In order to create an effective registration and housing process, the meeting professional must know the meeting's vision, goals, and objectives, and these should be clearly tied to the organization's overall strategic planning. With the potential attendees' profile, the meeting professional can determine an acceptable price range for registration, hotels, and other meeting features.

Registration is more than collecting money and information about attendees; it encompasses data management for the entire meeting or event. Housing describes the process of providing accommodations for the attendees, which means understanding their expectations, wants, and needs. Combined, these two service elements create the first impression of event quality and value, as well as contributing to overall attendee satisfaction and perceived ROI. Both services can be provided by in-house staff or by third-party vendors; each option has advantages and limitations.

This chapter highlights options for planning and implementing registration and housing programs, as well as introducing registration and housing data and analysis. In addition, it outlines ways to monitor and adapt registration and housing needs throughout the event cycle to meet the needs of the organization and attendees. For the purpose of Part One in this chapter, the focus will be on registration; however, meeting professionals commonly include housing with registration, especially when a room block is being utilized and/or the organization is paying for all or a significant portion of the housing. Part Two of this chapter will cover housing.

PART ONE Registration

Technology has revolutionized the registration process through the use of application service providers (ASPs), which offer customized services as well as in-house systems customized specifically for the host organization. The rules of processing are similar to those of the past, but the means by which the registration process is completed by the end-user and the interface with the meeting organizer have changed. The primary goal of registration is to create a positive experience for the potential attendee that will continue to the end of the meeting.

Registration Processes

Registration is a complex process, with three distinct phases: pre-meeting, onsite, and post-meeting. Each phase has distinct activities and personnel requirements. At least one person, usually the meeting professional, needs to be dedicated to overseeing the entire registration process—through design, implementation, answering registration inquiries, and reporting and analyzing data. Policies and procedures may be developed by a meeting-planning team, and when external resources are used to provide the registration process, the contracted vendor may influence those policies and procedures.

key points

Registration Process

- Pre-meeting
- Onsite
- Post-meeting

Pre-Meeting Phase

Before a meeting takes place, the meeting professional should determine what registration information is to be collected, how it will be collected, and what will be done with the information. During the pre-meeting phase for registration, the meeting professional may initiate in-person meetings with the organization's leaders and key stakeholders to understand and establish desired outcomes for the registration process. This information will be used to guide the selection of a service provider (if one is used), establish the registration process, identify the level of customer service needed, and determine the data reporting and analysis services.

In addition to demographic information, e.g., age, gender, and education, the registration process might collect information about job titles, employer, years of experience, personal interests, previous attendance, and other information. While the needs analysis profiles the target audience—those people for whom the meeting is hosted—the registration data provides verifying profile details, as well as essential information for future initiatives and meetings. However, the meeting professional should determine how data might benefit the organization before making the request. Registrants often resent or reject questions that seem impertinent, invasive, or irritating.

Once a decision has been made about the information to be collected, begin creating, planning, and implementing the registration system, policies, and procedures. Some registration systems include: website, telephone, or a printed form that can be completed and submitted via fax or mail. A website is the most common registration system, as it offers the most convenience for participants. With each registration option, payment procedures need to flow through a secured process.

Web-based software-as-a-service (SaaS) registration systems centralize attendee data and make it accessible from anywhere. **Online registration** offers a powerful, integrated method for automating and organizing the registration process. An efficient registration process

FIGURE 10.1 Registration Anywhere, Anytime A user-friendly registration process should be made as simple as possible. Today's participant desires to access a website anywhere and at any time with minimal effort. This is the first touchpoint the potential attendee has with the meeting.

means the experience of the attendee begins on a positive note, setting the stage for the meeting (see Figure 10.1). To make the process as seamless as possible, both internally and externally, select a registration platform that addresses attendees' needs, while being easy to use and within the budget.

key points

Advantages/Limitations of Third-Party Vendors

Advantages

- Saves the meeting professional time
- Provides software and process expertise
- Provides cost-effective troubleshooting

Limitations

- May cause time delays in data release
- May be more expensive than a small organization can handle
- May not provide adequate privacy protections and data security

Choosing a Service Provider

In the past, options for registration were limited to bank/wire transfers, credit cards, or mailed checks pre-event, as well as cash, credit cards, or checks onsite. The limitations of these options included bank fees, exchange fees, and payment being held for three to six weeks in order to be cleared through the bank process. There were occasions when registration did not clear and the meeting professional was faced with the daunting task of collecting fees. With advances in technology and sophisticated service providers, the registration process has become significantly streamlined for the registrant and more efficient. Often registering and paying for an event can be accomplished in as little as 10 minutes.

Meeting professionals now have the option of creating their own registration site or using a third-party vendor. A third-party vendor is an individual or company offering a valuable tool, service, or resource to contribute to the meeting's success. Registration vendors can provide different levels of service, from creating a simple website which is then monitored by the meeting professional, to creating and administering the registration site, as well as providing data and analysis from the registration process.

A third-party vendor is well versed in the registration software, including being able to fix, quickly and cost effectively, any issues that arise. This frees up a significant amount of time for the meeting professional. Although a third-party vendor saves the meeting professional time by administering the registration software, any requests for information about registrations need to go through the vendor, which may result in having to wait for data required for effective decision-making. Even if a regular reporting schedule is set up, situations can develop where a quick decision is required without all of the necessary data. The cost of hiring a third-party vendor could be prohibitive for smaller events or events that do not achieve predicted attendance numbers. Finally, using a third-party vendor means attendee data is not restricted to the event staff, which raises privacy issues.

As with any other part of the event planning cycle, the RFP should be used to secure the vendor that best matches the organization's needs. The meeting professional needs to collect proposals from several different vendors to compare the benefits and features each offers. The industry standard for this particular RFP has been created by the Convention Industry Council's APEX initiative and is titled "Housing & Registration." Additionally, using the "Event Specifications Guide," from the same source, provides guidelines for building a robust RFP. When the RFP is specific and clear, vendors submitting a proposal have an ideal opportunity to address the priorities, needs, and preferences detailed by the meeting professional.

key points

Sources of Third-Party Registration Services

- CVent (www.cvent.com)
- eventbrite (www.eventbrite.com)
- RegOnline (www.lanyon.com)

Identifying Potential Registrants

In the initial research for the meeting, at least one target audience will be determined, which is the key audience for whom the meeting is being produced. Depending on the type of meeting, these people could be mandated by their organization to attend, may have an interest in the meeting's topic, or may want to engage in professional networking with other attendees.

All registration policies should be established very early in the planning process, including the categories of attendees. Categories of attendees may be determined before or shortly after contracting with a third-party vendor to handle the registration process. How the registration site is set up will depend, in part, on the different types of attendees expected and may also dictate some registration policies. These policies impact revenue, customer service, and onsite logistics, and they serve as a guide in the overall planning process. They should include registration rules, hotel reservation methods, and the policies for cancellation, refund, and substitution. Once policies have been established, e.g., with advance notice of 14 days, 80 percent of the registration fee can be refunded, the procedures for enacting the policies can be determined. A third-party vendor will have suggestions to make regarding policies and procedures, based on the registration system utilized.

key points

Registration Categories

- Attendee
- Exhibit staff
- Suppliers
- Customers
- VIPs
- Board or committee members
- Vendors
- Meeting staff
- Media
- Student/faculty
- Government
- Speakers
- Guests

Preparing & Delivering Customer Service

Prior to collecting attendee demographics, frequently asked questions (FAQs) should be documented and readily available, along with any communication intended for confirmed attendees. Communication to confirmed attendees should reflect the registrant's profile, meeting-related purchases, program information, important meeting policies, and any payment transactions. Special visa or translation information should be made available for international participants.

Onsite policies and procedures also need to be determined, including: onsite badge requirements, other credentials, and education session/special event ticket design. Typically, all attendees wear a badge, which clearly indicates authority to access onsite areas. Badges also foster networking, which is one of the key reasons the attendees register for meetings.

Several factors must be considered when determining what demographics, information, and/or logos should be displayed on the badge or tickets for education sessions or special events. One option is to embed attendee information on the badge, either in a chip or bar code allowing the attendee to "capture" attendance verification for continuing education units (CEUs) or professional development hours (PDHs). Specific information may also be embedded to control access to sessions where space is limited and attendees are required to register and, at times, pay an additional fee in advance. This information can also be used for attendance counts to assist with future planning. A lead-retrieval vendor has the software and equipment necessary to provide this service.

The meeting professional must carefully consider the online registration system's set-up and flow. In addition to basic contact information, set-up may also include meal/dietary restrictions, special needs, housing (if using a room block), and any requirements related to persons with disabilities. If a third-party vendor is utilized to build the registration site, this vendor's expertise will be

FIGURE 10.2 Customer Service Representative Assisting Potential Attendee The availability of a customer service representative (CSR) is vital to customer satisfaction for a complex meeting. The CSR will assist anyone having a question or difficulty in registering for the meeting, and will answer unique questions that are not answered thoroughly via the posted FAQs.

SUSTAINABILITY *in* **Practice**

Online registration and payment have quickly become the norm in the meeting profession, as they are more convenient. Additional opportunities exist, though, for reducing paper, plastic, and resource waste in onsite registration and reporting operations. Tips include the following:

- Reduce or eliminate literature bags and packets; migrate this information to mobile apps or other online options.
- Print badge information on recycled paper.
- Collect lanyards, badge holders, and inserts for reuse and recycling at the end of the meeting.
- Use compostable lanyards, badge holders, and badge inserts.
- Replace wayfinding signage with electronic signage or make signs durable so they can be reused at future events.
- Donate leftover bags, giveaways, and décor to local charities.

—Susan M. Tinnish, PhD

valuable in creating a balance between collecting useful information and maintaining a site that is welcoming and easy to navigate. The site should be interactive, allowing the registrant to complete fields and make choices. However, when possible, personal and business information for repeat attendees should be populated automatically, as this reduces manual data-entry errors and creates a streamlined user experience. Additionally, registration forms should be kept as brief as possible with relevant and concise questions.

The customer service team, or a designated individual, should have in-depth knowledge of the registration details encompassing the event. This team or individual will assist and provide advice to potential attendees. Customer service representatives should be prepared to answer a variety of questions about the meeting, have knowledge related to additional fees, and assist attendees in registering (see Figure 10.2). A list of frequently asked questions (FAQs) should be developed and made available when answering phone calls. A list of potential questions and answers uploaded to the website is effective for communicating with registrants, although some questions may need phone follow-up.

key questions

FAQs for Potential Attendees

- What arrangements are available to accommodate my disability?
- How can I review the program prior to the convention?
- How do I connect with people who share my interests?
- How do I get continuing education credit at the meeting?
- How do I find and select sessions that are unique to my needs?
- How do I select a hotel?
- What should I wear at the meeting?
- Where can I find travel information about getting to the meeting site?
- Are there activities for children?
- Will there be special onsite resources and opportunities for first-time attendees?

Organizations often offer reduced registration, special services, or housing fees for advanced registration. As the "early-bird" deadlines approach, a spike in general inquiries should be anticipated. Continuous review of the marketing timeline will also assist in preparing the customer service representatives for answering and responding to inquiries. Cash handling procedures, credit card transactions, and wire transfers should be reviewed and monitored on a weekly basis.

Onsite Phase

The ease of getting registered onsite and/or picking up attendee materials for those who registered in advance will set the tone for the rest of the event experience. To achieve success with onsite registration processes, onsite registration area layouts, signage, electrical service, Internet connectivity, and staffing should be carefully planned, reviewed, and confirmed (see Figure 10.3). To reduce the number of last-minute adjustments, the registration logistics should be completed one to two months prior to the meeting's start date.

Crowd Management

When designing the registration area(s), the meeting professional will review the facility floor plans to establish the best location(s). The onsite inspection allows time to examine the entrances and exits to see if the registration area will be able to handle the anticipated traffic flow. Depending on the registration categories and their relative size, the meeting professional must decide whether or not there will be an area for each category or just for pre-registration and onsite registration. Some considerations for designing the registration area include the number of attendees, anticipated registration times, number of pre-registered attendees, anticipated onsite registration, materials

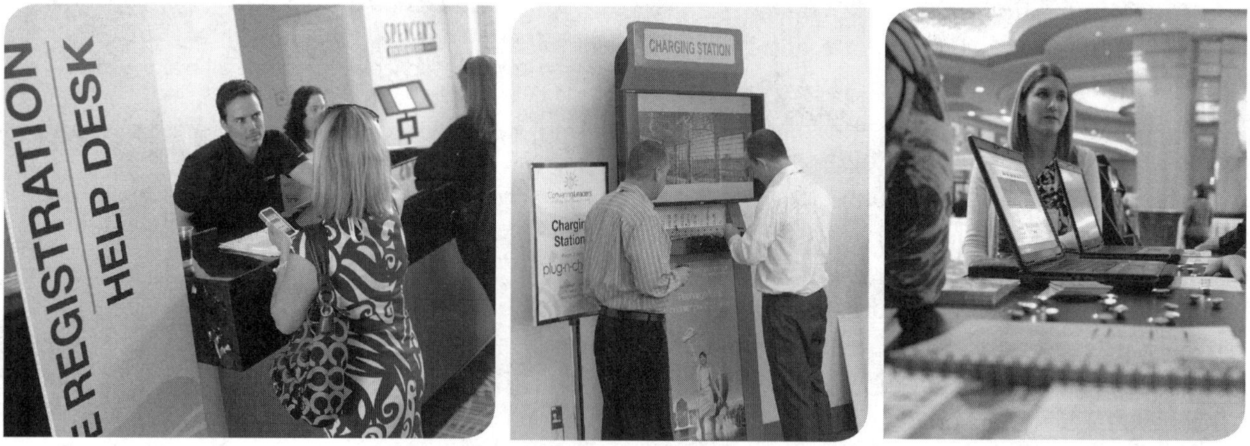

FIGURE 10.3 Onsite Registration Area Attendees appreciate a variety of services that can easily be incorporated into the design of the registration area. A help desk provides attendee assistance with technology issues, the charging station offers power outlets for attendees with portable electronics, and computer banks allow attendees to register onsite or check email.

FIGURE 10.4 Registration Area The location and arrangement of the registration area creates an ambience and an important early meeting touchpoint for attendees.

to be given out, session start times, and number of staff. Typically a registration area will be separated into the following smaller areas: alphabetical counters for pre-registered attendees; onsite registration; event questions; badge reprinting; and registration problems/issues. Regardless of the design, the ultimate goal of the registration area is to move the attendees through as quickly as possible.

Even the best-designed registration areas will have to deal with multiple attendees arriving at the same time. In order to reduce confusion and increase the efficiency of registration, queuing (waiting in line) needs to be considered. This system will differ from meeting to meeting and may be altered at different times during the registration process. For example, during slower times for registration, a straight-line queue in front of each area may work well. During peak registration times, a serpentine queue, which is a continuous feed to multiple counters, will keep individuals moving and be more efficient (see Figure 10.4). The use of stanchions (poles and ropes) can assist in creating a queue. In addition, the meeting professional should consider the attendees' perception of their wait, which can be influenced by the design. For example, using straight lines for a large event could result in very long lines. As an attendee approaches the line, he/she will perceive that registration is going to be slow. In this situation, the serpentine queue would be more effective and improve the attendees' perception. The meeting professional might arrange for hors d'oeuvres or beverages to be circulated, which can enhance the registration experience for attendees. At peak times, entertainment or screens that display the event's schedule or interesting information will keep individuals enjoyably occupied while standing in the queue.

key points

Organization of Registration Counters

- Alphabetical by name
- Onsite registration
- Questions
- Badge reprinting
- Resolution of registration problems/issues

Most meetings require signage to assist attendees in navigating the venue. This signage should be concise and set in prominent, high-traffic areas. Signage also needs to be large enough to be seen from a distance of several feet and high enough to be visible over the heads of the crowd. Sample signage with directional cues may read "Badge Pickup," "Course Registration," "Customer Service," "Hotel Information," "VIP Registration," "New Registrations," or "Registration Hours" (see Figure 10.5).

FIGURE 10.5 Registration Area Signage Informative signage assists attendees in locating the areas of interest within the meeting facility. Positioning an individual in high-traffic areas during peak crowd movements reinforces informational and directional signage. In this photo, the individual with an "Ask me" sign enhances the meeting experience and adds a personal touch.

Badge/Material Distribution

If the registration was successful, the majority of attendees will have pre-registered, so upon arrival at the event, they simply need to check in and pick up relevant event materials, e.g., badge, ribbons, tickets for special events/sessions, and programs. The materials can be pre-packaged, with the badge printed before the attendee arrives. Badges typically provide the person's name in large letters, and perhaps title or membership status, employer, and point of origin. Ribbons are an effective means of identifying certain categories of attendees (see Figure 10.6).

An alternative badge process is to allow attendees the opportunity to print their own badge insert (see Figure 10.7). This reduces the number of staff needed in the registration area, freeing them up to perform other duties. A self-serve registration area will need laptops and printers. At least one printer for every four laptops is recommended for convenience; this reduces the wait time for attendees and allows some time to fix malfunctioning printers.

Onsite registration will take more time, which is the reason for encouraging attendees to pre-register. If the meeting professional anticipates a large number of onsite registrations, the area will need to reflect

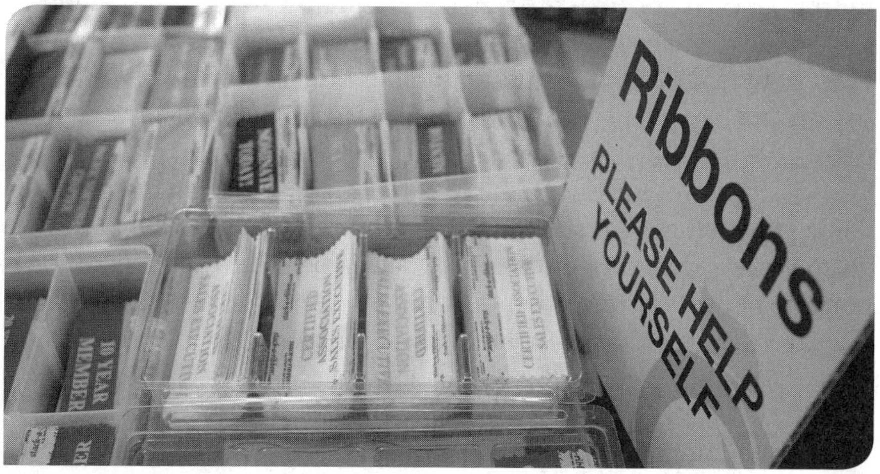

FIGURE 10.6 Available Ribbons At the badge pickup location, an assortment of ribbons for various categories of leaders and attendees provides easy identification of attendees. The self-adhesive, color-coded ribbons can be attached to the badge holder.

FIGURE 10.7 Badge Print and Pickup Area The badge and registration materials pickup area can be onsite at the convention center. Another option, providing the check-in service at contracted hotels, is convenient for the attendees, but may require additional trained staff, as the staff there will receive the same FAQs the registration staff will receive at the convention center.

this in terms of size, equipment, and staff. Using the original registration form will allow the meeting professional to collect data that will be comprehensive and can be added to the event's history. The equipment necessary in the onsite registration area will consist of laptops for attendee registration and staff, and printers. For attendees the laptops should be on high-top tables; this will speed up the registration process.

Temporary Staff

Considerations for staffing the registration area include: event size, arrival patterns, number of pre-registered attendees, and anticipated number of onsite registrations. A very general rule for staffing is one staff member for every 100 expected attendees. Additionally, the registration area may need four to five well-trained staff to assist with problems and to run errands as needed. These people need to be familiar with the registration system, the registration form, the FAQs, and possible issues that may surface.

The manner in which temporary staff are allocated throughout the event will depend on several factors. Meetings generally use a combination of paid and unpaid (volunteer) staff. The paid staff can be full-time meeting professionals or employees of the organization, and/or part-time meeting professionals. Employees will have a deeper understanding of the overall event, including its goals and objectives, and have a more holistic view of the event. Unpaid staff,

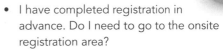

key questions

FAQs at the Meeting

- I have completed registration in advance. Do I need to go to the onsite registration area?
- Do I need to wear my badge to attend sessions or other events?
- How do I find where a session is located?
- How do I find my friends and colleagues?
- Where can I find out about potential employers?
- Can I record sessions?
- How do I get a copy of the paper presented in a session?
- What online tools are being provided? How do I get connected?
- Why is there a chip or a barcode on my name badge?

FIGURE 10.8 Student Gaining Experience at a Meeting Many organizations partner with educational programs to provide students with experience at a meeting. This opportunity is a valuable experience and an enhancement of students' education.

or volunteers, usually have an interest in the meeting industry and are looking to gain experience; some volunteers are interested in the meeting itself or are looking for volunteer hours, e.g., retired persons or students (see Figure 10.8).

Regardless of the type of staff, training will be necessary. Any policies and procedures related to the event should be easily accessible to all. Training should be done before registration is open so everyone is able to distribute the appropriate event materials and answer general questions about the event. Designated staff should be trained to handle data entry and the specific procedures to process payments and checkout. Reviewing safety procedures with the event security is a top priority once arriving onsite.

Reporting & Analyzing Registration Data

Once registration opens, the role of a meeting professional shifts from research and design to implementation of procedures and policies. The data being collected should be reported and analyzed frequently, well before the meeting and after the meeting concludes. Analysis of data from the previous meeting, if the organization has such data, will help the meeting professional develop an effective plan for a future meeting. However, analysis of registration data as it begins to come in allows the meeting professional to update the plan as necessary, e.g., adjusting function sheets, food and beverage guarantees, workshop materials, and many other details. The data can indicate whether objectives will be met and goals achieved. The data can also indicate if adjustments are necessary to stay within budget.

Weekly Reporting

Communicating registration data weekly to key stakeholders is a crucial part of ensuring the event stays on target with goals and objectives. The **pace report**, also known as a build-up report, provides a snapshot of registration activity at any given time, based on guidelines established during registration set-up. The pace report analyzes and compares registration trends against historical data and anticipated values. Weekly reports should include demographics, selected educational sessions, if applicable, and numbers by categories. In addition, the report should include revenue collected.

Report & Budget Review

While budget review and analysis will take place throughout the planning process, immediately after the event concludes the meeting professional will oversee final analysis of registration reports. The analysis begins while the meeting memory is fresh and will determine if expenses and revenue matched forecasted amounts. The meeting professional and key stakeholders should take time to reflect on reports and analysis, evaluate any new meeting features that were utilized, identify challenges encountered, and make recommendations for future meetings. Making the ROI determination is a complex process that is essential to business continuity.

Besides knowing what the registration data can tell about the meeting, the meeting professional needs to analyze the data to determine current trends. To do this, the meeting professional may need to utilize additional opportunities to generate and collect data. Meeting attendees, for instance, might participate in a brief online survey during the event to explain why they attended the entire event, but did not use the housing block for overnight accommodations. They might explain why they did not use the established airline discounts when making travel arrangements. When attendees are only registered for part of the event, they might explain what prompted that decision. Online surveys, accessed via mobile apps or at computer stations throughout the meeting venue, could provide additional information that explains the trends. Trying to guess why attendees make the decisions they do can be quite misleading, so collecting this additional data is useful in assessing the value of meeting arrangements.

The data should be analyzed to ensure all payments are received and appropriately processed, and to eliminate duplicate entries or other errors. If a registration vendor was used, the vendor's reports must be monitored carefully by the meeting professional to catch potential errors, misidentified participants, and trends that may not be obvious to the vendor, who is less familiar with the meeting stakeholders. As post-event reporting wraps up, the meeting professional will often work with the vendor to determine a date to officially close the event. At this time, refunds no longer are processed and the accounting books are considered finalized.

key points

Data Examples from Registration Process

- Number of registrants by type (e.g., attendee, exhibitor, staff)
- Number of registrants by date
- Number of registrants by length of stay (e.g., full event, half day)
- Number of registrants that paid full price
- Number of registrants that attended free of charge
- Geography of registrants
- First-time registrants in comparison to repeaters
- Titles and organizations represented
- Selection of meeting functions (e.g., workshops, receptions, meals)
- Accommodation requests
- Registrations listed by demographic information (if applicable)

PART TWO Housing

key points

Housing Processes

- Building a room block
- Contracting hotels
- Managing housing policies & procedures
- Managing room blocks
- Reporting

Housing describes the all-encompassing process of providing accommodations for attendees. The housing process can be divided into five steps: building a room block; contracting with hotels; managing housing policies, procedures, and room blocks; and reporting.

Like registration, housing can be done by a third-party vendor or handled in house. A local destination marketing organization (DMO) can provide housing services, and may be a good resource for many other aspects of event planning. Often organizations utilize internal, **in-house systems** to manage registration, housing, or both, and thereby track all attendee and exhibitor information. While in-house databases

Options	Advantages/Limitations
Direct—Attendees contact a hotel directly to make a reservation. There is no contract between the meeting organizer and the potential attendee.	**Advantages** • Effective for small meetings requiring only one hotel • No contract needed; available options can be marketed to attendees • No financial liability to the meeting organizer **Limitations** • Higher and varied rates may deter attendance • Availability may be limited and not accommodate all participants
Direct with Group Rate—Organization negotiates a group rate with the hotel to hold a block of rooms specifically for meeting participants; attendees directly contact the hotel to make a reservation within the group block.	**Advantages** • Effective for small meetings requiring only one hotel • Discount rate due to contractual agreement must be requested by attendee when reserving accommodations **Limitations** • Potential financial liability (attrition/cancellation) to the meeting organizer
In-House with Group Rate—The organization negotiates a group rate with the hotel to hold a block of rooms specifically for meeting participants; the meeting organizer manages the housing process.	**Advantages** • Ideal for a small to mid-sized meeting requiring one or more hotel(s) • Meeting organizer controls entire housing process **Limitations** • Requires full-time management and may involve additional staffing • Potential financial liability (attrition/cancellation) to the meeting organizer
Housing Provider with Group Rate—The organization negotiates a group rate with the hotel to hold a block of rooms specifically for meeting participants; a third-party company hired by the meeting organizer to manage the entire housing process takes reservations, works onsite to handle attendee questions, and provides comprehensive reports.	**Advantages** • Effective for mid-sized to large citywide meetings requiring multiple hotels with multiple price points • Ability to manage the entire housing process • Technology utilized to manage the housing process **Limitations** • Cost per reservation to the meeting organizer or meeting attendee • Potential financial liability (attrition/cancellation) to the meeting organizer
DMO with Group Rate—The organization negotiates a group rate with the hotel to hold a block of rooms specifically for meeting participants; the destination's local organization responsible for promotion, travel, meetings, and tourism may provide information on local resources and services, and may offer housing management.	**Advantages** • For any size meeting; more beneficial for citywide events • Established relationships with hotels and hospitality services • "Package" of hotels for citywide events **Limitations** • May have limited services that still require in-house staff management • Potential financial liability (attrition/cancellation) to the meeting organizer

FIGURE 10.9 Options for Housing Reservations Several options are available to the meeting professional to secure accommodations for attendees. The options here include one non-contract approach (direct) and four others that involve a contract but feature differing roles, responsibilities, and execution arrangements for attendees making reservations.

allow direct and immediate access to all data, these systems may not be as flexible as some third-party vendor systems. Additionally, setting up a database and maintaining it effectively can be demanding tasks. When selecting a third-party vendor, the meeting professional must be certain all monetary transactions, areas of responsibility, policies, and procedures are firmly established at the beginning of the partnership. Including housing arrangements on the registration form is a common practice worldwide.

Building the Room Block

Prior to signing hotel contracts, the method of making reservations should be determined. Five options are available to facilitate housing for a group. Figure 10.9 outlines the advantages, limitations, and general process for each housing method to assist in determining the best solution for a meeting.

A **room block** is the total number of sleeping rooms that is utilized and attributable to a meeting, and the size and content of the room block should be determined prior to contracting with each hotel. The following elements are considered when developing the room block.

The bell staff and the hotel registration desk form an early impression of the meeting experience. The ambience of the lobby area and greetings of staff are some of the first touchpoints in the meeting experience and should be considered when selecting appropriate hotels. Figure 10.10 provides a glimpse of the beginning of the experience.

key points

Elements of Building a Room Block

- Group history
- Guest-room types
- Rates/hotel mix
- Peak and shoulder nights

FIGURE 10.10 Hotel Lobby The traveling attendee will form an early impression of the meeting at the hotel registration desk. Welcome signage strategically placed in the hotel lobby provides the attendee with an overview of meeting events and locations. It is the beginning of the meeting experience.

Group History

A group's history of previous meetings helps a hotel understand the meeting's goals and attendee expectations. If this is a first-time meeting without historical data, the meeting professional might use data from a similar event to provide basic information about housing needs. This will communicate to the hotels the total dollar value of the meeting to assist in negotiations, e.g., best room rates, terms, and concessions. This history can be grouped into four categories:

- **Arrival/departure pattern**—A description of arrival and departure activities of the attendees
- **Food and beverage history**—The amount of money spent on breakfasts, lunches, receptions, refreshment breaks, and any other event involving group food and beverage
- **Outlet history**—Amount attendees spend inside of the hotel, e.g., restaurants, shopping, and entertainment
- **Affiliate revenue**—Revenue generated in the hotel from an affiliate meeting (also as known as an in-conjunction-with or ICW meeting) during the meeting's dates. Typically these are events hosted by exhibitors or sponsors, or pre- or post-meetings held at the same hotel(s) as the meeting.

Housing Bell Curve

A **peak night** is the date that the meeting has the highest demand for rooms, typically the highest attendance date of the meeting. Figure 10.11 illustrates this concept using a bell curve. In this example, there are 3,800 rooms needed on peak night, or 100 percent of the room block. Shoulder nights are the dates/nights before and after the meeting. Leading up to and post meeting, rooms are often needed; however, the need is not for as many rooms as on the peak nights of the meeting. The ending time of the last event and the ability to return home will influence arrival and departure patterns, and availability. The group history and patterns will assist in developing the block requirements per night.

The bell curve formula tracks the number of rooms blocked per night, expressed as a percentage of the peak night block. A bell curve is an effective tool in determining the number of rooms to block per night. Most effective when portrayed graphically, the bell curve shows arrival numbers for each day of the meeting, building up over the first few days and cascading downward following peak nights ("Guide to Room Block," 2014; Bracken & Shure, 2006).

Guest Room Types

Some meetings will have minimal room type requests and can contract **run-of-the-house (ROH)** rooms, i.e., rooms assigned at random and based on availability at the time of check-in. If the meeting requires specific room types, this should be defined in both the RFP

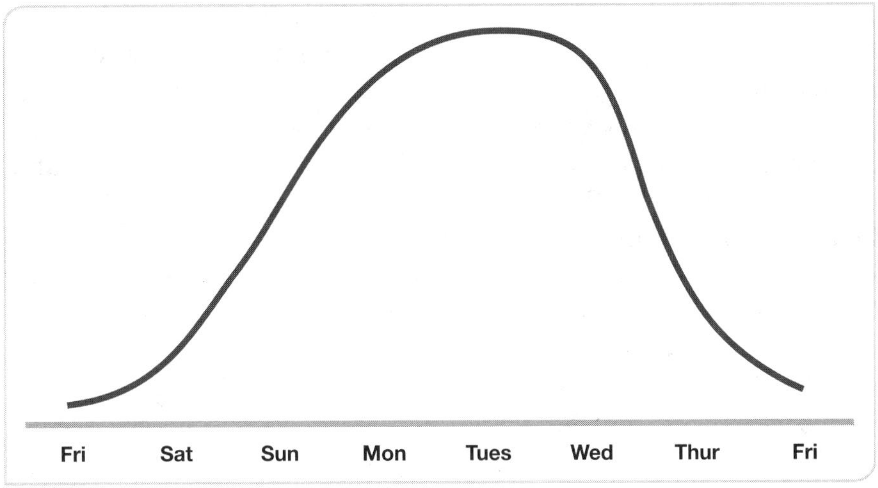

	Shoulder Nights				Peak Night	Shoulder Nights		
Day of Week	**Fri**	**Sat**	**Sun**	**Mon**	**Tues**	**Wed**	**Thur**	**Fri**
Number of rooms per day	76	570	1,900	3,420	3,800	3,420	760	114
Percentage of Peak	2%	15%	50%	90%	100%	90%	20%	3%

FIGURE 10.11 Bell Curve Formula The bell curve indicates when and how many room-nights will be needed for each night of the meeting. Using this example, a total of 14,400 room-nights are projected to be required over the meeting dates. Given the number of rooms required, multiple hotels will probably be contracted to complete this room block.

and contract. Additionally, consideration must be given for attendees with disabilities who require an accessible room. The following are standard room types:

- **Single**—room for one person with one bed of single, double/full, queen, or king size
- **Double**—room for two people with one bed of double/full, queen, or king size
- **Double/double**—room for two people with two beds of single or double/full size
- **Triple**—three people occupying a double/double room
- **Quad**—four people occupying a double/double room
- **Parlor suite**—hotel living room, usually with a sofa bed, connected to an adjoining sleeping room
- **Parlor suite+2**— hotel living room with two connecting rooms identified as singles, doubles, or double/doubles

Rates/Hotel Mix

Rates heavily influence an attendee's decision to attend the meeting and could determine the number of nights an attendee will stay at the contracted hotel. In order to negotiate the lowest possible room rate, the past rate history can be used to determine the best options. An annual meeting may expect a 3 to 7 percent rate increase per year, depending on the host city, demand for space, and rates at comparable properties. Typically, rate negotiation is based on the total dollar value the meeting brings to the hotel—including group and individual participant spending and affiliate or ICW spending.

Larger meetings require the use of more than one hotel, which can be accomplished by working with the local DMO. One of the services the DMO provides is to compile meeting requirements and share them with local hotels that meet the identified needs. Alternatively, meeting professionals can contract individually with area hotels. Accommodation options should offer attendees a range of prices and types, e.g., hostels, one star, two star, and luxury hotels. Offering diversity in accommodations increases the satisfaction levels of attendees, as they will be able to choose a hotel that is affordable. A consideration when utilizing multiple hotels is the proximity to the meeting's location. The hotels should be easily accessible; when the hotel is not within walking distance, the meeting organizer must offer shuttle service. Even when hotels are within walking distance of the meeting venue, alternative transportation must be planned.

Additional Considerations

A number of variables need consideration in constructing a room block that is realistic and achievable. Of course, the historical data is important in decision-making, since there are financial ramifications when actual performance fails to meet contractual obligations. The program format, meeting dates, and the destination itself are factors in building a room block that meets the group's needs.

Program format A significant predictor of room-night needs is the meeting's format. The schedule of events is a useful tool to determine arrival and departure patterns. For example, to determine the number of rooms on peak night, calculate the number of sessions offered on a given day, estimate the number of attendees per session, and multiply the results of those two factors for an estimated overall attendance. The results can then be adjusted to accommodate the group's preference for sharing rooms and the number of attendees within driving distance. Additionally, if the program begins with a morning session and the attendees are expected to fly to the destination, the first day will likely be a peak night for a multi-day meeting. If the meeting, though, begins in the evening, some may choose to fly in for the second day, deciding that the opening reception in the evening is insufficient to draw them to the destination early. The program, of course, must be developed with the needs and preferences of the target audience in mind, as well as the appeal of the destination and the hotel accommodations.

SUSTAINABILITY *in* Practice

Housing providers play an important role in sustainable meetings. The meeting's accommodation providers facilitate many energy-reduction, water-conservation, waste-reduction, and social-responsibility initiatives. Linen-reuse programs, in-room recycling, elimination of bottled water, or donation of unused room amenities/toiletries require the cooperation of the housing provider's staff, as well as attendees. Some lodging providers may even offer guest incentives for participation in these types of programs. Housing providers are responsible for generating their share of energy, carbon, water, and waste data toward the meeting's overall ecological footprint. Successful implementation requires collaboration between the meeting professional and housing providers from contracting through the post-event report (PER).

—Susan M. Tinnish, PhD

Dates An important consideration in developing a room block is the dates of the meeting, which will affect the arrival and departure patterns. For example, if a meeting is held during spring break or over a holiday weekend, some attendees may choose to extend their stay, accompanied by family or other guests. Other attendees may avoid meetings near holidays, so the meeting professional must consider the group's preferences. Since travel costs and availability of seats on flights and other transportation methods vary with the time of week, this is another consideration for housing arrangements.

Destination The geographic location of meetings influences transportation decisions and this may make a difference in the need for hotel accommodations. When an early morning or a late evening event is scheduled, additional hotel rooms may be necessary. Caution must be exercised in overestimating, as this may not be true for all attendees (Bracken & Shure, 2006). A resort or city known for attractions may increase the number of attendees who will be accompanied by family or other guests, and this can have an impact on the shoulder night numbers as well as the type of rooms the registrants seek. Appealing destinations may encourage additional overnight stays, so all attendees will not arrive the day before a meeting and leave as early as possible following the meeting. Extended stays of a day to a week are not uncommon, so extending favorable room rates to accommodate these decisions may be very attractive to attendees. How long a negotiated room rate is available to attendees must be determined at the time of contract negotiation with individual hotels.

Contracting the Hotel

The details relating to the meeting and attendees are provided to the hotel in the RFP prior to contract negotiations. Once the needs are met and terms are agreed upon, the contract can be signed. Housing for the meeting is a significant element, as it provides accommodations for attendees and is a major revenue source the hotel uses to offset other costs, e.g., complimentary meeting space, F&B pricing, and concessions agreed to during negotiations. Each detail should be included in the contract.

A contract clause addresses a specific aspect of the agreement by the involved parties. Depending on the meeting requirements, contracts with hotels can vary in length and number of clauses. Some clauses may be required and some specifically preferred. Contract clauses not only protect the organization and the hotel, but can protect attendees as well.

key points

Typical Hotel Contract Clauses

- Attrition
- Cancellation
- Cancellation & attrition fee calculation
- Deposit fees required
- *Force majeure*
- Room block audit
- Room block review
- Walk/relocation clause

Cut-Off Dates & Room Block Reviews

A **cut-off date** is a designated date when a hotel will release any unsold sleeping rooms in a room block and make them available to the general public. The date is typically three to four weeks (some venues will require up to six weeks) before the first arrival date, at which time the attendees will no longer have the ability to book rooms at the group rate. The hotel may agree to accept reservations at the contracted group rate, based on room availability, after the cut-off.

A room block review should be conducted and contractually agreed to at the 90-, 60-, and 30-day mark prior to the official cut-off date (for meetings planned well in advance, such as an association's annual meeting). This allows both the hotel and the meeting professional to review the pickup compared to the previous year's pace and avoid the possibility of attrition and pickup issues by releasing rooms back to the hotel or securing additional rooms at the contracted rate as needed.

Attrition & Slippage

Attrition is the failure to occupy all contracted rooms within an allowable shortfall, which requires financial compensation from the host organization to the hotel. Typically, the contract will specify a percentage of the block that must be achieved. Slippage is the "reduction in the number of rooms used from the original reserved block" ("APEX Industry Glossary," 2011). It is often measured from the cut-off date and the room block counts at that time. To calculate the slippage percentage, take the actual room-night pickup and divide it by the contracted room-night for a specific day. The amount of financial compensation that will be due is the difference between the reduced room block and the actual rooms booked. The contract should clearly state the exact price of an unoccupied room per night and when rooms can be released prior to cut-off dates.

Additionally, the contract should outline options for any mitigation, resale of rooms, or ability to rebook a future meeting by the host organization. In recent years, hotels have become more assertive in collecting attrition fees rather than booking future events to offset the calculated fees. The reason for this action is the budgeted revenue for the hotel is not realized, which affects the current financial bottom line. Thus, vigilance is required by the meeting professional to monitor reports carefully and maintain close communication with the hotel representative. In the end, the organization may be charged full rate for each room that was unoccupied.

Walk/Relocation Clause

A **walk/relocation clause** protects the attendee holding a confirmed room reservation from being denied accommodations upon arriving and being relocated to another hotel. This type of clause, along with any concessions to the individual if they are "walked," should be included in the hotel contract. The meeting professional should provide the hotel with a list of VIPs who should not be walked under any but dire circumstances and should be notified in advance.

"Comps"

"Comps" are complimentary hotel rooms. Hotels use this as a "reward" for maximizing room pickup. Comps are offered on a ratio basis and awarded post-meeting based on the total number of paid rooms occupied or "picked up." For example, for every 50 paid rooms occupied, the organization is awarded one comp night. While 1/50 has been the standard, the comp policy will vary by hotel and/or the size/value of the meeting. Comp nights can add up quickly and offer significant savings for the organization. The use of "comp" room-nights reduces housing expenses and is often applied to rooms required for staff, speakers, vendors, sponsors, or special guests.

Commissions & Rebates

While housing is a major source of revenue for the hotel, it can also be a revenue generator for the meeting organizer to offset meeting costs. Housing revenue can be generated in two ways: commissionable rate or rebate.

A **commissionable rate** provides a total cost with a commission included (percentage of total cost) that may be paid to the sponsoring group, a third party (e.g., a travel agent or an independent meeting planner), or a site-selection vendor.

A **rebate** is a set dollar amount rather than a percentage. The percentage is typically a per-room/per-night charge by the hotel and could be tied to offset specific expenses for the meeting, e.g., a shuttle bus program or a food and beverage event. The revenue may return to the host organization or a third-party vendor to offset specific or general expenses.

key points

Calculation of "Comps"

Using the information from Figure 10.11 (p. 187), the total room-nights has been calculated at 14,400; using the ratio of 1/50, a total of 288 rooms would be available to the meeting organizer and designated as "comp" rooms.

However, this calculation is made at the completion of the meeting and the "comp" room-nights are determined by actual occupancy over the course of the meeting with the rooms divided between the hotels in the block and based on the calculations by each hotel.

Concessions

A **concession** is "one party providing something of value to the other party in exchange for goods or services, pending certain conditions" ("APEX Industry Glossary," 2011). Concession items may be complimentary meeting space, discounted hotel rooms, suite upgrades, complimentary Wi-Fi, or any other goods or services of value. As with comps, an organization may include this cost savings in a budget or omit it from the budget with the assumption that a cost will not be incurred.

Maintaining the Room Block

Management of the room block starts the day housing opens and stops once all attendees have checked out of the hotel. During this phase, the meeting professional needs to be aware of factors that may encourage attendees to book **rooms outside the block (ROB)** or book **rooms outside the contracted hotel (ROCH)**. A ROB or ROCH is any room that is occupied by an attendee but was not booked through the housing reservation system. The meeting professional must be proactive in creating and communicating incentives to book a room within the block, which controls attrition liabilities to the host organization.

Protecting the Block

Once housing is open and attendees are able to make reservations, an organization will have to work to protect the block. An organization can do so by being prepared and planning ahead. Several factors may encourage attendees to book outside the block of rooms or outside the contracted hotel, including price, loyalty, convenience, and perceived value over that provided within the block. Protecting the block requires regular reporting from the registration provider and the housing arrangements provider, as well as the hotels. These data sources must be compared, to make certain the correct number of reservations are attributed to the meeting. Additionally, the reports provide data that allows the meeting professional to make adjustments as necessary to avoid slippage and attrition fees. When additional room-nights are required, early warning is essential and communication is a key ingredient to successful room block management.

Online Travel Sites

Attendees are often unaware that taking advantage of lower rates through alternative booking sites may not guarantee them a room at the hotel. Websites may offer lower rates than the organization's contracted block, e.g., Travelocity®, Expedia®, Hotels.com®, and even hotel websites. As a result of booking through these sites, the attendee may lose loyalty points, have to prepay for the entire stay, encounter

PROFESSIONAL DILEMMA

Your employer will reimburse only 50 percent of the cost of attending a professional development conference. You want to attend, but the conference is in Honolulu, Hawaii, with a fairly steep price tag for the registration fee, hotel costs, and travel to the islands. Even with the incentives offered for hotel and transportation, you found a rate on your own that is less than half the cost. However, this hotel is not in the room block. It is within walking distance, though, of a hotel that is in the room block and where the shuttle transportation picks up attendees for transport to the meeting facility. In fact, with the wonderful weather in Honolulu, you could walk from the meeting venue to this less expensive hotel. You hear through colleagues that the meeting host is concerned with attrition at this popular event. Do you make reservations through the deal you found or through the housing registration site? What is your rationale for this decision? If you stay outside the room block, is your use of the shuttle service ethical? What steps might the meeting organizer take to provide an incentive for you to stay within the room block for this meeting? What might the meeting host do that would make the deal you found much less attractive?

the inability to change arrival/departure dates, or be charged in full for a cancelled reservation. The meeting professional should "shop" these various sites to determine if they are offering reduced rates and notify both attendees and customer service of the pitfalls of this type of booking. Further, the meeting professional may have arranged for shuttle transportation between the hotels and meeting venue; if that shuttle is only available to attendees within the block, the attendee booking accommodation outside the block could be faced with additional expenses to attend the meeting.

Direct and Sub-Blocks

Groups associated with the meeting are more likely to contract with a hotel directly, rather than through the organization's housing service. These groups include exhibitors and/or sponsors; these groups could also arrange for a **sub-block**. Sub-blocks are contracted blocks of rooms designated for specific groups of meeting attendees. The challenge facing the meeting professional is determining whether or not the contracting organization has been made aware of the other group's direct booking. In many cases where organizations were faced with significant attrition fees, the primary culprit was a group either contracting directly with the hotel or not filling its sub-block. The meeting professional might add a clause to the contract, stating that a hotel cannot contract with an affiliated or industry group over the host organization's meeting dates without the organizer's approval.

Housing Pirates

Housing "pirates" or "poachers" are unauthorized, unaffiliated housing providers that offer rooms at reduced rates to attendees, often under the guise of an affiliation with the meeting. If successful, their efforts to siphon rooms from a block can result in attrition penalties as well as causing issues for the attendees (Bracken & Shure, 2006). The meeting professional should work with legal counsel when this type of activity is identified. In some cases the actions could be illegal while in other situations, unethical. A very fine line exists between ethics and legality and requires vigilance on the part of the meeting organizer (Waddle, 2009).

Creating Incentives

An **incentive** is a concession or reward for booking within the meeting block. Incentives can be monetary, which provides a way for an attendee to measure the value or benefit. Sometimes an organization will be creative and find other incentives that may be more of a benefit/value to the attendee. The use of incentives can help persuade attendees not to book outside the block or outside the contracted hotels. The goal is to keep the participants within the contracted block, thus minimizing the chance for attrition (see Figure 10.12).

Examples of some of the more popular and successful attendee incentives include:

- Increase the registration fee at the pre-planning stage and then offer registration discounts of that same amount only to those who stay within the block. This incentive helps to keep attendees inside the block and also protects the revenue received from registration fees.
- Allow attendees staying within the block to earn points toward products and services provided by the organization.
- If shuttle transportation is provided to the main meeting facility and/or other events, communicate that shuttles will provide transportation only to/from contracted hotels.

Housing Reports

The responsibilities of the meeting professional do not end once the meeting concludes. Key findings that provide data for future events are revealed in the post-meeting stage. Post-event reporting is perhaps one of the key elements in determining whether or not the event was successful. This stage requires the meeting organizer to analyze data, reports, and surveys to draw conclusions, and to provide a variety of reports to various interested stakeholders. This is one of the most critical stages to capture the group's history and trends for planning future events.

If a DMO or third-party housing provider is selected to manage housing, the vendor can provide real-time, up-to-date housing reports throughout the process. Customized reports may be available

FIGURE **10.12** **Comfortable Accommodations** The goal of the meeting professional is to select accommodations that meet the needs and expectations of the attendees. The amenities and services provided by the hotels are an important contribution toward creating and delivering a positive meeting experience.

as well. Reports may be sent on a weekly basis, but many housing vendors and DMOs also offer reporting via websites, making information easily accessible at any time. If the organization is not using a DMO or third-party vendor, the meeting professional should include in the hotel contract a schedule and delivery method for the housing reports to be sent directly to the meeting professional by each hotel.

Pre-Meeting

Prior to the meeting, daily, weekly, or monthly reports should be received. Careful attention to the common reports listed below will assist the meeting professional in managing the room block and help in addressing shortfalls or overbookings as they become apparent. Common reports include:

- summary of reservations confirmed by each hotel;
- room pickup by day for each hotel;
- rooming lists for designated sub-blocks;
- pickup by sub-block and total block pickup number to date; and
- rooms available (by category if not ROH) to date.

Room Audits

A **room audit** cross-checks the names of guests in the hotel against the most current registration list. Room audits are an effective way to find rooms outside the block (ROB). Miscoded rooms will be identified through an audit and this will result in the organization receiving credit toward fulfillment of room block requirements.

Some hotels may not be willing to share guest information with a housing provider (third-party vendor), as there could be privacy issues. In this case, the meeting registration list would be provided by the organization to the hotel to conduct the audit. To ensure that the housing provider will conduct the audit, a clause should be included in the contract. If the hotel is concerned with guest security, additional language can be written to protect the privacy of hotel guests. Audits can and should be conducted both pre- and post-meeting.

Post-Meeting

Gathering data post-meeting begins the last day of the meeting. For 60 to 90 days post-meeting, information about the meeting will be gathered and presented in a final report, which is used to create the group history for future meeting planning.

Post-meeting reporting is critical for ROI determination and the planning of future meetings. A post-meeting report is more detailed than the reports received leading up to the start of the meeting. The information obtained in the post-meeting report is used to create the meeting history and analyze trends. Items that can/should be included in a final report include:

- Total pickup—maximum number of rooms picked up by the group
- Room pickup by day
- Booking pace report
- Pickup report by category and sub-block
- Number of no-shows, comps, and cancellations by day and total
- Individual hotel pickup report—a detailed report that breaks down the pickup at individual hotels, day by day. This will help develop the bell curve for the next event. Typically, the report includes the contracted block, the block after any adjustment has been made, final pickup, and audit results.
- Summary report—represented in numbers and compares information from previous meetings (if available). May include final number of reservations, reservation method used (form, phone, fax, website), breakdown of room occupancy by type, breakdown of attendee type, average rate, length of stay, and other specific information.
- Summary of recommendations—a short written report from the chosen vendor. May point out any significant changes, future recommendations, and general statistics from the meeting.

Closing Report

Prior to "closing the books" on the meeting, a comprehensive post-event analysis or closing report that includes the final analysis of the registration and housing information should be submitted to organization leaders. An executive summary is a short document that summarizes the detailed post-event reports in such a way that key stakeholders can quickly become familiar with the most significant findings and incorporate that information when making decisions for future business plans.

SUMMARY

The goals of the registration and housing process, whether in advance or onsite, are accuracy and efficiency. Both must be achieved within a certain time limit and budget. The precise methods of dealing with the people and the details must save time, minimize attendee and staff frustration, and provide necessary and accurate data.

Technology has a major impact on the manner in which each process is planned and implemented. The behaviors of attendees and the function of the organization, as well as the management of meetings, have changed and are ever evolving. Successfully orchestrating the registration and housing process is both a science and an art. With so many variables and options, today's meeting professional must depend on data and anticipated behaviors to strategically make both functions cohesive and seamless.

For all meetings, large or small, registration and housing are collaborative. The best practice is to develop a working partnership with the hotels, the DMO, and/or the vendors specializing in these aspects of meeting management, to effectively manage the risk and ensure the meeting is successful in satisfying the needs of the attendees and other stakeholders (Carlisle, 2006; Bracken & Shure, 2006).

CONTRIBUTING AUTHORS

Amanda S. Rushing, CMP, Aff. M. ASCE
Director, Conference & Meeting Services
American Society of Civil Engineers

Linda M. Robson, PhD
Assistant Professor
School of Hospitality Management
Endicott College

KEY WORDS

attrition
concession
cut-off date
incentive
in-house system
online registration
pace report
peak night
room audit
room block
rooms outside the block (ROB)
rooms outside the contracted hotel (ROCH)
run-of-the-house (ROH)
sub-block

DISCUSSION QUESTIONS

1. Why should meeting organizers collect demographic information on their attendees? How could they use this information?
2. Explain the best way to determine the success of the registration and housing process.
3. Choose one type of housing reservation procedure for an event of 500 attendees. What makes this type of a procedure better than other options? Defend your answer.
4. What is a bell curve and how does that curve provide a visual reference to the housing trends for a meeting?

11

Exhibitions and the Role of Face-to-Face Marketing

Julia W. Smith, CEM, CTA
Senior Vice President, National Sales
Global Experience Specialists (GES)

Main Topics

- History of Exhibitions
- Exhibition Producers
- Selling Exhibit Space
- Knowing the Exhibition Audience
- Floor Plan Design
- Exhibition Schedule
- Exhibition Logistics
- Measuring the Return on Investment
- Future of Exhibitions

Learner Outcomes

Upon the completion of this chapter, the student should be able to:

1. Describe the main types of exhibitions.
2. List the types of exhibition organizers/producers.
3. Discuss the economic impact of exhibitions.
4. Identify trends impacting exhibitions.
5. Outline the value of an exhibition within a meeting.

CMP INTERNATIONAL STANDARDS

Domain A. Strategic Planning
Skill 2. Develop Sustainability Plan for Meeting or Event
SubSkills. 2.01, 2.02
Domain D. Financial Management
Skill 7. Manage Event Funding and Financial Resources
SubSkill. 7.04
Domain G. Meeting Or Event Design
Skill 19. Develop Plan for Managing Movement of Attendees
SubSkill. 19.01
Skill 22. Manage Meeting or Event Site
SubSkills. 22.01, 22.02, 22.03, 22.04
Domain I. Marketing
Skill 29. Manage Meeting-Related Sales Activities
SubSkill. 29.01

FIGURE 11.1 Outdoor Exhibition Space The CONEXPO-CON/AGG exhibition, held in Las Vegas, Nevada, provides attendees with an array of off-road equipment used in construction that is too large for any exhibition facility.

A meeting or event may have an **exhibition** component (also known as an **exposition**, **trade show**, or **trade fair**). An exhibition is "an organized presentation and display of a selection of items." Exhibitions may be permanent displays or temporary, but in common usage exhibitions are "considered temporary and usually scheduled to open and close on specific dates" ("APEX Industry Glossary," 2011).

Exhibitions are typically defined as **business-to-business (B2B)** events or **business-to-consumer (B2C)** events. A B2B exhibition offers industry-specific products or services, and attendees must qualify to attend the exhibition either through membership in a sponsoring association or by meeting other criteria. Corporate events may include an exhibition, and would fall in the B2B category. Educational programs may be a part of the exhibition program. Attendees and exhibitors may be domestic and/or international. The average length of a U.S. B2B exhibition is between two and four days.

B2C exhibitions, also known as public exhibitions or consumer shows, generally charge admission or sell tickets. They are open to the public (or segments of the public). At the exhibition, direct sales and order-taking may occur, provided sellers follow local rules including collection and reporting of applicable taxes. Attendees of B2C shows tend to be local or regional; most of these public events are held in venues where parking and concessions are available. The National Association of Consumer Shows (NACS) represents producers of home, automobile, sportsmen, RV, boat, craft, and other public shows.

Exhibitions are described as **horizontal exhibitions** if they include many types of products and services from one or more industries. For example, a "home and garden show" will have a wide variety of exhibitors featuring everything from outdoor floral options to indoor paint or furniture. A **vertical exhibition** is more limited in scope, focusing on a targeted segment of an industry. Many technology shows offer software solutions for specific types of business or needs and would be considered vertical exhibitions.

Exhibitions provide a temporary marketing environment for exhibitors to present products, services, and educational materials to attendees. Exhibitions are held in convention centers, exhibition halls, meeting rooms, hotel ballrooms, auditoriums, schools or government buildings, or open areas located adjacent to a meeting or event. Exhibitions can use outdoor space (e.g., parking lots) for display of machinery or other large items, and can be held at fairgrounds. For example, Figure 11.1 depicts the CONEXPO-CON/AGG exhibition, a mega-off-road equipment industry exhibition that has acres of outdoor exhibit space in addition to an indoor exhibition area.

The Center for Exhibition Industry Research (CEIR) "has been highlighting the importance of exhibitions in today's business environment. CEIR produces primary research studies that prove the effectiveness and efficiency of exhibitions as a marketing medium" (CEIR, 2013, para. 1). CEIR research estimates that 25,000–30,000 exhibitions are held worldwide each year, about half of which occur in the U.S. and Canada (Ducate & Breden, 2013, p. 16). CEIR is a non-profit organization with the mission of advancing the growth, awareness, and value of exhibitions and other face-to-face marketing events by producing and delivering research-based knowledge tools.

According to a 2012 study commissioned by members of the Convention Industry Council (CIC), meetings represent nearly $300 billion in annual direct spending, "providing a platform to educate, introduce new ideas, and innovate to achieve results across every business sector" ("The Economic Significance," 2012, p. 1). Exhibitions provide a key component of both the financial and educational value of meetings. The *2014 CEIR Index Report* indicates that more than two million organizations exhibited in 2013 at B2B exhibitions attended by 68 million professionals (p. 19).

key points

Additional Economic Statistics

- In 2013, gross exhibition revenues from B2B exhibitions exceeded $11 billion ("CEIR Index Report," 2014, p. 19).
- In 2012, exhibitors contributed $24.5 billion to the U.S. economy in direct spending ("Exhibitor Direct Spending Estimate," 2014, p. 1).
- In 2012, attendees contributed $44.8 billion to the U.S. economy in direct spending ("Attendee Direct Spending Estimate," 2014, p. 1).

History of Exhibitions

The Union of International Fairs (UFI), an international trade organization, found that the "historical traditions of trade go back to ancient Egypt, the Greek civilization, and the Roman Empire, when journeying traders met local producers in market places and bazaars." The term fair comes from the Latin word *feria*, meaning "religious festival," and in the Middle Ages these festivals usually took place near a convent or church. The UFI history goes on to note that the term currently used in Germany to describe large trade fair companies, *Messe*, "derives from the Latin term *missa*, or religious service, at which the priest, on pronouncing the final words 'ite, missa est,' declared the religious service at an end, thus giving the sign for the opening of the market, usually held in the church square" (UFI, "Foreword," para. 2).

The UFI history continues:

> The process of industrialization, which began in the 18th century, required new sales and distribution channels, thus affecting the trade fair business. During the 18th and 19th centuries, fairs indeed evolved from sites for direct sales to sites displaying a broad range of available goods: Only samples of much more diverse product ranges were exhibited. These fairs were known as Sample Fairs (from the German *Mustermesse*), initiated for the first time by the Leipzig Fair. These sample fairs, with a wide range of investment and consumer goods, dominated the fair scene in Europe up to the middle of the 20th century. (UFI, "Basic Knowledge," 1.1.3., para. 2)

In the U.S., Chicago and Philadelphia opened facilities to commemorate "world's fairs." In essence, these events highlighted global industrial advances, and the concept rapidly multiplied. By 1914, the exhibition business was sufficiently strong to warrant the formation of the National Association of Convention Bureaus (Dallmeyer & Ducate, 2006, p. 38). Convention bureaus and other destination marketing organizations (DMOs) promote specific destinations, with a goal of attracting exhibitions, conventions, and other visitors to their cities and venues.

As a result of the growth and increased awareness of the value of exhibitions, the National Association of Exposition Managers (NAEM) was formed in 1928. Later, the name was changed to International Association of Exhibitions and Events (IAEE). IAEE has over 9,000 members representing organizations or individual categories, and they are responsible for hosting, organizing, and sponsoring exhibitions worldwide (IAEE, n.d.).

Exhibition Producers

Exhibitions may be sponsored or produced by trade associations or other member organizations, private companies, entrepreneurs, multimedia organizations, and third-party meeting/exhibition organizers.

A trade association may offer an exhibition in conjunction with its annual conference or other large meetings, serving all or a portion of its membership. An association exhibition provides an opportunity for meeting attendees to see new products and services and gain skills through hands-on demonstrations. Attendance at an association-sponsored exhibition usually is limited to registered meeting attendees, members, or qualified guests of the exhibitors. Revenue from exhibition and other sponsorship opportunities may represent a major portion of an association's non-dues income.

A member-based organization, e.g., an automobile dealers' association, may sponsor an exhibition to attract new potential customers and gain media attention. Corporations sponsor exhibitions for particular user groups or client bases, e.g., Microsoft® sponsoring a developers' conference with exhibits. They also may sponsor exhibitions for their own employees, e.g., hardware or drugstore chains may sponsor a private exhibition to teach employees how to display seasonal products.

Exhibition organizers other than associations are referred to as "for-profit" exhibition producers. Entrepreneurs who identify a niche market or identify an emerging trend and design an exhibition to appeal to that audience, either B2B or B2C, often launch new exhibitions. There may be a meeting component attached to help potential attendees justify attendance and gain more value. Exhibitions launched by multi-media organizations frequently are designed to appeal to the readership of one of the organization's publications, e.g., a sports equipment exhibition for the readers of a sports magazine. Third-party meeting/exhibition organizers may be engaged to manage an exhibition for another group, e.g., an association without the in-house staff to manage the work, or they may launch or purchase existing events, managing or owning a portfolio of meetings and exhibitions.

key points

Potential Sources of Revenue

- Sale/rental of exhibit space
- Sale of sponsorships and advertising
- Registration/entry fees

A primary reason for an organization to host an exhibition is its financial value and return. For many associations, the exhibition is a major economic engine, as well as providing member value and education.

All direct and indirect expenses must be offset in order to realize a profit. Entrepreneurs and media companies sponsor exhibitions to derive new sources of revenue, and an exhibition that is not producing a profit will have a short lifecycle. Other viable reasons for offering an exhibition include extending member or reader value and fostering loyalty through meeting attendance.

Selling Exhibit Space

The exhibit-space sales cycle varies from event to event. Some exhibition organizers start marketing for the next year's event prior to the completion of the current year's exhibition. Others assign exhibit space during or after the exhibition, using a first-come/first-served process, a lottery system, or appointments that may be established via a **priority-points** system. Floor plans are developed using a software program, e.g., EXPOCAD®, AutoCAD®, or a web-based sales system, making it simple to reconfigure the floor plan as sales are completed. Exhibition space often is sold as part of a total sponsorship package designed to give a participating organization a fully integrated marketing program with access to the selected audience year-round. Exhibit and sponsorship sales may be handled by an organization's staff, or by a third-party organization specializing in sales.

In the U.S., exhibit space is generally sold or rented by the square foot. However, internationally it is common to sell space by cubic content. According to IAEE, "cubic content is a unit of measurement allowing display materials and products to occupy 100 percent of the exhibit space purchased, regardless of sightlines, up to a height established by the exhibition's rules. While full use of cubic content space is common on an international level, U.S. show organizers remain divided on the idea" ("Evaluating," 2011, p. 3).

Exhibition organizers produce an exhibitor prospectus (online or print) that includes the audience profile, prior attendance breakdowns by category, and other data that will help an exhibitor make the decision to participate. A sophisticated exhibition sales associate will provide compelling customized audience data to help close an exhibit sale.

Knowing the Exhibition Audience

A 2014 CEIR study focused on what attendees want from training sessions. The study listed product "interaction" and "information to take away" at the top of the respondents' list of preferences. The design of an exhibition that meets attendee expectations requires an in-depth understanding of the audience. Attendees and potential attendees should be surveyed regularly to ensure the exhibition organizers understand attendee decision-making power, purchasing roles, shopping styles, and learning styles, as well as having an overall audience profile. Studying and understanding generational differences guides exhibition organizers/producers to target elements like content delivery methodologies and traffic patterns on the exhibition floor ("Exhibition Floor Interaction," 2014, p. 2).

CEIR cites looking for new products as the primary reason attendees give for visiting exhibitions (the leading reason for over 25 years), followed by gaining insights into industry trends and networking with vendors and colleagues ("Exhibition Floor Interaction," 2014, p. 10).

Floor Plan Design

An exhibition is designed around a grid layout or floor plan, which includes exhibit spaces (known as **booths** or **stands**), aisles (often referred to as gangways outside the U.S.), permanent elements like columns and entrances, and feature areas. Exhibitors purchase or rent the use of exhibit space from the organizer or producer for the length of the event. Exhibitors either bring in exhibits, equipment, samples, and other items for display within the space or rent these elements from an exhibition supplier, who typically delivers the rented items to the booth/stand onsite.

In the U.S., booth areas are most often constructed of an interlocking pipe and drape system (see Figure 11.2), which allows booths to be installed quickly and at a reasonable cost. Pipe and drape booths consist of an 8-foot-tall back drape and two sections of side rail, which generally are a maximum of 4 feet tall. Figure 11.3 shows booths constructed of a modular, hard-wall system. Outside the U.S., exhibitions may be held in facilities with more permanent stand or shell scheme configurations. U.S. booth spaces are generally based on a 10-foot-deep × 10-foot-wide grid (although they can be 8 feet deep × 10 feet wide, or 9 feet deep × 10 feet wide); international booths/stands are laid out in meters (3.05 × 3.05 meters is the equivalent of one booth/stand space).

FIGURE 11.2 Pipe and Drape Booths/Stands Pipe and drape to designate booths/stands is used primarily in the U.S., as can been seen at the League of California Cities exhibition.

Floor Layout Factors

The layout of an exhibition floor plan is influenced by a number of factors. An exhibition organizer should have an understanding of the unique needs of the current and targeted exhibitors, as well as knowl-

FIGURE 11.3 Hard-Wall Booths/Stands This figure shows hard-wall booths/stands installed at the 2014 MAGIC show in Las Vegas.

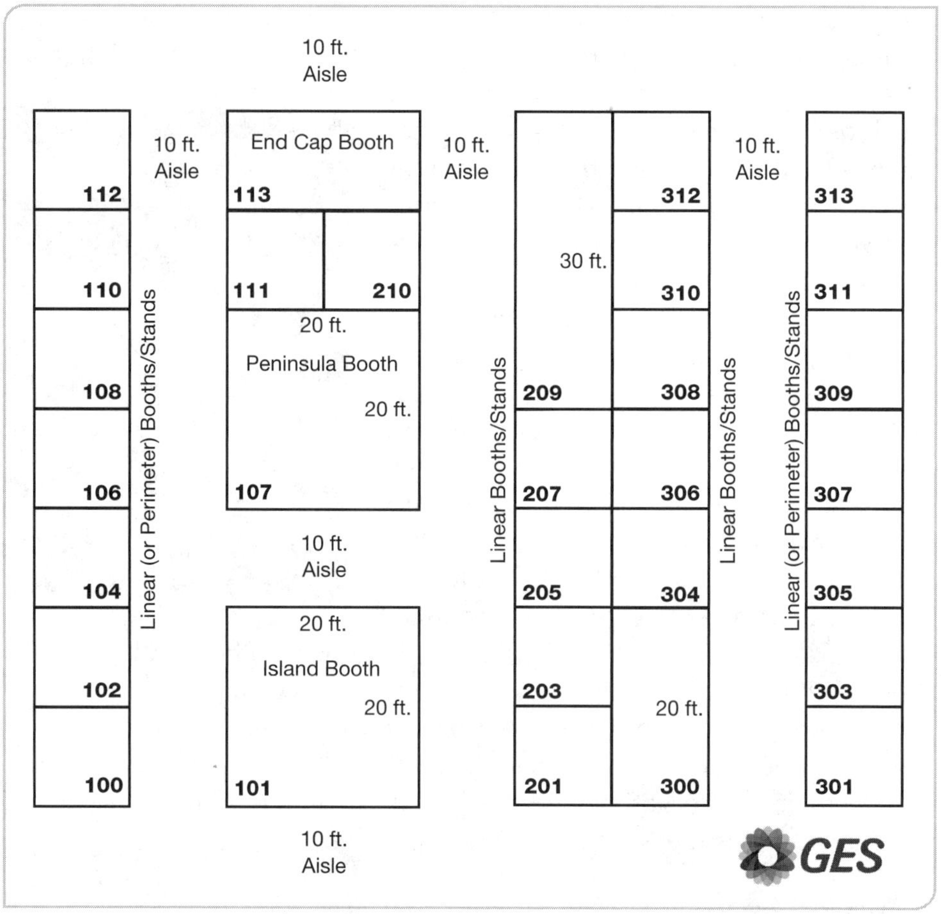

FIGURE 11.4 Floor Plan
A sample floor plan showing several types of booth/stand configurations.

edge of the facility. A facility site visit is an important part of the strategic planning process, as is collaboration with the facility's event coordinator and selected providers, e.g. **official services contractor (OSC)**.

Utilities The location and availability of utilities within the structure may be required to meet the specifications for the exhibit. Electricity, water, and compressed air can be accessed from floor ports, columns, or the ceiling. The locations and capacity of utility outlets will influence how a floor plan is designed.

Safety Compliance with local fire and safety regulations is required for such elements such as the minimum aisle size and number of accessible entrances and exits, as well as locations of fire alarms, fire extinguishers, and fire-hose cabinets. Regulations can vary from location to location and venue to venue. In the U.S., exhibition floor plans require approval by a fire inspector or fire marshal tasked with reviewing the plan to ensure that it meets local and state codes and regulations.

Logistical needs The logistical needs of individual exhibitors, as well as the dimensions of the spaces needed, must be considered. Logistical needs can include ceiling height or infrastructure for hanging signs or access to water or drains.

Facility layout The physical makeup of the facility, e.g., locations and sizes of columns, locations of entrances and exits, and permanent installations such as concession areas and digital signage, are important considerations in developing the floor plan (see Figure 11.4).

Feature areas Feature areas, e.g., association booths, food service seating areas, or registration areas, are designed to be located on the exhibition floor.

Types of Booths/Stands

There are three basic types of booth/stand configurations: linear, peninsula, and island.

Linear booth/stand A **linear booth/stand** is based on the 10-foot × 10-foot (or 3.05-meter × 3.05-meter) configuration. Linear booths are a maximum of one booth deep, though they may be sold in multiples, e.g., a 10-foot × 30-foot booth. Linear booths face just one aisle (with the exception of corner booths, which border two aisles). Linear booths that are located against the interior walls of an exhibit hall are also called perimeter booths.

Peninsula booth/stand A **peninsula booth/stand** generally includes a minimum of four booth spaces, featuring aisles on three sides, and with the fourth side bordering other booth areas. An **end cap** is the equivalent of two booths sold as a peninsula, so that the 10-foot × 20-foot (or equivalent) booth "caps" the end of the aisle, e.g., booths 113 and 212 would form an end cap booth/stand space in Figure 11.4. Many U.S. shows do not permit end caps, as it can be difficult to enforce standard **line-of-sight** rules.

key points

Types of Booths/Stands

- Linear
- Peninsula
- Island
- Perimeter
- End cap

FIGURE **11.5** **Large Island Booth** This photo captures large island booth areas at the Los Angeles Auto Show.

FIGURE **11.6** **An Exhibit for Servicing Association Members** An association-sponsored booth (PMA Centre) at the Produce Marketing Association's Fresh Summit.

Island booth/stand A stand-alone configuration or **island booth/stand** comprises a minimum of four booth spaces and faces aisles on all four sides (see Figure 11.5, p. 207). Large islands for indoor or outdoor exhibit space can also be referred to as "bulk space."

Exhibition organizers generally publish rules on how exhibitors can use their exhibit space(s). For example, regulations may include height, line-of-sight, hanging sign, and staffing restrictions, and local ordinances that govern specific types of products or processes in the exhibit spaces, e.g., safe food handling or fuel levels in vehicle displays.

Exhibits may be as simple as products or literature displayed on a table, or as elaborate as multi-level custom structures with hanging signs or lighting features. Budgets for exhibits can range from the nominal to millions of dollars to design, build, transport, and install.

key points

Sample Feature Areas

- Food and beverage service
- Demonstrations
- Internet and charging stations
- Publication bins
- Member services booths (see Figure 11.6)
- Poster sessions (see Figure 11.7)
- Lounges
- New product areas

Feature Areas

Feature areas generally refer to areas on an exhibition floor designed to help drive traffic, attract attendance, and meet the needs of the audience(s).

Feature areas may be sponsored by an exhibiting company or managed and paid for by the exhibition organizer based on the perceived value. When strategically selected and located, feature areas will enhance the attendee experience, increase the attendee "dwell" time on the exhibition floor, and increase exhibitor ROI.

Pavilions

Pavilions refer to groupings of booth spaces on an exhibit floor that have commonalities such as product type or country of exhibiting companies. Booths within a pavilion are grouped together to help attendees shop efficiently, or to share resources and save money. A pavilion organizer may purchase an area within an exhibition and help coordinate the needs of the participating exhibitors, subletting the space and coordinating the logistics. International pavilions are a common way for international exhibitors to test an exhibition or marketplace, as participation is relatively affordable and the logistical aspects are managed by a third party who understands the nuances of exhibiting in other countries. Pavilions may also be used to showcase new exhibitors or new products.

Exhibition Schedule

When held in conjunction with a meeting, a closely coordinated schedule helps to maximize exhibit traffic without drawing away from critical meeting elements. If exhibit hall traffic and the quality of the exhibit hall attendee are not perceived as adequate, exhibitors may not return.

Ways to enhance exhibition hall traffic include scheduling of "non-competitive" or exclusive exhibition hours, i.e., time that does not conflict with other meeting events. In addition, exhibition organizers might offer some or all of the following on the exhibition floor: receptions, refreshment breaks, meal service, meetings, educational sessions, and product or process demonstrations. Locating attendee

key points

Exhibition Hall Enhancements

- Receptions
- Refreshment breaks
- Meal service
- Educational sessions
- Product demonstrations
- Internet stations
- Charging stations
- Seating areas
- Career listings

FIGURE 11.7 "Virtual" Film and Poster Stations The kiosks in the exhibition hall at the American Society of Cataract and Refractive Surgery meeting allow physicians to view films and posters of surgical and procedural developments in a virtual environment.

resources on the exhibition floor may also attract attendee traffic; resources might include Internet stations, meeting rooms, seating areas, charging stations, and career listings.

Co-Location

As marketers become more discriminating in their selection of exhibitions, many mature exhibitions are looking for new ways to remain viable. One way is to co-locate with another meeting and/or exhibition that complements the meeting/event and provides a fresh audience source.

Co-location may be as simple as executing the two events in the same facility (or city) over shared dates. Or, it could include sharing resources like space, staff, suppliers, prospects lists, common areas, and social events. Exhibitions with overlapping audiences may exhibit at each other's events, or sponsor pavilions with crossover exhibitors. A new launch event may try to capitalize on the success of a larger event by locating in the same city and marketing to the established exhibition's attendees.

Exhibition Logistics

To ensure the success of meetings and exhibitions programs, the meetings, sales, marketing, communications, and operations departments must all work in concert, executing a carefully coordinated business plan. The teams must share a clear vision about the meeting's goals, budget, messaging, branding, and execution. Cooperation and clarity of ownership are critical in formulating the planned activities.

key points

Planning Activities

- Development of goals
- Budget alignment
- Site and venue selection
- Selection of vendors, suppliers, and other support services
- Schedule development
- Periodic checking for consistency of promotional messages

Site and Venue Selection

Many components impact the selection of the meeting and exhibition site and venue. When an exhibition is a part of a meeting, additional elements must be considered, including:

- Availability of suitable exhibit space with gross square footage to accommodate the exhibition's needs. Gross square footage is defined as the total available space within an exhibit hall or other area excluding physical encumbrances such as pillars. Net square footage is the total space available for sale or use after all aisles, cross aisles, and any other official needs, such as registration areas, are subtracted from the gross.
- Availability of dates, including suitable time to accommodate exhibition move-in and move-out
- Suitable physical components for the exhibition's unique needs, e.g., dock space, **marshaling yard**, access to utilities, freight elevators, ceiling height, floor load capacity, and accessibility to meeting rooms

- Positive labor environment (see Exhibition Labor Force)
- Potential conflict with competing exhibitions
- Hotel-room block capacity for attendees and exhibitor personnel

Exhibition Service Providers

A variety of vendors or suppliers provide services to ensure an exhibition's success. Many services are provided for the exhibition organizer, exhibitors, attendees, host facility, and sponsors, or any combination of these participants. Several categories of suppliers or vendors may be part of the exhibition.

key points

Categories of Suppliers & Vendors

- Exclusive
- Recommended or preferred
- In-house
- Non-exclusive or discretionary
- Exhibitor-appointed contractors (EACs)

Exclusive **Exclusive** service means the service is provided solely by a designated provider.

Recommended or preferred **Recommended or preferred** service implies a "stamp of approval" from the exhibition organizer or venue.

In-house An **in-house** service provider has a presence within the facility and is onsite.

Non-exclusive or discretionary The services offered by **non-exclusive or discretionary** suppliers can be provided by a variety of contractors, as long as they follow the exhibition's rules and regulations, and are appropriately qualified and insured. For example, audiovisual services may be provided by the official or recommended supplier, or by a company selected by an exhibiting firm.

Exhibitor-appointed contractor (EAC) An **Exhibitor-appointed contractor (EAC)** is a contractor selected by an exhibitor to provide certain non-exclusive services for a specific booth space, e.g., installation of a complex exhibit.

Financial and service incentives may exist for exhibitors to use providers selected by the exhibition organizer. Incentives may include lower negotiated pricing or earlier access to the facility to set up the exhibit.

Support Suppliers/Vendors

Many support suppliers/vendors are required to execute a successful exhibition. The following suppliers represent a small example of potential participants.

Official services contractor (OSC) The OSC is also known a **general services contractor (GSC)**. As the demand for fully integrated marketing programs has exploded, OSCs have expanded their offerings to include measurement and marketing, experiential event development, brand development, and more. OSCs are selected by the exhibition organizer to support the needs of the organizer and exhibitors; some of their services are considered exclusive (e.g., material handling) while others are optional or discretionary (e.g., booth construction or booth installation labor).

Audiovisual (AV) contractor The AV contractor may provide many services, including event technologies, equipment rentals, sound and stage elements, custom lighting, content delivery, speaker services, digital signage, and virtual meetings. Audiovisual is a line of business that may be provided by the OSC or by an AV contractor. A venue may have an in-house provider or a recommended contractor that pays the venue a percentage of the revenue earned or provides other services in return for the recommendation. An in-house contractor may have an office and equipment storage space onsite and the in-house services are promoted by the facility. Audiovisual services are usually not exclusive, which means an exhibitor can select an alternative provider, if certain rules are followed, e.g., providing proof of insurance.

Caterer Generally, hotels and convention centers have catering services onsite that are considered both in-house and exclusive. A consistent provider of these services that knows the kitchen facilities, operates the concession stands, develops menus, and manages the food servers and staff is beneficial to the facility and exhibit organizer.

Security/crowd control Security is an important part of an exhibition, ensuring that only properly credentialed individuals have access to the exhibition floor, and there is a response plan in place for security issues and other emergencies. Convention centers and hotels have in-house security staff, but meeting professionals and exhibition organizers are usually able to use an outside security firm to replace, manage, or supplement the in-house staff for use within their leased space.

Telecommunications Traditionally, telecommunications services, e.g., networking, telephone, voice, data, and Internet services, are in-house and are frequently exclusive. Some venues permit an exhibition organizer to bring in a telecommunications or networking consultant or provider to assist with complex networking and connectivity demands.

Utilities Electrical and plumbing utilities are provided either by an in-house provider or facility staff, or by the OSC or another approved electrical provider. For safety and insurance reasons, licensed contractors must follow strict guidelines when providing utilities and other equipment.

key points

OSC Traditional Services

- Floor plan development
- Design and creative services
- Booth design
- Rental or sale of exhibit structures
- Banner and sign production
- Shipping/logistics services
- Material handling
- Electrical and plumbing
- Installation and removal labor
- Sign hanging and lighting
- Furniture and carpet rental
- Booth and aisle cleaning

PROFESSIONAL DILEMMA

A mature exhibition has been losing exhibitors and attendees steadily over the course of the last three events. A new exhibits manager has been hired to replace the long-time exhibits manager, who recently left for a different position. The exhibition has been held in the same city and venue for five years and is contracted for two more. What kind of changes should the new exhibits manager consider? What stakeholders should he/she consult? Where can he/she obtain information regarding what is working and what is not? Do opportunities exist for change although the exhibition must stay in the same venue? Can the exhibition organizer reverse the declining trends of the exhibition? Why or why not?

Photography The exhibition organizer selects an official photographer. Photographers and videographers are selected to capture important moments of the meeting and exhibition, and collect footage and images for marketing and social media use. Exhibitors also benefit from professional images of their exhibit booths. Additionally, video capture of meetings and exhibitions can provide a potential revenue stream via sales to those interested parties who were unable to attend all or part of the meeting.

Floral Meetings, exhibitions, and individual exhibits may be enhanced by the use of floral arrangements and greenery. The selected florist is usually not in-house and is in the category of recommended or official, but not exclusive.

Temporary labor Temporary labor sources can help an exhibition organizer meet onsite needs such as greeters, registration or information desk staffing, bag stuffing, or ushers.

Rigging/sign-hanging A unique skill set is required to safely install overhead exhibit features such as banners, hanging signs, truss work, and custom lighting and this is done by rigging specialists. These services may be provided by an in-house or exclusive contractor, or by the OSC as an exclusive service.

First aid To assist with medical emergencies, most facilities have guidelines for minimum coverage by either nurses or emergency medical technicians (EMTs) during an exhibition, including move-in and move-out times.

Shipping/logistics (domestic and international) The movement of materials from location to location in a timely fashion and at a fair price is the job of shipping or **logistics providers**, who handle domestic or international transportation. Logistics providers who work with

SUSTAINABILITY *in* Practice

Exhibitions present a number of unique challenges for green meetings. The first is scale; exhibitions can generate enormous amounts of waste including booth components, signage, accessories, product samples, handouts, and shipping materials. The second is securing cooperation and collaboration from a wide variety of participants. To create a sustainable exhibition, the meeting professional must collaborate, plan, and execute a variety of programs with a number of key stakeholders including:

- Destination
- Venue
- Hotel
- Exhibitors
- Exhibitor appointed contractors (EACs)
- Attendees
- Official services contractor (OSC)
- Exhibition organizer
- Caterer

The third challenge is formulating a plan to eliminate, recycle, or reuse/repurpose the massive amounts of physical material that is present at an exhibition, including the exhibits, samples, and collateral material. The fourth is minimizing natural resources usage associated with the move-in, set-up, breakdown, and move-out processes.

Specific areas that meeting professionals can address that are relevant to creating a more sustainable trade show or exhibition include:

1. Transportation, including travel of participants and shipping of exhibits; often the weight of an exhibit is less important than how it can be crated and shipped.
2. Exhibit design, including reusability, size, weight, and use of nonrenewable or hazardous materials
3. Food and beverage served, e.g., sustainable menu items, recyclable service items
4. General services, e.g., carpeting, signage, and plastics
5. Collateral, e.g., printed vs. available electronically
6. Waste diversion through donation or recycling of leftover samples and booth materials

The RFP and contracting process are opportunities to allocate responsibility and set expectations among the various stakeholders. Additionally, the exhibition organizer must ensure that everyone involved is working toward the same sustainability goals. Working with various stakeholders early helps gain buy-in for a more sustainable exhibition.

—Susan M. Tinnish, PhD

shippers to move materials between countries are often referred to as **customs brokers** or **freight forwarders**, as they assist with the process of moving materials through the customs process and are conversant in the regulations particular to the countries in question. Logistics providers use a variety of methods of transportation to move materials, e.g., ocean containers, airplanes, trucking and van lines, or local carriers, and deliver materials to the OSC's warehouse or directly to the exhibition site. From that point, the OSC provides material handling services to move the materials from warehouse or dock to the exhibitors' booths, store empty containers, return them to the exhibitors' booths at the close of the exhibition, and load the materials back onto outbound carriers at the close of the exhibition.

Exhibition Labor Force

Exhibitions typically rotate between cities, facilities, and venues, and the requirements for each event change with every occurrence. The production schedules for facilities and OSCs can fluctuate dramatically from week to week due to rotation, market and economic changes, and world events. Therefore, both depend upon temporary labor forces to supplement their part- and full-time staffs when work demand swells.

Work rules are quite complex and vary from location to location. In the U.S., a variety of labor unions claim jurisdiction over particular types of work in different locales, and OSCs and venues are signatory to labor agreements that guarantee certain work rules, pay schedules, and benefits to members of the unions that are engaged to work. Examples of unions that service the exhibition industry include teamsters, carpenters, riggers, decorators, sign painters, electricians, plumbers, and stagehands. Hotels and convention centers may employ housekeepers, food-service workers, bellmen, and others. The labor environment, pricing, and skill set can influence the city rotation selected by events. In recognition of this, cities with long-standing reputations for restrictive union rules and high costs, such as Chicago and Philadelphia, have endeavored to institute labor reforms that are more favorable for exhibitors and OSCs.

Measuring the Return on Investment

Face-to-face marketing continues to be an important part of the marketing mix, and exhibitions are a cost-effective way for exhibiting individuals and organizations to gain access to pre-qualified, targeted audiences. Potential exhibitors evaluate exhibitions based upon the audience profile, total attendance figures, estimated costs of participation, value of potential contacts, visibility, sales, and other elements that figure into the ROI calculation. An "ROI Tool Kit" was developed in collaboration between the PCMA Education Foundation, CEIR, International Association of Exhibitions and Events (IAEE), and

Marketing Communications/Sales Tactic (N=298)	Primary Methods Used Today
Company website	83%
Exhibiting at business-to-business exhibitions	76%
In-person visits to existing customers	75%
In-person visits to prospective customers	73%
Direct email	58%
Telephone calls to existing customers	57%
Telephone calls to prospective customers	54%
In-person corporate events (seminars, road shows, etc.)	52%
Social media outlets	49%
Print advertisements	46%
Public relations	42%
E-newsletters	39%
Online advertisements/E-media	38%
Sponsorships	36%
Online meetings/forums	28%
Exhibiting at business-to-consumer exhibitions	27%
Direct mail in general	22%
Direct mail that drives traffic to an online location	22%
Mobile devices	20%
Other	2%

FIGURE 11.8 Marketing Communications/Sales Tactics Research ranks business-to-business opportunities at an exhibition as second in effectiveness and, as a result, a strong marketing tactic ("Marketers Find Exhibitions," 2011. Center for Exhibition Industry Research. Reprinted with permission.).

Exhibit Surveys to provide exhibitors with tips and a more formal process for calculating ROI.

According to a 2011 study by CEIR (see Figure 11.8), exhibiting is second only to the company website in a list of primary marketing, communications, and sales tactics ("Marketers Find Exhibitions," p. 1).

Future of Exhibitions

The introduction of new technologies has had a major impact on meetings and exhibitions. While people remain committed to the face-to-face interaction of a meeting, technological advances are beneficial to meeting and exhibition organizers because they allow continuing contact and marketing efforts.

Virtual Trade Shows

A **virtual trade show** or exhibition is a hosted online event, generally in a web environment, designed as a marketplace to connect particular buyers and sellers. When virtual trade shows were first explored in the mid-1990s, some professionals were concerned that they would replace face-to-face events eventually. However, as the industry has evolved, virtual trade shows typically are held in conjunction with and supplement or extend the life of actual exhibitions.

key points

Trends and Recommendations

- Using data to design customized experiences
- Maximizing tie-ins with social media and technology
- Creating an experience that attendees *can't get anywhere else*
- Surveying audiences, responding quickly, and making them feel heard

Impact of Technology

As generations raised on technology enter the workforce, exhibitions must continue to reinvent themselves. According to John Graham, president and CEO of the American Society of Association Executives (ASAE), "One of the things ASAE has noticed is how the digital environment brings an added dimension to the attendee experience at trade shows through different expectations about what is delivered, what platforms the experience is delivered through, and in the case of social media, the ability to share their experiences immediately" ("Scenarios for the Future," 2013, p. 9).

PCMA's *PMM5 Postscript* (Tinnish, 2007b) lists the following technologies as ways to revitalize exhibitions: blogs, Flickr®, online maps, microsites, podcasts, social media, and webcasts. Mobile apps and other technology features contribute to extend the life of an exhibition to a 365-day virtual event. E-commerce platforms make doing business easier, whether simplifying ordering services for exhibitors or helping to close a sale onsite. Scheduling and matchmaking programs offer attendees the opportunity to plan their schedules, outline their exhibition visit, and arrange meetings in advance of their trips.

Hosted Buyer Programs

A hosted or VIP buyer program is a way to guarantee a core of qualified buyers, with all or part of the exhibition hours dedicated to private pre-scheduled meetings. An example is IMEX America, a major annual event in the travel and meetings industry, which hosts thousands of qualified buyers from around the globe, covering their travel and accommodation expenses.

Interactive Communities

Building a community is one method for drawing an audience and gaining event loyalty. Many pop-culture exhibitions, e.g., Anime Expo, Comic-Con, PAX, and VidCon, have active online communities that build excitement for the events. Finding ways to maintain and enhance that community year-round helps to extend the lifecycle of an exhibition and provides additional educational and content sharing opportunities.

SUMMARY

Exhibitions in all their iterations have survived for centuries by providing face-to-face marketing environments that bring buyers and sellers together. While individual exhibitions have come and gone as a reflection of changing market needs, the exhibition still is a highly successful and proven way to do business. An exhibition held in conjunction with a meeting provides an extension of the educational experience that adds measurable value to the attendee and the exhibitor.

KEY WORDS

booth/stand
business-to-business (B2B)
business-to-consumer (B2C)
co-location
customs broker
end cap
exclusive provider
exhibition
exhibitor-appointed contractor (EAC)
exposition
freight forwarder
general service contractor (GSC)
horizontal exhibition
in-house provider
island booth/stand
linear booth/stand
line-of-sight
logistics provider
marshaling yard
non-exclusive or discretionary provider
official services contractor (OSC)
pavilion
peninsula booth/stand
priority-points
recommended or preferred provider
trade fair
trade show
vertical exhibition
virtual trade show

DISCUSSION QUESTIONS

1. What value can an exhibition add to a meeting or event?
2. What feature areas could enhance traffic on the exhibition floor?
3. What information does an exhibition organizer need to know about potential attendees?

12 Bring Meetings to Life: Event Technology

Anthony Miller
Chief Marketing Officer
Lanyon

Richard D. Reid
Vice President, Digital Services
Freeman

Rich Tate
Director of Marketing & Creative
Alford Media Services, Inc.

Rebecca Ferguson
Content Marketer

Main Topics

PART ONE DESIGNING THE MEETING EXPERIENCE: EVENT TECHNOLOGY

- Shaping Technology to the Audience
- Before the Event
- During the Event
- After the Event
- Big Data and Event-Management Software

PART TWO BACK TO THE BASICS: AUDIOVISUAL SERVICES

- Video
- Audio
- Lighting
- Associated Technologies and Services

Learner Outcomes

Upon the completion of this chapter, the student should be able to:

1. Identify relevant event technology tools and services that are available to meeting professionals.
2. Describe how event technology is used to shape the meeting experience.
3. Explain the collaboration of event technology paired with meeting management that translates to return on investment.
4. Discuss event technology tools and services available for planning before, during, and after the meeting.
5. Distinguish audiovisual service components that are common in production.

CMP INTERNATIONAL STANDARDS

Domain A. Strategic Planning
Skill 2. Develop Sustainability Plan for Meeting or Event
  SubSkills. 2.01, 2.02
Domain G. Meeting or Event Design
Skill 18. Manage Technical Production
  Subskills. 18.02, 18.03, 18.04

Meeting professionals have something in common with military generals, firefighters, and airline pilots—they all have one of the top 10 most stressful jobs of 2014 (Adams, 2014). The good news is, the meetings industry is evolving and event-management technology is proving to be the meeting professional's new best friend. From event technology to audiovisual services, there are now tools at the meeting professional's fingertips to help relieve this stress, and make the job easier and more strategic. These technologies are at the forefront of a new era in the meetings industry that allows for delivering more dynamic and personalized attendee experiences, as well as automating manual tasks and demonstrating the true value of meetings through real-time data and analytics.

PART ONE Designing the Meeting Experience: Event Technology

Now more than ever, meeting professionals must grasp the effect technology has on the meetings profession. As of 2014, research shows 87 percent of American adults use the Internet and 68 percent connect via mobile devices (Fox & Rainie, 2014). With the rise of adults who are comfortable with and capable of using technology, opportunities open for meetings to connect with attendees in various ways. To begin, the meeting professional must determine the most effective means to reach the preferred audience.

Shaping Technology to the Audience

There are several generations using technology today—specifically Baby Boomers, Gen X, and Millennials. How and where each generation uses different types of technology are crucial pieces of information that should help meeting professionals apply technology to enhance the meeting experience.

Use of Technology	Baby Boomers	Gen X	Millennials
	Born: 1946–1964	Born: 1965–1981	Born: 1982–2004
Experience	Novice	Tech savvy	Very digital
Internet usage[1]	88%	93%	97%
Smart phone owners[2]	40%	68%	81%
Social networking[3]	65%	78%	90%
Downloading apps[4]	11%–25%	40%	56%

1 Internet users in 2014. (2014, January) Pew Research Center. Retrieved from http://www.pewinternet.org/data-trend/internet-use/latest-stats

2 Lella, A. (2014, February). Why are Millennials so mobile? ComScore. Retrieved from https://www.comscore.com/Insights/Blog/Why_Are_Millennials_So_Mobile

3 Social networking fact sheet. (2013, September). Pew Research Center. Retrieved from http://www.pewinternet.org/fact-sheets/social-networking-fact-sheet

4 Rainie, L. (2012, March). Baby Boomers and technology. Pew Research. Retrieved from http://www.pewinternet.org/2012/03/28/baby-boomers-and-technology

FIGURE 12.1 Technology Use Across Generations Three generations attend or exhibit at meetings and events today. Each generation has different learning needs and styles, interests, and skill levels. The challenge for the meeting professional is to satisfy the expectations of each group so all are comfortable at a meeting.

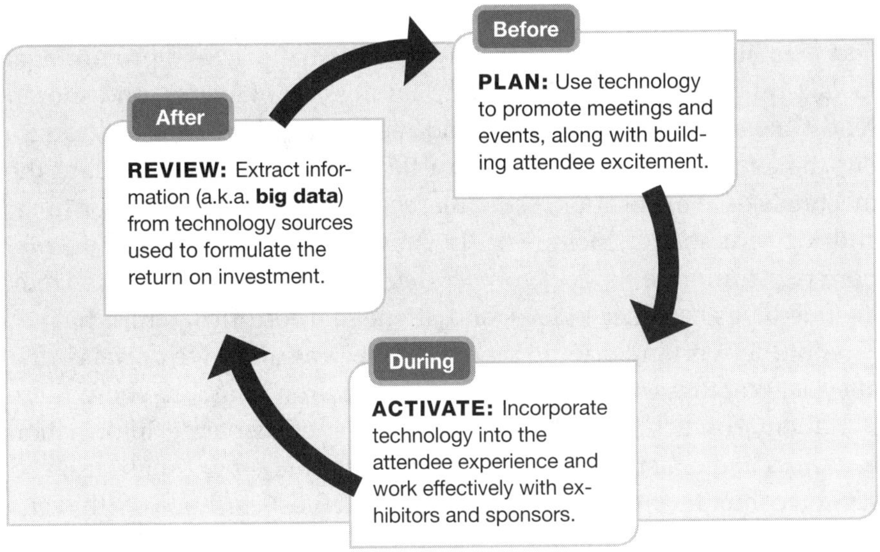

FIGURE 12.2 Technology Use Throughout the Event Lifecycle A defined plan for the use of technology before, during, and after the meeting or event should have high priority in the strategic planning process, as well as in each area of planning.

For example, Millennials have grown up with technology from a young age and have been surrounded by rapidly advancing technologies. Gen-Xers are considered tech savvy and are the first generation to fully embrace the Internet (Nisen, 2013), whereas Baby Boomers tend to be novices in experience with technology. Figure 12.1 illustrates the technology usage across generations, as a guide in shaping the way technology should be used at meetings and events.

At its core, event technology benefits meeting professionals as much as the attendees, exhibitors, and sponsors. Consider technology use throughout the event lifecycle as a gateway to an improved event experience from every angle—before, during, and after the event (see Figure 12.2).

Before the Event

Preparing for meetings and events includes a variety of tasks related to event logistics including venue selection, budgeting, promotion, registration, and presentations. Event technology enables the meeting/event professional to manage these tasks all in one place with transparency across the organization.

Selection of Technology Tools

Choosing the right event technology provides the meeting organizers and attendees with tools that streamline and elevate an event. Well-established and emerging technologies make connecting event organizers, session presenters, and attendees easy and more intuitive. There are numerous pre-meeting, organizational, and communication tools that provide content collection and management, access, and information sharing prior to the event.

Meeting websites and attendee portals Websites are the fastest and easiest way to deliver key information needed by attendees, sponsors, and exhibitors. The event website is one of the primary promotional tools, providing the first and lasting impression of events, and should reflect the same brand imagery and messaging that is used throughout the event. Content included on the website needs to explain the meeting's date(s), location, schedule, session highlights, sponsor titles, and logos; it should include a directory of exhibitors, hotel information, registration links, and contact details. Other optional pieces may include blogs, speaker videos, and attendee directories, which help to promote networking prior to the event. **Meeting attendee portals** bring attendee resources together in one online environment. Pre-show, these portal environments can house many types of disparate information resources like registration information, electronic program guides, and session content from prior events. Figure 12.3 lists technology that can be considered when building an event website.

key points

Checklist for Mobile Apps

- Raise awareness early by promoting the mobile event app with the website launch and email marketing.
- Send communications to attendees encouraging the use of the mobile app for setting up appointments and networking.
- Start a game through the app that begins before the event and finishes onsite.
- Use mobile apps to solicit real-time feedback from attendees.

Mobile apps With mobile usage on the rise, resources need to be aligned to provide access to information by attendees in a variety of platforms. These include event websites and online registration that are universally accessible on mobile devices and optimized for mobile viewing. To maximize the attendee experience, creating a **mobile app** is essential. Apps, which are accessible from smartphones or tablets, enable attendees and exhibitors to connect, schedule one-on-one meetings, and more. For meeting professionals, mobile apps enable event management on the go, distribution of event content, surveying attendees, lead management, and other tasks. Use the Key Points checklist as a guide for going mobile.

Presentation management and speaker resource center Presentation management services provide streamlined organization of presenter materials for meetings. Typically, presenters submit their materials in advance via a secure website. This tool also gives the person responsible for organizing the content a centralized environment that allows him or her to check status and communicate with event speakers.

Virtual event A virtual event is a specific kind of event website, which provides an online, interactive experience that can happen before,

FIGURE **12.3**

Key Technology Tools With a website as the primary vehicle to disseminate meeting information, the tools associated with Internet-based communication are many and varied, and technology continues to evolve. Professional meeting management requires continual vigilance and creativity to attract an increasingly technology-savvy audience.

Content management system (CMS) A CMS enables easy publishing, editing, and uploading of content to implement and maintain event websites.

Web buttons A web button serves as the call to action, e.g., to register or to download mobile apps.

Mobile-friendly sites As mentioned above, with 68 percent of adults in the U.S. accessing the Internet via a mobile device, it is important to make event websites optimized for mobile devices to be accessed anytime, anywhere.

Social media Embed links to the meeting or event's social media sites for easy networking, e.g., via Twitter® and Facebook®.

Search engine optimization (SEO) Use key words and phrases to boost the event website's rankings in search engine results.

during, or after an event. This type of website provides many of the same elements present in a physical event, including educational presentations, networking, and sponsorship opportunities. A "virtual preview" offered pre-meeting creates interest and raises attendance.

During the Event

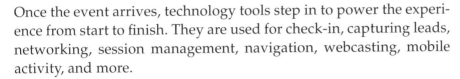

Once the event arrives, technology tools step in to power the experience from start to finish. They are used for check-in, capturing leads, networking, session management, navigation, webcasting, mobile activity, and more.

Onsite Technology Tools

During an event, there are a number of exciting tools, which provide convenience to the event organizer and help engage and interact with audiences in exciting ways.

Onsite check-in An essential way to alleviate long check-in lines and confirm attendance in advance is **onsite check-in.** This may be administered in two ways: self-service or during hotel registration. With self-service, attendees who register online may print a confirmation barcode from home or the office, then scan it onsite at self-service kiosks to quickly check in and print a badge and session schedules. Alternatively, arrangements can be made with partner hotels to set up event check-in during hotel registration.

Mobile apps The secondary usage of mobile apps takes place throughout the live event. Attendees can use the mobile app to access session and speaker information, maps, and personalized schedules onsite, allowing for real-time updates should schedule changes occur. Mobile apps also enable content to be distributed to attendees in real time, e.g., presentations, videos, surveys and polls, and social media.

Lead retrieval Think of **lead retrieval** simply as an exchange of information between attendees, exhibitors, sponsors, and event organizers. Lead retrieval facilitates capturing and managing contact information referred to as "leads," to develop existing and future sales or networking opportunities. Exhibitors/sponsors can acquire and manage these leads during events with real-time mobile badge scanning using Quick-Response (QR) Codes, 1-D barcode, or **near-field communication (NFC)** technologies.

Social media The use of social media at meetings and events should focus on engaging, communicating, and connecting with attendees. This applies to event-to-attendee, attendee-to-event, as well as attendee-to-attendee communication across platforms, e.g., Facebook®, Twitter®, LinkedIn®, YouTube®, Instagram®, and blogs. When building

key points

Social Media Strategies

- Integrate the selected social media platforms with the event website.
- Share content and collateral by uploading to the platforms.
- Create a #hashtag for your event.
- Use social media for customer service—attendees will provide opinions, both negative and positive, on these platforms.

the social media meeting strategy, the following options should be reviewed from an event technology perspective.

Gamification In basic terms, **gamification** means using games, social media, and incentives to create attendee engagement. For example, a scavenger hunt can be created on the show floor via the mobile app to increase exhibitor booth visits or collateral exposure. Or, points leading to prizes can be awarded for posting on social media platforms or providing speaking feedback. Event technology provides various ways to motivate more interaction and attendee involvement, delivering an enhanced event experience.

Presentation management and speaker resource center When presenters arrive onsite, presentation management systems provide access to presentation materials for last-minute updates and changes prior to session presentations. Once deployed, these systems typically provide tools to help meeting organizers make sure presentation materials are distributed to session meeting rooms.

e-Poster systems Another type of presentation management system is the **e-Poster system**, which extends the reach of onsite paper posters. These systems make posters available electronically to onsite and online attendees.

FIGURE 12.4 Wayfinding Kiosk Wayfinding kiosks/touchscreens can be strategically located throughout a venue to help attendees find their way. Alternate routes within the facility can help in managing crowds, assisting those with limited mobility, and even identifying emergency exit routes. User-friendly interface designs can be incorporated to push information to mobile devices.

Digital signage The **digital signage** system distributes information throughout the venue to stand-alone or networked electronic displays. Providing accurate and timely information is key for a successful event. These versatile electronic systems support multiple media options, e.g. text, graphics, video, and animation, while allowing instantaneous updates of information. Depending on where these displays are placed, they can provide timely and convenient access to meeting room schedules, weather and travel information, social media updates, sponsorship and advertising, and general event information.

Interactive applications Digital signs can also be set up with touchscreen interactivity. This is an increasingly common way to create interaction with the audience; it entices attendees to stop and engage with content like gaming, education, or general event information.

"You are here" **wayfinding** kiosks are a specific type of digital signage display that provides navigation information to venue attractions like the exhibition hall, using convenient touchscreen technology. With this type of display, attendees are quickly able to find booths, facility services, and session meeting rooms (see Figure 12.4).

Digital capture/streaming Providing attendees with a number of versatile ways to access a live meeting creates a unique opportunity to reach a wider audience. An on-demand or **real-time webcast** solution digitally captures audio, video, text, and graphics from live

PROFESSIONAL DILEMMA

An event is approaching in four months and planning has delayed the event website launch. The meeting professional wants to begin email marketing to announce online registration, providing a link to the unfinished event website. In his/her mind, every day wasted is a registration lost. The individual overseeing registration wants to wait until the event website is complete, the registration system has been tested, and all pertinent event information, e.g., location, dates/times, sessions, keynote speakers, and partner hotels, is uploaded. To ensure the best user experience and alleviate confusion, many questions arise. The meeting professional has the deciding vote. What is your choice and why? Would your answer change if you knew the online registration was already tested and working properly? Why or why not?

presentations for playback via the Internet or local area network. This content, when delivered via websites or within mobile applications, is highly customizable and can be made available 24/7, essentially extending the reach of events after they have concluded.

During the event, having twice as many people show up might sound like a good problem to have, but it is a problem, nonetheless. By capturing and **streaming** live content, event organizers have the ability to simultaneously broadcast to virtual viewing areas where audiences can watch live session-room presentations on remote screens and listen in with the use of wireless headsets.

key points

Onsite Technology Tools

- Onsite check-in
- Mobile apps
- Lead retrieval
- Social media
- Digital capture/streaming
- Simultaneous interpretation
- Audience response system (ARS)
- Mobile applications
- Virtual events

Simultaneous interpretation No matter where in the world an event takes place, **simultaneous interpretation** services give international attendees the ability to overcome language barriers by allowing them to hear a message delivered in one language translated into another language in real time. These systems create a multi-lingual environment by incorporating wireless, radio frequency or infrared equipment and combining it with microphone and participant **name-handling technology**. This digitally controlled group discussion system allows the moderator to control a discussion and identify the individual and microphone location from a video control monitor (Welker, 2006).

Audience response system Keeping an audience engaged in a presentation can be challenging in today's climate of "what's in it for me?" An **audience response systems (ARS)** connects presenters with their audience by allowing audience members to respond to surveys or ask interactive questions using small, handheld response keypads provided to the audience in advance. Presenters embed questions or surveys in presentation slide decks and with the use of wireless radio frequency identification (RFID), the audience uses a keypad to provide immediate responses.

Audience participation through **short-message service (SMS)** and mobile applications has also become increasingly popular since attendees generally have access to their own mobile device. While this method of ARS interaction is generally easier to accommodate, instantaneous access to feedback could be delayed because of network latency or availability. One advantage to SMS and ARS is the availability of immediate tabulation of responses and closing reports. Additionally, the systems can be kept active after the meeting, for data analysis and sharing.

Mobile applications With more than three billion mobile broadband users in the world by the end of 2014 (ITU, 2014), there is a good chance that event attendees will be bringing along their smartphones and tablets to the next event they attend. There are a number of types of mobile event apps that will lead the way. Event-based mobile apps benefit both the meeting organizer and the attendee by eliminating the need to provide and carry the sheer bulk of printed materials associated with a meeting.

Meeting organizers can make immediate updates to content and provide real-time announcements and reminders to their audience. Attendees are able to access relevant show content on their own devices and have the ability to review and manage their personal session schedules. As with the use of wayfinding kiosks, the use of mobile applications can allow users to search for specific exhibitors and use built-in mapping to find their way to booths that feature products in which they have an interest. Newer generations of mobile applications also incorporate social media and gamification elements. Twitter® integration, for example, allows users to view all tweets using the event hashtag and may offer the ability to tweet directly from within the app. Typical gamification features include the use of leaderboards and scavenger hunts to encourage participation and collaboration between event attendees.

Virtual events Coupled with content collected via digital capture, virtual events provide the perfect extension to the physical event by providing an interactive online experience. Attendees can visit virtual website venues such as auditoriums, exhibit halls, lounges, and resource libraries. They can also interact with speakers and exhibitors through a variety of methods, including text and video chat windows, moderated Q&A sessions, and social media.

After the Event

Once the meeting is over, meeting professionals are responsible for collecting, summarizing, and sharing valuable event data and metrics. Understanding how the event was successful and what value the event contributed to the organizer has become a critical part of strategy and success. Meeting professionals measure the success of the event experience and the return on investment (ROI).

The use of event technology can help to validate the value that meetings bring to an organization, attendees, and sponsors. Specifically, event technology contributes with surveys, communities, and reporting.

Once the meeting has concluded, technology allows meeting professionals to extend the meeting far beyond the three or four days in which it physically takes place. These tools provide an opportunity to take a one-time experience and expand the life by providing access to those who missed it, as well as those who wish to revisit content.

key questions

ROI Measurement Questions to Ask

- If it is a customer-based meeting, how many leads and how much potential revenue did the event generate for sales? Utilize a customer relationship management (CRM) system for integrated data and analytics, i.e., pairing data with the analytics.
- If it is an internal meeting, how did the event help educate or train the employee to make them more effective in their role?
- In all areas, what was the ROI for attendees? Was the event of value to them? Did they learn something new and/or meet someone of value to them?

Online surveys Surveying attendees for opinions and feedback is the doorway into realizing the true attendee experience at meetings. Online surveys offer a fast and simple means for collecting this vital information. Figure 12.5 provides technology ideas for changing manual tabulation of surveys to an automated process.

Online communities Creating persistent **online communities** through the event's website can help attendees stay connected after the event. Online communities help to create a dialogue within groups formed around common interests, content, organizations, or ideas that keep the conversation going after the event. When seeking an online community software platform, meeting professionals should ensure that the software integrates with event-management software, organization-management systems, customer databases, content-management systems (CMS), or customer relationship management (CRM) systems being deployed. Additionally, the interface of the software should be user-friendly for all experience levels.

Online reporting Intuitive and comprehensive online reporting is vital to measuring the success of meetings and events. The data can be dissected to distinguish attendance records, surveys, speaker engagement, and total meeting spend including hotel, food and beverage, and vendors.

- Electronic formats optimized for smartphones and tablets provide easy access.
- Pre-populated multiple choice or yes/no answers shorten response time and time spent analyzing the response data via automated reporting.
- Send test surveys to event organizers in advance to check for accuracy and improved delivery performance before they reach attendees.
- Provide an open area for comments as this allows attendees to provide feedback that may not have been considered.

FIGURE 12.5 Automation of Survey Responses This figure provides ideas for the transition to an automated survey system, which will provide better analytics and more useful information.

Big Data and Event-Management Software

The term "**big data**" refers to the information organizations capture, store, share, and analyze across the business. Meeting and event analyst Chris Dwyer, director of research and vice president of operations with Ardent Partners, said, "Big data is really just another word for business intelligence. It basically means taking data and converting it to actionable strategies" (Lanyon, 2013, p. 3).

For meeting professionals, big data can be collected through portals to gather attendee demographics, psychographics, session participation and evaluation, exhibitor visits, budget cycles, buying behaviors, and social media participation. Other areas may include hotel data, meeting feedback, and email marketing. All of this information is traveling through **event management software** such as registration systems, radio-frequency identification (RFID) chips, mobile apps, appointment schedulers, meeting cards, travel-management systems, communities, social media, and survey tools.

Consolidation is key—having a central software solution in place allows meeting professionals and stakeholders access to data in a seamless process. This contributes to greater efficiencies as less time and money is spent organizing and merging data.

As Dwyer also stated, big data is "using business intelligence to make strategic moves to improve events" (Lanyon, 2013, p. 3). Examples include 1) reviewing attendees' spending patterns for sales revenue, or 2) analyzing how many meetings contributed to an organization's ROI. Big data helps to endorse decisions for creating

FIGURE 12.6 Main Stage The main stage is the backdrop and focal point of a meeting. Technology and audiovisual support are the anchors, allowing all attendees to see and hear the proceedings as the program and entertainment unfolds.

new events or revising existing events based on total spend, attendees' needs, vendor costs, and more. By interpreting, managing, and evaluating event information, meeting professionals and stakeholders are able to plan for the future. Since every meeting and organization is different, the collection of data based on goals and objectives should be planned before the meeting to receive the biggest benefit of big data.

Event technology continues to excite this industry with innovative ways of awakening meetings and events. However, bringing these event experiences to life through technology would not be possible without the assistance of audiovisual services. In the next part of the chapter, we explore how audio, video, and lighting deliver meaningful experiences to attendees.

Back to the Basics: Audiovisual Services PART TWO

Audiovisual services are traditionally made up of three basic components: video, audio, and lighting. There are many variations of these three basic elements along with many related technologies and services like gobos, atmospheric effects, staging, and scenic pieces. Together, these individual pieces work seamlessly in conjunction with each other to present a fully immersive experience to the audience, as seen in Figure 12.6.

Video

Video encompasses a variety of formats including standard and high-definition digital video in numerous formats, high-resolution graphics, and 2D or 3D animation. Video, graphics, and animation are accessed via computers, tablets, or dedicated digital storage devices (Carter, 2014).

Projection

Projection is the most visible and high-profile component of video services. Projectors range in size and capability from simple, portable models up to extremely expensive and feature-packed projectors that are used to display the biggest, brightest, and clearest images possible. Projectors use bright, conventional, LED (light-emitting diode) bulbs and lasers to provide the light source that projects images on a screen. Projector placement can be either in the rear, i.e., behind the screen and not usually visible to the audience, or in the front of the screen in plain view of the audience (see Figure 12.7, p. 230). Front or rear projection is selected with consideration for a number of factors, including the size and shape of a venue, architectural elements, and audience orientation. Flat-screen monitors and

FIGURE 12.7 Stacked Projectors This figure shows the projectors through which the visual images come to life on the screen(s) and engage the audience.

LED panels are used for video display. The projectors, **monitors**, or LEDs receive video or graphics through a variety of sources like a computer, router, or switcher system.

Switcher

Even simple shows have more than one source of graphics or video, so a **switcher** or router is required to display each individual output on the screen. Basic switchers can take several inputs from different sources like a computer or video device and then send those signals to the screen. A set of buttons on the front of the switcher allows a technician to "punch" between the different sources. As the switchers become more complex and more expensive, additional features allow for more advanced effects to be used, like seamless transitions or a static graphic image. High-end switcher systems have enormous capabilities and have the ability to generate real-time special effects, picture-in-picture windows, text generation, and **green screen** effects. These systems require dedicated and specially trained technicians. A router is normally used in conjunction with a switcher and it routes signals from one device to several devices.

Digital Video

Playback of digital video is accomplished by using computers or dedicated digital playback devices. If video, graphics, or animation can be played back on a computer or tablet, they can most likely be shown on the screen at an event in a wide range of resolutions. Computers are standard sources for graphics like PowerPoint® or Keynote® presentations and there are even customized computer graphics systems like WATCHOUT that are designed specifically for creating and playing rich graphics or video content at live events. Tablets and smartphones are also being used to supply video and graphic content, often wirelessly during meetings.

Recording

Recording the entire meeting is an important part of many events. The highest quality recording comes from using dedicated, high definition, digital recording devices. While there are a variety of these devices available, they all work the same way essentially. Signals are routed from the switcher system to the recording device and a technician ensures that the entire meeting is recorded digitally in high definition. In larger or more complex shows, multiple devices will be used for backup and to record **isolated (ISO) camera feeds**. Quite often, a client will use this raw digital video to edit together a version of the meeting for other uses like streaming or archive purposes.

Cameras/IMAG

Cameras are a very import source of visual content at events. They are used to enlarge the speaker on the screen through **image magnification (IMAG)** so the audience can see him or her more clearly, and they also capture speakers from multiple angles. Cameras can be outfitted with different lenses to accommodate use either close or very far away from the stage. When multiple cameras are in use, a dedicated switcher system with an operator in place can switch between the different views, at the request of the technical director who is "calling" or directing the show.

Audio

Audio for live events is as much of a science as it is an art. Getting clear, even sound in a variety of venues with different acoustics and architecture requires talented and well-trained audio engineers.

Speaker Systems

Achieving crystal-clear sound is accomplished through a variety of technologies, with speaker systems being one of the most crucial (see Figure 12.8, p. 232). Speakers come in all shapes and sizes, but for corporate events, both **conventional** and **line-array speaker systems** are the most common. Conventional speakers are individual loudspeaker boxes with a traditional combination of woofers and/or tweeters, whereas line-array speaker systems are a series of loudspeaker elements that are configured in vertical lines and are programmed to provide a controlled, linear sound field. These line-array speakers are

FIGURE 12.8 Truss, Speakers, and Lighting The truss is installed from "hang points" in the ceiling and provides a safe structure to hang speakers, lights, and other equipment used to create the show.

used almost exclusively for live concerts, but events in large venues or outdoors can benefit greatly from these types of speaker systems. Additionally, to reach every part of a ballroom or event space properly, delay or repeater speakers are needed. These speakers are placed in locations to fill in where the main system does not reach, and the audio engineer programs the audio feed so that the sound will be synchronized with the rest of the speakers.

Soundboard

Audio consoles or **soundboards** provide the command and control for all of the audio sources (see Figure 12.9). Everything that makes a sound will be sent to the audio console before it is sent out to the speakers. The audio engineer will use the audio console to ensure that all of the sound is clear and that the levels are even. Everything from wireless and wired microphones, video sources, sound effects, and music playlists are all controlled, mixed, and routed by the **front-of-house (FOH) audio engineer** via the audio console. Additional audio engineers are present on larger events to monitor wireless microphones and crew communications and to mix the audio for musical acts.

Bands and entertainment acts often require additional, specialized audio equipment including backline gear, which includes items like guitars, amplifiers, drum kits, and other instruments. These acts also need extra speakers called monitors that sit at the front of the stage and face away from the audience. The band members use these monitors so that they can hear themselves when they perform. Quite often, a separate audio engineer is needed to mix the audio being played through the monitors. Additionally, bands and entertainment acts often need special microphones and microphone stands along with other special audio gear for their performances.

Microphones

Although wired and wireless microphones serve the same purposes, they require dramatically different set-ups and equipment to make them work. Wired systems utilize XLR audio cables that send the signal from the microphone to the audio console. Each microphone requires its own cable. Wired microphones are generally easy to set up and do not require a lot of additional equipment to function. Wireless or "RF" microphones use radio waves to send audio signals to the audio console via specially tuned antennas. Wireless microphones allow the presenters to have more freedom to move and reduce wire clutter, but are more complex to set up and must adhere to certain Federal Communications Commission (FCC, in the U.S.) frequency ranges. Many shows will use a mix of both wired and wireless microphones.

Music is an important part of any event. Whether it is walk-in music that plays before the event or specially scripted and timed sound effects, the audio engineer must be prepared to play audio from a variety of sources. Computers play a big role in the playback and organization of music clips, playlists, and sound effects in formats like .mp3, .wav, or .aif, to name just a few. Dedicated digital audio playback systems are

FIGURE 12.9 Audio Console The sound engineer controls the audio from this console, which is connected to microphones, speakers, and other media programmed for the show.

made just for playing back sound effects and music clips at the touch of a single button. Compact disc (CD) players, smartphones, iPods®, and tablets can be used as audio sources. The audio from the various video sources must also be routed to the audio console from backstage and the playback technician must work with the audio engineer to ensure that the audio levels are just right.

Lighting

Lighting is a special part of any event. It can add excitement and emotion to an otherwise plain or drab environment. Dramatic lighting can create mood and add splash, but it also provides the necessary illumination for the presenters to be seen by the audience and for the cameras and video to be viewed properly on the screen.

Lighting instruments come in all shapes and sizes and each serves a different specific purpose (see Figure 12.8, p. 232). Conventional lights use bulbs as their light source, while LED instruments have different combinations of light-emitting diodes that generate light. Conventional lights are used for creating an even wash of light across the stage, and, when combined with colored gels, can be used for up-lighting drape or scenic elements. While conventional lights can achieve different colors, they are hard to change quickly. Conventional lights can be dimmed up and down when they are connected to a dimmer rack. This rack is controlled by the lighting console and changes the electrical current sent to the lights to adjust the brightness.

LED lights are cooler and more energy efficient, and can be programmed to change color instantly by the lighting designer via a lighting control console. LED lights are versatile and provide lighting designers access to new levels of creativity in lighting design.

Additionally, there is an entire category of robotic (moving) lights that can spin and turn. These lights can be programmed and controlled to move slowly or quickly, change colors, display patterns, and be dimmed up and down. Moving lights provide dynamic effects and flashy displays, can be used to highlight specific points on a stage or in a room, and can be programmed to hit specific cues during a show.

The **lighting control console** is the lighting designer's artist's palette. Lighting consoles run the gamut, from very basic with simple controls, to extremely feature-rich digital workstations that are used to create fantastic and complex light shows.

Associated Technologies and Services

The end effect of a well-integrated technology component is enhanced with the final "dressing." The creativity of many individuals involved in the installation of the assembled pieces of equipment ensures the experience is maximized and memorable.

SUSTAINABILITY *in* **Practice**

The primary function of AV is to provide and operate lighting, audio, video, and other related equipment for meetings. A meeting professional must carefully consider the AV company and the equipment used and whether the company and equipment meet sustainability goals. Requiring suppliers to offer a few options will assist in making the most sustainable choices.

Suppliers It is important to develop an awareness of a manufacturer's dedication to sustainability and that the equipment is the most efficient in terms of energy usage. Other factors require consideration in selecting an AV supplier.

- Commitment to meeting/event sustainability, e.g., in the form of a policy or in the form of ISO-standard compliancy (ISO 14001, ISO 20121)
- Onsite recycling to support the meeting waste-reduction goals
- Limited use of hazardous substances in electrical and electronic equipment
- Limited use of packaging materials
- Support of sustainable transportation methods, e.g., green freighters
- Proper waste management
- Proper disposal of equipment, e.g., e-waste, batteries, videotape
- Local hiring practices that support the local economy (economic sustainability) and give back to the local community (social sustainability)
- Support of internal sustainability practices
    - Internal administrative/office processes, e.g., electronic communication and documentation, as well as two-sided printing
    - Commitment to reuse, e.g., packaging materials
    - Corporate social responsibility (CSR) initiatives

Equipment Factors to consider in evaluating equipment include life span, energy consumption, and cooling requirements.

- **Lighting** The most important aspect of environmentally sustainable lighting is a switch to light-emitting diode (LED) lighting. The upfront cost of LED lights is slightly higher, but light quality is not sacrificed and the life span is approximately 40 times longer than that of incandescent lighting; LED requires less solid and manufacturing waste. Careful planning and meeting design will help ensure that the proper amount of lighting is used (Pulse Staging & Events, 2007).
- **Audio** State-of-the-art equipment is essential for energy conservation.
- **Video** Several businesses and organizations deal with their obsolete electronic equipment in an environmentally, ethical, cost effective, and accountable manner, which includes erasing data and recycling materials.
- **Generators** Solar-powered generators or traditional generators using a blend of biodiesel fuel are now available to support outdoor meetings and events.

—Susan M. Tinnish, PhD

Scenic

The term "scenic" refers to a variety of elements that are used to dress up a set. Pipe and drape are the most basic scenic elements and they can provide a consistent background behind a stage. They can also be used to integrate screens or other scenic pieces into the set design. Other scenic elements can be custom-built pieces that match the theme of the event, and numerous pre-built, modular scenic systems can be arranged to create patterns and structures behind or around the stage. Large, stretched fabric that is similar to a screen can be used as a blank palette for the lighting designer to turn into almost anything with lights, patterns, and even video elements.

Rigging

Rigging refers to a **truss** (see Figure 12.8, p. 232) and other structures that are hung or supported by structural points in the ceiling; rigging can also be attached to a truss and other structures that are supported on the ground to raise equipment like speakers, screens, lighting, projectors, and scenic elements into the air. When using rigging from the ground, special motors are used to raise and lower the truss or structures from the floor up to the ceiling. Specially certified riggers are often required to hang and raise truss structures.

Staging

In the audiovisual industry, staging refers to the physical stage and accessories. Stages can be built from pre-fabricated, modular panels that come in standard sizes and heights or can be custom built for a specific use. Many venues like theaters already have integrated stages. Stages can be customized with different levels and generally require stairs and ramps for safe access and egress.

Much like stages, the seating for an event can be customized. When a client feels that traditional banquet-style seating or theater-style seating will not be right for the event, specialized seating can be employed. Risers and multi-level platforms can be erected that provide the entire audience with a dramatic and unobstructed view of the stage.

SUMMARY

Event technology plays an integral role in meetings and events for meeting professionals, attendees, exhibitors, and sponsors before, during, and after the event. The various stages of the event rely on different technologies to create greater efficiencies for meeting professionals and better event experiences for attendees than ever before.

By collecting and capturing business intelligence (a.k.a. big data) through event technology and event-management software, meeting professionals take giant leaps to improving meetings and events. This correlates to return on investment (ROI), improved cost savings, and enhanced attendee insights. The use of the right technology can take an event to the next level by providing relevant tools for the event organizer and his or her audience. These tools enhance the gathering, organization, and sharing of content and make communication and collaboration for event attendees seamless and intuitive.

There are a number of solutions that extend the life of the event before, during, and after the actual physical event. With proper use of these tools, a three- or four-day event can live on 365 days a year. Video, audio, and lighting, along with a variety of associated technologies and services, are used seamlessly together to provide a memorable experience for the audience and to present the intended messages clearly. Separately, each individual part of the audiovisual puzzle tells part of the story. While the individual disciplines require their own special equipment and expertise, they must work as a synchronized unit in order to provide a complete experience.

CONTRIBUTING AUTHOR

Jim Carter
Information Technology Specialist
Alford Media Services

KEY WORDS

audience response system (ARS)
audiovisual
big data
conventional speaker system
digital signage
e-Poster system
event-management software
front-of-house (FOH) audio engineer
gamification
green screen
image magnification (IMAG)
isolated (ISO) camera feed
lead retrieval
lighting control console
line-array speaker system
meeting attendee portal
mobile app
monitor
name-handling technology
near-field communication (NFC)
online community
onsite check-in
real-time webcast
rigging
short-message service (SMS)
simultaneous interpretation
soundboard
streaming
switcher
truss
wayfinding

DISCUSSION QUESTIONS

1. A meeting professional needs to inform attendees that a speaker session has been moved from one room to another the morning of the session. Describe three ways event technology can be used to alert attendees.
2. After a meeting takes place, the meeting professional requests attendee information on exhibitor booths visited. Explain the event-reporting technology that will supply this data.
3. A client informs you that he/she will have two different computers with content for the show and some videos to play off a DVD. There will only be one screen in the room. What kind of device will be needed to display properly each of these different sources on one screen?
4. Your client has a presenter who likes to walk around the stage when she speaks. You already know that the stage is 30 feet wide and that there will be at least 1,000 people in attendance. To ensure that she can move freely, be seen by everyone in the room, and be heard clearly, what combination of audiovisual technologies will be needed?

13

Food and Beverage Fundamentals

Erin R. Peschel, CMP
Events & Project Manager
Hospitality Democracy

Main Topics

- Determining Food & Beverage Requirements
- Selecting the Menu
- Planning Meal Functions
- Selecting Service Options
- Choosing Seating Arrangements
- Managing Beverage Service
- Purchasing Beverage Options
- Managing Liability Exposure
- Verifying Gratuities and Service Charges

Learner Outcomes

Upon the completion of this chapter, the student should be able to:

1. Explain the importance of determining food and beverage requirements for meetings.
2. Describe the factors to consider when selecting the menu for a meeting.
3. Identify the different types of foodservice events in the meetings industry.
4. Evaluate the various styles of service for meetings with food and beverage.
5. Categorize the different arrangements for alcohol to be offered at meetings.
6. Critique the importance of controlling the liability associated with the service of alcohol at meetings.

CMP INTERNATIONAL STANDARDS

Domain A. Strategic Planning
Skill 2. Develop Sustainability Plan for Meeting or Event
SubSkills. 2.01, 2.02
Domain G. Meeting or Event Design
Skill 16. Coordinate Food and Beverage Services
Subskills. 16.01, 16.02, 16.03, 16.04, 16.05

Most meetings will need some type of food and beverage (F&B) service. It can be as basic as dry snacks and nonalcoholic beverages for a refreshment break or as elaborate as an elegant, multi-course, sit-down gala dinner. The manner in which F&B is served can make the difference between memorable and mediocre (Shock, 2006).

F&B arrangements for meetings should support the objectives of the event and meet attendees' needs. The role of food service during a meeting will change due to a variety of factors, which should be considered when making F&B arrangements. For example, attendees at a corporate three-day training meeting need to be alert and comfortable; this requires balanced, nutritious, and appealing menus. However, an association holding a gala awards dinner has different objectives where the menu must be remarkable and create a celebratory atmosphere without the same regard for nutrition.

A catering manager works for the facility hosting the meeting and assists the meeting professional when making foodservice arrangements. However, the services of a third-party or outside caterer can be engaged if the facility does not have an exclusive caterer. Whether working with the facility's caterer or a third-party contractor, the meeting professional will provide the meeting's goals and objectives, as well as a history of the group's F&B preferences. The caterer, in turn, provides the meeting professional with options that will satisfy expectations, stay within budget, and comply with sustainability standards. In addition to the basics of date, time, and location, many questions should be answered through the RFP process, discussion, and the event specifications guide (ESG).

This chapter outlines the menu planning process, explores the various types of F&B service, and identifies key strategies to guide the decision-making process for food service that supports the meeting's objectives.

key questions

Questions to Ask About the F&B Function

- What is the meeting budget?
- How will the guests arrive?
- Will the meeting have a theme?
- Will VIPs be attending?
- Will the meeting be formal or casual?
- What time of day will the meeting take place?
- What are the demographics of the attendees?
- What type of service is preferred, e.g., buffet, table service?
- Is the meeting for business, networking, or social purposes?
- Will entertainment or presentations take place during the meeting?
- Will other scheduled activities precede or follow the meeting, e.g., a reception, a dance? (Shock, 2006)

Determining Food & Beverage Requirements

Food and beverage is one of the largest expenses associated with a meeting and extends beyond menu selection. The focus should be on creating a memorable experience. Achieving or exceeding the guests' expectations should be a high priority for the caterer and the meeting professional.

Once the meeting professional has outlined the requirements and expectations, and disclosed budget parameters, the catering manager will prepare menu proposals for the event(s). When the selections are confirmed, typically through the ESG, **banquet event orders (BEOs)** are made by the caterer for the meeting professionals' review and sign-off.

Operational Constraints

Selecting the destination and venue for the meeting are among the first decisions the meeting professional makes; selecting the caterer (when that is an option) and the menu(s) are decisions that come much later in the planning process. The destination offers both opportunities and challenges throughout the planning process, e.g., shrimp may be readily available at a coastal destination in parts of the world, while heavily spiced foods are the norm in other locations. The venue may offer a unique atmosphere but may also come with a variety of space constraints. Meeting professionals and the caterer must consider the movement of attendees to/from and within the space, and will decide if additional staff are needed to realize a smooth traffic flow, based, in part, on the menu and service style ordered.

The choice of the main course is important and serves as the starting point for selecting the rest of the meal. If the choices on the standard menu do not seem appropriate for the meal function, it is appropriate to ask for a customized menu proposal. When selecting F&B offerings, consider the geographic location of the meeting. Each region of a country has its own specialties and many attendees will appreciate the opportunity to sample the specialty foods and flavors indigenous to the location. On the other hand, the meeting professional will also need to consider some alternatives to heavily spiced foods, foods served raw when that is not the norm throughout the world, and other unique F&B treatments. Unique orders can be processed along with requests for special accommodations for a disability, e.g., no peanuts or peanut oil for people with an allergy to that specific food.

FIGURE 13.1 An Outdoor Luncheon Many venues provide the opportunity to enjoy the outdoors for a meal event, which allows attendees to be refreshed and enjoy the location.

If an outdoor venue is considered, an alternative location should always be planned in preparation for the possibility of inclement weather (see Figure 13.1). An agreement should be made with the caterer about when a decision is needed if the site needs to be moved indoors. Most caterers ask for a 24-hour notice, but this standard may be negotiated.

Calculations for Space Requirements

Most venues provide capacity information for available meeting space. However, meeting professionals should verify the calculations to determine if the stated capacity will be comfortable for attendees based on the meeting requirements, e.g., staging, aisles, dance floor,

	Comfortable Arrangement	Tight Arrangement	Uncomfortable Arrangement
Suggested Space Requirement per Person			
	13.5 sq. feet (1.25 sq. m)	12.5 sq. feet (1.16 sq. m)	11.5 sq. feet (1.07 sq. m)
Table Diameter	**Number of People per Table**		
60 inches (153 cm)	8 people	9 people	10 people
66 inches (168 cm)	9 people	10 people	11 people
72 inches (183 cm)	10 people	11 people	12 people

FIGURE 13.2 Arrangement Guidelines for Meal Functions with Round Tables
The figure provides the calculations for determining space, number of tables, and guests for a dining experience.

buffet, and AV components. If the initial space is restrictive, alternative space should be considered. Figure 13.2 provides the suggested space requirements for round-table seating at meal functions with common table sizes.

Selecting the Menu

The menu impacts the experience of the attendee. It will influence style of service, staffing, décor, equipment, room layout, and space utilization. Many meeting professionals begin with the menu selection rather than considering all the options and variables, whereas an efficient planning process would involve the catering manager with a full discussion about the variables associated with the space, the meeting's objectives, and options for F&B service.

The catering team will know the house specialties, current trends, budget constraints, and what works best in the space. This expertise can be invaluable, and partnering with them early in the process will make F&B planning and execution much smoother.

The Group

Even though the catering team can provide excellent ideas for the meeting, some information about the attendees will be required to help the team present the best options for the meeting attendees.

Group profile Maintaining a historical group profile, including feedback from meeting attendees and the F&Bs that were popular, successful, and appreciated, assists in menu selection. When historical information is not available, time should be spent surveying potential attendees to obtain information about their needs and preferences. It is time well spent for the large meeting, especially when the F&B will be formal and/or extensive.

Age and gender Building the demographic profile of the attendees provides essential information for planning F&B menus and style of service. Age and gender influence not only what people eat, but also how much they eat in a given setting.

Political or religious affiliations If this is a consideration for the meeting organizers and their stakeholders, it should also guide menu selection. For example, politically active groups may require only sustainable food products, while some religious groups' beliefs do not allow consumption of certain food products or may specify changes in the preparation process. These standards for F&B are critical considerations for many people and should be honored when appropriate and possible to do so.

Food Allergies and Dietary Restrictions

Knowing the group profile will guide menu selection, as attendees, due to allergies, health-related issues, or lifestyle, may not consume certain foods.

A nonprofit organization, Food Allergy Research & Education, cites several studies suggesting that the number of people with food allergies is increasing. A summary of research findings from 2006 through 2011 estimates that up to 15 million Americans have food allergies ("Facts and Statistics," n.d.). A food allergy is an adverse immune response to a food protein. Although most food allergies are relatively mild, some food allergies can be life threatening and should be taken seriously. People diagnosed with a severe food allergy may carry an injectable form of epinephrine (EpiPen®).

Since allergies and dietary choices are increasing among meeting attendees, selecting menus to meet a variety of attendee needs has become more challenging.

Several options are available to manage food allergies and dietary restrictions. First, ask attendees, when they register, if they have food allergies or dietary restrictions. Second, communicate with the caterer about food options that will meet specific needs of the attendees and communicate the importance of labeling buffets to include ingredients. Another precautionary step is to communicate with the caterer about the importance of the service staff having clear knowledge of the food being served and how to handle food allergy requests and dietary considerations.

key points

Common Allergenic Foods

- Milk
- Eggs
- Fish
- Wheat
- Peanuts
- Tree nuts
- Soybeans
- Crustacean shellfish

Nutrition

Nutrition is an important consideration for all meetings, but especially for groups that will be at a hotel or conference center for several days during a convention. Since virtually all meals during their stay will be consumed on the premises, special attention must be paid to nutritional requirements when planning menus. Many attendees will appreciate that alternatives are provided (Shock, 2006).

The current trend in food service is to use fresh ingredients instead of processed foods that contain preservatives and other additives. Today's consumers want fresh choices. Additionally, attendees are requesting healthier, more nutritious foods, although many attendees see eating out as an opportunity to change their routines and splurge a little. The key to satisfying attendees' nutritional needs, as well as their expectations for a special dining experience, is to serve a variety of foods in appealing combinations and appropriate portions.

Meeting professionals should be aware of the following common diets:

- **Lacto-ovo vegetarian**—This term describes the diet of an individual who does not eat meat, but may consume animal by-products, such as dairy foods and eggs.
- **Lacto vegetarian**—This term describes the diet of an individual who does not eat meat and eggs, but may consume dairy foods.
- **Vegan**—This term describes the diet of an individual who does not consume or utilize any animal products or by-products, including meat, eggs, dairy, honey, leather, fur, silk, wool, cosmetics, and soaps.
- **Kosher**—This term describes food prepared according to Jewish dietary laws and restrictions.
- **Gluten free**—This term describes food that excludes the protein gluten.
- **Diabetic**—This term describes the diet of an individual with diabetes, who must have a proper balance of carbohydrates, protein, and fat. Scheduling meal functions is very important for the diabetic attendee.
- **Religious preferences**—Many faith-based groups restrict consumption of certain F&B groups. Knowing the group profile will assist in making appropriate decisions. When the group profile does not include religious preferences, the meeting professional must trust the attendee to make his or her dietary restrictions known. The meeting professional encourages this communication by prominently listing a question about such restrictions on the registration form.

key points

Common Diets

- Lacto-ovo vegetarian
- Lacto vegetarian
- Vegan
- Kosher
- Gluten free
- Diabetic
- Religious preferences

Planning Meal Functions

Food and beverage will be ordered for traditional meals (breakfast, lunch, dinner/supper), as well as refreshment breaks, usually in mid-morning and mid-afternoon. However, the meeting might call for F&B service at odd hours, such as early morning and late

FIGURE 13.3 A Continental Breakfast Fresh bagels are a mainstay for a continental breakfast, along with other traditional items.

evening. Additionally, the meeting professional should be aware of dining schedules at the destination, as well as the dining expectations of attendees. When standard dining times are outside the anticipated arrival and departure schedules for most of the attendees, dining can become an issue for some travelers. The meeting professional could make arrangements for early arrivals and late departures or at least inform attendees so they can make their own arrangements.

Breakfast

Approximately 18 percent of adults skip breakfast in the U.S. (Institute of Technologists, 2012) while, historically, as many as 50 percent of attendees will skip breakfast at a meeting (Pizam, 2005, p. 211). They may prefer to sleep later or prefer to exercise. While this can be difficult to predict for a meeting that has no history, solid historical data helps estimate the number of attendees who will participate in breakfast, so the catering manager can plan accordingly and not waste food and money. There are several choices for breakfast meals.

Continental breakfast In the U.S., a **continental breakfast** is popular because it is fast and encourages prompt attendance at morning meetings (see Figure 13.3). The typical menu can be upgraded upon request. At least one attendant and a buffet table should be set for every 100 attendees. The typical breakpoint for setting up a second buffet is 120 attendees. Continental breakfasts usually run for 30 to 60 minutes. Many guests arrive within the last 15 minutes, so the tables should be replenished for this wave of attendees.

key points

Continental Breakfast Menu

- Coffee
- Tea
- Juice
- Bagels
- Muffins
- Danish
- Croissants

Full breakfast buffet A **full breakfast buffet** features two or three types of meat, two or three styles of eggs, one potato dish, three to six types of bread or pastry, cereals (cold and hot, with nonfat and whole milk), fresh fruit, yogurt, juices, coffee, and tea (see Figure 13.4, p. 246). A full breakfast buffet should be planned for approximately one hour.

FIGURE 13.4 Full Breakfast Buffet This photo depicts a full breakfast buffet where guests are seated at tables in the meeting room. Notice the use of serpentine tables for the buffet table to add additional visual interest to the presentation of food.

English breakfast An **English breakfast** includes the same foods as a full breakfast buffet and features action stations at which foods such as waffles, omelets, or crepes are made to order. It also should last about one hour.

Full served breakfast Some occasions call for a seated, served breakfast, e.g., an opening breakfast to kick off the meeting, an awards presentation, or a special speaker. This format, of course, will require more time for service and increase the number of servers (Shock, 2006).

Refreshment Breaks

The human body and brain react to movement, which can be achieved through breaks. These changes in meeting environment may provide a comfortable and productive opportunity for thought processing and networking, thus enhancing the meeting experience. Shifting focus, changing position, or any large muscle movement (standing, clapping) can be done in lieu of formal breaks. In a time-crunched environment, the meeting professional may be tempted to limit or restrict breaks; however, this is detrimental for meeting attendees. Breaks offer benefits for the following reasons:

- **Refreshing and attending to physical comfort**—The most traditional reason for a break is as a time to refresh and take care of physical needs. Participants cannot pay attention or be involved if they are uncomfortable.
- **Tightly packed, efficient meetings are not ideal**—The most efficient meeting may not serve an organization's long-term purposes. Allowing downtime in the agenda encourages people to mingle, share ideas, and swap stories. The term "the hallway track" is often used to refer to the benefit of informal conversation that occurs in the hallways, away from the organized meeting (see Figure 13.5).

The meeting budget will dictate what can be served. Many breaks include beverages only. Costs for breaks may be quoted per person or on a consumption basis. Paying for coffee by the gallon and pastry by the dozen is usually more cost effective than paying a per-person price (see Figure 13.6). The meeting professional usually requests that the set-up be completed at least 15 minutes prior to the scheduled break time, as a session may end early. The meeting professional must determine the quantity of F&B to order for breaks, and, while onsite, verify that what was ordered was actually delivered. When the master account is examined after the event, the meeting professional must check that F&B was charged appropriately (Shock, 2006).

FIGURE 13.5 Networking during a Refreshment Break Refreshment breaks should be of sufficient time to allow for networking—discussing the session just attended and visiting with other attendees about the next part of the meeting.

When people are hungry, they are more likely to become irritable. Well-balanced meals with adequate portion sizes leave attendees calm, satisfied, and ready to go back into session. Thoughtful consideration of refreshment-break menu options also makes a difference to help to stave off hunger, elevate the mood, and thereby enhance learning (Dallas, 2011).

LUNCHEONS

Luncheons provide attendees the convenience of remaining on the property and ready for the afternoon sessions. Prompt service is important in order keep the afternoon's programming on schedule. Approximately a 90-minute time period should be scheduled for a seated luncheon.

FIGURE 13.6 Refreshment Break This photo is an example of a beverage station where attendees can be served from both sides of tables configured end-to-end, thus avoiding lines.

If time is an issue, part of the meal can be pre-set prior to attendee arrival, such as salads and desserts. Luncheon buffets are also another option when time is compressed and allow attendees to attend to other activities or priorities. The catering staff can provide a variety of options for both hot and cold buffets. If the intention is to keep attendees on the exhibit floor or if they are moving to another location, box lunches are a popular option (Shock, 2006).

Receptions

Receptions refer to events where seating is limited and have the purpose of allowing attendees to mingle and network (see Figure 13.7). Receptions can be held as stand-alone events or held before or after a meal. Many meetings have an opening reception, often followed by a dinner. Such receptions allow people to gather and be seated at the same time instead of straggling into the banquet room.

FIGURE 13.7 An Elegant Reception The creative presentation of food accompanied by a floral display as the centerpiece significantly adds to the elegance and ambiance of a reception. The height of the centerpiece here makes it a dramatic focal point of the presentation.

The types of hors d'oeuvres to serve at a reception will depend on the available budget. When the budget is small, dry snacks, raw vegetables with dip, and cubed cheese with crackers may be appropriate. When additional funding is available, hot and cold hors d'oeuvres set on attractively decorated buffet tables strategically placed around the room will increase the free-flow movement of guests and encourage networking.

When budget constraints are important, providing distractions reduces the consumption of food and drink, e.g., dancing, entertainment, or music. A comfortable atmosphere for conversation can be interfered with when the volume of music exceeds a certain volume level. Typically, seating is limited at a reception to discourage guests from sitting and eating (Shock, 2006).

Today's chefs are constantly looking for new and creative options to help the meeting professional impress attendees. The meeting professional should work closely with the catering manager and the culinary team to create an experience for attendees that meets the goals of the meeting, but stays within budget.

Dinners

A plated dinner service is used for a more formal event. The chef should be consulted in creating the menu for this type of service. Since this is often the last event of a meeting, it should be a memorable experience—a spectacular dessert is often a great strategy to close the experience. Typically two hours are allotted for a formal dinner and may increase when entertainment, a program, or dancing is included (see Figure 13.8, p. 250).

SUSTAINABILITY *in* **Practice**

People Planet Profit

Menus No matter what the meeting's goal, inclusion of local, sustainable, and/or organic F&Bs signals a concern for attendee health, wellbeing, and productivity, as well as the environmental commitment of the organizer. Today's attendees expect to be able to choose good-tasting, fresh, and healthy foods that meet their dietary needs and preferences. These needs and preferences may be related to fitness goals, food allergies or sensitivities, or ethical concerns, e.g., a desire for meat- or dairy-free, hormone-free, non-genetically-modified, and low-carbon-impact foods. Most caterers and restaurants are attuned to these needs and are able to propose menus that include locally produced, seasonal, and organic options, sustainably caught seafood, and fair-trade coffees and teas. They do so within budget, using creative strategies such as reducing meat portion sizes or creating a signature hors d'oeuvre.

Service How the food is served is almost as important as what is on the menu. Sustainable practices include using china, silverware, glasses, and linens, instead of disposable plates, cups, and utensils whenever possible. This also sets a more elegant tone. If disposables must be used, biodegradable alternatives are widely available, but the meeting professional should make sure that composting is feasible in the meeting's location before making the investment. Requesting that water be served in pitchers or bubblers and avoiding pre-filling glasses is becoming a common practice that reduces both cost and waste.

Disposal Careful ordering and monitoring of attendance helps reduce waste; food and food-service waste that does occur should be recycled or donated. For instance, live plants or flower arrangements can be donated to a nursing home or school. Despite common misconceptions, unopened F&Bs can be donated to food pantries and shelters in many locations; however, appropriate precautions are recommended, such as flash freezing or refrigerating vulnerable foods. Under the federal Good Samaritan Act, good-faith food donations are protected from liability.

—Deborah R. Popely

A buffet dinner is an alternative option when a program is scheduled throughout the event. Traffic flow of attendees going through the buffet line is a critical consideration; however, this style allows guests to eat at their own pace. The addition of various themed stations with different menu items adds interest. This type of service must be carefully planned so that movement in the room does not interfere with the program.

FIGURE 13.8 Formal Dinner Setting This photo represents the ambience that can be created in a hotel ballroom with décor, lighting, and table settings, complete with audiovisual support to permit guests to see and hear the program that unfolds on the stage.

Current F&B Trends

Incorporating trendy F&B into an event is a great way to provide something new that will give attendees a unique experience. Again, knowing the group profile will guide decisions when integrating trendy foods. The meeting professional must be able to determine whether the attendees will appreciate a new or exotic experience (see Figure 13.9); otherwise, a lot of expense and time could go into planning a special meal that does not interest the attendees.

Keeping up with current trends can be a challenge. The meeting professional will consult industry publications for annual trend articles and be observant of foods served in restaurants; both methods can be a good source of new ideas. One trend that seems to be here to stay for the long term is healthy foods that include sustainable food options. There are a number of benefits to using sustainable food options. They minimize fossil fuel consumption, use locally grown foods, provide fresh food, often with improved flavor, and highlight local food specialties.

> **key** points
>
> **Top 10 Food Trends**
>
> - Locally sourced meats and seafood
> - Locally grown produce
> - Environmental sustainability
> - Healthful kid's meals
> - Gluten-free cuisine
> - Hyper-local sourcing, e.g., restaurant gardens
> - Children's nutrition
> - Non-wheat noodles/pasta, e.g., quinoa, rice, buckwheat
> - Sustainable seafood
> - Farm/estate branded items (Johnson, 2014, p. 27)

When planning daylong meetings, the food offered can greatly affect attendees' energy and concentration levels. Consider integrating "brain

FIGURE 13.9 Offering Something Different Surprise your attendees with unique options for a refreshment break. Healthy options are usually well received after a time of learning. An espresso bar, a smoothie station, or a popcorn treat will bring delight to attendees and help to add to the meeting experience.

food" in refreshment breaks as a step in creating a productive meeting, e.g., granola, blueberries, bananas, yogurt, peanut butter, dark chocolate, and energy bars. Integrating these foods is another step toward creating a productive meeting (Vining, 2011).

Selecting Service Options

The next step in planning a successful F&B function is to determine the style of service that best suits the event and the F&B selected. Considerations when selecting a service style include: program schedule, attendee expectations, site opportunities or challenges, time constraints, and budget. Figure 13.10 (p. 252) describes service types that range from the most causal to the most formal, with brief descriptions.

Service Ratios

When planning the food service, the meeting professional should ask how many tables will be assigned to each server and clarify the timing of service steps. Then, the meeting professional can create a comprehensive schedule that integrates service times with the programming schedule and any other special requirements. When details have been decided, the information can be verified by checking the BEO.

When the F&B function will be having introductions, speakers, or presentations, a request should be made to have the servers either out of the room or positioned at the rear of the room. In addition, request

Service Type	Description
Cafeteria Service	In this service option, attendees carry their own trays and select food from a display counter(s). It is similar to buffet, but service attendants serve food.
Butler Service	American style is a method of service where servers move among guests to serve food and beverages to guests (Goldblatt, 2001). Australian style is a method of service where servers hold a platter for the guests to serve themselves (Goldblatt, 2001).
Family-Style	Platters and bowls of food are set on the dining tables, from which guests serve themselves. Guests pass the serving dishes to each other.
Russian Service	The food is placed on platters in the kitchen or back-of-the-house. Tureens are used for soup and special bowls for salad. Servers place the appropriate plate in front of guests for each course. Servers return with the platter of food and serve moving counter-clockwise around the table, serving the food from the guest's left with the right hand. With this style of service, the server controls portions.
American Service/Plated	The food is plated in the kitchen and placed before each guest. Side dishes are used for bread and salad. Food is served from the left, beverages from the right, and all items are removed from the right.
French Service	This type of service is similar to Russian service. However, in this pattern of service, platters of food are prepared in the kitchen. Once in the dining room, servers serve the food from the platters to individual plates, then serve the plated food item from the guest's left.
Pre-Set Service	A pre-set service option allows plated food to be placed on the banquet tables prior to the seating of guests and reduces serving time. This type of service works best with plated menu items that can be served at room temperature. Consulting with the chef is important in making the menu selection to determine the length of time the item will remain fresh and retain a fresh appearance. Generally, pre-set items can withstand 20 to 30 minutes before the event begins.
Synchronized service (Also Known as Hand Service)	This service requires one server for each seated guest. The waiters carry only one plate to the table and, upon signal from the service captain, the plates are set in front of the guests simultaneously. When plate covers are used, they are lifted simultaneously (Culinary Institute of America, 2009, p. 157). This style of service is efficient, elegant, and costly due to the requirement for additional servers.
Buffet Service	The buffet service option works well in the right setting and for the right event. An assortment of foods is offered on display tables and is self-served. The guests are moving around, which tends to make the event less formal. Sufficient space is required to minimize the wait time and accommodate lines of people so the buffet tables should be positioned in a way to allow unrestricted flow and service. Generally, one buffet set is needed for every 100 guests. For more efficient service, have a separate dessert table away from the main buffet tables or provide dessert service with a coffee station later in the meal.

FIGURE 13.10 Description of Service Types The various types of services are outlined in this figure. Service styles are often mixed to add interest to the dining experience.

that at least one **banquet captain** remain in the room after the meal has been served, since assistance may be needed during the course of the program. The servers should be able to answer questions from guests with regard to the ingredients and preparation method of each menu item. This is particularly important when dealing with special accommodations, e.g., allergies to shellfish.

Setting the expectations of service requires an advance discussion and agreement with the catering manager. Figure 13.11 lists the rec-

	Minimum Service Level	Optimum Service Level	Table Service—Pour Wine with Limited French Service	Full French or Russian Service
Rounds of 8	1 server per 4 tables (1:32 ratio)	1 server per 3 tables (1:24 ratio)	1 server per 2 tables (1:16 ratio)	1 server per table (1:8 ratio)
Rounds of 10	1 server per 3 tables (1:30 ratio)	1 server per 2 tables (1:20 ratio)	2 servers per 3 tables (1:15 ratio)	1 server per table (1:10 ratio)
Bussing Staff	1 busser per 4 servers (1:4 ratio)	1 busser per 3 servers (1:3 ratio)	1 busser per 3 servers (1:3 ratio)	1 busser per 2 servers (1:2 ratio)
Buffet Service	1 server per 40 guests; 1 busser per 2 servers	1 server per 40 guests; add 1 busser per 2 servers		

FIGURE **13.11** **Recommended Service Staff for Optimal Service** Service ratios vary from facility to facility and depend upon the amount of spend for the event. Each caterer has a basic standard that should be reviewed during negotiations. Upon reaching decisions on menu selection(s), service types, and service expectations, ensure the details are contained in the written contract. This figure provides suggested ratios of servers to guests from several facilities.

ommended service staffing levels, which can change from facility to facility. The service level is negotiable and an additional charge may be assessed when a request is made to increase staffing and service levels. When a buffet format is planned, the meeting professional should arrange to have the room captains release guests by table, which helps to avoid lines and long wait times at the buffet stations. These details must be in writing and should be outlined in the BEO.

Catering Guarantee

One of the greatest challenges is to provide the catering manager with an accurate meal **guarantee** or the final number of guests expected. The head table guests and staff members should be included in the guarantee. Weather, popular speakers, or unusual locations may cause attendee fluctuations from year to year and skew traditional attendance patterns. It is the combination of historical data and current local situations that should be considered to calculate the final guarantee. During the planning stage, the catering manager will note the anticipated number of guests on the BEO and will request a guaranteed number of attendees between 48 and 72 hours prior to the event.

To ensure quality of service, guarantees should be as accurate as possible; also, this is the number that will determine the F&B charges. The average no-show factor is 3 percent, but that varies by the group and the destination. A guarantee that is too conservative can result in decreased service and altered menu options for the overflow.

Guarantee Count	Over-Set Percentage	Food & Beverage Plan
20 guests	20%	24 guests
50 guests	15%	58 guests
100 guests	10%	110 guests
200 guests	7.5%	215 guests
400–1,000 guests	5%	420 for 400 guests 1,050 for 1,000 guests
Over 1,000 guests	3%	1,030 guests

FIGURE 13.12 Suggested Over-Set Percent of Guarantee Count This table provides general guidance for over-set calculations, which should be discussed with the catering representative during contract negotiations and included, in writing, in the final contract.

The **over-set guarantee** is the percentage of guests that the caterer will prepare for beyond the guarantee number to accommodate additional or unexpected guests. The calculation is negotiable. However, an average over-set is 5 to 10 percent. The meeting professional must refer to the F&B section of the catering or venue contract for the negotiated over-set percentage. Typically, as the guarantee number increases, the over-set percentage decreases as indicated in Figure 13.12.

Choosing Seating Arrangements

key points

Common Seating Arrangements

- Formal
- Casual
- Open seating

Several seating options are available when planning an F&B event. Seating arrangements can have a significant impact on meeting objectives, as well as on the overall experience of the attendee. Historical information and feedback from attendees are good guides to selecting the seating arrangement for the event. Of course, the nature of the program, should the function include a program, might also determine the seating arrangements.

Formal Seating

The **formal seating method** means the meeting organizer pre-determines where each guest will be seated. This method requires a seating list in alphabetical order and table chart for staff or volunteers to guide guests to the proper table. Escort cards may be used to indicate which table the guest has been assigned; place cards located at each table indicate precisely where the guest is to sit. The meeting professional should arrange for a check-in table outside of the room to allow for distribution of guest badges and escort/place cards. In some cases, the use of radio frequency identification (RFID) badges, a reader, and a flat-screen display may replace the **escort cards**. The reader catches the code on the back of the badges as the attendee or guest approaches the room entrance, and the flat screen displays the corresponding table for that guest.

Another seating method often used for large and/or formal banquets is a **ticket exchange**. This allows guests to turn in a ticket by a pre-determined time to self-select a seat. This method can be accomplished in advance with a web-based or software-based registration system, and allows for a more accurate calculation of attendees, thereby saving on the cost of the event (Shock, 2006, p. 410). However, the event would need to be a multi-day event to allow the meeting professional adequate time to inform the chef about the tickets exchanged.

Casual Seating

The most casual method of arranging attendees for an F&B function is to **self-select seating** (see Figure 13.13). This allows attendees to socialize with whomever they choose. This method is most often used for breakfast and lunch functions. If networking is the objective for the meal, tables may be designated by signage allowing sub-groups to sit together and network.

A casual, reception-style setting may also be used for networking events that provide hors d'oeuvres. With this style, the room is set with some seating (usually smaller tables of 4–6 seats), cocktail tables, and soft-seating lounge chairs. The smaller groupings encourage guests to mingle, network, and socialize (Shock, 2006).

FIGURE 13.13 Networking Luncheon This networking luncheon included a box lunch and guests could be seated at a table of their choice.

PROFESSIONAL DILEMMA

Your association is hosting a prestigious annual meeting for 3,000 members. However, you also have a new CEO who does not know the members very well and wants to make a good impression. She asks for a one-hour, casual reception with "serve yourself" hors d'oeuvres prior to a highly attended formal evening meal. She wants a "cook-out" feel, reminiscent of a dude ranch, with a well-known country-western entertainer. You can't imagine anything less likely to be well received by the attendees. They are used to a formal affair, with expert service complete with expensive wines and an elegant dessert. What will you do—provide what the CEO wants or try to talk her out of it? What if you can't talk her out of it? How can you handle this event so your attendees eagerly anticipate it?

Open Seating

Open seating is an alternative for meetings that do not have a history or that have too many variables to determine an accurate guarantee. Open seating allows guests to sit anywhere in the room and provides one or more extra tables that are covered with tablecloths, but not completely set. Should the number of attendees go over the over-set guarantee, the service staff can rapidly activate the partially set tables and the paid count increases by the number of additional attendees that are served. However, with this type of arrangement, the meeting professional must accept that the additional guests may not be served the same meal as the rest of the group (Shock, 2006).

Managing Beverage Service

Careful selection of both alcoholic and nonalcoholic beverages can add to the success of a reception or catered meal. Again, the group profile will guide the decision-making process. The choice of whether to serve alcohol with a meal will depend upon the budget, the impression the host wishes to convey, and the guests' expectations.

The gender and average age of the group may influence many decisions. For example, younger guests may drink more than others, while older guests may prefer higher-end liquors. Consumption of wine and beer is more common than it once was. The location and season also influence preferences, e.g., individuals at an outdoor event will consume more white wine, while red wine is more popular in the winter.

The average consumption per person is three beverages during a two-hour reception. When wine is served with dinner, most caterers use a standard formula of one half-bottle of wine per person. However, when possible, the best situation is to obtain the history of the group for an accurate estimate.

Signature or themed beverages are popular, especially when the guests are from out of town. If the event has a theme, a signature cocktail can add to the overall experience. Additionally, a signature beverage can be a cost-saving option as opposed to a full-service bar. For a unique experience, beverages can be paired with the foods, encouraging guests to try combinations they may not have had before. Of course, nonalcoholic choices should be provided at any F&B function that serves alcohol.

The catering manager is a good resource on the latest trends in F&B and should be able to advise the meeting host on cost-saving measures. For example, if a keg of beer is trendy and fits into the meeting's theme, it could result in cost savings. Additionally, most facilities charge a corkage fee for beverages brought into the facility. This additional charge can significantly increase the cost of beverage service.

Purchasing Beverage Options

Several factors should be considered when selecting beverage options. Demographics of the attendees, event time, purpose of event, budget, and other activities before and after the event will impact the selection of beverages. Understanding and managing beverage service is critical to the overall success of an event and limiting liability issues for the host.

Cash or No-Host Bar

A **cash** (no-host) **bar** is one at which the guest pays the bartender directly or presents a ticket for each drink, obtained from a cashier. Tickets may be the same price for all drinks or the tickets may be color-coded according to a pricing structure for the available beverages.

Most facilities place a minimum on the number of drinks sold per bartender. If the minimum dollar amount is not reached, the organization pays the difference. The minimums should be negotiated at the contracting stage.

The per-drink price may or may not include a **gratuity** and may be only for house brands, rather than premium or name brands. The meeting professional must determine what will be served and what is included in the price.

Beverage consumption with a cash bar is generally much lower than when a host is paying the bill. When the reception is scheduled to follow a meeting, approximately half of the meeting attendees will stay for the event. Consumption typically averages one and a half drinks per person for a one-hour cash bar function (Shock, 2006).

Open or Host Bar

When a sponsor is hosting the reception as an **open** (hosted) **bar**, consumption increases, as does cost. A reception that occurs at the end of meeting with an open or hosted bar and hors d'oeuvres will find approximately 80 percent of the group in attendance, with the

FIGURE 13.14 **Bar Set-Up** This figure shows the bar area, which will include a bartender to serve guests with an array of options.

average consumption of two to two and a half beverages per person for a one-hour open bar (see Figure 13.14).

Per-person package The organization pays a flat amount per person for a set number of hours. Package options may include beer and wine only, or various types or brands of alcohol. The number of attendees for which the sponsor is charged will be based on the guaranteed number or the number of guests who attend, whichever is higher. When purchasing the per-person package, costs are known prior to the event and based on the guarantee. This method is most profitable for the facility.

On consumption The cost for the **on consumption** (per beverage) charge method is totaled at the end of the event and a single check is presented to the host. The meeting professional should negotiate the prices per beverage in advance. A common method to control cost and limit consumption is to provide the guest with a specific number of drink tickets. At the end of the event, the number of tickets collected determines the cost. Some problems, though, are inherent in this method. Some attendees may collect numerous tickets from attendees who do not drink or use only one ticket. This allows, or even encourages, alcohol indulgence. It might also allow underage drinking, if the audience consists of young adults, as well as older attendees.

Limited consumption bar With this method, the host organization establishes limits to the open bar, which may include a time limit, a fixed total cost, or limited selection, e.g., beer, wine, and soft drinks. When the limit is reached, the bar closes or is converted to a cash-only basis.

Beverage Service Charges

Generally, prices for alcoholic beverages are subject to service charges and sales taxes. Additionally, the venue may have bartender charge of \$100–\$150 per bartender and for a set amount of time. Should the host authorize extending the time, additional fees may be added to the final total. Depending on the flow of guests arriving, one bartender is needed for every 50–100 guests.

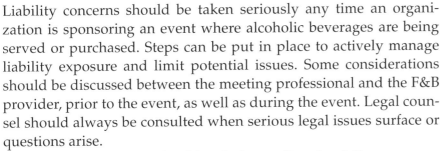

Managing Liability Exposure

Liability concerns should be taken seriously any time an organization is sponsoring an event where alcoholic beverages are being served or purchased. Steps can be put in place to actively manage liability exposure and limit potential issues. Some considerations should be discussed between the meeting professional and the F&B provider, prior to the event, as well as during the event. Legal counsel should always be consulted when serious legal issues surface or questions arise.

The catering contract should include wording that follows responsible alcohol service procedures, including but not limited to

- avoiding service to noticeably intoxicated guests;
- requiring the catering manager to request valid identification for any individual who may appear to be underage; and
- providing an indemnification and hold harmless clause that releases the host organization from liability that might accrue because of alcohol consumption.

Before the Event

The meeting professional should help protect the host organization from unnecessary liability exposure by following numerous steps before the meeting.

- Know the state liquor laws of the state.
- Verify the facility is licensed to serve liquor, e.g., ask for a copy of its liquor liability insurance certificate.
- Specify in the contract that the facility has control of the sale and serving of alcohol.
- Coordinate with the supplier on volume served for each category of alcoholic beverage, e.g., 1 ounce per mixed drink, 5 ounces per glass of wine, and 12 ounces per beer.
- Request that bartenders use **pour-control methods** rather than free-pouring to manage drink strength and limit costs.
- Limit alcohol distribution to trained servers.

- Limit the time of receptions serving alcoholic beverages to 90 minutes without food service.
- Arrange a drive-home service.
- Check liquor liability insurance—most general liability policies cover general host liability, which protects non-commercial servers of alcohol.

During the Event

Even during the event, the meeting organizer and beverage servers can take steps that limit liability exposure for their employers.

- Serve food that is high in protein, low in salt, and mild-to-moderate in spices.
- Monitor guests for intoxication issues or underage drinking. Correct the situation as quickly as possible when these issues do occur.
- Provide nonalcoholic alternatives.
- Close the bar before the end of the meeting and begin service of nonalcoholic beverages, including coffee and tea.
- Communicate to the catering manager when the bars must do a **hard close**.
- For groups that tend to linger, have the house lights brought up to full bright and diplomatically begin to encourage guests to depart.

Additionally, the meeting professional should monitor guests at the conclusion of the event for anyone who needs assistance. For receptions with many guests, contact a taxi or ask the concierge to stage taxi cabs near the entrance. If a shuttle bus program is part of the meeting, pickup stations should be clearly marked and the transportation partner should have staff onsite to direct guests to the shuttle stations.

Verifying Gratuities and Service Charges

Gratuities and service charges can be a substantial component of the F&B costs of a meeting, so the meeting professional should know the amount, how it is computed, and how gratuities are distributed. Typically, for large groups, a service charge will be added to the total bill and only part of the charge will be given to the servers. Generally, tax is added to service charges. However, in the U.S., tax requirements vary by state. The meeting professional must carefully search, prior to the meeting, for tax laws at the country, state, regional, and local levels. During the negotiation phase, the meeting professional should discuss service charges with the catering manager.

SUMMARY

A majority of meetings include some type of food and beverage function. F&Bs, and the manner in which they are served, can help make the meeting memorable and productive. When planning for F&B, the catering manager will assist the meeting professional in making appropriate selections. Meeting professionals should provide the catering manager with the meeting's objectives, as well as a history of the group's F&B preferences. Other details, including date, time, location, budget, entertainment, and presentations, will influence F&B decisions. The key to satisfying the attendees' nutritional needs, as well as their expectations, is to serve a variety of food in appealing combinations and appropriately sized portions. The catering manager can work with the meeting professional to develop menus that are creative, nutritious, and satisfying.

Service quality is just as important as food quality. Service at a sit-down function should be timed and efficient, especially if a program is planned. A variety of service standards and strategies can be deployed to meet the program's objectives and the attendees' needs.

The sponsoring organization providing alcohol service could be held liable if any guests become intoxicated and cause injury to anyone or damage to property, or if liquor is served to underage guests. Meeting managers should take appropriate precautions to ensure that the facility and caterer are following all applicable laws.

CONTRIBUTING AUTHORS

This chapter is a revised and updated version of Patti Shock's work in *Professional Meeting Management*, 5th ed., published in 2006 by the Professional Convention Management Association.

Kimberly S. Severt, PhD
Associate Professor
Department of Human Nutrition
& Hospitality Management
The University of Alabama

Patti Shock, CPCE, CHT, CGSP
Academic Consultant
The International School of Hospitality

Donnell G. Bayot, Med, CPCE, CHT
Director of Academic Affairs
The International School of Hospitality

KEY WORDS

banquet captain
butler service
cafeteria service
cash bar
continental breakfast
English breakfast
family-style
French service
gluten free
gratuity
guarantee
hard close
kosher
on consumption
open bar
over-set guarantee
reception
Russian service
ticket exchange
vegan
vegetarian

DISCUSSION QUESTIONS

1. If the facility has an exclusive caterer, but the organization (meeting host) needs a meal with a unique cooking method, what should/will the host organization and facility do to meet the meeting's objectives?
2. Plan a three-course meal in your location with sustainable foods. What food selections did you make? How might you alter these selections if attendees indicate they have common food allergies?
3. A common problem at meals combined with meetings is the need to see the screen (when AV is used) and the speaker when all of the attendees are seated around a round table for the meal. What options for this meal can you share, where all attendees can see the presentation, but eat comfortably at the same time?
4. Sharing meals that are uneaten with local charities and shelters is common. What are the potential risks associated with this practice and how might the meeting professional manage these risks appropriately?

Onsite Management 14

Susan A. Sabatke, CMP
Meetings Director
International Dairy-Deli-Bakery Association

Main Topics

- Onsite Management Functions
- Event Specifications Guide
- Communication Plan
- Communication Systems
- Signage
- Directing Meeting Activities
- Controlling Meeting Performance
- Record Keeping
- Staffing and Project Teams

Learner Outcomes

Upon the completion of this chapter, the student should be able to:

1. Explain the importance of an event specifications guide, including key components of final instructions to facilities and suppliers.
2. Discuss the purpose of pre-convention, post-convention, and daily logistical meetings and staff briefings.
3. Identify the three functions of event signage and how to effectively determine placement.
4. Implement an onsite communication plan.

CMP INTERNATIONAL STANDARDS

Domain A. Strategic Planning
Skill 2. Develop Sustainability Plan for Meeting or Event
SubSkills. 2.01, 2.02
Domain B. Project Management
Skill 4. Plan Meeting or Event Project
SubSkill. 4.06
Skill 5. Manage Meeting or Event Project
SubSkill. 5.03
Domain E. Human Resources
Skill 11. Train Staff and Volunteers
SubSkill. 11.01
Skill 12. Manage Workforce Relations
SubSkills. 12.01, 12.02
Domain G. Meeting or Event Design
Skill 17. Design Environment
SubSkill. 17.03
Skill 22. Manage Meeting or Event Site
SubSkills. 22.01, 22.02, 22.03
Skill 23. Manage Onsite Communications
SubSkills. 23.01, 23.03

Meeting professionals expend considerable time and energy during the development phase of a meeting, which is then followed by onsite implementation. Successful execution of a meeting plan is based on effective and timely communication of the goals and objectives, along with all necessary logistical details, to various members of the onsite team. If information is not communicated in an effective and timely manner, the work of planning the meeting may be compromised or rendered ineffective.

The meeting professional must manage communications effectively, both within the meeting-management team and with a multitude of suppliers who support the production of a memorable, smoothly running meeting.

Onsite Management Functions

Successful onsite implementation of a meeting can be compared to a beautifully performed orchestral piece. The meeting professional, like a symphony orchestra conductor, follows the score (the meeting plan) and coordinates the efforts of the orchestra (staff, volunteers, exhibitors, vendors, and other partners) to create a harmonious and extraordinary experience for the attendees.

Just as the symphony conductor must plan, direct, organize, and control all aspects of the performance, the meeting professional must have a clear and concise plan that describes how the meeting will unfold (see Figure 14.1). The plan should include a narrative that provides an overview of the organization along with the goals and objectives of the meeting and function schedules, i.e., day, time, room, set-up, and requirements for each function. This plan must provide complete details on all aspects of the meeting, so as to organize and direct the team while maintaining control (Tinnish & Ramsborg, 2008d, p. 113).

Event Specifications Guide

The event specifications guide (ESG) is also referred to as a staging guide. The "APEX Industry Glossary" (2011) defines the ESG as "the preferred term for a comprehensive document that outlines the complete requirements and instructions for an event. This document is typically authored by the event planner and is shared with all appropriate vendors as a vehicle to communicate the expectations for a project."

The purpose of an ESG is to provide the meeting professional with one comprehensive document containing the required information for the venue and other vendors or partners involved in the meeting. Some meetings may require more than one ESG if more than one facility is involved. A citywide meeting may require several ESGs: one for the main or headquarters hotel(s), one for the overflow hotels, and

FIGURE 14.1 Onsite Arrival of Meeting Professional Once onsite, the meeting professional will meet with the team from the facility. Some team members will be well known to the meeting professional by this point in the meeting's preparation, but others will be newly introduced.

one for the convention center or the location where individual events will take place (Mutnik, 2006).

An ESG can be prepared as one single document or as a compilation of several documents. Whatever the chosen format, each section of the ESG should be self-explanatory because some onsite staff will not require every detail of every component of the meeting. Only key personnel need the entire ESG.

Sections of an ESG include a general overview of the meeting sponsor and attendees, a profile of the meeting, a detailed schedule and listing of all onsite requirements, a list of key personnel involved in the meeting, staff responsibilities, and any policies of the sponsoring organization that relate to the meeting. Figure 14.2 (p. 266) provides more details about which meeting components are included in each section of the ESG, as well as other documents. The usual locations for these documents are described in Figure 14.3 (p. 267).

The information provided by the meeting professional in the ESG must be clear and concise and describe how the meeting will proceed. In essence, the ESG encompasses the full operational guidelines of the meeting and must be shared with all of the key individuals. This guide is the diary of every detail, as authorized by the meeting professional.

The ESG comprises a number of comprehensive function sheets. Each function sheet provides explicit instructions, pertaining to a single, scheduled event, session, or activity within the scope of the meeting, including all food and beverage requirements, audiovisual support, and function room set-ups. The final function sheets should be sent to the venue's convention services manager (CSM) or event manager (EM) at least five to six weeks prior to the meeting. This is the minimum time needed for the facility to review, question, and communicate the requirements to all the various departments onsite,

FIGURE 14.2 Essential Onsite Meeting-Management Documentation The event résumé and event specificiations guide (ESG) are two comprehensive documents outlining the complete requirements and instructions for the meeting or event. The remaining documents in the table are subsets and/or supporting documentation necessary to use and have readily available throughout the meeting or event.

Event Résumé	Event Specifications Guide (ESG)
✔ Meeting profile (inclusive of event name & published start/end dates) ✔ Attendee profile/exhibitor profile ✔ Key contacts ✔ Billing instructions ✔ General set-up considerations ✔ General expectations ✔ CSR policy & initiatives ✔ Transportation ✔ Shipping ✔ Housing list ✔ Exhibition component	✔ Function sheets ✔ Banquet event orders (BEOs) ✔ AV orders ✔ Electrical orders ✔ Telecommunications orders ✔ Room sets ✔ Signage list and distribution ✔ Furniture orders ✔ Utility orders ✔ ADA compliance ✔ In-conjunction-with (ICW) meetings
Staff Guide	**Communication Network**
✔ Contact information ✔ Assignments ✔ Delineations of responsibilities ✔ Frequently asked questions (FAQs) ✔ Orientation ✔ Facility(ies) map(s) ✔ Arrival/departure dates, times, flight itineraries	✔ Radio or mobile phones ✔ Walkie-talkies ✔ Channel identification & assignments ✔ Identification of key vendors on network ✔ Calling tree in case of emergency, cancellation, or change of the location of an event
Program Schedule	**Safety/Security/First Aid**
✔ List of speakers w/travel itinerary, arrival/departure dates & time ✔ Contracts ✔ Special needs ✔ AV requirements	✔ Risk-management plan for medical and other emergencies ✔ Primary contacts for emergency departments in host city & each venue ✔ Mobile phone, email, home phone, office phone for primary contacts ✔ Meeting room key distribution list ✔ Security schedule ✔ Personnel access list & times access is permitted to secured areas ✔ Lost & found
Production Schedule	**Supplies & Shipping**
✔ Move-in/move-out dates & times ✔ Rehearsal schedule ✔ Set-up—lights, AV, staging, other equipment, registration, exhibition hall	✔ Shipping manifest ✔ Distribution list of incoming & outgoing shipments ✔ List of office supplies & equipment
Meeting Apps	**Volunteer/Temporary Staffing**
✔ Program schedule, i.e., electronic version of final program book ✔ Daily schedule of events ✔ Facility maps ✔ Push notification procedure, e.g., cancelation or change in location ✔ Exhibitor data ✔ Calendar ✔ Social media feeds	✔ FAQs ✔ Training program (inclusive of safety/first aid plan) ✔ Orientation ✔ Identification of supervisors ✔ Escalation policy to staff ✔ Schedule of events ✔ Facility(ies) map(s) ✔ Interpretation skills list
Attendee Manifest	**Contracts**
✔ Attendee manifest list ✔ Emergency contacts (obtained from registration forms)	✔ All contracts associated with the event ✔ Electronic access ✔ Licenses and permissions

Headquarter Office	Speaker's Ready Room	Registration Desk
✔ Event résumé ✔ ESG ✔ BEOs ✔ Final program ✔ Frequently asked questions (FAQs) ✔ Facility(ies) map(s) ✔ Contact information for staff & suppliers ✔ Delineations of responsibilities for staff and volunteers ✔ Contracts with all suppliers	✔ Final program ✔ Contact information for staff who are assigned duties related to speakers ✔ Back-up of speaker's presentation ✔ Handouts ✔ Evaluation forms or apps ✔ Facility(ies) map(s) ✔ Instructions for speakers ✔ FAQs, specifically for speakers ✔ Staff/volunteers to "meet & greet"	✔ Contact information for staff ✔ Delineations of responsibilities for staff and volunteers ✔ Frequently asked questions (FAQs) ✔ Facility(ies) map(s) ✔ Final program ✔ Local information ✔ Badge pickup process ✔ Onsite registration ✔ Cash management system process ✔ Coat check process, when applicable
Information Desk	**Each Room for a Presentation**	**Signage**
✔ Local area brochures & maps ✔ Hotels information ✔ Transportation information ✔ Final program ✔ FAQs ✔ Facility(ies) map(s)	✔ Final program ✔ Back-up of speaker's presentation ✔ Introduction in writing for speaker (unless speaker introduces self) ✔ Evaluation forms ✔ Handouts ✔ Contact information for AV technician	✔ List of signage ✔ List of times, locations, & responsible person for placement ✔ International symbols visible

FIGURE **14.3** **Locations for Meeting-Management Documentation** Documents for the meeting may be provided in hardcopy or digital format. Some documentation may be needed in specific locations, e.g., at the head table in a meeting room, where a speaker may look for a copy of the final meeting program.

prior to returning a copy to the meeting organizer for final approval and signature. The facility will generate banquet event orders (BEOs) (see Appendix 4, p. 329), which are forms used to provide details to onsite staff reflecting requirements for each function at the venue.

Communication Plan

Successful onsite operations depend upon a well-defined plan for project management. Excellent project management is contingent upon thorough and frequent communication with staff, meeting venues, hotels, and suppliers.

Pre-Departure Meeting

A week or two prior to the departure for the meeting venue, the meeting professional should hold a **pre-departure meeting** with the organization onsite. The purpose of this meeting is to review key information about the meeting facilities, program, and logistics. The goal is to orient staff to all aspects of the meeting and provide clear expectations of each team member's responsibilities. The background information outlined in the Key Points box on the next page should be provided to onsite staff.

Once onsite, staff should tour the facility and become familiar with the meeting space, emergency exits, and all public areas. This is often organized as part of the **pre-convention meeting.**

key points

Onsite Staff Orientation

- Map of the area where meeting will be held with all venues highlighted
- Emergency plan for both medical and non-medical emergencies
- Floor plans of event venue(s) with details of specific events/activities in each space
- Summary of events and room assignments
- Onsite staff and support personnel job responsibilities

Pre-Convention Meeting

The pre-convention meeting is an essential meeting between the meeting professional and onsite meeting staff with the facility's key decision-makers and outside contractors. The purpose of the pre-convention meeting is to reconfirm all written and verbal details of the meeting, review the meeting arrangements, and provide an opportunity for all onsite staff and suppliers to ask any questions pertaining to the program. The pre-convention meeting is a time to resolve any last-minute issues. This meeting should establish the expectation that everyone involved in the execution of the meeting will operate as one team. Contractors must be included in the pre-convention meeting; their experience with other groups gives them an extensive knowledge base that allows them to contribute worthy recommendations and suggestions to the discussion.

A pre-convention meeting should be scheduled no later than 24 hours prior to the first meeting function, even for small meetings. For large meetings or citywide conferences, the pre-convention meeting may be held one week in advance, to allow participants an opportunity to review the information in detail before the start of the event.

Depending on the size and complexity of the program, separate pre-convention meetings may also be set up with individual supplier sub-groups, such as the OSC, DMC, multiple hotels in a citywide room block, and the transportation provider.

key points

Pre-Convention Meeting Participants

- Staff members, including members of meetings team
- Facility convention services personnel
- Facility sales manager
- Catering manager when the event includes food and beverage
- Audiovisual representative, if AV is required
- IT representative, if computer and networking are involved
- Sales and operations managers of destination marketing organization (DMO), if involved
- Safety/security representative(s) from all facilities and local municipal authorities, if applicable
- Key vendors, e.g., official services contractor (OSC), transportation company, destination management company (DMC)
- Others as appropriate

Pre-Convention Meeting Agenda

- Welcome and introductions
- Brief profile of organization and meeting overview
- Review of contracted room block and actual pickup
- Number of guests expected, main arrival and departure dates
- VIPs and special considerations
- Procedures for master account
- Meeting room activity update
- Food and beverage activity update
- Security/emergency preparedness plan
- Overview of facility services
- Review of function sheets and BEOs (with selected staff members)

Daily Onsite Meetings

Once the meeting begins, **daily onsite meetings** are important to maintain clear, frequent communication with the meeting team and suppliers' staff. These meetings provide the opportunity to discuss changes to the program, food and beverage orders, AV needs, and more. They are also times to review operations from the previous 24 hours and discuss possible improvements in communication or strategies for the following day's events. While these meetings offer an excellent opportunity to manage problems, they also provide a forum to build camaraderie and recognize team members for jobs well done (see Figure 14.4).

There are typically two types of daily briefings—logistical and staff—though if time is short, the meetings can be combined. Logistical meetings are typically led by the meeting professional and attended by key facility and contractor personnel, while staff meetings tend to include key members of the onsite staff.

If finding time during a hectic meeting schedule makes convening the staff each day too difficult, the meeting professional should develop creative solutions to share information and update the group. Flipcharts in the staff office can be used to highlight the day's activities and areas needing additional focus, while nightly emails provide an opportunity to recap the day's events and recognize staff accomplishments and support of the meeting's goals (Drew & Cooper, 2006).

key points

Daily Onsite Staff Meeting

- Evaluate the previous day's events and discuss any unresolved issues
- Review the current day's activities and highlight any cancellations/changes/additions/concerns
- Discuss the following day's activities
- Review responsibilities and procedures
- Reemphasize communication lines
- Congratulate members of the team (Drew & Cooper, 2006, p. 560)

FIGURE 14.4 Daily Onsite Meeting The daily meeting will include a review of what has happened to date and any changes that are recommended for the rest of the meeting. Care must be taken to have key team members at these meetings.

SUSTAINABILITY *in* Practice

While onsite management is at the heart of effective meeting execution, issues of sustainability are more nuanced and subtle. A meeting professional must consider the environmental, social, and economic consequences of typical onsite management practices.

Using the lens of sustainability, meeting professionals should grapple with the following issues related to onsite management.

- **Minimizing use of natural resources** Water and energy should be minimized in all onsite functions. Air quality should be protected.
- **Health and safety** The health and safety of attendees, volunteers, exhibitors, sponsors, and staff is the responsibility of the meeting organizer, as well as the venue.
- **Meeting-management practices** The meeting organizer's onsite office should be operated in a way to encourage sustainable practices.
- **Accessibility** Marketing materials, registration, the venue, and even access to technology can marginalize attendees. Failing to address access and inclusion-related issues can limit registration, engagement, and event growth, and may impact satisfaction.
- **Inclusivity** From marketing materials to selection of speakers, the people with visible positions during a meeting send a message about the organization's culture and diversity. Inclusivity is promoted by considering issues such as cultural, racial, and gender differences.
- **Harassment and discrimination** The meeting professional should promote equality to minimize complaints by attendees, volunteers, exhibitors, sponsors, and staff.
- **Fairness and equity in sourcing** Purchasing meeting-related services and products should be accomplished against a backdrop of transparency and fairness. Purchases should represent a strategic and effective use of funds. Sustainability means considering issues such as fair trade items, child labor, local purchases, and transportation. Labor practices of suppliers, although not immediately related to meetings, are viewed as a second-level concern around sustainable supply chain management. Considering the wide range of social and economic issues is an aspect of sustainable purchasing, hiring, and contracting, and will involve tradeoffs and complexity concerning fairness and equity (McKinley, 2014).

The sustainability team should address sustainability issues onsite. A well-prepared team will be able to deal with most issues and make changes as the need arises.

—Susan M. Tinnish, PhD

Post-Convention Meeting

At the conclusion of the event, the meeting team and key facility and contractor personnel should participate in a **post-convention meeting**. This meeting provides the opportunity for the organization to receive candid feedback on the logistics planning and onsite management of the meeting and to openly thank the supporting teams.

A staff debriefing can be held onsite or soon after the event, while details remain fresh. This debriefing gives staff the opportunity for input and allows the leadership a forum for extending a special thank you for everyone's contribution to a successful event. A "lessons learned" session during the various post-convention meetings provides an opportunity to make recommendations for future meetings and process improvements.

key points

Post-Convention Meeting Agenda

- Congratulate members of the team.
- Critique the facilities' performance and recommend improvements.
- Identify outstanding efforts made by the facilities' employees.
- Ask what information could have been provided earlier, or in a better way, to help the facility prepare for the meeting.
- Review the master account (Drew & Cooper, 2006, p. 560).

Communication Systems

Establishing a system for communicating with staff, facility contacts, and vendors is imperative. Without a well-designed communication plan, troubleshooting problems and quickly resolving issues as they arise onsite may become difficult.

Two-way and group communication technologies are developing as rapidly as other meeting technologies, so the meeting professional will benefit from expert advice in this area from technical contractors.

Staff members who need to be accessed frequently should be determined at the outset. Typically, key meeting personnel from the organization, facility, and suppliers are in constant contact and need to be accessible around the clock (see Figure 14.5). All onsite team members should have a list of key contacts, with instructions on how to reach them, so that the appropriate individuals can be contacted quickly, especially in the case of an emergency.

FIGURE 14.5 Communicating with Team Members A variety of technologies could be utilized to keep team members informed throughout the meeting, but smartphones and tablets are common.

Regardless of the communication equipment chosen, the meeting professional should arrange a test run in advance of the meeting to determine dead spots, coverage distance, and any interference that may cause issues. This test run allows time to make necessary adjustments prior to the start of the meeting.

Signage

key points

Types of Signage

- Identification
- Informational
- Directional

Clear and effective signage is needed to communicate with attendees and is critical to the success of any meeting. Signs serve to inform, protect, and direct people efficiently throughout the venue, while incorrect use of signage can result in confusion, frustration, and risks to personal safety. Figure 14.6 shows a situation in need of signage for effective crowd movement management, while Figure 14.7 demonstrates the use of directional signage.

Identification signs include the name of the event and the location of places, e.g., pressroom, general session, exhibit hall, and other function space.

Informational signs provide background data and/or instructions for the attendee. A sign displaying the exhibit hours is informational, as are signs with instructions denoting that the session may not be recorded.

Directional signs assist attendees in moving safely and efficiently throughout a venue as they attend general sessions, breakout sessions,

FIGURE 14.6 Crowd Management Moving hundreds or thousands of visitors in a locale that is not familiar territory can lead to chaos for attendees. Succinct signage facilitates orderly movement to various locations in the meeting space and is an important customer service at meetings.

FIGURE 14.7 Signage Augments Crowd Management Directional signage provides attendees with guidance on moving from one point to another.

meal functions, and other activities. Not all directional signs require copy—international symbols can often provide sufficient information to direct traffic (see Figure 14.8).

The proper placement of signage is critical to its function. It is important to anticipate such things as what the attendees are doing at the moment they encounter each sign, whether they are moving or standing still, what they may be carrying, and where their attention is directed when they encounter a particular sign. Knowing this type of information will help guide sign design and placement.

FIGURE 14.8 International Symbols As the world becomes smaller and the number of meetings and events attract international attendees, the signage must utilize a set of symbols that are globally recognized. The American Institute of Graphic Arts makes these symbols available for download at no charge to enhance communication and direction.

Directing Meeting Activities

The onsite meeting professional is responsible for directing all activities that occur onsite. In order to be effective, the meeting professional must be certain that all staff and volunteers have a clear understanding of their roles and responsibilities during the event.

To ensure that all expectations are clear, the meeting professional should develop a schedule outlining the daily responsibilities of each staff and volunteer member. This schedule should include the event or job location, date(s), exact times, and detailed responsibilities. Compiling a detailed schedule for each staff member and volunteer is time consuming during the planning stage but worth the effort once onsite. Amply sharing information with staff and volunteers results in a smooth and effective onsite management process.

In addition to written schedules, training sessions should be organized for staff and volunteers to discuss expectations and answer any questions they may have. Staff and volunteers should receive copies of all materials that will be distributed to attendees during the event and participate in a tour of the facility. Advance training should be planned for staff and volunteers on the basic facility questions, e.g., location of meeting rooms, restrooms, telephones, in-house restaurants, ATMs, shops, and emergency contacts. Additionally, preparing a list of frequently asked questions (FAQ) assists staff and volunteers with knowledge about the meeting. Meeting attendees expect staff and volunteers to answer these types of questions. The meeting professional has a responsibility to ensure that all staff and volunteers are adequately prepared and informed.

Controlling Meeting Performance

The size and nature of the partnerships created to execute one event should never be underestimated. Like the screen credits that roll at the end of a film, the list of people working together to execute a flawless meeting is long and impressive, e.g., staff, volunteers, venue partners (catering, operations, AV, security), hotel partners, OSC, Internet provider, transportation company, DMO, interpreters, photographer, and more. All work together to achieve the same goal—the execution of a successful meeting or event.

The final phase of onsite logistics is quality control. When onsite, meeting professionals must lead and motivate the team to ensure that everyone is doing all that is required to successfully implement the meeting. This is achieved by ensuring that meeting rooms are correctly set, speakers are briefed and ready to present, AV equipment is functional and presentations are loaded, attendees are greeted in a friendly manner and given event related materials, meals are served as ordered and are of the quality and quantity expected, and that attendees are networking, learning, and generally having a "good time" in a safe environment.

The meeting professional should use the daily onsite meetings to ensure that quality service levels are being attained and that any unexpected challenges have been correctly and completely handled.

PROFESSIONAL DILEMMA

A meeting professional contracts a destination management company (DMC) to coordinate all of the aspects of the closing-night party, including venue rental, catering, décor, transportation, and entertainment. The DMC was hired on the basis of a very impressive proposal and references from previous clients attesting to the company's ability to deliver a fantastic event. Two months into the planning, the meeting professional realizes the DMC overstated its capabilities and the references were perhaps more enthusiastic than warranted. What should the meeting professional do at this juncture to salvage the success of the closing-night party?

Communication is the best way to implement quality control and attain the desired results (see Figure 14.9).

The meeting professional will hear comments, suggestions, and criticisms. A procedure should be in place for staff to address delicate issues in a professional, efficient manner. This procedure should be presented during the pre-departure staff meeting, i.e., at a meeting held at the organization's office before staff and volunteers depart to the meeting's venue, and reviewed during onsite staff training. The meeting professional and/or staff should address grievances immediately, consistently, and thoroughly; a summary of these grievances should be addressed at the daily onsite meeting.

FIGURE **14.9** **Reviewing the Digital Format of the ESG** The trend is toward using a digital format for the ESG and other meeting documentation. This photo depicts the ease of answering a question in reference to a speaker requirement when all meeting details are available through the use of a mobile app.

Record Keeping

Onsite record keeping is the foundation of post-event evaluation as listed in the Key Points box on this page. These data should be documented for various meeting components as they occur. Careful post-event documentation will also streamline the reconciliation of final invoices.

Any information gleaned from the event will be useful in the planning process in the future. All changes should be documented, even minor issues, as staff may forget these and they may recur in the future.

key points

Post-Meeting Documentation

- Changes made to the ESG, including any services ordered but not provided. These should be documented in writing to the appropriate vendors.
- Final versions of the BEOs that include any changes made onsite.
- Actual meals consumed versus the guarantee; helps in establishing future F&B events.
- Actual beverages consumed for beverage orders billed on consumption.
- Attendance estimates for general sessions and breakout sessions; helps in planning future meeting space.
- Staff assistance; where additional help was needed or coverage was solid.

Staffing and Project Teams

Selecting knowledgeable event partners who understand the organization's goals and objectives is critical to the overall success of the meeting. An effective partner understands the needs of the organization, communicates solutions, and works within a specified budget. This team is an extension of the organization's staff and should be chosen wisely.

Some partners are pre-selected for the meeting professional. Hotels, convention centers, and DMOs generally assign a primary contact person to each meeting. The role of the CSM and EM is to assist the meeting professional with the coordination of meeting details and services before, during, and after a meeting. In addition, the CSM will identify which facility vendors are preferred and which are exclusive.

Local DMCs provide a wide range of services including tours, spouse/guest programs, transportation, décor, entertainment, printing services, VIP and attendee gifts, temporary staffing services, and offsite event coordination and management. A knowledgeable and resourceful DMC is an invaluable resource that can save the meeting professional money and staff time during the planning and execution phases of the meeting.

FIGURE 14.10 Volunteer Guiding an Attendee with Directions A well-oriented volunteer can be a valuable asset to the meeting when providing assistance to an attendee with a direction question.

Working with Volunteers

Peacy (2006) states that "managing volunteers is like managing employees in that volunteers need clearly defined jobs, orientation and training, supervision, and recognition for a job well done" (p. 122). Associations and government agencies are more likely to utilize volunteers than corporations, and some destination-based organizations may have volunteers as well.

Volunteers, when utilized, play a vital role in executing a successful meeting (see Figure 14.10). The meeting professional must consider the capabilities of and limitations of volunteers in comparison to paid staff. This will help determine which roles fit volunteers and which roles must be filled by staff. Volunteers should be placed in positions where they have the competencies to be successful. Determine when training and guidance are required and supply that well before the meeting. Provide support and direction to harness the passion that volunteers have for the organization (Peacy, 2006).

SUMMARY

Communication is the key to successful onsite meeting management. A complete ESG with explicit instructions, regular meetings with key event management staff, and a comprehensive communications strategy are used to ensure uniform knowledge and performance among various members of an onsite meeting team. Once this solid foundation is laid, expectations are effectively communicated, and staff and volunteers are properly trained, onsite meeting management can be a very rewarding experience. Not only will the goals and objectives of the organization be met, but the attendee experience will be positive and expectations exceeded.

KEY WORDS

daily onsite meeting
directional sign
identification sign
informational sign
post-convention meeting
pre-convention meeting
pre-departure meeting

DISCUSSION QUESTIONS

1. What is the purpose of the event specifications guide and who should receive a copy of it?
2. Who should be present at the pre-convention meeting and why?
3. What should be accomplished during a daily onsite meeting?
4. Prepare a list of signs for a meeting. How will the placement of signs and their content assist attendees to navigate around the venue(s) and remain safe?

15

Post-Meeting Follow-Up

Darlene W. Somers, CMP
Senior Meetings Manager
Association Management Center

Michael J. Dzick, CQIA, CMQ/OE
Conference Manager
The American Society for Quality

Main Topics

PART 1 CLOSING THE MEETING

- Return Shipment
- Rental Equipment
- Gratuities and Tips
- Post-Convention Meeting
- Paying the Bills
- Post-Event Report (PER)
- Thank You Letters
- Attendance Certificates
- Registration Reports
- Data Gathering With an Eye to the Future

PART 2 THE SCIENCE OF EVALUATION

- Meeting Evaluation
- Evaluation Planning
- Data and Samples
- Methods of Data Collection
- Data Sources
- Levels of Evaluation

Learner Outcomes

Upon the completion of this chapter, the student should be able to:

1. Develop detailed plans for organizing the return shipment and returning rented equipment.
2. Discuss the different data to be gathered from the hotel or meeting facility and the data's importance to future planning.
3. Discuss the reconciliation process of invoices from all vendors.
4. Identify possible data sources and data-collection methods.
5. Define the different levels of evaluation.

CMP INTERNATIONAL STANDARDS

Domain A. Strategic Planning
Skill 2. Develop Sustainability Plan for Meeting or Event
SubSkills. 2.01, 2.02
Domain A. Strategic Planning
Skill 3. Develop Business Continuity or Long-Term Viability Plan of Meeting or Event
SubSkills. 3.01, 3.02, 3.03
Domain B. Project Management
Skill 4. Develop Evaluation/Audit Procedures
SubSkill. 4.07
Domain F. Stakeholder Management
Skill 13. Manage Stakeholder Relationships
SubSkill. 13.03
Domain G. Meeting or Event Design
Skill 14. Develop Program
SubSkill. 14.04
Domain H. Site Management
Skill 22. Manage Meeting or Event Site
SubSkill. 22.04

The meeting that volunteers and staff planned for so long is finally over. The last attendee has left and the facility and meeting staff are moving on to the next meeting. Everyone involved is eager to return home and to the office. However, the work of the meeting professional is far from over. Prior to leaving the facility, the meeting staff must manage return shipments, disburse tips (if doing so), and make sure all rented equipment is returned properly. In addition to the work onsite to close the meeting, the meeting professional has many other tasks to complete upon return to the office. Invoice reconciliation and data gathering via the meeting evaluation process are major tasks in the post-meeting workload.

Meeting evaluation is a process that spans the entire length of the meeting-planning cycle. The scope of meeting evaluation should not be limited to the identification of whether attendees were satisfied with a meeting. Limiting the evaluation process to that perspective only sells short the contribution a thorough meeting evaluation could have for future meetings. A robust evaluation plan, when carried out effectively, produces information that can help with every aspect of the meeting-planning process. For that reason, the evaluation plan is a crucial element of the meeting process that should not be overlooked or minimized.

key points

First In, Last Out

A standard practice for a meeting professional is to be the first person to arrive onsite and the last person to leave, ensuring all aspects of move-in and move-out go smoothly.

PART ONE Closing the Meeting

Closing a meeting is usually a very busy time with everyone anxious to leave; the meeting staff is tired and wants to return home, and the facility staff is preparing the space for the next event. However, plans and systems need to be in place and ready to implement to ensure that the process of move-out and wrap-up is as efficient as move-in.

Return Shipment

Meeting professionals determine, in advance, the final outcome for each item used at a meeting. Some items, such as final program books, may be needed for future use when applying for grants or soliciting advertising. However, it may not make sense to ship certain items back to the office, e.g., dated signs or sponsored tote bags. A better choice may be to donate these products to a local charity or arrange with a local recycling company to pick up excess materials, rather than incurring return shipping fees and storage costs.

If the meeting professional has a multi-year contract with a decorator or official services contractor (OSC), the vendor may be able to ship and store items for the organization to use the following year. Additionally, the event facility may have a service that will manage outbound shipping, or the meeting professional may choose to manage the process. Regardless of the method, the meeting professional must monitor the tasks associated with shipping and the costs that will be incurred.

If the process is managed within the host organization, the inbound shipment to the event site should have included a return shipment packet and supplies, e.g., packing tape, permanent markers for labeling, and paper or bubble wrap to secure box contents. The packet may contain various blank shipping forms, **bill of lading** forms, return address labels, and blank content inventory forms with numbers for each box. A thorough packet will make compiling the information for the return shipment more efficient. The use of content inventory forms will help the meeting professional determine insurance values and amounts for the outbound shipment. Multiple methods of shipping may be necessary should certain items have time-sensitive delivery dates (see Figure 15.1).

FIGURE 15.1 Preparing for an Outbound Shipment Boxes and other pieces of equipment used to produce the meeting are placed on pallets, shrink-wrapped with plastic, and loaded for transport.

Walking away after affixing shipping labels on sealed and numbered boxes without transferring the care of the shipment to a responsible party can lead to missing items and/or delayed shipments. The return shipment process in not complete until it has been accepted by the storage facility, picked up from the OSC, or transferred to a vendor's vehicle (see Figure 15.2).

FIGURE 15.2 Loading of Audiovisual Freight An 18-wheel semi truck was backed into the exhibit hall to load the audiovisual and technology equipment that was used to produce the meeting.

Paperwork related to the return shipment, e.g., bill of lading receipts and completed content inventory forms, should be hand-carried back to the office, separate from the shipment. As an alternative, the meeting professional might photograph or digitally scan and upload copies of all paperwork. The meeting professional should create a shipping manifest that includes the contents of each box and tracking numbers of packages that are being shipped via a private carrier.

key points

Top Secret

Do any of the event products contain highly sensitive research data or unannounced product photographs? If they are one-use items that are not required to be retained for future use, shred the items prior to departing the event site.

For shipments leaving from a country different from that of the host organization, the meeting professional must be extremely knowledgeable regarding customs rules and guidelines. Additional time may be needed for the shipment to clear customs inspections at several points along its journey. The meeting professional may choose to engage the services of a **customs broker** to facilitate the process; the customs broker's expertise is to provide customs clearing services to shippers of goods to and from another country.

Upon delivery of the return shipment, the meeting professional will ensure that all boxes and their contents have been received intact. Should there be missing boxes, missing items, or damage to the shipment, the meeting professional should contact the shipping vendor immediately.

Rental Equipment

The meeting professional may have used rental equipment, e.g., computers, office equipment, and furniture, during the event. The pickup date, time, and location of these items should have been clearly indicated in all rental paperwork and confirmed with the vendor when the items were initially delivered. If the vendor is unable to pick up the items at the assigned time, alternative arrangements should be made to secure the safekeeping of the rented items until claimed by the vendor.

Gratuities and Tips

The words "**tip**" and "**gratuity**" are often used interchangeably, but there is a distinction. A tip is defined as a "voluntary and selective amount of money given at will for special or excellent service" ("APEX Industry Glossary," 2011). Tips are usually given as tokens of gratitude when service staff renders services, e.g., bellmen, valets, drivers, food servers, and other facility personnel. The tip is usually provided by the customer.

A gratuity is defined as a "voluntary payment added to a bill to signify good service" ("APEX Industry Glossary," 2011). Standard practice at hotel and event facilities is to add a gratuity to the food and beverage bill. This is typically an established percentage of the total bill and should be clearly outlined on any orders and invoices.

Regardless of the level of service, this gratuity will be included on the invoice, depending on the country and the facility's practices. Also, in some states in the U.S., tips and/or gratuities are taxable. State and local laws determine this practice. In some cases, a gratuity may only be taxable if it is added to the invoice automatically. In some states, how the gratuity is paid out to the servers will determine whether it is taxable.

The meeting professional must understand tax liabilities at the meeting destination to avoid unanticipated expenses. Additionally, tips and gratuities should be taken into account during the budgeting process.

key points

There are many reasons that the practice of tipping is worth getting right; one of them is easy to remember: TIPS means **T**o **I**nsure **P**rompt **S**ervice.

Recipients of Tips

A standard procedure for meeting professionals is to maintain a list of facility staff who went beyond the normal job responsibilities to ensure a smooth and successful meeting. The list is generated by the meeting professional in collaboration with the onsite staff and the facility's convention services manager (CSM). The CSM is a valuable resource to identify employees who demonstrated extraordinary efforts, but may have been unseen, e.g., overnight set-up crews. Tipping, for the most part, is an accepted and expected practice, but standards are strongly dictated by local culture. When in doubt, asking the CSM is a prudent course.

Typically, high-ranking facility staff, e.g., directors or vice presidents, are not included in a tip list. The CSM can explain the distribution or sharing of the food and beverage gratuity among the service staff, if at all. This has a bearing on the names of individuals on the organization's tip list. If the facility is owned and operated by a government entity, rules may be in place preventing an employee from accepting a cash tip. Gift cards or other items may be acceptable alternatives. Again, the meeting professional should speak with the CSM about the rules for tips and gifts in advance of the meeting. When tips are an expectation for quality service, the meeting professional may need to inform attendees about the practice in premeeting information materials.

Amount to Tip

The meeting professional's organization may also have a policy in place regarding tips, or there may a cultural expectation on the part of the organization's management team, e.g., cash tips may not be reimbursable for employees providing the tip. A clear direction on the topic should be established prior to the creation of the event budget. If tips are a part of the organization's culture, there should be a line item in the budget.

If there is a specific amount budgeted for tips, the following criteria helps to determine the amount of the tip for each individual.

- Number of food and beverage functions
- Number of meeting rooms used

- Complexity of room set-ups
- Number of room set-up changes
- The amount of lead time given for requested changes
- Overall performance and attitude of facility staff

Alternatively, an organization may determine tip amounts based on the following calculations.

- Set dollar amount per attendee
- Set dollar amount per sleeping room
- Percentage of total bill
- Percentage of total meeting

Method of Tipping

key points

Show Me the Money!

Where does the actual cash for the tips come from? The facility may be able to provide cash "paid out" for the purpose of tipping, which is generally charged to the group's master account.

Anytime cash is being handled and disbursement made, there should be checks and balances in place. The entire tipping process should be completely transparent to members of the organization. The meeting professional should disburse tips to facility staff with a colleague standing as witness to the entire process. There should be no question that any cash obtained by the meeting professional for the purpose of tipping ends up in the hands of those it was designed to reward.

To ensure transparency, the list of tipping recipients should be agreed on in advance. Additionally, at least two staff members should witness the transfer of money to the facility staff. If it is not feasible to distribute tips individually, the meeting professional may give the bulk of the tips to the CMS, with a list of recipients and the amounts to be presented to the employees. A copy of the tip list should be retained for the permanent files.

Tipping at Resorts or in International Settings

Depending on the location, tipping may not be part of the culture, may already be included in the facility charges, or may already be included in the attendee's guest-room rate. The meeting professional should ascertain in advance the tipping policy of the facility and should research the cultural attitude toward tipping. If the meeting organizer is covering tips for facility staff, the meeting professional should inform all attendees in advance, if appropriate.

Post-Convention Meeting

A **post-convention meeting** should be scheduled within two days to a week after the event, whenever possible. The date and time should be included in the critical path with appropriate facility staff, and should be confirmed prior to the meeting. The goal is to capture the most current information. The attendees of this meeting typically include key

SUSTAINABILITY *in* Practice

Most leftover meeting materials can be used again, but many items still get left behind or put in the trash. Materials could be reused or donated to local non-profits and schools. Reusable materials range from large items, e.g., furniture, appliances, and equipment, to smaller items, e.g., product samples, plants, bottled water, giveaways, and unopened food and beverages. Many cities have non-profit reuse centers that collect used building materials, hardware, and appliances for resale. Hotel toiletries can be donated to disadvantaged families and unopened food and beverages can be donated to food pantries and shelters in many locations. Some convention centers, hotels, and caterers may push back, based on fear of liability, but under the federal Good Samaritan Act, good-faith food donations are protected. Many facilities have enterprise-wide policies and procedures for donating unused food and beverages, so the quality and safety of the food and beverages are excellent. During the planning process, even before contracts are negotiated, the meeting professional should ask for information about the facility's ability and willingness to reuse and donate.

—Deborah R. Popley

stakeholders, e.g., the meeting professional, CSM, and other facility department heads. If the meeting was a citywide event, a representative from the local destination marketing organization (DMO) or convention and visitor's bureau (CVB) may be in attendance.

While this is not the time to point fingers and place blame if things have gone awry, it is the appropriate time to share expectations that have been met or exceeded. If expectations have not been met, specific details should be referenced, e.g., situation, names, dates, and times. These details will help the facility make improvements. If expectations were exceeded, those details should be shared as well. The meeting professional should ask the facility staff for a critique of the efforts by the meetings staff. Sharing honestly will help both groups improve.

Paying the Bills

The reconciliation of all invoices is a process that requires detailed and focused scrutiny. The facility personnel preparing the invoice may not be thoroughly knowledgeable regarding the contract, or any subsequent agreements between the parties. The meeting professional must maintain excellent notes during the meeting, should any additional charges be authorized. If any other event staff has authority to approve additional items during the event, accurate notes are critical.

1. All aspects of guest-room booking and occupancy
    a. Pacing of reservation booking, e.g., How many rooms were booked per week?
    b. Percentage of single-occupancy vs. double-occupancy rooms
    c. Number of suites booked and occupied
    d. **Pickup numbers**, e.g., nightly quantity of guest rooms occupied in the block
    e. Number of reservation cancellations
    f. Number of no-shows, i.e., guests holding reservations who failed to check in
    g. Guest-room audit, i.e., number of attendees booking rooms outside contracted hotels (ROCH)
2. Revenue generated at the hotel by group's attendees
    a. Room service
    b. Food and beverage outlets
    c. Gift shop
    d. Catering revenue generated by affiliates of the group
3. Number of security reports, e.g., physical injuries, theft, or other incidents
4. Amount of commission and/or rebates earned, if applicable

FIGURE 15.3 Hotel Data to Collect This non-inclusive list of data to capture from the hotel is essential as well as helpful in determining the value of the business to the facility. The meeting professional armed with specific data leverages the negotiation process and helps to obtain the best overall value proposition for future meetings.

A good way to minimize and correct errors in billing is to schedule a daily onsite review of all items charged to the master bill, e.g., a report detailing the number of guest rooms billed nightly, no-shows from the previous night, catering invoices for the day, and the daily rental of audiovisual equipment.

The facility contract should have listed very specific terms of payment for the master bill. Typically, for events based in the U.S., all undisputed charges are due 30 days from the date of invoice receipt. The facility should be made aware of disputed charges immediately and payment should be sent to the facility for the total amount of undisputed charges. Disputed charges may include a food and beverage event that did not belong to the group, or a charge for a suite that should have been complimentary according to the contract. The facility will research the disputed charges and either send documentation to explain or remove the charge. The host organization must adhere to the specific terms of payment in order to maintain a good credit history. If an attrition or performance penalty has been added to the invoice and more detailed information is necessary from the facility, the payment of undisputed charges should be paid according to the contractual agreement.

The invoice provided by the facility should contain complete backup documentation for all charges, e.g., individual catering checks attached to the catering section and guest-room folios attached to the guest-room section. Some facilities will include commissions or rebates due the group as a credit on the invoice, while others pay commissions or rebates only after the master bill has been paid in full. The details should be clearly outlined in the facility contract.

Any staff that had incidentals, i.e., expenses other than room and tax, billed to their room should be provided a copy of their personal guest-room bill during the invoice reconciliation period and can report any billing errors regarding room charges. Prior to the event, the meeting professional or the employee's supervisor should inform the staff person of which incidental expenses are covered by the organization.

If the event took place outside the U.S., the facility might have required 100 percent of anticipated charges in advance. In this case, the invoice from the facility should be scrutinized carefully, even if it shows a zero balance due.

Post-Event Report (PER)

As much data as possible should be collected from the facility and other vendors to improve future planning for the meeting professional and the organization. Information about the meeting (see Figure 15.3) is also a powerful tool in negotiating future contracts with other venues or vendors.

Hotels generally provide the meeting professional with a post-event report; however, the report should be requested in the contract or at the pre-convention meeting. Some groups will provide the hotel with their own version of a post-event document, especially if there are specific items that the group needs to have tracked. The industry accepted practice is to use the APEX **post-event report (PER)** format, which can be found at the Convention Industry Council's website. The expectation of such a report should be shared with the facility well in advance of the meeting so that they have an opportunity to ensure the requested items are being tracked. Additionally, data from outside vendors should be compiled and referred to in planning future meetings (see Figure 15.4).

1. If the group used Internet services, the supplier should provide a report noting daily bandwidth use, number of users on the service each day, and any other data gathered regarding usage.
2. The decorator should provide a list of exhibitors that added additional rental equipment or had challenges before, during, or after the exhibition.
3. The decorator should provide a list of donation items left from the decorations in the exhibition, e.g., floral bouquets to donate to a local hospital.
4. The audiovisual provider should detail exhibitors ordering additional equipment for their booths.
5. If the group used a mobile application, the application vendor should provide a robust report including details regarding usage.

FIGURE 15.4 Vendor Data to Collect Services provided by the various contracted vendors can be a major portion of the budget. Collecting data from each contracted vendor provides the meeting professional with information to evaluate the service, compare and negotiate a reasonable cost for the services rendered, and identify areas that can be altered to control or decrease costs.

Thank You Letters

Thank you letters are an important part of the post-meeting process. Many facility staff and other suppliers bring copies of thank you letters to their annual reviews to showcase their talents and efforts. Rules do not exist regarding who should or should not receive a thank you letter. As long as the letters are sincere and speak to specific ways the recipient helped to make the event a success, they will be greatly appreciated. A handwritten note is always received more gratefully than a generic letter (especially by volunteers). The cost of thank you cards or meeting-specific letterhead and postage/stamps should be included in the budget; these items are often overlooked.

Thank you letters may be sent to all volunteers, DMO or CVB personnel, and outside vendors who participated in the event. As a bonus, sending a copy to the recipient's supervisor is a welcomed gesture.

In addition to the thank you letter, each speaker should receive an attendee evaluation of his or her session and a thank you gift, if this is the group's custom. Exhibitors should also receive thank you letters with information on final registration numbers. This is an excellent time to provide exhibitors with information about next year's program, as well.

Attendance Certificates

Many attendees will need simple certificates of attendance to prove attendance at the meeting or to be reimbursed for expenses. These certificates range from generic forms with no personalization to very specific forms listing the number of continuing education credits or units earned. In an effort to be green, meeting organizers can include this certificateon the meeting website, which results in less paper waste and reduced printing costs.

Registration Reports

Accurate registration reports should be kept in the weeks or months leading up to the meeting dates and a final report should be produced once the group has final statistics. The final report should include data from each aspect of the meeting and should be combined with other historical data to determine trends, both positive and negative (see Figure 15.5).

Data Gathering With an Eye to the Future

Determining the success of an event cannot be done without a thorough review of the data gathered from the various stakeholders of the event. The hotel, convention center, exhibitors, staff, volunteers,

1. Category breakdown by registration type, e.g., member, non-member, one-day, exhibitor
2. Pacing of the receipt of registrations
3. Registration method counts, e.g., number registered online vs. fax, or mail-in
4. Breakdown by attendee geographic data, e.g., various states, countries
5. Onsite registration counts, i.e., breakdown by date of registration
6. Number of no-shows, i.e., attendees who registered, but did not attend
7. Total revenue generated
8. Counts for various social events or meal functions

FIGURE 15.5 Registration Data to Collect Registration data collected is probably the most important set of analytics to capture. The information is used to track registration activity for future meetings, an integral part of the budgeting process, and is helpful in determining marketing strategies to continue an attendance-building program.

attendees, and outside vendors all have good information to share regarding their unique perspective on the event and suggestions for future improvements. Future planning should always include a review of data gathered from evaluations of previous events.

The Science of Evaluation — PART TWO

Evaluation is a "systematic process to determine the worth, value, or meaning of an activity or process" (Phillips, 1983, p. 36). When evaluating a meeting, the goal is to determine to what level the objectives of the meeting were met and how the process might improve in the future. This cannot be done without clear and measurable objectives that are established at the outset of the meeting-development process. Once objectives are established, many methods and tools are available to evaluate the meeting.

When developing an evaluation plan, three main groups should be considered: the participants who attend the meeting, the stakeholders who support and execute the meeting, and partners who exhibit at or sponsor the meeting.

Meeting Evaluation

Effective meetings are developed and held to serve needs that are discovered and validated through the needs-assessment process. Once it is established that a need exists, and once it is decided to develop a meeting to satisfy that need, meeting stakeholders want to understand whether the meeting successfully did so. It is important early in the process to develop a communication plan for evaluation efforts—from the beginning through the use of the "lessons learned." The plan must include a strategy for how the information gleaned from the evaluation process which measures the effectiveness of the meeting or event, will be integrated into future programming. Thus, the results from the evaluation process become the basis for the next needs assessment. The needs assessment and evaluation create a circular process with a view toward future meetings. The needs assessment and evaluation are critical components in creating the meeting experience.

The information produced from a successful evaluation can be extremely helpful with strategic planning because it provides supporting data that meeting professionals can leverage while advocating for improvements. Meeting professionals do not always have final say (and sometimes have little say) in how different aspects of a meeting are designed and executed. Evaluation data arms meeting professionals with documentation that can help to give them a stronger voice in strategic planning.

Evaluation Planning

Evaluation planning involves more than just designing a questionnaire or set of interview questions. A true evaluation plan has one main objective, and that is to investigate what is unknown or assumed and increase understanding of it. Often organization personnel make assumptions about a meeting or its attendees and treat those assumptions as established facts, e.g., "People come to this event to hear the keynote speakers. Everything else is less important to them." If assumptions like this are left unchallenged, the entire meeting-planning process could be focused in the wrong direction. For that reason, the development of an effective evaluation plan is critical.

Collection of Data

When choosing what data to collect, the meeting professional should focus on the data that can be analyzed and utilized effectively. If the location and facility of an event were established and unable to be changed, the collection of data on location preference would be a waste of time and should not be included in the plan. Taking this type of approach not only avoids wasted time, but also helps to manage expectations.

Various methods exist to collect information, but most involve asking people for their opinion. A request for feedback also carries with it an assumption that the feedback will be used. No evaluation plan should have the goal of incorporating every single piece of feedback that is received, but it should be developed with an appreciation for the expectations that feedback providers hold.

Goal of Evaluation

When developing an evaluation plan, the goal of evaluation should be clearly identified. This could be tied directly to the meeting's

PROFESSIONAL DILEMMA

Imagine a scenario in which you become part of a planning team that is working on an annual meeting that has been held for several years. Early on in the process, you become aware that the evaluation data that has been collected over the years is either missing or stuck in a file that is never used. In looking through some of the folders, you discover several well-prepared documents that reflect valid opinions with many very good and plausible suggestions to improve the meeting from an attendee perspective. Additionally, there are several notes from speakers that provide ideas that would assist speakers in being able to deliver better presentations with more focus on attendee needs. How would you approach this situation? What approach would you take if the leader of the team you were working on placed no value on the evaluation process?

objectives. A meeting professional should also consider the type of data to collect, method of collection, and from whom to collect it. Lastly, the level of evaluation that will occur must be determined. The subsequent sections of this chapter will explore each of these elements and identify aspects to consider when addressing each.

Data and Samples

Data collection is vital to being able to evaluate a meeting. The who, what, and how for data are key to determine in the collection process.

Types of Data

When conducting an evaluation of meetings there are two types of data involved: hard data and soft data.

Hard data, also known as **quantitative data**, is information that is represented numerically, to which one might assign scores or rank, or from which one might determine averages and frequencies ("APEX Industry Glossary," 2011). An example of hard data can be found when compiling the results from the registration process. The value of this type of data is that it is more objective than soft data. Hard data provides specifics in numbers and tells what the numbers may mean and what factors may have had bearing on the numbers.

Soft data, also known as **qualitative data**, consists of descriptive information that is a record of what is observed ("APEX Industry Glossary," 2011). Often presented in narrative form by the respondent, soft data is more subjective and open to interpretation or assumption than hard data. However, hard data can be easily manipulated and misread. The value of soft data is that it can often provide a greater depth of information than hard data.

key points

- Quantitative data = hard data
- Qualitative data = soft data

Sampling

The group of individuals or other elements that data is collected from is referred to as a "sample." Generally, a sample is used when every single member of the target data source cannot be included in the study. When selecting a sample, the meeting professional should select representatives who accurately reflect the diversity of the group they represent. Collection methods can be used to gain feedback from attendees, suppliers, and other stakeholders and there are different methods by which to sample members of each of these groups.

Methods of Data Collection

There are many different methods by which to collect feedback from various groups. Each has advantages and disadvantages and each is more appropriate in some instances than others. This section discusses the more commonly used methods.

Questionnaires and Surveys

Questionnaires can provide a very good method for requesting feedback from attendees of a meeting or partners, e.g., exhibitors and sponsors. Questionnaires are particularly useful when attempting to gather feedback from a large number of people. One drawback to using questionnaires is that they can be restrictive. Using questionnaires can be a good way to find out how people feel about a meeting, but the results of a questionnaire may do little to identify why those feelings are held. Surveys are similar in composition to questionnaires. The questionnaire is typically delivered in person, where the respondent is asked to provide answers to various questions and the person recording the responses marks the questionnaire form accordingly. A survey is rarely delivered in person; the respondent marks the survey form directly and submits the form when it is complete. The questionnaire is useful when meeting face to face is preferable and precise recording of responses is important to data analysis (see Figure 15.6). Surveys are much easier to utilize, but respondents have the opportunity to provide incomplete or unusable responses.

FIGURE 15.6 A Questionnaire or Survey Completed Onsite Frequently face-to-face interaction will be effective in obtaining data onsite, while the attendee can provide "fresh" information about the meeting experience. This method is labor intensive; however, it yields immediate feedback.

After-Action Reviews

An **after-action review (AAR)** is a structured review, often called a "debriefing process" in the meetings industry, to analyze what happened, why it happened, and how the attendees and those responsible for the meeting can do better. An AAR begins with a clear comparison of intended vs. actual results achieved (Headquarter, Department of the Army, 1993). Conducting an AAR with the planning team and other stakeholders can be an extremely effective method of identifying strengths and opportunities that exist for a meeting.

Interviews

One way to collect individual feedback from people is to conduct interviews. Interviews can be conducted with stakeholders and can be done before, during, or after a meeting. In this format, the person conducting the interview can use either open- or closed-ended questions. This format also allows for the interviewer to ask follow-up or clarifying questions to ensure that the responses being given are accurately understood. The ability to clarify responses is a significant advantage of the interview format. One disadvantage is that it can be time consuming, making it difficult to get feedback from a large number of people.

Focus Group

Another method that is similar to conducting interviews is to conduct **focus groups** with a small group of people. The meeting professional should carefully consider whom to include in the focus group so that group make-up does not improperly influence the feedback being given. Focus groups are similar to questionnaires and surveys, in that they can be conducted before, during, or after a meeting. As when conducting interviews, the focus group facilitator must manage the participation in a way that does not unintentionally influence the comments. Focus groups are similar to interviews in the way that they provide detailed feedback and deeper understanding of the views shared (see Figure 15.7).

FIGURE 15.7 Focus Group in Session Bringing a group of people together for the specific purpose of exploring and evaluating a meeting or event builds the data bank that can be integrated into the overall evaluation and communication plan.

FIGURE 15.8 Data-Collection Kiosks Space permitting, data-collection kiosks provide easy access for attendees so they can share information onsite. This configuration is very large and in a highly accessible area. When strategically placed in a high-traffic area, kiosks will significantly increase the feedback obtained for evaluation purposes.

Focus groups are typically made up of 6 to 10 people and are led by a facilitator. The facilitator keeps the discussion within the scope of its intent and ensures that everybody in the group is able to contribute with no one person or set of people dominating the discussion. The focus group discussion is typically recorded (audio only or video) and the meeting professional must determine who will analyze the recordings. Multiple focus groups may be held to capture an adequate sampling number. Focus groups can be a time-consuming and challenging format by which to get feedback from large numbers of people.

Electronic Analysis

As technology continues to advance, meeting professionals have an ever-increasing number of electronic tools to utilize throughout the evaluation process. Access to these tools is more tied to the availability of funds than with the other methods discussed, but as technology advances, many of these tools are becoming more practical in terms of cost and availability. For example, Google® Analytics, NVivo™, and MeetingMetrics™ are among the options that can be used to analyze data for future planning (see Figure 15.8).

Web Trends Tracking

Meeting professionals might employ electronic means to monitor trends in web navigation, searches, and other activities on the meeting's website. Analysis of this data can produce information such as topics of interest and the effectiveness of meeting promotion and marketing tactics. This type of analysis can be conducted post meeting to track participant behavior and engagement with items such as: content from the meeting, post-meeting discussion groups, and reaction to the meeting through various social media outlets.

Badge Scanning

Tracking can be done during the meeting through the use of attendee badges or nametags that are coded and are able to be scanned, i.e., RFID technology. In instances where meeting professionals have access to the equipment and software needed for this type of tracking, it can produce real-time and highly accurate data on behaviors such as: what exhibit booths are getting the most visits, what sessions are getting the most attendees, and even how attendees are navigating the facility (see Figure 15.9).

FIGURE 15.9 Mobile Device or Badge Scanner This example of a mobile device or badge scanner provides real-time and accurate information for either the meeting organizer or exhibitor. Control of access to "ticketed" events can be monitored through this technology.

Mobile Apps

One particular tool that has made huge inroads into the meetings industry is the mobile app. Mobile apps that are designed for and tailored to meetings have a great number of capabilities that can be used within the evaluation process (see Figure 15.10). These capabilities include, but are not limited to, polling attendees, rating various

FIGURE 15.10 Mobile App Meetings often encourage downloading mobile apps for participants before, during, or after the meeting. It is one avenue to connect with participants during post-event follow-up. This technology can provide communication during the event, control access to certain meetings or events, and allow polling within a meeting room. The application of this technology is unlimited.

elements of a meeting, and providing discussion boards for electronic comment and response. An audience response system (ARS) incorporated into a presentation provides the presenter and audience real-time feedback and provides a unique opportunity better meet the needs and interests of the audience.

Data Sources

When considering the different methods by which to collect data, the meeting professional should attempt to appropriately match the method with the source(s) providing the feedback. Figure 15.11 identifies four main sources to consider when developing an evaluation plan; each has different and unique information, and some methods may help uncover this information more effectively than others. The four main sources of data for meetings are attendees, suppliers, other stakeholders, and artifacts.

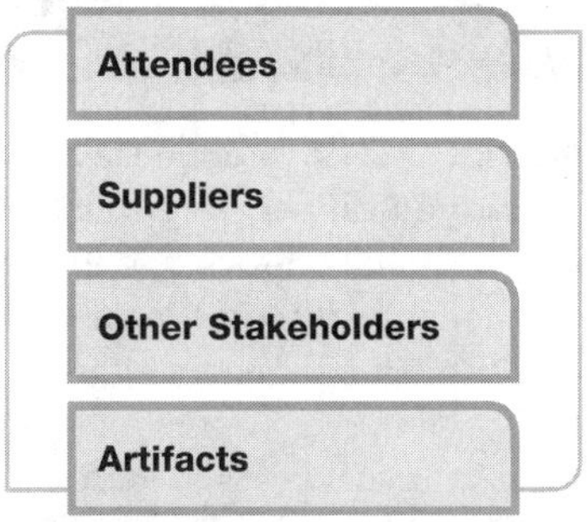

FIGURE 15.11 Common Sources of Data This figure identifies the four most common sources of data for evaluation purposes. The method to collect data should be consistent and align with the expectations of the groups being queried.

Selection of the appropriate data-collection method(s) is best made when developing an evaluation strategy as opposed to after the meeting has taken place. The challenge to the meeting professional is to select method(s) appropriate for the setting, the specific meeting, and the time and budget constraints of the organization (Myhill & Phillips, 2006, p. 699).

Attendees

The size of the meeting being evaluated has significant influence on the best data-collection method to be used for this group. Meetings with a large number of attendees naturally lend themselves to electronic surveys and RFID tracking. Questionnaires, interviews, and focus groups can be used for large meetings, but generally capture feedback from a relatively small percentage (sample) of attendees. Managers of smaller meetings often use interviews and focus groups to garner feedback from attendees, as well as questionnaires.

When soliciting feedback for meeting evaluation, one commonly overlooked group is made up of potential participants who did not attend. It may not seem logical at first, but non-participants can provide valuable insight into how the meeting or organization is perceived. Non-participants could be contacted via surveys, questionnaires, interviews, and focus groups. If these non-participants are at geographically dispersed locations, electronic focus groups (via videoconferencing technologies) may be useful.

Suppliers

Those people who are essential to the delivery of the meeting, the suppliers, are a rich source of data about the meeting's success and onsite processes. This group includes internal stakeholders such as members of the meeting-planning team, general staff, and management; it also

SUSTAINABILITY *in* **Practice**

While anecdotes and examples can be compelling, sustainability reporting is becoming increasingly data-driven. Crucial data can be lost unless meeting professionals think ahead about what information will be captured, from whom, and during what time frame. Questions about the meeting's sustainability initiative should be included in post-event surveys for attendees and other stakeholders. Partners such as hotels, food and beverage providers, printers, and travel services should provide data about energy and water conservation, waste reduction and diversion, and local economic and social impacts related to the meeting. Number and type of floral decorations delivered to a local hospital is an example of the type of data point, and the level of detail, that the final report should contain. Ideally, sustainability reporting requirements should be included in RFPs and contracts, as well as the post-event report (PER) and post-convention meeting agenda.

—Deborah R. Popley

includes external stakeholders such as speakers, the meeting facility staff, and service contractors. To gain information from suppliers, the meeting professional might use different methods for segmented groups, e.g., use interviews with audiovisual technicians, surveys with exhibitors, and personal interviews with the decorating team.

A combination of data-collection tools may also be useful. For example, the meeting professional might start with a questionnaire and follow up with interviews or focus groups to help clarify the feedback received from the questionnaire.

The exhibitor's perspective of the meeting is all about what participation yields in terms of new business for the exhibitor. If it costs an exhibitor $2,000 for a booth at the meeting, plus another $4,000 for transportation, booth materials, and staffing, the initial investment to exhibit would be $6,000. With that level of investment, it is only reasonable that the exhibiting organization expects a tangible benefit exceeding the initial investment. Using interviews, as well as surveys, for exhibitor data collection can be useful for strengthening relations and perhaps turning an exhibitor into a future sponsor.

Other Stakeholders

When the media is invited to the meeting, reviewing what the media representatives say about the meeting can be an excellent source of data. Tracking how many media representatives attended, how many asked questions or interviewed speakers, and how many followed the meeting with a newspaper, radio, or other kind of news story provides useful information for many meeting hosts.

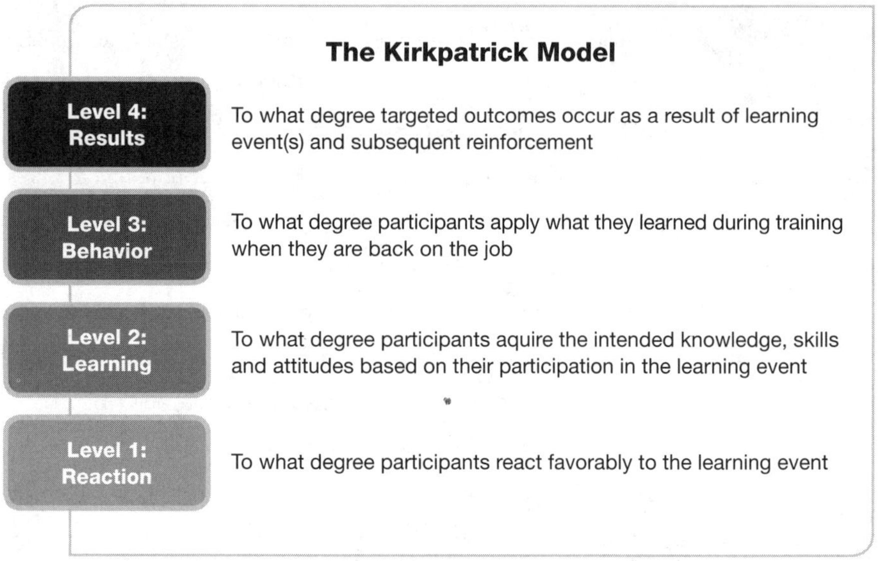
The Kirkpatrick Model
Level 4: Results
To what degree targeted outcomes occur as a result of learning event(s) and subsequent reinforcement
Level 3: Behavior
To what degree participants apply what they learned during training when they are back on the job
Level 2: Learning
To what degree participants aquire the intended knowledge, skills and attitudes based on their participation in the learning event
Level 1: Reaction
To what degree participants react favorably to the learning event

FIGURE 15.12
The Kirkpatrick Levels of Evaluation The four-level approach is useful in objectively analyzing the effectiveness of a meeting, and provides a roadmap to maximize organizational outcomes of both current and future meetings.

Stakeholders who were important to the meeting's success, but who were not in attendance, are also a source of data. These might include planning committees, boards of directors, or insurance providers. This group may be small, with very few members, so interviews with these stakeholders would not only yield useful data, but could be a cost-effective tool to maintain strong relations with them. Perspectives from additional stakeholders can be valuable when making return on investment (ROI) projections, especially when those stakeholders are the supervisors of employers of attendees. They have the perspective of behavioral change and actual results from professional development and discipline-specific training. Interviews even months after the meeting can be extremely important for in-depth exploration of meeting success.

The perspective shared by sponsors can be very different from that of other groups included in the evaluation process. When collecting feedback from these stakeholders, the meeting professional is acknowledging that the main indicator of success for sponsors is ROI. However, they may not have a focus on tangible new business, as exhibitors do. Sponsors look for name and brand recognition, positive relations with the host organization and their attendees, and the opportunity to network with potential clients and suppliers. Business may result directly from sponsorships, but the tendency is to look at sponsoring as a relationship-building prospect. The sponsors will want some sort of report from the meeting professional that provides evidence of relationship-building and return on investment. Meeting professionals often provide visual evidence, e.g., video or photographs, as well as written evidence with critical data. Providing this information quickly and thoroughly is an expected part of the sponsor/meeting organization partnership.

ARTIFACTS

This chapter has indicated numerous artifacts in the various reports the meeting professional should collect as part of the evaluation process. Closing reports from the various suppliers, e.g., hotel, meeting facility, and AV provider, will prove valuable. Additional artifacts include any printed materials the host organization generated for the meeting, electronic communication systems, and registration information. Additionally, though less commonly, artifacts might include presentation materials provided by speakers, social media posts by attendees about the meeting, citations in research from presentation materials at the meeting, and many others.

How attendees used recycling bins provides information, as do other observable behaviors, including what attendees buy at local retail establishments. Video of various parts of the meeting can be examined for contents, a process known as content analysis, and that can provide interesting behavioral data. Recordings of discussions can also be analyzed for contents, as can email and other electronic "conversations." However, some artifacts, while data rich, are also beyond the scope of meeting evaluation due to a lack of resources committed to this purpose. Considering the investment, though, perhaps more resources should be devoted to meeting evaluation.

Levels of Evaluation

The level of evaluation that exhibitors and sponsors are looking for is often more involved than that of other groups engaged in the meeting-planning process. There are many different levels of evaluation and different schools of thought as to how many levels exist.

In the 1950s, Donald L. Kirkpatrick developed a model for training evaluation that consisted of four levels, and more recently the model has undergone revisions (see Figure 15.12) (Kirkpatrick & Kirkpatrick, 2007). In the 1970s, Jack J. Phillips (1997 & 2003, p. 12) created a multilevel model of evaluation to determine the return on investment for training and development programs (see Figure 15.13).

At its essence, the "level" of evaluation has to do with just how much information is being sought. At the most basic level, there is

Reaction and planned action—Measures participant's reaction to the program and outlines specific plans for implementation

Learning—Measures skills, knowledge, or attitude changes

Application and implementation—Measures changes in behavior on the job and specific application and implementation

Business impact—Measures business impact of the program

Return on investment—Compares the monetary value of the results with the costs for the program, usually expressed as a percentage

FIGURE 15.13 The Phillips Return on Investment (ROI) Levels The Phillips approach looks at evaluation from a business perspective and emphasizes the need to place a monetary value on the impact of training (Phillips, 2003, p. 12. Reprinted with permission).

evaluation of how many people attended, how much money was spent, and how much money was made. Evaluations that probe deeper are aimed at trying to determine the reaction and level of satisfaction that each group had. Further probing can seek to determine whether behaviors were changed as a result of the meeting and whether those behaviors were implemented and/or led to significant results. The most complex evaluations aim to accurately calculate and reflect the return on investment that was achieved by participating in the meeting. This level of evaluation is tuned to results, in terms of changed behaviors, improved productivity, and achievement of learner outcomes.

The accurate measurement of the reaction to and satisfaction with a meeting can be very powerful, as well as challenging to evaluate. While the highest level of evaluation has a corresponding level of complexity, the return for this effort is establishing the extended results of the meeting. Evaluating meetings to this level can produce extremely valuable information, but often requires skill, time, and resources that are unavailable to many meeting professionals.

Analysis

A key aspect of the evaluation process involves analyzing the data that is received. The goal of this analysis is to turn the data collected into information that can be used and made actionable. This is done through the conclusions that are drawn once the data has been scrutinized. This element of the evaluation process can present challenges and pitfalls, which, if not addressed sufficiently, could lead to inaccurate or incomplete conclusions. One approach is to have multiple people examine the data independently and see if they draw similar conclusions. This involves more resources, but the results can add considerably to the accuracy of conclusions drawn from the data.

Meeting professionals may want to seek the services of a research consultant to help develop an evaluation plan and to train staff on appropriate analysis techniques. Data-analysis software is available, and some basic analysis techniques are easily acquired. With sophisticated apps now available, visual as well as written data can be analyzed successfully, but data analytics is becoming a complex field with the growth of technological aids. Keeping up with the nuances and advances in data analytics is beyond the reach of many meeting professionals who must maintain professional knowledge and skills in so many areas.

Data Segmentation

Data segmentation involves the isolation and analysis of certain pockets of data in order to draw specific conclusions. In this approach, the characteristics of respondents may suggest which segments of the data to isolate and examine more closely. Comparing the questionnaire responses of first-time meeting attendees with the **aggregate results** that came from all respondents would provide an example of how this approach could be applied. This method of analysis often leads to valuable discovery. For example, the host organization may discover that first-time attendees are generally less satisfied than those who have attended an annual meeting in previous years, or the opposite may be true.

When designing questionnaires, a common practice is to include questions that relate to specific aspects of a meeting; also include a question that asks for the respondents' overall satisfaction with a meeting. This type of design can be very helpful when analyzing and segmenting data. An example of this approach could be demonstrated by segmenting or separating out the responses of those who gave a very high overall rating and comparing the segmented results with the aggregate results that came from all respondents. The opposite approach could also be taken by segmenting the results that came from attendees who provided a very low overall rating.

SUMMARY

This chapter has focused on the work conducted by the meeting professional at the conclusion of the event. That work ranges from closing out the event onsite, shipping items back to the office, and thanking various personnel for their efforts. For several weeks after the event, invoice reconciliation will be a large part of post-event work. This chapter also discussed the science and method of evaluating an event.

The purposes and benefits of evaluating a meeting are numerous. The two most important reasons to evaluate a meeting are to determine whether and to what degree the meeting objectives were met; further, evaluation should identify ways the meeting can be improved in the future. An effective evaluation process can help implement improvements by providing meeting professionals with supporting data that can be leveraged when advocating for improvement initiatives.

The four main groups to consider when developing an evaluation plan are attendees, suppliers, other stakeholders, and artifacts. There are numerous methods that can be used to collect feedback from these groups, and each has advantages and limitations. The evaluation process can produce both hard and soft data. Both types of data are valuable and should be used together when evaluating a meeting or event.

Analyzing data that is collected is a critical step in the evaluation. Misinterpreting data and drawing conclusions that are inaccurate or incomplete can be easy mistakes to make during the evaluation process. The data collected should be viewed from as many different angles as possible in order to ensure that the conclusions drawn from the evaluation process are accurate and complete.

KEY WORDS

after-action review (AAR)
aggregate results
bill of lading
customs broker
data segmentation
evaluation
focus group
gratuity
post-convention meeting
post-event report (PER)
qualitative data
quantitative data
tip

DISCUSSION QUESTIONS

1. What are the necessary actions to take when organizing a return shipment?
2. Who should receive a receive a tip, and in what amount?
3. What is the difference between disputed and undisputed items on an invoice?
4. What data should be included in the post-event report from a hotel?
5. What levels of evaluation data are most important to various stakeholders?

16

Career Building in the Meetings Profession

Brian L. Miller, EdD
Associate Professor
Department of Hotel, Restaurant,
& Institutional Management
University of Delaware

Main Topics

- Developing Meeting-Management Skills
- Standards in the Meetings Industry
- Ethics and Professionalism
- Ethical Issues in the Meetings Profession
- Industry Issues Into the Future—2020

Learner Outcomes

Upon the completion of this chapter, the student should be able to:

1. Identify skills and attributes needed by meeting professionals.
2. Explain ethical behaviors impacting meetings.
3. Organize, by the level of importance, future trends predicted to impact the meeting professional.
4. Summarize the future roles and expectations of meeting professionals.

CMP INTERNATIONAL STANDARDS
Domain A. Strategic Planning
Skill 2. Develop Sustainability Plan for Meeting or Event
SubSkills. 2.01, 2.02
Domain K. Professionalism
Skill 30. Exhibit Professional Behavior
SubSkill. 30.01

Over the last decade the meetings industry has been in a transition. During this time meeting professionals have scrambled to compete in highly uncertain economic and political environments. The organizations hosting meetings, as well as the attendees at these gatherings, are looking for a greater return on investment (ROI) of time and money. Travel has become more cumbersome and attendees' options for their meeting dollars are more numerous. All of these factors have pressured the meeting professional to do more with less.

In the past, many organizations hosting meetings expected in-house meeting professionals to carry out the logistical elements of planning, organizing, and executing their meetings. However, employers and clients today are expecting measurable results for their stakeholders and consequently are placing higher demands on the people who plan and execute their meetings. These changing job expectations require a paradigm shift for meeting professionals who now must be deliberate in executing their roles as strategic partners in addition to performing logistical functions of the job.

The chapters in this book have been selected to provide the learner with best practices used in the meetings industry. The knowledge gained by studying these topics will enable future meeting professionals to position themselves as strategic partners in the meetings industry. This chapter attempts to provide a roadmap toward developing a successful career in this profession, identifies key industry **competency standards**, summarizes ethical and professional behavior expectations, and presents 10 issues that will affect the meeting professional as we move toward the year 2020.

Developing Meeting-Management Skills

As the meetings profession continues to evolve, success will belong to the meeting professionals and suppliers who have the knowledge, experience, and perspective to:

- understand the specific purpose behind every meeting and event in which they are involved;
- design meetings and events to reflect and respect attendees' learning needs and styles;
- maximize attendees' pre-meeting, onsite, and post-meeting experiences with respect to networking and learning; and
- organize and deliver services in ways that effectively meet the strategic objectives of the host organization and attendees' expectations.

What are the traits, characteristics, and skills that future meeting professionals will need? How will you begin building and refining that knowledge base and skill set? Five key actions are provided for your consideration as you embark on a successful career in the meetings and events industry.

Create a Plan

Moving ahead, create a plan for your own professional development and career advancement. In a longitudinal study of 10,000 meeting participants that began in 1979 and tracked attendees through 2010, researchers found that the average participant has held 10.8 jobs (Bureau of Labor Statistics, 2012). Through deliberate introspection, you can assess your personal and professional strengths. This should develop a strategic perspective on how to approach your job and will lead you to a plan for building networks, identifying learning opportunities, enhancing your skills, and developing weaknesses until they no longer hinder your career advancement.

key points

Actions for Building a Career

1. Create a plan
2. Complete a personal SWOT analysis
3. Move outside your comfort zone
4. Build a network
5. Expand your skills

Complete a Personal SWOT Analysis

The acronym SWOT stands for "strengths, weaknesses, opportunities, and threats." Throughout this text, SWOT has been applied with a professional perspective to risk, project, budget, and marketing management. You can apply the SWOT strategy to yourself, as well. Begin by identifying your career goals for 5, 10, and 15 years ahead, and beyond. The analysis will help you identify internal strengths and weaknesses, as well as the external opportunities and threats that you may face (Quast, 2013) (see Figure 16.1). In a competitive job market, you should consider yourself to be a brand looking for opportunities to add value to the employers and clients with whom you chose to work.

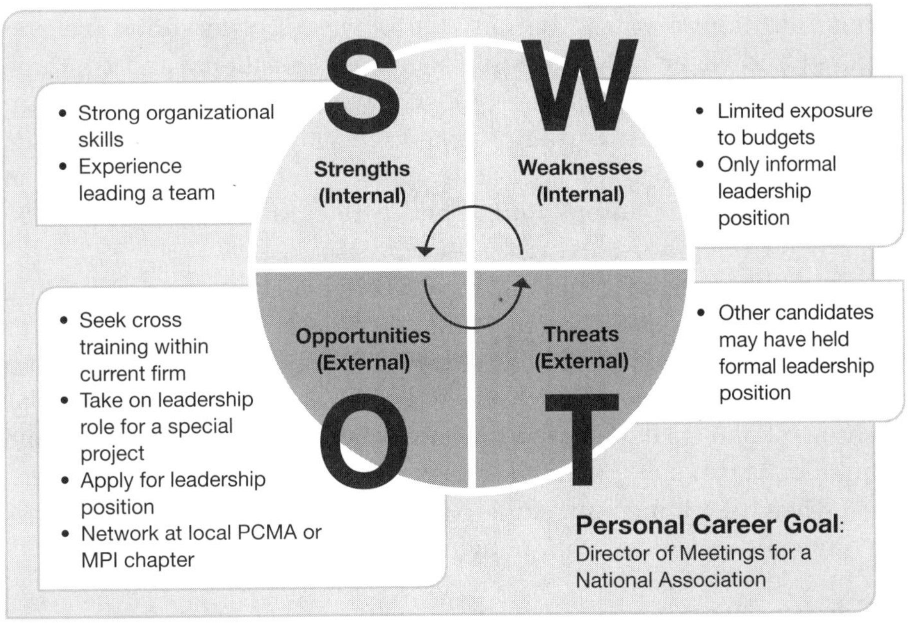

FIGURE 16.1 Example of Personal SWOT Analysis Using the SWOT analysis as a personal exercise, complete an analysis of your future personal goals to guide your thought and decision-making process. This exercise requires introspection and awareness of career opportunities that await you in your quest for the "perfect" entry-level position in the meetings industry (Adapted from Mind Tools, 2014).

Get Out of Your Comfort Zone

In shifting from logistics to a more strategic focus, meeting professionals are broadening their view to encompass the significance of a meeting to all of its stakeholders. Becoming a strategic partner often requires young professionals to move out of their comfort zone in order to reap success. For many of us, getting out of our comfort zone leads to feelings of uncertainty and fear, but after doing it, we often feel pleasantly surprised with how well we handled the situation and are eager to meet another challenge. As an aspiring young professional in the meetings profession, you will meet people with all types of experiences. Network with each and every person who crosses your path, force yourself to seek out others, and continue to look for opportunities to add value to everything you do by challenging yourself in new and sometimes uncomfortable situations. Cultivate a reputation for asking questions, rather than having all of the answers. Professionals, especially those with years of experience, often enjoy sharing their lessons learned. You will benefit from these career stories and make a friend in the sharing.

Build a Large and Evolving Network

Business and professional networking is widely recognized as the lifeblood of the meetings industry. At its best, networking is about bringing colleagues and professional partners together to share information, ideas, and opportunities, secure in the knowledge that if the substance is sound, commercial success will follow.

Networking is not easy and it requires a plan. Successful networking will require you to harness the power of observation, be prepared and eager to learn from others, ask questions, and continue the conversation (see Figure 16.2). Networking is not always about getting business cards from people higher up the corporate ladder. As a matter of fact, that is usually the least effective thing you can do. Instead, keep an open mind and realize that there is a lot to be learned from others, including your peers.

key points

Benefits of Networking

- Share information
- Get new ideas
- Look for opportunities
- Obtain new knowledge
- Meet new people

In addition to the traditional means of networking, such as meeting people at work, social events, and conferences, there are a number of social media platforms that allow young professionals to build a large and evolving network. LinkedIn® is an example of a popular social media site that is used to connect business professionals to one another. When using social media, remember to be prudent and honest when describing your skills, experiences, and contacts with others within and outside of your network.

Expand Your Skills

Expanding your skills and competencies is an essential building block for your future professional success. As meeting professionals strive to position themselves as experts in the creation of impactful adult

FIGURE 16.2 Networking at a Student Created Trade Show A potential employee has presented his résumé to a recruiter. Recruiters at the trade show allow students an opportunity to practice presenting themselves professionally, providing a succinct self-introduction, and expressing their career goals.

learning experiences and networking opportunities, they must also become committed lifelong learners themselves. This should include the continuous pursuit of the latest knowledge, ideas, techniques, and strategies within their discipline as well as beyond that narrow focus. The content needed to be successful in the future will change continually, but expanding your knowledge and skills will increase your business acumen and lead you to become a valued team member and a strategic partner to your stakeholders. You may become a driving force behind change, but only by knowing what is going on around you, listening to others, and networking with people who need to hear your ideas and solutions.

Standards in the Meetings Profession

The path taken to become a meetings professional has proven to be very diverse. Industry leaders come from all kinds of academic and professional experiences. Some 25 years ago, there were few academic programs offering courses of study in meetings and events. According to a database compiled through a grant from the PCMA Foundation (2014), over 430 academic institutions now offer courses directly related to the meetings profession worldwide (Cecil, Reed, & Reed, para. 1).

Hosting meetings requires a variety of business skills and competencies. Academic programs offering hospitality degrees require students to take a variety of courses, many of which are not directly focused on meetings. So how do people starting their careers begin to put together a professional development plan to ensure that they are focused on the right **knowledge, skills, and abilities (KSA)** needed for the meetings industry? The acronym KSA refers to the activities that are deemed to be required to perform a specific job competently. Phelan and Mills (2011) published the results of a small study that identified five domains decided by academics and industry professionals to be essential to be successful in the meetings profession. Additionally, two professional organizations for the meetings profession, Meeting Professionals International and the Convention Industry Council, have created industry standards of KSA for the meetings profession. These two sets of standards are Meeting and Business Events Competency Standards (MBECS) and Certified Meeting Professional International Standards (CMP-IS), respectively.

Meeting and Business Event Competency Standards (MBECS)

Meeting Professionals International (MPI) in collaboration with the Canadian Tourism Human Resource Council (CTHRC) worked together to build a "comprehensive summary of knowledge and skills that should be possessed by experienced meeting and business event experts" (MBECS, 2011, p. 5), resulting in MBECS. The results of this project were in response to the industry's request for metrics to measure the value of curricula for industry professionals by a collection of international boards, governmental bodies, task forces, and MPI staff. The standards include 12 domains and 33 individual skills. Domains include strategic planning, event design, and site management. Individual skills include engaging speakers, developing mission and goals, and designing the site layout.

For industry professionals, these standards should be used to learn about the industry, recognize and promote your skills to clients, enhance your performance, and plan your professional development.

Certified Meeting Professional International Standards (CMP-IS)

In 1985 the Convention Industry Council (CIC) rolled out the Certified Meeting Professional (CMP) designation. The purpose of the program is to enhance the knowledge and performance of industry professionals, promote the credibility of the profession, and enhance a uniform standard of practice ("CMP International Standards," 2011).

Periodically, the CIC conducts an industry job analysis to update the knowledge and skills deemed important for competent performance as a CMP. The CIC also partnered with the CTHRC and used MPI's MBECS to develop the CMP-IS ("CMP International Standards," 2011). These standards include 10 domains, e.g., strategic planning, meeting and event design, and site management.

The CMP credential is recognized around the world and is a mark of excellence in the industry. The certification's qualifications include education, professional experience in the industry, and an examination.

The CMP program aspires to increase professionalism in the meetings profession by promoting standards, stimulating the advancement

SUSTAINABILITY *in* **Practice**

The pressure for sustainable meetings will only increase in the future. Meeting professionals must scan the internal and external environment to gauge the interest and pressure for the organization to create more sustainable meetings. In the future, meeting professionals will see the following trends:

- A holistic focus (whole systems thinking) on sustainability, the economy (profit), the environment, and society (people) will replace more simplified concepts of greening.
- Savvy meeting professionals will increase their abilities and organizational capacity. This requires new knowledge acquisition, assimilation, and transformation within their organizations.
- The supplier community will help drive change. Suppliers have the opportunity to move from the status of vendor to trusted advisor by providing advice and education to meeting professionals.
- Scrutiny and debate will be invited (and should occur) to avoid greenwashing a situation where meetings may set the bar too low (goals not sufficiently aggressive) or where meetings may not accomplish sustainability goals. This criticism will help sustainable meetings improve and create true impact.

Sustainable event planning will be embedded in the meetings industry. Early adopters will have their professional identity tied to sustainability. Eventually, sustainability will become a standard part of the meeting planning process—requiring no extra thought or preparation. This paradigm shift will occur within the larger context of society and also within the meetings profession as planners and suppliers support a more sustainable future.

—Susan M. Tinnish, PhD

of knowledge and increasing the value of CMPs to their employers and customers. As your career progresses, seriously consider studying for and earning appropriate certification to position yourself as an expert in the meetings profession.

Ethics and Professionalism

In a world of instant gratification, intense competition, and fluctuating economies, ethics is sometimes seen as less important than other business essentials. In reality, business and personal ethics play a vital role in all business endeavors. Allegations of unethical behavior can ruin a business and professionally ruin an individual. For this reason, ethics

key points

Ethical Influencers

- Family
- Religion
- School
- Work
- News
- Politics
- Pop culture
- Life experiences
- Professional organizations

is not just a "do-gooder" personal choice, but also an essential business practice. Protect your professional reputation by cultivating and demonstrating strong ethical standards professionally and personally.

Your ethical principles will also help maintain the meetings industry as a profession. For this reason, those employed in the meetings profession must help develop, support, and enforce a professional code of ethics in their own organizations, as well as throughout their professional networks and meetings-related associations. Although many ethical standards are not currently legislated by law, a renewed effort to legislate minimum levels of corporate ethical behavior is growing, due to numerous scandals and unlawful business actions. Recent scandal and business disruption in Las Vegas caused by the General Services Administration (GSA) (Miller, 2012) should be a wake-up call that both meeting professionals and suppliers should evaluate the ethics of their behavior regularly.

Defining Ethics

Ethics is often very difficult to define and to discuss; everyone knows unethical behavior when they see it. The dictionary defines ethics as "a system of moral standards or values" (Neufeldt, 1996). Based on a definition like this, people instinctively know that they should behave ethically and avoid unethical behavior. Moral standards vary from person to person, not because some people are "bad" and others are "good," but because individual moral standards are developed from various influences encountered throughout our lives.

Influences vary not only from person to person, but between groups within which we identify ourselves—from generational differences to social group memberships. However, professional ethics refers to a set of rules provided to an individual by an external source and provides a common and consistent set of principles for ethical behavior of those who are employed in a profession—in this case, meeting professionals.

Professional Ethics

Professional ethics concerns situations that people face while carrying out their job-related duties. The responsibility for ensuring ethical behavior in the workplace rests not only on management, but on our own actions as well. Unethical behavior on the part of a single person in a business can affect the reputation and success of the entire business.

Unfortunately, many think that the enforcement of ethics is someone else's job. Certainly, revealing unethical behavior can put the whistleblower in an uncomfortable or awkward position. Being ethical is not always easy. Being ethical takes a strong constitution, but if ethical behavior is adopted throughout a single business or an entire industry, it will become the rule and not the exception.

Ethical Issues in the Meetings Profession

Ethical issues arise with many variations. Two common examples are familiarization trips (a common DMO/CVB promotion strategy), and gift giving. Since ethical issues are situational, meaning that some unique circumstances make an ethical decision-making process difficult, most associations in the meetings profession, such as PCMA, have created a code of ethics. Professionals use this code to guide their actions.

However, professionals also benefit from creating their own code, based on their values, culture, social orientation, and experiences. Often we do not know how we might act in a specific situation until that situation actually occurs. Hypothetical codes are useful, but limited. In that case, sharing the ethical dilemma with peers and supervisors may help you make the best ethical choice.

Familiarization Trips

One of the more typical ethical transgressions involves **familiarization trips** or "FAM trips." Hotel companies or DMOs often invite meeting professionals on an all-expenses-paid trip to visit and tour the city and/or hotel properties. FAM trip organizers should qualify meeting professionals—that is, verify that the meeting professional has business to bring to the destination or hotel company in the foreseeable future. Not to do so is an ethical violation on behalf of the organizer. A meeting professional who is less than truthful in completing the FAM trip application so that he/she gets a free trip to a destination when he/she has no intention of bringing future business to that destination is breaching the ethical code. What is your advice to these meeting professionals (see Figure 16.3)?

FIGURE 16.3 Meeting Professionals on a Familiarization Trip A group of meeting professionals was invited to experience the facilities and service of Gaylord Opryland. A FAM trip is more than just looking at the convention facilities; it is experiencing the city of Nashville, Tennessee, and activities that would take place outside the hotel. Potential clients for this destination participate in the FAM trip to learn about places to host events and points of interest for attendees and exhibitors.

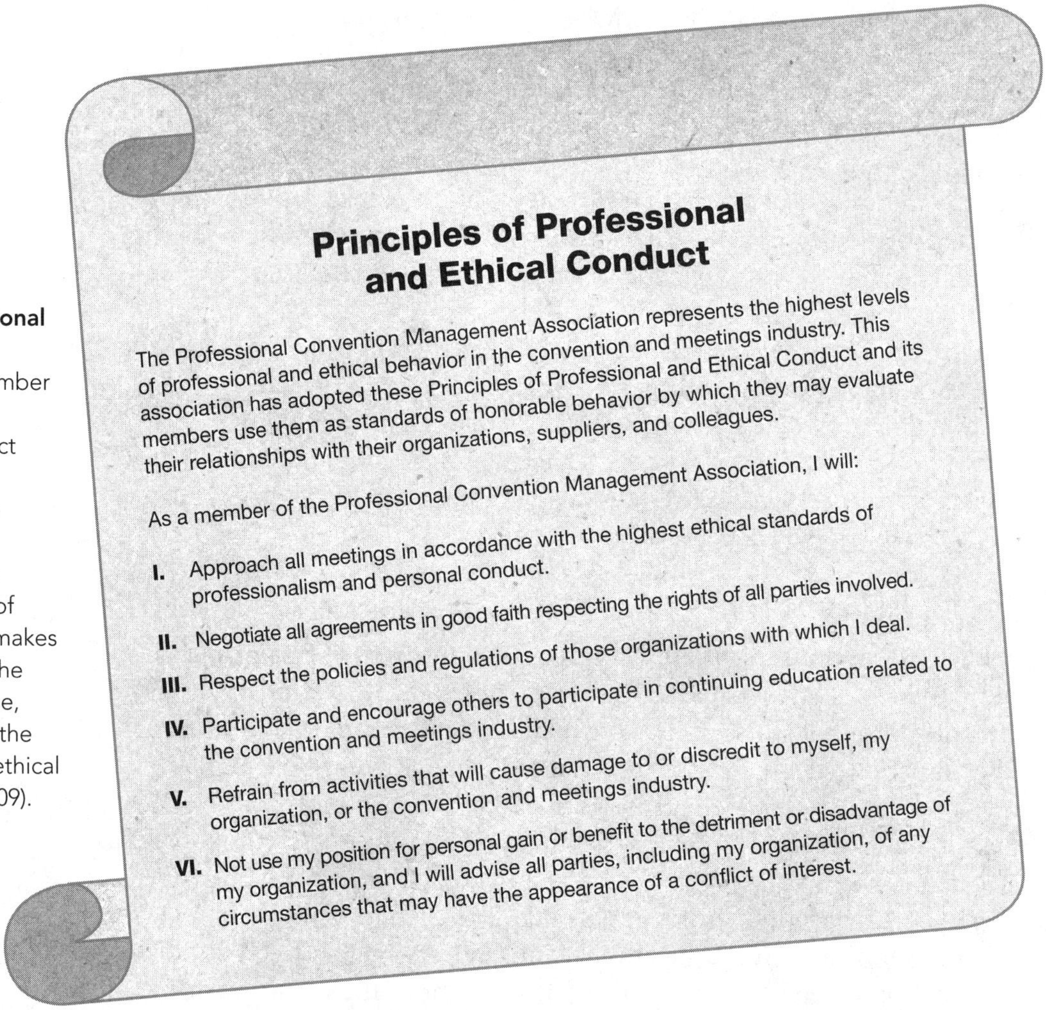

Principles of Professional and Ethical Conduct

The Professional Convention Management Association represents the highest levels of professional and ethical behavior in the convention and meetings industry. This association has adopted these Principles of Professional and Ethical Conduct and its members use them as standards of honorable behavior by which they may evaluate their relationships with their organizations, suppliers, and colleagues.

As a member of the Professional Convention Management Association, I will:

I. Approach all meetings in accordance with the highest ethical standards of professionalism and personal conduct.

II. Negotiate all agreements in good faith respecting the rights of all parties involved.

III. Respect the policies and regulations of those organizations with which I deal.

IV. Participate and encourage others to participate in continuing education related to the convention and meetings industry.

V. Refrain from activities that will cause damage to or discredit to myself, my organization, or the convention and meetings industry.

VI. Not use my position for personal gain or benefit to the detriment or disadvantage of my organization, and I will advise all parties, including my organization, of any circumstances that may have the appearance of a conflict of interest.

FIGURE 16.4
Principles of Professional and Ethical Conduct
Most professional member organizations have a code of ethical conduct or code of ethics with which members agree to abide. Generally, a leadership committee discusses allegations of ethical breaches and makes a decision regarding the organization's response, such as discontinuing the membership of an unethical party ("Principles," 2009).

GIFTS

In some cultures, the exchange of gifts is a polite and even necessary part of conducting business. However, exchanging gifts can create an ethical conundrum. One issue with gift giving is the timing of the gift. For example, a gift given by a hotel to a meeting professional on the day before a decision is to be made about whether to choose that hotel or another property may be construed as a gift intended to influence the decision—also known as a bribe. A gift given by the same hotel to the meeting professional while the meeting professional is onsite for the meeting may be considered standard business practice. If it is given after the meeting is over as a token of appreciation, the gift may be perceived as a gracious and polite gesture. Another issue with gift giving is whether the gift is intended for the meeting professional personally or is intended for the benefit of the company or organization as a whole. Finally, the nature and cost of the gift can add to the level of uncertainty about appropriateness.

To avoid even the hint of impropriety, some organizations have created ethical guidelines that do not allow their staff to accept any personal gifts, or that place a dollar value on the personal gifts that can be accepted. Meeting professionals must understand and abide by the policies of their organizations. Meeting professionals who own their own companies should develop policies and procedures for the giving and acceptance of gifts that are in keeping with industry standards.

PCMA Code of Ethics

In addition to a code of ethics found in many private and public companies, most industry associations have a common standard of requiring all members to follow the industry's code of ethics. Figure 16.4 is the PCMA "Principles of Professional and Ethical Conduct." The "Professional Ethics Checklist," found on page 316, is part of the Professional Dilemma for this chapter. Both ethical documents have been adopted by the Board of Directors of the Professional Convention Management Association.

Industry Issues Into the Future—2020

Associations that support and represent the meeting profession are challenging their members to shift the focus from "the meetings business" to "the business of meetings." There is no doubt that tomorrow's meeting professionals will have to understand the issues and language that drive their organizations, whether they work independently or directly for associations, corporations, or government agencies. The following 10 issues are predicted to have a continuing and significant impact on the business of meetings. As a young professional interested in a career in the meetings profession, these should be on your radar as you move toward the year 2020 and beyond.

key points

Industry Issues—2020

1. Economic uncertainty
2. Mass customization
3. Co-location
4. Event marketing
5. Networking innovation
6. Procurement and strategic sourcing
7. Focus on risk management
8. Sustainability
9. Barriers to travel
10. Changing technology

Economic Uncertainty

Unfortunately, when the growth of the economy slows, unemployment rises, the growth of new business is stagnant, and the demand for meetings and events shrinks. In the years following the catastrophic events of 2001, the world economy has gone through three economic downturns; each has had a negative impact on the attendance of thousands of meetings held annually around the world. Global economic uncertainty is especially challenging to the meetings profession due to the extended booking window in which most large conventions and events are planned. As a result, there is a growing consensus that the world's economy will continue to see shorter economic cycles. To remain competitive and relevant during the economic downturn, meeting professionals will need to be creative and look for more opportunities to add value for their constituents.

Shorter booking window A 2013 poll of meeting professionals, conducted by MPI, found that 53 percent of respondents believe that

FIGURE **16.5** **Learning Lounge** The interaction that takes place in this learning lounge provides an outstanding opportunity to connect with other professionals, pursue dialogue on a wide variety of topics, and engage with learning that occurs outside the meeting room.

lead times for booking meetings will continue to get shorter, e.g., an increase of 13 percent between 2013 and 2014 (Pofeldt, 2014, p. 2). This trend creates challenges for meeting professionals who are responsible for finding adequate venues and hotel rooms for their attendees. The consistent development of efficient and effective tools and strategies to manage meeting logistics in a shorter time frame is imperative to be successful and remain competitive.

Mass Customization

Since early 2000, meeting professionals have worked diligently to design meeting agendas that enhance audience participation and encourage interaction. Educational sessions are now being designed to activate discussion using creative and innovative learning tools. The objective is to create a stimulating environment that engages learners with one another. These changes in the approach to adult education were undertaken in an effort to create a more learner-centered educational experience at meetings (see Figure 16.5).

Dynamic content delivery As we move forward, meeting professionals will need to go beyond learning styles to develop strategies that allow attendees to have more input in creating topics and determining how, and in which portions of the meeting, they want to participate. Attendees will continue to utilize personal tools and electronic devices.

Although projecting what these tools will be in the not-too-distant future is quite difficult, meeting professionals must quickly embrace new technology. Keeping up with changes and learning new technology interface skills is imperative.

Virtual meetings are not likely to take the place of face-to-face meeting attendance, yet meeting professionals will need to ensure that virtual meeting tools become an option to grow participation in their meetings and perhaps increase revenue from meetings (see Figure 16.6). Attendees in the future will demand access to all educational sessions when they want and using the medium of their choice.

Co-Location

Co-location refers to holding two at-least-somewhat-related events at the same time and in the same venue. The benefit of doing this is to create economies of scale, with a variety of common features of the meetings to be shared by multiple organizations. What makes the co-location concept work is when there is an overlap of interest between the meetings and events. Some of the common characteristics for co-location to be successful include:

- some overlap, but not too large an overlap, of attendees or exhibitors;
- meetings/events have some relationship to each other;
- the value proposition works for both organizations; and
- joining resources should increase overall attendance.

Experts agree that the co-location arrangement is unlikely to be permanent, as at some point, the value to one or the other organization

FIGURE 16.6 Virtual Meeting in Action This photograph shows an attendee participating in a virtual meeting in the "Aspiration Café" at the technology area of the Professional Convention Management Association's Convening Leaders annual meeting.

PROFESSIONAL DILEMMA

You are a meeting professional who has circulated an RFP for your organization's annual meeting to three potential destinations. The DMO at each destination has responded with a thorough proposal. In one proposal, the DMO suggested a wonderful idea for a meeting theme that has excellent potential for marketing purposes. Your site selection committee has chosen a different proposal, but they told you to use the theme suggested by the DMO with the losing proposal. While the theme idea is superior, would using it be ethical if your meeting does not go to that destination?

Professional Ethics Checklist

All activities in the meetings and conventions industry should exemplify the highest ethical standards of professional and personal conduct. When faced with making an ethical decision, take this test. If you answer "yes" to all of these questions then the proposed solution is probably ethical.

Yes	No	
❑	❑	Is it ethical and legal?
❑	❑	Is it an action for which you can accept full responsibility?
❑	❑	Are you willing to be held accountable for the consequences of this decision?
❑	❑	Is it the right thing to do?
❑	❑	Would your decision be the same if you knew everyone would learn about it—especially those you admire and respect?
❑	❑	Is it consistent with PCMA's Principles of Professional and Ethical Conduct?

Professional Ethical Values

- **Integrity** Strive to behave ethically, honestly, morally, and with unquestionable character.
- **Respect** Be committed to developing trust and respect from your colleagues and clients through your actions and behavior.
- **Credibility** Make decisions in good faith. Don't let your actions damage or discredit you or the organization for which you work. (PCMA, 2009)

will be lost. However, meeting professionals should be creative during uncertain economic times and look for opportunities to add value to both their affinity groups and to their host organization.

Event Marketing

As competition for meetings and events continues to grow, marketing events will become even more complex. This will require meeting professionals of the future to get more creative and technologically savvy. For example, while printed copies of marketing materials for meetings are being drastically reduced, creating hard copies of your marketing materials for your best attendees may be the answer to reach, engage, and connect with them. The rules for marketing to your constituents are changing rapidly; however, the number one rule in future marketing remains certain—customer engagement. There are five relatively new rules that focus on engaging attendees; each should be considered and carefully explored (see Figure 16.7).

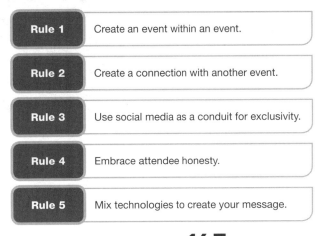

Rule 1	Create an event within an event.
Rule 2	Create a connection with another event.
Rule 3	Use social media as a conduit for exclusivity.
Rule 4	Embrace attendee honesty.
Rule 5	Mix technologies to create your message.

FIGURE 16.7 Rules of Engagement for Attendees Common-sense rules of attendee engagement continue to be an integral part of marketing a meeting. Future meeting professionals must cultivate skills with new technologies and knowledge of emerging trends to engage an increasingly savvy audience.

Create an event within an event Within most meetings there are many activities going on simultaneously, e.g., registration, exhibits, breakout sessions, and traveling to and from venues on shuttle buses. There are plenty of periods of time when attendees are not engaged in a formal meeting activity. These down times provide a great opportunity to create a mini event. For example, if your event utilizes a shuttle service, this could be a perfect opportunity to promote a video about a product, service, or innovation. Another example would be to create a unique and exclusive environment that builds relationships with attendees (see Figure 16.8).

Create a connection with another event Connect with suppliers or other event organizers that go beyond or have a connection with your attendees. Look for opportunities to build value with another event (similar to co-location) that will allow access to a new segment of potential attendees for your meeting or event.

FIGURE 16.8 Imaginarium—An Event Within an Event Sponsors often create an event within an event, as has Tourism Toronto, by attracting customers to a unique environment while building a strong relationship with customers. These events are usually "by invitation only."

FIGURE **16.9** **A Strategically Placed Networking Function** The innovative use of a planned meal function provides opportunities for attendees and exhibitors to meet new people and build a professional network. The active engagement of individuals at the table adds value that can be fostered long after the meeting or event has concluded.

Use social media as a conduit for exclusivity Membership has its privileges, the saying goes. Use your social media platform to provide exclusive deals or freebies by participating. For example, run a promotion on Instagram™ promising the first 50 attendees who upload and tag a picture of your event an invitation to a special backstage experience during your opening ceremony, an early entrance to a VIP reception, or a special consulting invitation with a supplier.

Embrace attendee honesty Most meetings and events use standard comment cards to hear what attendees have to say. However, often this feedback is only seen by a few of the meeting's organizers. Plan opportunities for your attendees to provide real feedback in real time. If you take the time to set up and track virtual communities with the comments and feedback open to the public, you will be amazed as to how much of that content can be used in constructive ways, from improving the meeting to providing real, honest testimonials.

Mix technologies to create your message Whatever your message and whatever your meeting, mix up how you build your marketing message. If the marketing mantra in the future is attendee engagement, you will need to create your marketing messages using a variety of technologies. Your marketing strategy will be evolving but it will need to be innovative and relevant. In other words, "mash up" your message in ways that have never been "mashed up" before.

Networking Innovation

Networking at meetings, conferences, and events is often ranked as the most important reason for attending meetings (Yoo & Chon, 2008). However, when thinking about the value proposition that meeting professionals identify for their meetings, effective networking is very hard to do. In the future, it will be imperative that meeting professionals continue to discover and experiment with innovative ways to improve the outcomes of attendee networking activities. Lutz (2014) provides three suggestions for meeting professionals to generate stronger networking outcomes for attendees (see Figure 16.9 and the Key Points box on this page).

key points

Networking Outcomes

- Use data to enhance connections.
- Move networking sessions from hallways to meeting rooms.
- Strategically use meal functions for networking. (Lutz, 2014)

Procurement and Strategic Sourcing

The two biggest costs meeting professionals face when planning meetings are the costs for the venue and hotel rooms. Due to fluctuations in the economy, rates for both since early 2000 have cycled up and down, causing a flurry of activity amending contracts to account for economic shifts in either direction. **Strategic sourcing** is a procurement process that continuously improves by re-evaluating the purchasing activities to reduce costs, while maintaining or improving the value-to-cost relationship (Institute for Supply Management, 2014). When developing this procurement protocol, the meeting professional must go beyond a single negotiation tactic and move toward building a partnership with suppliers that adds value to both the host organization and the supplier. Hospitality lawyer Greg Duff offers three pointers:

1. Conduct market research to understand the trends in a market.
2. Focus on upgrades and amenities that the hotels have control over.
3. Build flexibility into the meeting development, e.g., dates and location. (Dosh, 2012)

Focus on Risk Management

Risks associated with the hosting of meetings come in all types and from a variety of sources, from failure to comply with a contract to natural disasters. As the industry moves toward the next decade, meeting professionals will spend more time identifying and assessing potential risks that are associated with their meetings and events. Too often the strategy meeting professionals take is more reactive than proactive approach (Russell, 2014b).

Sustainability

As we move into the future, there continue to be many good reasons to locate events at sustainable meeting facilities and to align meeting-management policies with sustainable best practices. It will continue to make sound business sense to align the business of meetings with the future of the planet (Boo & Park, 2013). In fact, meeting professionals should be harnessing the economic power of the global meetings industry to help point the way to a more environmentally sustainable future for all attendees. The bottom line for attendees and host organizations alike is that a well-designed facility that deploys the latest in sustainable architecture and operations is a more comfortable environment. The more comfortable the environment, the better the results for attendees and host organizations (Boo & Park, 2013). Global warming will continue to challenge meeting professionals to do their part in developing sustainable best practices at their meetings. This will require the adoption of smart policies and procedures to truly sustain the planet and our presence on it.

Barriers to Travel

In addition to the pressure put on attendance by the ease and availability of virtual meetings, business travelers have a whole range of barriers that have made traveling more difficult. Additionally, there are the added stresses of potential man-made and natural disasters and world political disruptions that impact travel. When organizing meetings, it is important to select destinations that are safe and affordable in both time spent traveling and cost; these factors will continue to be important to attendees (Yoo & Chon, 2008). Meeting professionals in the future will need to evaluate the extent to which these barriers impact travel for their attendee base, to look for creative solutions that ameliorate these barriers, and to ensure that they are able to grow and build attendance.

key points

Barriers to Travel

- Cost
- Time
- Feeling of isolation
- Lack of personal comfort

Changing Technology

In the near future, meetings and exhibitions are projected to offer a totally personalized experience that is tailor-made to the needs of the attendees. As part of that effort, meeting professionals will utilize necessary technological tools to make the event fully interactive for attendees, so they can engage with and influence the content of the event. Some of the emerging trends that will continue to evolve and become more prevalent in the future include:

- streaming live video simultaneously with face-to-face meetings and events;
- managing and engaging attendees through social networking before, during, and after the meeting; and
- downloading presenters' presentations to mobile devices before, during, and after the meeting.

SUMMARY

This chapter has focused on what meeting professionals can expect in order to achieve success and stay ahead of the curve. The landscape and scope of responsibilities that meeting professionals carry out is dynamic and exciting, and has been in flux since the beginning of the new millennium. As we move quickly toward 2020, the pace of this change is expected to accelerate. In the first section of the chapter the focus was on developing your professional skills, such as completing a personal SWOT analysis, and on the importance of behaving in an ethical and professional manner. The second part of the chapter presented trends and issues that the meetings profession will face as we move toward the next decade.

The bottom line for the meetings industry is that our professionals become strategic partners with their constituents, stakeholders, vendors, and colleagues. This will require you to be dedicated to seeking creative ways to effectively and efficiently develop, host, and execute meetings.

KEY WORDS

competency standards
familiarization (FAM) trip
knowledge, skills, and abilities (KSA)
strategic sourcing

DISCUSSION QUESTIONS

1. What will the industry look like beyond 2020?
2. What global issues will impact meetings in the future?
3. Who will attend meetings and how will meeting professionals market to them?
4. How will technological changes in society affect meetings in the future?

POSTSCRIPT

On behalf of all the meeting professionals who have diligently contributed to this book and the Board of Directors and staff of the Professional Convention Management Association, we wish you only the very best for a successful career in this fantastic and dynamic industry.

Appendices

Appendices 1, 2, & 3. © 2014. Glen C. Ramsborg. Adapted from Beal, Bohlen, & Raudabaugh, 1962; Beck, 2006; Bergevin, Morris, & Smith, 1963; *Convention Industry Council Manual*, 2008; Endean, 2014; Owen, 2012; Robinson, 1979; and Seaman & Fellenz, 1989.

Typology of Room Sets: Captivating, Engaging, and Communicative

Captivating	Strengths	Challenges
Meeting Pods Designed for a number of small groups in one room, allowing participants to move from one meeting to another. **Optimal Capacity** 10–30 people; maximum 60 people. Depends on room size. **Set-Up** 2 rectangular (6 ft. x 30 in. or 8 ft. x 30 in.) tables are placed side by side to create a "pod" with up to 2–3 rolling chairs at each table. One end remains open for facilitator to record proceedings. Several pods are interspersed throughout the room (see Figure 4.16, p. 61).	• All-way communication • Interactive, not hierarchic. • Participants are mobile. Hands-on participation possible. • Appropriate for teamwork, negotiations, brainstorming, strategic planning, Q&A interaction, and training. • Appropriate technology includes individual computers, white boards, and flip charts at each table.	• Highly informal; unstructured. • Space-intensive. • May be unsettling for attendees unfamiliar with configuration. **Meeting Format Examples** • Role Play • Buzz Sessions • Break-Out Sessions
Captivating	**Strengths**	**Challenges**
Interactive Circle Chairs are aligned in a circular pattern, forming a learning circle for group interaction. Facilitator is seated with participants, or steps to the center. **Optimal Capacity** Less than 20; maximum 40. **Set-Up** All chairs face toward center of circle. No lectern, no table.	• All-way communication. • Intimate, open setting with participants facing one another. • All participants equal. • Fosters unity and connectedness. • Appropriate for group therapy, personal sharing, team building, and consensus building. • Set-up is fast and easy; any space appropriate.	• Lacks writing surface. • Use of audiovisuals and technology may be awkward. • Takes up large amount of floor space. • Participants may feel exposed. **Meeting Format Example** • Fish Bowl
Engaging	**Strengths**	**Challenges**
Boardroom or Conference A single but extensive solid rectangular surface provides seating on all four sides, with workspace for each participant. **Optimal Capacity** Less than 20; maximum 40. Approximately 30 sq. ft. per person. **Set-Up** Rectangular tables (6 ft. x 30 in. or 8 ft. x 30 in.) combined to create single large rectangular table. Minimum of 2 ft. workspace per person. No chair within 1 ft. of shared corner. Leader placed opposite to entrance door. Along the wall of entrance door, provide seating for observers. (See Figures 4.12 & 4.13, p. 59).	• Both one-way and two-way communication possible. • Formal, executive level. • Encourages total group interaction as well as dialogue among participants. • Good visual lines of communication. • Writing surface for everyone. • Strategic seating available. • Fixed boardroom table often available.	• The longer each side, the harder it is to see others along side. • Formal, immobile. **Meeting Format Examples** • Seminar • Committee Meeting • Board Meeting • Break-Out Sessions
Engaging	**Strengths**	**Challenges**
U-Shaped Rectangular tables are placed together to form the shape of a "U." Participants sit facing one another on the outside of the horseshoe. **Optimal Capacity** 12–24; maximum 40. Approximately 35 sq. ft. per person. **Set-Up** Rectangular tables (6 ft. x 30 in. or 8 ft. x 30 in.) placed in 3-sided "U" shape with chairs on outside or both sides, if necessary. Allow a minimum of 2 ft. workspace per person. No attendee within 1 ft. of shared corner. If outside seating only, skirt on inside (see Figure 4.14, p. 59).	• Interactive, two-way, face-to-face communication, with excellent sight lines. • Facilitator has close access and communication with participants from inside the "U." • Center of "U" available for audiovisual presentation. • Appropriate for presenter-discussion format. • Sufficient workspace for each participant. • No preferential seating; equality among participants; unifying.	• Onsite review of set-up is crucial. • Space-intensive. • Use of AV as some people will need to turn chairs around to see the screen. **Meeting Format Examples** • Colloquium • Committee Meeting • Debate

Continued

Engaging

Hollow Square Long rectangular tables form a square with an internal open space.

Optimal Capacity 12–24; maximum 40. Approximately 30 sq. ft. per person.

Set-Up Join two (2) or more 6-ft. or 8-ft. tables per side to form a square, leaving an open but inaccessible space in the center. Allow a minimum of 2 ft. of workspace per person. Chairs are placed on all four sides of square.

Strengths

- Two-way, face-to-face communication.
- Appropriate for group discussion, problem-solving, decision-making.
- Appropriate for both small and mid-size groups.
- Provides both appropriate distance and excellent sight lines for all.
- No hierarchy evident.
- Facilitator guides discussion.

Challenges

- Inaccessible and unusable center space.
- Space-intensive, perhaps costly.
- Not appropriate for audiovisual presentations or video conferencing.

Meeting Format Examples

- Seminar
- Symposium
- Group Discussion
- Committee Meeting

Communicative

Banquet Style Circular tables allow for meal-centered meeting and group discussion. If staggered in rows, at least half of each circle has a clear view of front of the room; movable chairs allow others the opportunity to face the presenter.

Optimal Capacity Depends on room capacity and table size. No more than 12 per table, depending on size of table. Approximately 13.5 sq. ft. per person.

Maximum Capacity Unlimited.

Set-Up Align tables for minimum distance of 9–10 ft. between centers of adjacent tables (see Figure 4.15, p. 60). For a **crescent round** set-up, place chairs around only one half of table for viewing of presentation at front of room.

Strengths

- Versatile
- Appropriate for networking, socialization.
- Allows for both food and meeting.
- Easy conversion from meeting to dining and vice versa.

Challenges

- Viewing of visual aids awkward.
- Simultaneous discussion at multiple nearby tables may be noisy.
- Some audience members must move chairs to view speaker.

Meeting Format Examples

- Seminar
- Symposium
- Group Discussion
- Committee Meeting
- Debate

Communicative

Theater (Amphitheater) Padded, stacking chairs are lined in rows facing the front or a focal point of a room.

Optimal Capacity Unlimited, depending on size of space.

Room Requirements (calculation for space per person)

- > 60: 12–13 sq. ft.; 1.1–1.2 sq. m.
- 60-300: 11–12 sq. ft.; 1.0–1.1 sq. m.
- < 300: 10–11 sq. ft.; 0.93–1.0 sq. m.

Set-Up Horizontal, semicircular, chevron, or herringbone rows of chairs face a single focal point and are offset for visibility. First row is no closer than 6 ft. from edge of platform or twice the vertical dimension of the viewing screen. Row length is limited to 14 chairs or 30 ft. long with 24 in. between rows. Avoid center aisle. No tables (see Figures 4.9 & 4.10, p. 58).

Strengths

- One-way communication; attendees are audience members.
- Formal, provides opportunity for elaborate staging.
- Maximizes seating capacity, highly efficient.
- Projection presentation, teleconference appropriate.

Challenges

- Participation restricted.
- Limited space for personal belongings, no space for writing.
- Difficult for speaker to maintain close communication with audience.
- May appear crowded, or if seats are empty, significance may be undermined.

Meeting Format Examples

- Keynote Address
- General Session
- Staged Performance
- Executive Presentation
- Interview
- Lecture

Communicative

Classroom A series of tables and chairs face the front of a meeting room where a speaker is the focal point.

Optimal Capacity 40–50; maximum dependent on room size.

Room Requirements (calculation for space per person)

- > 60: 22–23 sq. ft.; 2.0–2.1 sq. m.
- 60–300: 20–21 sq. ft.; 1.9–1.95 sq. m.
- < 300: 17–18 sq. ft.; 1.6–1.7 sq. m.

Set-Up 6 ft. or 8 ft. x 18 in. tables with standard seating placed in rows facing focal point. Rows are 24 ft. or less, with aisles on both sides. Distance between tables at least 3.5 ft. Chevron style angles tables inward for sight lines. Allow 2.5–3 ft. of table space per person (see Figure 4.11, p. 58).

Strengths

- Offers both one-way and two-way communication, both audience experience and small group interaction.
- Appropriate for training, lecture-presentation of some duration, and Q&A session with presenter.
- Business-like atmosphere.
- Individual workspace available.
- Comfortable for participants.
- Projection presentation, teleconferencing, video conferencing appropriate.
- Easy set-up.

Challenges

- Engagement with speaker challenging. Gap between speaker and audience.
- Microphones necessary.
- Not spatially efficient.
- Collaboration between tables unlikely.

Meeting Format Examples

- Workshop
- Lecture
- Seminar

Meeting Formats

Formal		Informal		Participant-Driven	
Goals		**Goals**		**Goals**	
• Dissemination of information • In-depth understanding • Decision-making Expertise and content primary; structured.		• Exposure to various points of view • Critical thinking • Cooperation and collaboration • Self-expression Process and participation valued; moderated.		• Engagement • Experience • Intellectual and imaginative stimulation Reflective, relatively unstructured, spontaneous, open-ended.	
Lecture Single individual controls one-way information to stimulate, inspire, entertain, or rapidly transfer information to large audience.		**Forum** Large, public, open discussion of an issue.		**Brainstorming** Creative generation of ideas pertinent to the topic, initially without order, editing, or evaluation. This immediate, spontaneous response to a question or problem can be accomplished alone or in a group; may be linguistic or imagistic. Quantity of responses more important than quality.	
Strengths	**Challenges**	**Strengths**	**Challenges**	**Strengths**	**Challenges**
• Integration of ideas, in-depth knowledge of expert.	• Typically academic, audience may be passive. • Limited interaction.	• Democratic, all may contribute, variety of voices heard. • Appropriately paired with another program, e.g., panel discussion, lecture.	• Conducive setting important. • Moderator must manage audience.	• Avoids premature challenges. • Incorporates the improbable in generating a wide variety of ideas.	• Messy, inefficient, time-consuming. • Risky for individuals. • Group can stifle ideas. • Requires facilitation.
Seminar Small group engages in in-depth study of a specific topic. Facilitated by recognized authority.		**Group Discussion** Small group converses about a topic of mutual interest and knowledge.		**Silent Meeting** Deep consideration of a topic by a small group practicing silence, i.e., meditation, study, or writing, and spontaneous oral contribution.	
Strengths	**Challenges**	**Strengths**	**Challenges**	**Strengths**	**Challenges**
• Expert leader, committed and active participants. • Thorough and researched study.	• Time commitment. • Highly focused topic.	• Both teamwork and leadership skills developed, individual voices heard. • Most common to 21st century.	• Involvement of members may be unequal. • Reaching productive results may be lost in talk.	• Promotes reflection in a corporate setting. • Encourages creative and personal expression. • Unusual.	• Not for self-conscious or inhibited individuals. • Without a facilitator, meeting may fail.
Debate Two teams argue opposing sides of an issue. Format preordained. Evidence, logic, and persuasion are used.		**Fish Bowl** A two-part discussion group, with the smaller "inner circle" of 4–5 people discussing a topic and the larger "outer circle" of as many as 20 observing. Roles switched periodically.		**Role Play** An unrehearsed portrayal of a problematic situation in which participants assume various roles. Followed by analytic discussion.	
Strengths	**Challenges**	**Strengths**	**Challenges**	**Strengths**	**Challenges**
• Stimulating, appropriate for controversial topics, audience assesses and judges.	• Few participants, limited time. • Arguments may be slanted.	• Stresses both listening and speaking skills. • Gives participants the opportunity to evaluate process and content. • Improvement implicit. Simulates discussion.	• Some performance anxiety possible. • Assessment by observers can be hurtful. • Focus easily derailed. • Moderator key to success.	• Allows participants to gain insight into others' attitudes and experience; promotes empathy. • Roles need to be assigned. • Involving. • Engaging.	• Audience in observation role. • Some may feel performance anxiety. • Can easily veer off track. • Requires alert and careful direction.

Continued

Formal	Informal	Participant-Driven
Interview Expert or celebrity responds to questioning by an individual before an audience. **Strengths** • Celebrity appeal of interviewee. • Personalizes topic or issue. • Opportunity for impromptu follow-up questions. **Challenges** • No audience participation. • Success largely depends on skillful interviewer.	**Buzz Session** Several small groups meet simultaneously for short periods of time to discuss a topic or perform a task, returning their contribution to the larger group. **Strengths** • Focused and purposeful. • Efficient. • Encourages contribution of everyone. • Group problem solving. • Increases rich generated ideas. **Challenges** • Not effective for complex issues. • Participants easily distracted by other groups. • Eavesdropping on other group discussions possible.	**Simulation** Self-paced, interactive instructional technique in which the learner has the opportunity to practice a skill in the model of a real-world process or situation. **Strengths** • Highly relevant to learner, fully experiential. • Provides opportunity for safe testing of the unfamiliar and new. • Learner performance can be tracked. **Challenges** • Model must be accurately and carefully designed. • Costly. • May not easily translate to reality.
Panel Discussion A selected group of experts discuss a complex topic before an audience. Moderated. One- or two-way communication. **Strengths** • Varying approaches and points of view presented. • Appears informal, conversational. **Challenges** • No audience participation. • Expertise of panel members must be balanced. • Significant planning and skillful moderation required.	**Committee** A small group appointed to perform a specific task unsuitable for an individual or for a large group. **Strengths** • Efficient, action-oriented. • All members responsible. • Group plans, studies an issue, and reports findings. **Challenges** • Time and distance may interfere with participation. • Group dynamic may negatively impact productivity.	**Technology Center** Open space filled with various cutting-edge technology experiences available to the learner. **Strengths** • Learner-initiated. • Involving. • Experiential. **Challenges** • Training may be needed. • Costly. • Solitary.
Colloquy A panel discussion including equal numbers (3–4) of both experts and audience members. Appropriate for problem/solution or controversial topic. **Strengths** • Audience is represented. • Rapport between audience and experts established. **Challenges** • Selected audience members must be well informed and prepared to participate.	**Learning Communities** A combination of individuals with shared interests. Grow out of listservs or social media groups, e.g., LinkedIn or Facebook. Synonyms include study groups, action research teams, communities of practice, birds of a feather, conversation circles, or round-table discussions. **Strengths** • A virtual and in-person complement. • Tested concept from education community. • Ongoing resource supporting varied participation. **Challenges** • Sustained participant leadership. • Managing renegade conversations.	**Unconference** A participant-driven, self-organizing meeting; audience creates the agenda. Generally focuses on specific theme and features open discussion. **Strengths** • Participant-driven agenda maximizes relevancy. • Creative and open conversation; share insights. **Challenges** • Requires explanation of how and why the format works in advance of the program. • "Selling" the idea to participants. • May be uncomfortable format for some participants.

Meeting Structures		
Characteristics	**Strengths**	**Challenges**
Exposition A public exhibition depicting an issue or featuring an artist or genre. The trade show provides companies with an opportunity to unveil and demonstrate their products. Demonstrations provide information regarding the use of a product or service, accompanied by oral and visual explanation.	• Typically open to the public. • Experiential, participatory. • Sensory, attention-getting exhibitions and field trips. • Demonstrations offer convincing motivation to use the product or service. • Revenue stream for host organization. • Business-to-business and business-to-customer relationships solidified.	• Attendance may be "trade only." • Travel (also a potential attraction). • Crowd management. • Time, skill, money, and talent required to create compelling exhibits. • Skilled and engaging demonstrators essential.
Convention/Congress Large gathering of members and representatives of an industry or organization convened for a common purpose. A recurring, regularly scheduled, perhaps mandated meeting that may last for several days with many internal meetings simultaneously scheduled. Organizational governance or business, future planning, continuing education, training, and networking are accomplished.	• Large number of individuals served at one time in one place. • Actions that require membership input can be accomplished in a timely manner. • Identity of organization is strengthened; membership is solidified. • A venue for marketing and sales. • Encompasses a variety of smaller, more focused meetings with varying purposes.	• Membership required; non-members may pay higher fee. • Travel (also a potential attraction). • Crowd management in appropriate setting.
Conference Participatory meeting designed for discussion or "conferring" on a topic or pressing issue. Also involves fact-finding, problem solving, debate, and presentation of research on a specific issue. Conference proceedings may be published. Convening may be annual or irregularly scheduled.	• Highly participatory and interactive. • Not as large or long as a convention. • Topic or issue is focused. • Develop plans promoting some idea.	• Membership required; non-members may pay higher fee. • Travel (also a potential attraction). • Crowd management in appropriate setting.
Symposium A formal meeting at which several specialists deliver short addresses or papers on a topic or on related topics. Recommendations concerning the problem under discussion are made. Moderated. May be scheduled or ongoing, online.	• Suitable for controversial or in-depth topics. • Audience is exposed to a thorough range of information or opinions from experts in the field. • Brief talks keep audience's attention. • Multiple experts prevent over-simplification.	• Formal; may be exclusive. • Interaction among speakers unlikely. • Audience does not participate. • Skillful moderator essential. • Securing competent speakers at same level may be difficult.
Workshop A meeting at which a group of people engage in intensive discussion and interaction regarding a particular subject or project. A training session of some duration in which participants develop knowledge in, and practice skills of, a particular discipline. **Institute** A short, intensive workshop or seminar on a specific subject. **Clinic** A brief, focused training, conference, or short course.	• Highly focused, purposeful. • Members share common purpose; exchange of information stressed. • Meaningful goals can be accomplished within allotted time. • Great potential for behavioral changes and process alterations.	• Measuring effectiveness difficult. • Intensive workload can preclude socialization, networking. • Time constraints may limit developing group cohesion. • Extensive planning and significant resources impact success. • Effective leader needed to maintain awareness of work within small clusters of larger group.

Banquet Event Order—281407

Account:	Association of XYZ	**Event Date:**	Tuesday, February 14
Group Post:	Mid-Year Assembly	**Contact:**	Jared Mason, CMP
Event Post:	Breakfast Buffet	**Phone:**	888-777-8888
Address:		**On-Site:**	888-444-5555

Deposit:	N/A	**Billing ID#**	H-XYZ	**Catering Src:**	Melinda French, CMP
CCHolder:	Direct Bill, Approved			**Convention Src:**	Jeffrey House, CMP
CCNum:		**F/B Min:**	$175,000		

***All events are subject to:** 18.5% service charge, 7% administrative fee taxed at 10.25%, 10% state & city tax, 3% bottled beverage tax, and applicable rental tax—subject to change.*

Date	Time	Room	Function	Set-up	Post	GTD	SET	Rental
February 14	7:00am–9:00 am	Grand Ballroom	Bfst	6:30am	YES	250	250	TBD

FOOD & BEVERAGE REQUIREMENTS

Selection of Chilled Fruit Juices
Sliced Fruit Display
Assorted Bagels
Assorted Cold Cereal with Whole or Skim Milk
Scrambled Eggs with Cheddar Cheese and Scallions
Thick-Cut French Toast with Vermont Maple Syrup
Applewood Smoked Bacon
Breakfast Link Sausage Oven Roasted
Hash Browns
Cream
Cheese, Butter, Marmalade, and Assorted Jams
Fresh Brewed Coffee and Assorted Teas
Iced Tea, Brewed Coffee, and Brewed Decaffeinated Coffee
$31.00 per person/++

AUDIOVISUAL REQUIREMENTS

Table lectern with microphone
3 wireless microphones for audience questions @ $190.00 each per day
1 Projection Package with Screen per quote
1 standing microphone (for announcements)
Music through house sound—patch fee $85.00
Client to provide CDs
House sound

SET-UP REQUIREMENTS

Six food buffets in Ballroom
Banquet tables—60" rounds, 8 guests per table
Linens—Black furnished by hotel w/ white napkins
See diagram provided by client
3 easels at room entrance

BILLING INSTRUCTIONS

Direct Billing to Master Account

Labor charges may apply. All audiovisual is subject to a service charge of 22% and 8% equipment tax PLUS $95.00 set-up fee. Audiovisual pricing is through in-house provider and will be invoiced separately.

VALUED GUEST: It is necessary for all event banquet checks to be signed upon conclusion of your event/events.

The final guarantee attendance must be received 3 business days (72 hours) prior to the event. Should the final guarantee not be received, the original guarantee will be the basis for billing charges. We will be prepared to over-set 3% of the final guarantee, up to 30 guests. Increases in guarantees within 72 hours are subject to approval and to additional delivery fee charges. To confirm this Banquet Event Order, please review carefully, sign below, and return to your hotel representative.

Organization Authorized Signature ______ Date

Hotel Representative Signature ______ Date

CMP-IS Mapping

A group of subject matter experts reviewed the content of each chapter with respect to the CMP-IS. A 50 percent or greater agreement was required by reviewers that the content, to some degree, met the Skill and SubSkills identified on the title page of each chapter. SubSkills not covered in the chapters are listed in italics.

DOMAIN A. STRATEGIC PLANNING

SKILL 1. Manage Strategic Plan for Meeting or Event

- ✓ 1.01 Develop mission, goals and objectives of meeting or event
- ✓ 1.02 Determine feasibility of meeting or event
- ✓ 1.03 Determine requirements to carry out meeting or event
- ✓ 1.04 Develop financial summary
- ✓ 1.05 Monitor strategic plan

SKILL 2. Develop Sustainability Plan for Meeting or Event

- ✓ 2.01 Implement sustainability management plan
- ✓ 2.02 Monitor strategic plan

SKILL 3. Develop Business Continuity or Long-Term Viability Plan of Meeting or Event

- ✓ 3.01 Develop evaluation plan
- ✓ 3.02 Measure return on investment
- ✓ 3.03 Evaluate/audit meeting or event
- ✓ 3.04 Evaluate effectiveness of risk management plan

DOMAIN B. PROJECT MANAGEMENT

SKILL 4. Plan Meeting or Event Project

- ✓ 4.01 Develop project plan
- ✓ 4.02 Develop quality standards, policies, and procedures
- ✓ 4.03 Develop theme for meeting or event
- ✓ 4.04 Develop procurement plan
- ✓ 4.05 Establish milestones and critical path
- ✓ 4.06 Develop integrated communication plan
- ✓ 4.07 Develop evaluation/Audit procedures

SKILL 5. Manage Meeting or Event Project

- ✓ 5.01 Manage critical path
- ✓ 5.02 Manage contracts
- ✓ 5.03 Manage implementation of the meeting or event

DOMAIN C. RISK MANAGEMENT

SKILL 6. Manage Risk Management Plan

- ✓ 6.01 Identify risks
- ✓ 6.02 Analyze risks
- ✓ 6.03 Develop management and implementation plan
- ✓ 6.04 Develop and implement emergency response plan
- ✓ 6.05 Arrange security

DOMAIN D. FINANCIAL MANAGEMENT

SKILL 7. Manage Event Funding and Financial Resources

- ✓ 7.01 Manage sponsorship and donor process
- 7.02 *Manage grant-funding process*
- ✓ 7.03 Manage registration process
- ✓ 7.04 Manage exhibit sales process
- ✓ 7.05 Manage miscellaneous funding sources

SKILL 8. Manage Budget

- ✓ 8.01 Develop budget
- ✓ 8.02 Establish pricing
- ✓ 8.03 Monitor budget performance
- ✓ 8.04 Revise budget

SKILL 9. Manage Monetary Transactions

- ✓ 9.01 Establish cash handling procedures
- ✓ 9.02 Monitor cash handling procedures

DOMAIN E. HUMAN RESOURCES

SKILL 10. Acquire Staff and Volunteers

- ✓ 10.01 Manage sponsorship and donor process
- ✓ 10.02 Recruit staff and volunteers
- 10.03 *Select best candidates and offer positions*

SKILL 11. Train Staff and Volunteers

- ✓ 11.01 Provide orientation
- 11.02 *Provide training*

SKILL 12. Manage Workforce Relations

- ✓ 12.01 Supervise staff and volunteers
- ✓ 12.02 Manage teams

DOMAIN F. STAKEHOLDER MANAGEMENT

SKILL 13. Manage Stakeholder Relationships

- ✓ 13.01 Identify, assess, and categorize stakeholders
- 13.02 *Manage stakeholder activities*
- ✓ 13.03 Manage stakeholder relationships

Domain G. Meeting or Event Design

SKILL 14. Develop Program

- ✓ **14.01** Determine program components
- ✓ **14.02** Select program content and delivery formats
- ✓ **14.03** Structure and sequence program components
- ✓ **14.04** Measure event success

SKILL 15. Engage Speakers and Performers

- ✓ **15.01** Determine event requirements for speakers and performers
- ✓ **15.02** Develop selection criteria/strategies
- ✓ **15.03** Select candidates
- ✓ **15.04** Secure contracts and communicate expectations

SKILL 16. Coordinate Food and Beverage Services

- ✓ **16.01** Determine food and beverage service requirements
- ✓ **16.02** Select menu(s)
- ✓ **16.03** Plan service style(s)
- ✓ **16.04** Select food and beverage provider(s)
- ✓ **16.05** Manage alcohol service

SKILL 17. Design Environment

- ✓ **17.01** Establish functional requirements
- ✓ **17.02** Select décor and furnishings
- ✓ **17.03** Coordinate meeting or event signage

SKILL 18. Manage Technical Production

- **18.01** *Determine requirements for staging and technical equipment*
- ✓ **18.02** Acquire staging and technical equipment
- ✓ **18.03** Install staging and technical equipment
- ✓ **18.04** Oversee technical production operation

SKILL 19. Develop Plan for Managing Movement of Attendees

- ✓ **19.01** Develop admittance credential systems
- ✓ **19.02** Select crowd management techniques
- ✓ **19.03** Coordinate accommodations
- **19.04** *Coordinate transportation*
- **19.05** *Manage protocol requirements*

Domain H. Site Management

SKILL 20. Select Site

- ✓ **20.01** Determine site specifications
- ✓ **20.02** Identify and inspect sites

SKILL 21. Design Site Layout

- ✓ **21.01** Design site layout

SKILL 22. Manage Meeting or Event Site

- ✓ **22.01** Create logistics action plan for site set-up and takedown
- ✓ **22.02** Set up site
- ✓ **22.03** Monitor site during meeting or event
- ✓ **22.04** Dismantle site

SKILL 23. Manage On-site Communications

- ✓ **23.01** Establish communications framework
- **23.02** *Determine and acquire required communication equipment and resources*
- ✓ **23.03** Specify communication procedures and protocols

Domain I. Marketing

SKILL 24. Manage Marketing Plan

- ✓ **24.01** Conduct situational analysis
- ✓ **24.02** Define target market segments
- ✓ **24.03** Select marketing distribution channels
- ✓ **24.04** Implement marketing plan

SKILL 25. Manage Marketing Materials

- ✓ **25.01** Determine needed marketing materials for event
- ✓ **25.02** Develop content and design parameters
- **25.03** *Produce marketing materials*
- ✓ **25.04** Distribute marketing materials

SKILL 26. Manage Meeting or Event Merchandise

- ✓ **26.01** Develop product(s) design and specifications
- ✓ **26.02** Determine pricing
- **26.03** *Control brand integrity*
- **26.04** *Acquire merchandise*
- **26.05** *Distribute merchandise*

SKILL 27. Promote Meeting or Event

- ✓ **27.01** Develop cross-promotional activities
- ✓ **27.02** Develop contests
- ✓ **27.03** Coordinate hospitality

SKILL 28. Contribute to Public Relations Activities

- ✓ **28.01** Contribute to public relations strategy
- ✓ **28.02** Contribute to publicity plan
- ✓ **28.03** Manage media relations
- ✓ **24.04** Contribute to implementation of publicity plan
- ✓ **28.05** Manage response to crises and controversies

SKILL 29. Manage Meeting-Related Sales Activities

- ✓ **29.01** Contribute to sales plan and objectives
- **29.02** *Conduct sales activities*

Domain K. Professionalism

SKILL 30. Exhibit Professional Behavior

- ✓ **30.01** Demonstrate ethical behavior

Glossary

A

advanced logistics The management of all logistics associated with individual meetings as well as meeting functions.

after-action review (AAR) A structured review or debrief process for analyzing what happened, why it happened, and how it can be done better by the participants and those responsible for the project or event.

aggregate results Data formed by the compilation or collection of information about a meeting in order to evaluate its success or identify areas for improvement.

authority Permission; right to exercise the power delegated by a principal to its agent.

B

big data An accumulation of data that is too large and complex for processing by traditional database management tools.

blog Short for weblog, a type of website that publishes entries in chronological order, upon which visitors can comment.

budgeting A process of planning and preparing estimated revenues and expenses in order to achieve financial goals.

business continuity A business process that ensures that an organization's critical business functions are not compromised when organizations experience opportunities or threats. Recent definitions include a focus on issues such as natural resource supplies, the cost of pollution, sustainable relationships with suppliers, and the economic distress of the communities in which an organization produces and sells products.

business-to-business (B2B) exhibition An exhibition offering industry-specific products and services, which attendees must qualify to attend based on organizer-defined criteria.

business-to-consumer (B2C) exhibition An exhibition that is open to the public or segments of the public where direct sales and order-taking may take place; an admission fee is often charged.

C

capacity Legal qualification, competency, power, or fitness, e.g., a person's capacity and authority to enter into a contract may be questioned.

communication flow A description of the manner in which content or information flows between the instructor, speaker, or facilitator and the attendees and/or learners.

competency standards A list of requirements for effective performance in a specific work area; often used as the basis for defining knowledge, skills, and appropriate application for those in the workplace.

condition of premises A contract clause that addresses the issue of the property's condition and any material deterioration or damage to the facility that occurred between the time the contract was signed and the commencement of the event. It may provide remedies or procedures to apply in the event of a change in condition. This clause is rarely used for short-term bookings.

congress center A facility, outside the U.S., whose purpose it is to host trade shows, public shows, conventions, and other large functions; it combines exhibition space with a substantial number of smaller meeting and event spaces.

conventional speaker system A series of traditional electroacoustic loudspeakers used in combination to project sound across a wide area, like a ballroom or arena.

corporate social responsibility (CSR) A form of corporate self-regulation integrated into the business and culture of an organization, which embraces responsibility for the organization's actions and encourages a positive impact on the environment, consumers, employees, communities, and other stakeholders.

creative director The person who focuses on the development of the visual messaging, staging, and artistic elements of a meeting.

crisis response team An individual or group of individuals who respond to an emergency or crisis for the purpose of managing the situation, and identifying and engaging the appropriate resources.

D

daily onsite meeting A time each day for the meeting/event staff to review the activities of the day, identify any issues that need to be addressed, and discuss any changes for the following day, used typically for multi-day meetings/events.

dashboard An interactive table of contents used in project management when communicating with multiple parties via the Internet.

data segmentation The isolation and analysis of certain pockets of data in order to draw specific conclusions.

deficit A shortfall, loss, or discrepancy in the financial situation of a meeting.

delivery stage The stage of meeting design in which the design for the meeting is put into action.

demographic Socioeconomic characteristics of a population expressed statistically, such as age, sex, education level, income level, marital status, occupation, religion, birth rate, death rate, average size of a family, average age at marriage, etc.

destination A geographic location where meetings or events are held.

development stage The stage of meeting design in which the design team develops meeting objectives and associated design elements.

digital signage Signs within the meeting facility projected digitally, as opposed to traditional signs on some of type of poster board.

direct competition Competition among suppliers who offer identical goods and services.

directional sign A sign designed to provide direction that helps attendees move from location to location within a large facility.

discovery stage The stage of meeting design in which the design team analyzes the environment and performs a stakeholder needs analysis.

due diligence The process of asking reasonable questions to assist in developing a risk-management plan appropriate to the organization and the meeting/event; this also applies to developing a contract for the meeting/event.

E

e-Poster system A system that displays digital posters on screens or similar display devices in place of traditional printed media.

e-RFP An electronic document (request for protocol) that stipulates what services the organization wants from an outside contractor and requests a bid to perform such services.

event-management software Software products that are used in the management of professional and academic conferences, trade exhibitions, and smaller events.

exclusive provider A contractor, designated by the venue, who has the right to provide all services within a given facility.

expenses The cost of the products and services utilized to host a meeting.

exposition A large public show, exhibit, or trade show; also referred as an exhibition.

F

face-to-face meeting A gathering of people in a common location for the purpose of learning, transacting business, or socializing.

familiarization (FAM) trip A visit by invitation only to provide a guided view of a destination, venue, and facility to better determine its appropriateness for a meeting/event.

focus group A small number of people (usually between 4 and 15, but typically 8) brought together with a moderator to focus on discussing or obtaining responses to formal questions about a specific product or topic. The results produce qualitative data (preferences and beliefs) that may or may not be representative of the general population.

forecast To use past or historical data to estimate information about the future, e.g., future attendance at a meeting or financial data.

front-of-house (FOH) audio engineer The main audio engineer who sits in the room, usually behind the audience, at front-of-house (FOH) and who is responsible for mixing, manipulating, recording, and reproducing all of the sound for an event.

G

gamification The process of using game, social, and reputation mechanics to drive desired behaviors at events, including driving attendees to engage with one another, with exhibitors, and with the event brand.

gap analysis A project-management tool to help determine what needs to be accomplished in order to meet the outcomes; also known as a discrepancy analysis.

gluten free A diet that excludes the protein gluten, which is found in grains such as wheat, barley, rye, and triticale (a cross between wheat and rye).

green screen A form of chroma key compositing, or chroma keying, this is a live or post-produced special effect for compositing (layering) two images or video streams together based on color hues (chroma range). Green is one of the most popular background colors but other choices are blue, orange, or purple.

H

hard close A specific time when the bar is closed at an event and can no longer serve guests alcoholic beverages.

hashtag A word or phrase preceded by a hash mark (#) and used within a message to identify a keyword or topic of interest and facilitate a search for it. It is used on social media websites.

hazard A source of danger or vulnerability causing concern for the safety and security of individuals or property.

high season A time of year when a destination is in highest demand, creating higher prices for goods and services.

horizontal exhibition An exhibition that displays many types of products and services appropriate to one or more industries.

hybrid meeting A blend of a face-to-face meeting and virtual meeting occurring in an Internet platform; also known as a blended meeting.

I

identification sign A sign designed to identify the meeting or event and any special features that may be of interest to the attendee.

incentive A concession or reward for booking a hotel room within the contracted room block for a meeting/event.

incremental budget A budget created by using past budget data or actual performance as a foundation and making incremental changes as necessary for the new budget period.

independent planner An individual or organization who plans meetings or events; also known as a third-party contractor.

indirect competition Competition among suppliers of different types of products that satisfy the same needs.

infographic An umbrella term used for illustrations and charts that instruct people in ways that would be difficult or impossible to accomplish in a text-only communication.

informational sign A sign designed to provide information for attendees about the program, changes to the program, or other vital details.

in-house system A system (usually computerized) within the organization for registering meeting attendees; also applies to handling reservations for lodging in hotels within the contracted room block.

in-kind donation Tangible (often consumable) items donated to a cause and separated from financial contributions.

intellectual property The ownership of intangible and non-physical goods, which include ideas, names, designs, symbols, artwork, writings, and other creations; also refers to digital media, e.g., audio and video clips, that can be downloaded online.

isolated (ISO) camera feed The live or recorded video from an individual camera used during an event. The isolated feed is the raw, uncut, and unedited video from that single camera.

K

knowledge, skills, and abilities (KSA) A series of narrative statements that are deemed to be required to perform a specific job competently.

L

learning objective A statement written that describes what the participant will be expected to learn at the conclusion of an educational event; "learner outcomes" refer to the results of activities conducted by the learner.

liability A legal responsibility for an incident or a monetary responsibility for services rendered.

line-array speaker system A system that is made up of a number of identical loudspeaker elements mounted in a line and fed in phase, to create a linear source of sound. They send sound waves farther than traditional horn-loaded loudspeakers, and with a more evenly distributed sound output pattern.

liquidated damages An amount of money the parties of a contract designate during negotiations for the injured party to collect as compensation upon a specific breach of the agreement.

low season A time of year when a destination is in low demand, creating associated prices for goods and services.

M

marketing The activity, set of institutions, and processes for creating, communicating, delivering, and exchanging offerings that have value for customers, clients, partners, and society at large.

marketing mix A combination of approaches to market a specific meeting, product, or service to the target audience.

marketing plan Product-specific, market-specific, or company-wide plan that describes activities involved in achieving specific marketing objectives within a set time frame.

measurement The activities associated with assessing the value of a meeting.

meeting attendee portal A virtual gateway that brings many different information resources together for a meeting in an online environment.

meeting client The person who organizes a meeting and is responsible for strategic goals and objectives.

meeting design The purposeful shaping of the form and content of a meeting.

meeting designer The person who applies social, behavioral, and cognitive science to the design of a meeting. The meeting designer leads the activities of a meeting-design team.

meeting environment The space in which people gather for a meeting.

meeting experience Term that emphasizes the holistic effects of the meeting on the attendee, including the emotional and intellectual effects of the meeting.

meeting structure In the meetings industry, the public name for the meeting is based on the structure, e.g., institute, convention, or symposium.

mitigate (mitigation) The efforts taken to reduce or minimize the risks at a meeting/event that have been predicted to have a potential impact on the organization.

mobile app Mobile software that is designed to run on tablet computers, personal digital assistants (PDAs), enterprise digital assistants (EDAs), smartphones, and cellphones.

monitor A video or audio device used to maintain a reference on the sound or video that is being sent out to the audience; audio feeds are also given to performers and referred to as monitors, but do not necessarily represent the sound sent to the audience.

N

name-handling technology A digitally controlled group discussion system that provides a given chairperson the flexibility and discretion to control a meeting by identifying the individual and microphone location from a video control monitor.

near-field communication (NFC) A method for smartphones and similar devices to establish radio communication with each other by touching them together or bringing them into proximity, usually no more than a few centimeters.

needs assessment A systematic process for determining and addressing needs or "gaps" between current conditions and desired conditions or "wants." The discrepancy between the current and wanted condition must be measured to identify the need appropriately.

negotiation A series of discussions between the buyer and seller that result in a contractual arrangement.

non-exclusive or discretionary provider Services provider at an exhibition, hired at the discretion of the organizer or exhibitor.

O

ongoing impact stage The stage of a meeting in which the activities and impact of the meeting are tied to other activities in an organization on an ongoing basis.

online community A virtual community where members communicate over the Internet, enabling people with like interests to connect with one another year-round; social media platforms use this format in developing chat rooms, discussion groups, etc.

online registration A process of registering for an event through a website before the meeting actually takes place.

onsite check-in Manual or automated assistance for attendee check-in at events, offering convenience and reduced wait times.

P

pace report A document that tracks the pickup of rooms or registration of attendees on a regular basis, which assists in developing a history year over year.

pandemic A disease that is prevalent over an entire country or the world.

pedagogy Refers to the art and science of teaching, training, and facilitation.

portfolio management The management and alignment of an organization's entire portfolio of internal and external meetings with organizational strategy.

portfolio manager A person who fosters connections between programs and some projects that are not interdependent, but are influenced by a common strategic goal.

pre-departure meeting A meeting for organizational staff that takes place prior to departing for the meeting or event. The agenda focuses on reviewing the onsite meeting details, roles, and responsibilities.

professional liability insurance Protection for professionals with a special expertise that is not covered by the general liability insurance of an organization.

profit (net income) The amount of money remaining after payment of all expenses.

program component One of several "building blocks" of the meeting concept; focuses on delivering specific outcomes and results in a cohesive program for attendees.

program format The form, design, or arrangement of the program delivery for individual program components.

program manager An individual who manages a variety of projects, other activities, employees, and resources which are interrelated and often interdependent.

program outcome The anticipated results from the learning that attendees will achieve through program attendance.

project A temporary and unique product, service, or initiative. From the perspective of the meetings industry, a project could be any meeting or event that meets the basic definition.

project charter A document that states a project exists and provides the project manager with written authority to begin work; it details project goals, roles, and responsibilities, primary stakeholders, and the level of authority for a project manager.

project management (PM) The process of planning, organizing, directing, and controlling resources for a project.

project manager The leader of the project team, who fosters collaboration through project-management tools and techniques between key project stakeholder groups.

project team A group of individuals, usually managers, who represent internal departments, functions, or offices, and work together to achieve the project objectives.

psychographic Analysis of consumer lifestyles to create a detailed customer profile. Market researchers conduct psychographic research by asking consumers to agree or disagree with statements on activities, interests, and opinions.

Q

Quick-Response Code (QR Code) Easily readable barcodes that when scanned with a QR decoder (usually available on smartphones) can be translated into a URL, a telephone number, a bit of text, or other data.

R

real-time webcast A live webcast, commonly referred to as streaming, that sends a signal straight to the computer or other mobile device without saving the data or transmission to a hard disk.

recommended or preferred provider A service provider identified by venue personnel that has worked well in the facility and meets the minimum expectations of performance.

relocation/walk clause Clause protecting a guest holding a confirmed sleeping room reservation who is denied accommodations at the hotel upon arrival and is relocated to another hotel.

revenue The money generated from the supply of products and services, including hosting a meeting, over a period of time.

risk assessment A process designed to safeguard the organization and various elements of a meeting by minimizing the amount or severity of harmful events that may occur.

room audit An effective process designed to find attendees who locate and occupy rooms outside the contracted room block with a hotel; the activity assists in avoiding attrition fees.

room set A configuration of tables, chairs, and other equipment that reinforces the communication flow and creates the ambience to enhance the meeting experience; e.g., theater style, classroom layout.

rooms outside the block (ROB) Rooms that are reserved by a conference attendee in a contracted conference hotel, but are not counted in the group's contracted block.

rooms outside the contracted hotel (ROCH) Rooms that are reserved by a conference attendee, but are not in a contracted hotel block.

S

scope creep A subtle process that begins with small adjustments to the project's original goals and results in the project becoming improperly defined, documented, or controlled.

search engine optimization (SEO) Improving a website's presence in organic search engine results.

short-message service (SMS) A text messaging service component of phone, web, or mobile communication systems. It uses standardized communication protocols to allow fixed line or mobile phone devices to exchange short text messages.

sourcing A business term referring to procurement practices, such as identifying, qualifying, and selecting potential providers of products or services.

speaker preparation/ready room A space set aside at the meeting venue for speakers to review presentations.

stakeholder Internal and external person, group, or organization that has an interest in, or is impacted by, another organization's actions.

strategic alignment Strategic alignment occurs when the activities taking place and the results achieved in an organization are in accordance with its stated aspirations, i.e., strategies, goals, and objectives.

Strategic Meetings Management Program (SMMP) One type of portfolio management that primarily focuses on cost reduction and efficiency. Companies with an SMMP use specialized software to centrally track all aspects of meeting spend across a department or an entire organization.

strategic sourcing A procurement process that continuously improves by re-evaluating purchasing activities to reduce costs, while maintaining or improving value to the relationship.

strategic thinking An approach to thinking and decision-making that takes into account the context of the organization's broader strategies and goals, which is not limited to high-level decisions that affect the whole organization, and is required of all leaders when they are contemplating any aspiration or initiative.

strategy A broadly defined direction and use of an organization's resources that achieves a unique and differentiated advantage for an organization; in fact, it advances an organization by aligning and organizing resources.

T

teaser An advertisement that attracts customers by offering something extra or free.

threat A source of danger or vulnerability causing concern for the safety and security of individuals or property; same as hazard.

total cost In regard to a meeting, can be described as the total expenses, i.e., fixed costs plus the variable costs, needed to produce a meeting.

touchpoint Any point of contact between the meeting organizer and potential attendee; from a marketing perspective, it is used to keep a product or meeting in front of audience.

triple bottom line A concept that incorporates the holistic view of sustainability (i.e., social, cultural, environmental, and economic) into business decisions; this holistic focus is also called "the three P's": people, planet, and profits.

truss A structure comprising five or more triangular units constructed with straight members whose ends are connected at joints referred to as "nodes." In audiovisual staging, the planar truss is the most common. It is used in long sections that can be interconnected to form different shapes and used to hang lights, speakers, projectors, or any other elements that need to be suspended from the ceiling.

V

vertical exhibition An exhibition that is limited in scope and focused specifically on an industry segment.

virtual meeting A gathering of people in an online environment for a common purpose.

W

waiver clause A clause that entitles both parties to take measures to prevent or reduce loss without prejudice to the rights of either party.

wayfinding Encompasses all of the ways in which people and animals orient themselves in physical space and navigate from place to place. Offering indoor maps for handheld mobile devices is becoming common, as are digital information kiosk systems.

work breakdown structure (WBS) An organized framework identifying the tasks, responsibilities, and time frame required to complete a project.

References

2012 economic significance study key findings. (2013). Convention Industry Council. Retrieved from http://www.conventionindustry.org/ResearchInfo/EconomicSignificanceStudy/ESSKeyFindings.aspx

2013 annual report. (2014). Professional Convention Management Association. Retrieved from http://pcma.org/docs/default-source/default-document-library/2013-annual-report.pdf?sfvrsn=4

2014 global meetings and events forecast. (2014). American Express Meetings and Events, p. 21. Retrieved from https://www.amexglobalbusinesstravel.com/wp-content/uploads/2013/11/2014_Meetings_Forecast_US_letter_final_LR.pdf

About the CIC. (2014). CIC facts. Convention Industry Council. Retrieved from http://www.conventionindustry.org/AboutCIC/CICFacts.aspx

Adams, S. (2014, January 7). The most stressful jobs of 2014. *Forbes*. Retrieved from http://www.forbes.com/sites/susanadams/2014/01/07/the-most-stressful-jobs-of-2014

Anderson, C. (2008, July 8). *The long tail: Why the future of business is selling less of more*. New York: Hyperion (Revised edition).

APEX industry glossary. (2011). Convention Industry Council. Retrieved from http://www.conventionindustry.org/standardspractices/apex/glossary.aspx

APEX post-event report template. (2005). Convention Industry Council. Retrieved from http://www.conventionindustry.org/Files/APEX/APEX_Post_Event_Report.pdf

APEX RFP workbook. (2012). Convention Industry Council. Retrieved from http://www.conventionindustry.org/StandardsPractices/APEX/RFPWorkbook.aspx

Arieff, A. (2014, January 28). To inspire learning, architects reimagine learning spaces. Retrieved from MindShift website: http://blogs.kqed.org/mindshift/2014/01/to-inspire-learning-architects-reimagine-learning-spaces/

Arvey, R. D. (n.d.). Why face-to-face meetings matter. White paper prepared for Hilton Hotels. Retrieved from http://www.iacconline.org/content/files/whyface-to-facebusinessmeetingsmatter.pdf

Ashe-Edmunds, S. (n.d.). How to develop a marketing plan budget. Retrieved from http://smallbusiness.chron.com/develop-marketing-plan-budget-39809.html

ASQ. (2014). *Total quality management (TQM)*. American Society for Quality. Retrieved from http://asq.org/learn-about-quality/total-quality-management/overview/overview.html

Attendee direct spending estimate, SM40.14. (2014). Dallas, TX: Center for Exhibition Industry Research.

Bain, B. (2005, November 4). Former president of the Long Island Convention and Visitors Bureau sentenced to 840 hours of community service, $10,000 in restitution for filing bogus expense reports. Retrieved from http://www.hotel-online.com/News/PR2005_4th/Nov05_LongIslandCVB.html

Batten, M. C. (2013). A history of associations. Canadian Society of Association Executives. Retrieved from http://www.csae.com/AboutCSAE/AHistoryofAssociations.aspx

Beal, G. M., Bohlen, J. M., & Raudabaugh, J. N. (1962). *Leadership and group action*. Iowa City, IA: University of Iowa Press.

Beck, J. (2006). The environment for meetings and events. In G. C. Ramsborg, et al (Ed.), *Professional meeting management* (5th ed., pp. 337–358). Dubuque, IA: Kendall/Hunt.

Bergevin, P., Morris, D., & Smith R. M. (1963). *Adult education procedures: A handbook of tested patterns for effective participation.* New York: Seabury Press.

Best practices for sustainability in the audio visual staging industry: greening the audio visual staging company. (2007). *Pulse Staging & Events*. Retrieved from the Meeting Professionals International website: http://www.mpiweb.org/cms/mpiweb/uploads/doclibrary/256398_1192009_90759_pm_.pdf

Betzig, V. (2006). Effectively managing your meeting's budget and financial success. In G. C. Ramsborg, et al (Ed.), *Professional meeting management* (5th ed., pp. 28–48). Dubuque, IA: Kendall/Hunt.

Bolman, T. (2006). The conference center difference. In G. C. Ramsborg, et al (Ed.), *Professional meeting management* (5th ed., pp. 213–219). Dubuque, IA: Kendall/Hunt.

Boo, S., & Park, E. (2013). An examination of green intention: The effect of environmental knowledge and educational experiences on meeting planners' implementation of green meeting practices. *Journal of Sustainable Tourism, 21*(8), 1129–1147.

Boone, M. (2009). The four elements of strategic value for meetings and events. White paper. Dallas, TX: MPI Foundation. Retrieved from http://www.mpiweb.org/cms/uploadedFiles/Education_and_Events/Webinar_Series/TheCaseforMeetings.pdf

Boone, M. (2012). Interview Part II: A discussion between Mary Boone and Liz Guthridge. Retrieved from http://www.maryboone.com/index.php?option=com_content&view=article&id=111:interview-part-ii&catid=79:thought-leadership

Bracken, S. & Shure, P. (2006). Housing and room block management. In G. C. Ramsborg, et al (Ed.), *Professional meeting management* (5th ed., pp. 375–397). Dubuque, IA: Kendall/Hunt.

Brady, K., Henson, P., & Fava, J. (1999). Sustainability, eco-efficiency, life-cycle management, and business strategy. *Environmental Quality Management, 8*(3), 33–41.

Brewer, C. (1995). *Music and learning*. Tucson, AZ: Zephyr Press.

Bureau of Labor Statistics. (2012, July 25). Number of jobs held, labor market activity, and earnings growth among the youngest baby boomers: Results from a longitudinal survey. Retrieved from U.S. Department of Labor website: http://www.bls.gov/news.release/nlsoy.nr0.htm

Carlisle, K. G. (2006). Taming the registration beast. In G. C. Ramsborg, et al (Ed.), *Professional meeting management* (5th ed., pp. 359–374). Dubuque, IA: Kendall/Hunt.

Carter, J. (2014, May). Ideal formats for video playback. Retrieved from Alford Media Services, Beyond Burgundy Blog website: http://www.alfordmedia.com/beyond-burgundy-blog-b3/ideal-formats-for-video-playback

Cecil, A. K., Reed, B. J., & Reed, L. R. (2014). Meeting-related programs in higher education worldwide. Unpublished database.

CEIR index report: An analysis of the 2014 exhibition industry and future outlook. (2014, 10th ed.). Dallas, TX: Center for Exhibition Industry Research.

Center for Exhibition Industry Research (CEIR). (2013). Welcome to the center for exhibition industry research. Retrieved from http://www.ceir.org

Centers for Disease Control. (2006, November 30). Risk management plan. Retrieved from http://www2a.cdc.gov/cdcup/library/templates/default.htm#.VEo4xRaK4ds

CMP international standards (CMP-IS). (2011). Alexandria, VA: Convention Industry Council.

Convention Industry Council. (2008). Function room and set-ups. In *Convention industry manual* (8th ed., pp. 323–340). Washington D. C.: Convention Industry Council.

Craig, T. & McNamara, T. (2014, June 2). Known unknowns in global supply chains. *Supply Chain Management Review*. Retrieved from www.scmr.com/view/known_unknowns_in_global_supply_chains/procurement

Cruz, S. (2012, April 23). Top ten U.S. convention centers. *USA Business Review*. Retrieved from http://www.businessreviewusa.com/business_leaders/top-ten-us-convention-centers

Culinary Institute of America, The. (2009). *Remarkable service: A guide to winning and keeping customers for servers, managers, and restaurant owners*. New York: John Wiley & Sons.

Dallas, M. E. (2011, September 16). Research reveals why hungry people get cranky. *HeathDay*. Retrieved from http://consumer.healthday.com/mental-health-information-25/behavior-health-news-56/research-reveals-why-hungry-people-get-cranky-656938.html

Dallmeyer, R. & Ducate, D. (2006). A history of exhibitions. In Kent, P. (Ed.), *Art of the show* (3rd ed., pp. 34–49). Dallas, TX: International Association of Exhibitions and Events™.

DeMers, J. (2013, May 14). The history of infographics. Retrieved from http://www.audiencebloom.com/2013/05/the-history-of-infographics-infographic/

Dopson, L. R. & Hayes, D. K. (2009). *Managerial accounting for the hospitality industry.* Hoboken, NJ: John Wiley & Sons.

Doran, G. T. (1981). There's a S.M.A.R.T. way to write management's goals and objectives. *Management Review, 70*(11), 35–36.

Dosh, C. (2012, September). CMP series: Give & take. *Convene, 26*(9), 73–80.

Drew S. & Cooper J. M. (2006). Effective meeting communications and onsite operations. In G. C. Ramsborg, et al (Ed.), *Professional meeting management* (5th ed., pp. 553–562). Dubuque, IA: Kendall/Hunt.

DuBois, D. & Gonzales, K. (2013). Destination marketing organizations. In G. C. Ramsborg, et al (Ed.), *The art of the show* (4th ed., pp. 123–137). Dallas, TX: International Association of Exhibitions and Events™.

Ducate, D. & Breden, C. (2013). Exhibitions defined. In G. C. Ramsborg, et al (Ed.), *The art of the show* (4th ed., pp. 15–22). Dallas, TX: International Association of Exhibitions and Events™.

Duffy, C. & McEuen, M. B. (2010). The future of meetings: The case for face-to-face meetings. Retrieved from https://www.hotelschool.cornell.edu/research/chr/pubs/perspective/perspective-15297.html

Economic significance of meetings to the U.S. economy. (2012). Convention Industry Council. Retrieved from http://www.conventionindustry.org/Files/2012%20ESS/140210%20Fact%20Sheet%20FINAL.pdf

Economics and Statistics Administration. (2014, September 12). Advance monthly sales for retail and food services. United States Department of Commerce. Retrieved from http://www.esa.doc.gov/economic-indicators/economic-indicators

Einstein, A. (1879–1955). Quote. Retrieved from http://www.gurteen.com/gurteen/gurteen.nsf/id/X0006F576/

Elkington, J. (1998, Autumn, Fall). Partnerships from cannibals with forks: The triple bottom line of 21st century business. *Environmental Quality Management, 8*(1), 37–51.

Email marketing. (2013). Retrieved from http://p5marketing.com/email-marketing-effective-strategy/

Endean, T. (2014). Skill 17: Design environment. In *Convention industry manual* (9th ed., pp. 174–190). Alexandria, VA: Convention Industry Council.

Esty, D. & Winston, A. (2009). *Green to gold: How smart companies use environmental strategy to innovate, create value, and build competitive advantage.* Hoboken, NJ: Wiley & Sons.

Evaluating and implementing cubic content into linear exhibit space. (2011). Dallas, TX: International Association of Exhibitions and Events™.

Exhibition floor interaction: What attendees want, AC40.14. (2014). Dallas, TX: Center for Exhibition Industry Research.

Exhibitor direct spending estimate, SM41.14. (2014). Dallas, TX: Center for Exhibition Industry Research.

Facility overview. (2014). McCormick Place. Retrieved from http://www.mccormickplace.com/facility-overview/facility.php

Facts and statistics. (n.d.). Food Allergy Research & Education. Retrieved from http://www.foodallergy.org/facts-and-stats

Figge, F., Hahn, T., Schaltegger, S., & Wagner, M. (2002). The sustainability balanced scorecard: Linking sustainability management to business strategy. *Business Strategy and the Environment, 11*(5), 269–284.

Finkel, C. L. (1987). *Total immersion learning environment.* New York, NY: Conference Center Development Corporation.

Fishkind & Associates. (2014). The fiscal and economic impact of the OCCC 2013. Retrieved from the Orange County Convention Center website: http://www.occc.net/community/

Fleming, N. D. (1995). I'm different; not dumb. Modes of presentation (VARK) in the tertiary classroom. In Zelmer, A., (Ed.) *Research and Development in Higher Education*, Proceedings of the 1995 Annual Conference of the Higher Education and Research Development Society of Australia (HERDSA), HERDSA, Vol. 18, pp. 308–313. Retrieved from http://www.vark-learn.com/documents/different_not_dumb.pdf

Fleming, N. D. (2001). *Teaching and learning styles: VARK strategies.* Christchurch, N.Z.: N. D. Fleming.

Foster, J. (2006, May 19). John's thoughts on attrition and cancellation. *VNUTravel.* Retrieved from http://vnutravel.typepad.com/migurus/2006/05/johns_thoughts_.html

Fox, S. & Rainie, L. (2014, February). The web at 25 in the U.S. Retrieved from Pew Research website: http://www.pewinternet.org/2014/02/27/the-web-at-25-in-the-u-s

Fryatt, J., Mora, R., Janssen, R., John, R., & Smith, S. (2012a). How-to guide: Hybrid meetings. Retrieved from Meeting Professionals International website: http://www.mpiweb.org/_secure/HybridHowTo.pdf

Fryatt, J., Mora, R., Janssen, R., John, R., & Smith, S. (2012b, September). Hybrid meetings and events. Dallas, TX: Meeting Professionals International. Retrieved from http://www.mpiweb.org/_secure/HybridResearch.pdf

Gardner, H. (2011, March 29). *Frames of mind: The theory of multiple intelligences* (3rd ed.). New York: Basic Books.

Global reporting initiative. (2012a). Global reporting initiative, GRI, sustainability reporting guidelines, G3. Retrieved from http://www.globalreporting.org

Global reporting initiative. (2012b). What is the event organizers supplement? Retrieved from https://www.globalreporting.org/reporting/sector-guidance/sector-guidance/event-organizers/Pages/default.aspx

Glynn, S. (2013, March 29). Music benefits both mental and physical health. *Medical News Today.* Retrieved from http://www.medicalnewstoday.com/articles/258383.php

Goldblatt, J. (2005). Advertising, public relations, promotions, and sponsorship. In *Special events: Event leadership for a new world* (4th ed., pp. 287–289). Hoboken, NJ: John Wiley & Sons.

Goldblatt, J. and Nelson, K. (2001). *The international dictionary of event management* (2nd ed.). New York: John Wiley & Sons.

Goodman, T. (Ed.). (2007). John D. Rockefeller as quoted in *The Forbes book of business quotations*. New York: Black Dog & Eventual Publishers.

Guide to room block management: How to avoid attrition charges (2014, rev. ed.). Twinsburg, OH: Experient, a Maritz Travel Company.

Guidelines for developing great RFPs. (2003, February 1). *MeetingsNet.* Retrieved from http://meetingsnet.com/religioussmerf/guidelines-developing-great-rfps

Hatch, S. & Kovaleski, D. (2010, April 20). Eruption disruption: Meetings scramble after flight cancellations. *MeetingsNet.* Retrieved from http://meetingsnet.com/corporate-meetings/eruption-disruption-meetings-scramble-after-flight-cancellations

Headquarter, Department of the Army. (1993). *A leader's guide to after-action reviews.* Washington, D. C.: U.S. Army Combined Arms Command.

Heinrich, R., Molenda, M., Russell, J. D., & Smaldino, S. E. (1996). *Instructional media and technologies for learning*. Englewood Cliffs, NJ: Merrill.

Hot environments: Health effects and first aid. (2014, June 12). Canadian Centre for Occupational Health & Safety. Retrieved from http://www.ccohs.ca/oshanswers/phys_agents/heat_health.html

HotelOnline (2007, September 11). Widow of Hollywood director-producer Moustapha Akkad sues Global Hyatt Corporation for Wrongful Death. Retrieved from http://www.hotel-online.com/News/PR2007_3rd/Sept07_MAkkad.html

Humphrey, A. (2005, December). SWOT analysis for management consulting. *Stanford Research Institute Newsletter,* pp. 7–8. Retrieved from http://www.sri.com/sites/default/files/brochures/dec-05.pdf

IACC quality standards. (2012, December 5). International Association of Conference Centres. Retrieved from http://www.iacconline.org/about/index.cfm?fuseaction=memcrit

Institute for Supply Management (2014). The future of purchasing and supply: Strategic sourcing. *ISM Report of Business.* Retrieved from http://www.ism.ws/pubs/content.cfm?ItemNumber=9721

Institute of Food Technologists (IFT). (2012, June 29). Skipping breakfast can lead to unhealthy habits all day long. *ScienceDaily.* Retrieved from http://www.sciencedaily.com/releases/2012/06/120629143045.htm

International Association of Exhibitions and Events™ (IAEE). (n.d.) [Website]. Retrieved from http://www.iaee.com/about/who-we-are/

ISO 9000—Quality management. (2005). Retrieved from the International Organization for Standardization website: http://www.iso.org/iso/home/standards/management-standards/iso_9000.htm

ITU. (2014, May 5). ITU releases 2014 ICT figures. Retrieved from http://www.itu.int/net/pressoffice/press_releases/2014/23.aspx#.U7K5pBaK4dt

James, J. (2012). Data never sleeps [infographic]. Retrieved from http://www.domo.com/blog/2012/06/how-much-data-is-created-every-minute/

Jantsch, J. (2009, November 18). What the heck is integrated marketing anyway? Retrieved from http://www.ducttapemarketing.com/blog/2009/11/18/what-the-heck-is-integrated-marketing-anyway/

Johnson, S. (2014, April). A full plate. *Corporate & Incentive Travel,* 32(4), 26–29.

Johnson, W. (2006). Program design and development. In G. C. Ramsborg, et al (Ed.), *Professional meeting management* (5th ed., pp. 265–282). Dubuque, IA: Kendall/Hunt.

Kirkpatrick, D. L. & Kirkpatrick, J. D. (2007). *Implementing the four levels*. San Francisco: Berrett-Koehler.

Knowles, M. S., Holton III, E. F., & Swanson, R. A. (2011). *The adult learner: The definitive classic in adult education and human resource development* (7th ed.). Florence, KY: Taylor & Francis.

Krotz, A. (2011). How to engage a customer before nailing the sale. Retrieved from http://www.microsoft.com/business/en-us/resources/marketing/customer-service-acquisition/how-to-engage-a-customer-before-nailing-the-sale.aspx?fbid=mmSJ-d477pn

Krugman, C. (2010). Contingency planning and business continuity. Presented at Meeting Professionals International CMM Program, Dallas, TX.

Lanyon. (2013, December). Big data: Transforming meetings and events with better intelligence.

Lewis, K. (2006). Site selection. In G. C. Ramsborg, et al (Ed.), *Professional meeting management* (5th ed., pp. 143–159). Dubuque, IA: Kendall/Hunt.

Lippman, P. (2010) Can the physical environment have an impact on the learning environment? ISSN 2072-7925 CELE Exchange 2010/13, OECD. Retrieved from http://www.oecd.org/education/innovation-education/entreforeffectivelearningenvironmentscele/46413458.pdf

Loomis, C. (2012, August). Feed your head. *Smart Meetings The Magazine, 11*(8), 56–62.

Lubin, D. & Esty, D. (2010). The sustainability imperative. *Harvard Business Review, 88*(5), 42–50.

Lundquist, I. (2011). *Results-driven event planning*. TLC Publishing: Roseville, CA.

Lutz, D. (2014, April). Net value. *Convene, 28*(4), 38.

Marketers find exhibitions an essential marketing and sales tactic, PE3.11.3. (2011). Dallas, TX: Center for Exhibition Industry Research.

MBECS (The). Meeting and Business Event Competency Standards. (2011). Canadian Tourism Human Resource Council. Ottawa, Ontario, Canada.

McEun, M. B. & Duffy, C. (2010, September). The future of meetings: The case for face-to-face. Retrieved from http://www.maritz.com/face2face

McKinley, S. (2014, April 9). Six major event sustainability issues and how to solve them. Event Manager Blog. Retrieved from http://www.eventmanagerblog.com/event-sustainability-issues#BVMI3ilrk0dI9cuC.99Carbon Emissions

Meeting and business events competency standards curriculum guide. (2012). Dallas, TX: Meeting Professionals International.

Meetings mean business. (2014). *Meetings Mean Business Coalition*. Retrieved from http://www.meetingsmeanbusiness.com/index.php#about

Miller, B. & Ramsborg, G. C. (2006). Writing effective program outcomes. In G. C. Ramsborg, et al (Ed.), *Professional meeting management* (5th ed., pp. 283–303). Dubuque, IA: Kendall/Hunt.

Miller, B. D. (2012, April 2). Final management deficiency report: Public buildings service. U. S. General Services Administration. Retrieved from *Washington Post* website: http://www.washingtonpost.com/r/2010-2019/WashingtonPost/2012/04/03/National-Politics/Graphics/GSAreport040212.pdf

Mind Tools. (2014). Corporate website. Retrieved from http://www.mindtools.com/pages/article/newTMC_05_1.htm

Morrison, M. (2007). PESTLE analysis tool. Retrieved from http://rapidbi.com/the-pestle-analysis-tool/

Morriss, P. G. B. (1925). *How to plan a convention*. Chicago: The Drake Publishing Company.

Munford, L. (2012, December 10). What is integrated marketing communications? Retrieved from http://www.braatheenterprises.com/virtualproject/business/marketing/what-is-integrated-marketing-communications/

Mutnik, G. E. (2006). It's showtime: Final instructions to the facility and your supplier team. In G. C. Ramsborg, et al (Ed.), *Professional meeting management* (5th ed., pp. 523–534). Dubuque, IA: Kendall/Hunt.

Myhill, M. and Phillips, J. J. (2006). Determine the success of your meeting. In G. C. Ramsborg, et al (Ed.), *Professional meeting management* (5th ed., pp. 711–724). Dubuque, IA: Kendall/Hunt.

Neufeldt, V. (1996). Webster new world college dictionary (3rd ed.). New York: Simon & Schuster Macmillan.

NFPA 1600 standard on disaster/emergency management, and business continuity programs. (2007). National Fire Protection Association. Retrieved from http://www.nfpa.org/catalog/product.asp?pid=160013

Nijja, N. (2012, June 15). How to leverage paid tactics in social media. Retrieved from http://greatfinds.icrossing.com/how-to-leverage-paid-tactics-in-social-media/

Nisen, M. (2013, May 25). How to know if you're too old to call yourself a millennial. *Business Insider*. Retrieved from http://www.businessinsider.com/definition-of-generational-cohorts-2013-5

Ogin, G. (2014). Ask the experts. Retrieved from http://www.physlink.com/education/askexperts/ae420.cfm

Oldham, K. (2009, October 13). WTO meeting and protests in Seattle (1999). Retrieved from http://www.historylink.org/index.cfm?displaypage=output.cfm&file_id=9183

Orange County Convention Center. (2014). Retrieved from http://www.occc.net/community/

Owen, H. (2012). *Open space technology: A user's guide.* (3rd ed.). San Francisco: Berrett-Koehler.

Palmer, B. D. & Jenkins, D. C. (2006). Hiring speakers and working with speaker bureau. In G. C. Ramsborg, et al (Ed.), *Professional meeting management* (5th ed., pp. 305–316). Dubuque, IA: Kendall/Hunt.

Patterson, L. (2009, July 21). Getting the biggest bang for your social media buck. Retrieved from http://www.chiefmarketer.com/web-marketing/getting-the-biggest-bang-for-your-social-media-buck-21072009

PCMA history. (2014). Professional Convention Management Association. Retrieved from http://www.pcma.org/pcma-defined/about-pcma/pcma-history#.U3V9AvZGiWU

PCMA professional ethics' checklist. (2009). Professional Convention Management Association. Retrieved from http://www.planninghelper.com/spv-131.aspx

Peacy, K. (2006). Committees, volunteers, and staff: Working together to make meetings successful. In G. C. Ramsborg, et al (Ed.), *Professional meeting management* (5th ed., pp. 115–128). Dubuque, IA: Kendall/Hunt.

Phelan, K. & Mills, J. (2011). An exploratory study of knowledge, skills, and abilities (KSAs) needed in undergraduate hospitality curriculums in the convention industry. *Journal of Human Resources in Hospitality and Tourism*, *10*(1), 96–116.

Phillips, J. J. (1983). *Handbook of training evaluation and measurement methods*. Houston, TX: Gulf Publishing Co.

Phillips, J. J. (2003). *Return on investment in training and performance improvement programs.* (2nd ed., p. 12). Boston: Butterworth-Heinemann.

Phillips, J., Myhill, M., & McDonough, J. (2007). *Proving the value of meetings & events: How and why to measure ROI.* Private publisher. ROI Institute and Meeting Professionals International.

Pine, B. J. and Gilmore, J. H. (2011). *The experience economy*. Boston, MA: Harvard Business Review.

Pizam, A. (Ed). (2012). *International encyclopedia of hospitality management* (2nd ed., p. 211). Florence, KY: Taylor & Francis.

PMBOK® Guide. (2013). *Project management body of knowledge (PMBOK® Guide)* (5th ed.). Project Management Institute. Newtown Square, PA: PMI.

PMI. (2014). *About PMI.* Project Management Institute. Retrieved from http://www.pmi.org

Pofeldt, E. (2014, Spring). MPI meetings outlook: 2014 spring edition. Meeting Professionals International. Retrieved from http://www.mpiweb.org/docs/default-source/research-and-reports/meetings-outlook-spring-web.pdf

Porter, M. & Kramer, M. (2006). Strategy and society: The link between competitive advantage and corporate social responsibility. *Harvard Business Review, 84*(12), 78–92.

Porter, M. & Kramer, M. (2011). Creating shared value. *Harvard Business Review, 89*(1/2), 62–77.

Preston, C. & Hoyle, L. (2012). E-event marketing. In *Event marketing: How to successfully promote events, festivals, conventions, and expositions* (2nd ed., 111–136). Hoboken, NJ: John Wiley & Sons.

Principles of professional and ethical conduct. (2009). Professional Convention Management Association. Retrieved from https://www.pcma.org/docs/pcma-defined-docs/code_of_ethics.pdf?sfvrsn=0

Prosci. (2014). *Change management series*. Prosci, Inc. Retrieved from www.change-management.com/prosci_change_series.pdf

Quast, L. (2013, April 15). How to conduct a personal SWOT analysis. Retrieved from http://www.forbes.com/sites/lisaquast/2013/04/15/how-to-conduct-a-personal-s-w-o-t-analysis/

Ramsborg, G. C. & Tinnish, S. M. (2008a, January). How adults learn, now: Meetings remix, Part 1. *Convene, 22*(1), 40–47.

Ramsborg, G. C. & Tinnish, S. M. (2008b, February). How adults learn, now: Meetings remix, Part 2. *Convene, 22*(2), 46–51.

Robinson, R. D. (1979). *An introduction to helping adults learn and change.* Milwaukee, WI: Omnibook Co.

Rottman, G. (2013, April 10). Making email marketing work for your conference. Retrieved from http://www.rottmancreative.com/inspiration/making-email-marketing-work-for-your-conference-20130410/

Russell, M. (2014a, March). 23rd annual meetings market survey. *Convene, 28*(3), 43–60.

Russell, M. (2014b, February). Re-thinking risk. *Convene, 28*(2), 71–75.

Scenarios for the future: Convention exhibits & trade shows of 2016. (2013). Chicago: PCMA Education Foundation. Retrieved from http://pcma.org/docs/default-document-library/conventionresearch.pdf?sfvrsn=12

Schiff, A. (2012, June 14). DMA: Direct mail response rates beat digital. Retrieved from http://www.dmnews.com/dma-direct-mail-response-rates-beat-digital/article/245780/#

Schweitzer, M., Gilpin, L., & Frampton, S. (2004). Healing spaces: Elements of environmental design that make an impact on health. *The Journal of Alternative and Complementary Medicine, (10)* Supplement 1, (S-71–S-83).

Seaman, D. F., & Fellenz, R. A. (1989). *Effective strategies for teaching adults.* Columbus, OH: Merrill Publishing Co.

Seattle Police Department. (2000, April 4). The Seattle police department after action report: World trade organization ministerial conference (p. 41). Retrieved from http://www.seattle.gov/police/publications/WTO/WTO_AAR.PDF

Service-providing industries. (2014). Retrieved from U.S. Bureau of Labor Statistics website: http://www.bls.gov/iag/tgs/iag07.htm

SGMP's history and future. (2013). Society for Government Meeting Professionals. Retrieved from http://www.sgmp.org/about/history.cfm

Shock, P. (2006). Food and beverage arrangements. In Ramsborg, G. C., et al (Ed.), *Professional meeting management* (5th ed., pp. 399–417). Dubuque, IA: Kendall/Hunt.

Silvers, J. R. (2008). *Risk management for meetings and events.* Burlington, MA: Butterworth-Heinemann.

Society for Human Resource Management. (2014). Retrieved from Society for Human Resource Management website: http://conferences.shrm.org/

TEDx Speaker Guide. (n.d.). Retrieved from http://storage.ted.com/tedx/manuals/tedx_speaker_guide.pdf

Tesdahl, D. B. (2012, November 1). Attrition reduction strategies. *Successful Meetings.* Retrieved from http://www.successfulmeetings.com/article.aspx?id=15448

The Center. (2014). The Bertalanffy Center for the Study of Systems Science. Retrieved from http://www.bcsss.org/

Tinnish, S. M. (2007a). Starting with a need. *PMM5 Postscript: New directions in learning*, #2. [PDF]. Chicago: Professional Convention Management Association.

Tinnish, S. M. (2007b). Trade show trends. *PMM5 Postscript: New directions in learning*, #23. [PDF]. Chicago: Professional Convention Management Association.

Tinnish, S. M. & Mangal, S. M. (2012). Sustainable event marketing in the MICE industry: A theoretical framework. *Journal of Convention & Event Tourism, 13*(4), 227–249. DOI: 10.1080/15470148.2012.731850.

Tinnish, S. M. & Ramsborg, G. C. (2008c, May). How adults learn, now: Synthesizing, composing, designing. *Convene*, *22*(5), 73–78.

Tinnish, S. M. & Ramsborg, G. C. (2008d, December). How adults learn, now: The final score. *Convene, 22*(12), 113–118.

Toups, E. (2006). Marketing and promotion: Strategy and collaboration for success. In G. C. Ramsborg, et al (Ed.), *Professional meeting management* (5th ed., pp. 61–82). Dubuque, IA: Kendall/Hunt.

Tweed, K. (2010, September 29). Sustainability practices are really risk management. *Green Tech.* http://www.greentechmedia.com/articles/read/sustainability-is-really-risk-management

UFI (The Global Association of the Exhibition Industry). (n.d.) Foreword. Retrieved from http://www.ufi.org/Public/Default.aspx?Clef_SITESMAPS=142&Clef_SITESMAPS=146

UFI (The Global Association of the Exhibition Industry). (n.d.) Basic knowledge. Retrieved from http://www.ufi.org/Public/Default.aspx?Clef_SITESMAPS=142&Clef_SITESMAPS=151&Clef_SITESMAPS=152

University of Tasmania. (2007, April 4). Thermal Comfort Guidelines. [PDF]. Revision Reference No. 1.0

Veach, K. (2011, September 30). Infographic: Going social with event marketing. Retrieved from http://info.livemarketing.com/blog/bid/74047/INFOGRAPHIC-Going-Social-with-Event-Marketing

Vining, S. (2011, Spring). The Science of food for thought: Enhancing meetings through food. *Meeting discoveries.* Leesburg, VA: The National Conference Center. Retrieved from http://www.conferencecenter.com/var/conferencecenter/storage/original/application/bac7dd451f999b70767b43ee4ae301a2.pdf

Waddle, J. (2009, March). Protect your association from room-block "pirates." *Associations Now*. Retrieved from the ASAE website: http://www.asaecenter.org/Resources/ANowDetail.cfm?ItemNumber=39139

Welker, H. (2006). Presentation technology for 21st century meetings. Retrieved from the Corbin Ball website: http://www.corbinball.com/articles_technology/index.cfm?fuseaction=cor_av&artID=3601

What is public relations? PRSA's widely accepted definition. (2011–12). Public Relations Society of America. Retrieved from http://www.prsa.org/AboutPRSA/PublicRelationsDefined

White, S. (1972). Physical criteria for adult learning environments. Washington, D. C.: Adult Education Association of U.S.A., Commission on Planning Adult Learning Systems, Facilities, and Environments. (ERIC Document Reproduction Service No. ED080-882).

World Commission on Environment and Development (WCED). (1987). *Our common future*. Oxford: Oxford University Press, p. 43.

Worldwide mobile phone users: H1 2014 Forecast and comparative estimates. (2014, January 16). Retrieved from http://www.emarketer.com/Article/Smartphone-Users-Worldwide-Will-Total-175-Billion-2014/1010536

Yoo, J. & Chon, K. (2008, August). Factors affecting convention participation decision-making: Developing a measurement scale. *Journal of Travel Research, 47*(1), 113–122.

Figure Credits

All figures reprinted with permission.

Abbreviations

PCMA Professional Convention Management Association
WSCC Washington State Convention Center

About the Editorial Team

Cecil © 2011. Photography by Jim Patterson. **Krugman** © 2013. Courtesy of Carol Krugman. **Miller** © 2013. Photography by Kathy F. Atkinson. **Ramsborg** © 2010. Photography by Eric Futran. **Reed** © 2013. Courtesy of B. J. Reed. **Sperstad** © 2007. Photography by James Tkatch. **Vannucci** © 2006. Photography by Jack Gentry. Courtesy of Metro State Office of Communications.

Chapter 1

1.1. © 2014. Photography by Jacob Slaton. Courtesy of PCMA.

Chapter 2

2.5. © 2009. Boone Associates. **2.6.** © 2013. Photography by Jacob Slaton. Courtesy of PCMA.

Chapter 3

3.3. © 2013. Photography by Jacob Slaton. Courtesy of PCMA.

Chapter 4

4.3. © 2009. B. J. Reed, EdD, CMP. **4.7.** © 2014. Courtesy of WSCC. **4.9.** © 2004. James Simpson Theatre. Courtesy of The Field Museum, Chicago, Illinois. **4.10.** © 2014. Courtesy of WSCC. **4.11.** © 2014. Courtesy of WSCC. **4.12.** © 2013. Photography by Isaac Maiselman. Courtesy of JW Marriott, Chicago, Illinois, a Marriott Convention & Resort Network Hotel. **4.13.** © 2014. Courtesy of WSCC. **4.14.** © 2014. Courtesy of WSCC. **4.15.** © 2014. Courtesy of WSCC (left). © 2011. Photography by Jacob Slaton (right). Courtesy of PCMA. **4.16.** © 2013. Courtesy of Châteauform' Château de Nointel, Val d'Oise, France. **4.22.** © 2014. Photography by Jacob Slaton. Courtesy of PCMA. **4.23.** © 2011. Photography by Jacob Slaton. Courtesy of PCMA.

Chapter 5

5.9. Kemal Taner/Shutterstock.

Chapter 6

6.1. © 2014. Courtesy of Orange County Convention Center. **6.2.** © 2012. Courtesy of McCormick Place. **6.3.** © 2012. Courtesy of Châteauform' Château de Nointel, Val d'Oise, France. **6.4.** © 2012. Courtesy of Hilton Chicago. **6.5.** © 2014. Courtesy of Residence Inn Portland Pearl District by Marriott. **6.6.** © Disney. Courtesy of Disney. **6.7.** © 2012. Photography by Ramon C. Purcell. Courtesy of The Westin Detroit Metropolitan Airport. **6.8.** © Disney. Courtesy of Disney. **6.9.** © 2014. Photography by Jacob Slaton. Courtesy of PCMA. **6.10.** © 2011. Courtesy of the International Association of Exhibitions and Events™. **6.11.** © 2012. Courtesy of Gaylord Texan Resort & Convention Center, a Marriott Convention & Resort Network Hotel.

Chapter 7

7.2. © 2014. Courtesy of the Risk and Insurance Management Society, Inc. (RIMS). **7.4.** © 2012. Courtesy of the Risk and Insurance Management Society, Inc. (RIMS). **7.6.** © 2014. Courtesy of the Risk and Insurance Management Society, Inc. (RIMS). **7.7.** © 2014. Courtesy of the Risk and Insurance Management Society, Inc. (RIMS). **7.11.** © 2014. Courtesy of SecuritasUSA. **7.12.** Michaeljung/Shutterstock. **7.13.** Gardar Olafsson /Shutterstock.

Chapter 8

8.1. Golden Pixels LLC/Shutterstock. **8.5.** Andrey_Popov /Shutterstock. **8.8.** Fotofrog/iStock (left). Imagefactory studio/Shutterstock (right). **8.9.** PaulPaladin/Shutterstock.

Chapter 9

9.6. © 2013. Courtesy of p5marketing. **9.8.** © 2012. Courtesy of iCrossing, Inc. **9.9.** © 2011. Courtesy of Live Marketing.

Chapter 10

10.1. Luna Vandoorne/Shutterstock. **10.2.** Goodluz /Shutterstock. **P. 177.** © 2014. Photography by Jacob Slaton. Courtesy of PCMA. **10.3.** © 2013. Photography by Jacob Slaton. Courtesy of PCMA. **10.4.** © 2011. Photography by Jacob Slaton. Courtesy of PCMA. **10.5.** © 2011. Photography by Jacob Slaton. Courtesy of PCMA. **10.6.** © 2013. Photography by Jacob Slaton. Courtesy of PCMA. **10.7.** © 2013. Courtesy of CONEXPO-CON/AGG & IFPE. **10.8.** Goodluz/Shutterstock. **10.10.** © 2013. Photography by Jacob Slaton. Courtesy of PCMA. **10.12.** Diego Cervo/Shutterstock.

Chapter 11

11.1. © 2014. Courtesy of CONEXPO-CON/AGG. **11.2.** © 2014. Courtesy of the League of California Cities. **11.3.** © 2014. Photography by Global Experience Specialists (GES). Courtesy of Advanstar Communications, Inc. **11.4.** © 2014. Courtesy of Global Experience Specialists (GES). **11.5.** © 2014. Convention Photo by Joe Orlando. Courtesy of the Los Angeles Auto Show. **11.6.** © 2013. Courtesy of the Produce Marketing Association. **11.7.** © 2014. Courtesy of the American Society of Cataract and Refractive Surgery. **11.8.** © 2011. Courtesy of the Center for Exhibition Industry Research.

Chapter 12

12.4. © 2013. Photography by Jacob Slaton. Courtesy of PCMA. **12.6.** © 2014. Photography by Alford Media Services. Courtesy of Vemma Nutrition Company. **12.7.** © 2014. Courtesy of Alford Media Services, Inc. **12.8.** © 2014. Courtesy of Alford Media Services, Inc. **12.9.** © 2014. Courtesy of Alford Media Services, Inc.

Chapter 13

13.1. © 2013. Photography by Jacob Slaton. Courtesy of PCMA. **13.3.** © 2013. Photography by Jacob Slaton. Courtesy of PCMA. **13.4.** © 2013. Photography by Jacob Slaton. Courtesy of PCMA. **13.5.** © 2014. Courtesy of WSCC. **13.6.** © 2014. Courtesy of WSCC. **13.7.** © 2013. Photography by Jacob Slaton. Courtesy of PCMA. **13.8.** © 2014. Photography by Jacob Slaton. Courtesy of PCMA. **13.9.** © 2014. Courtesy of WSCC. **13.13.** © 2013. Photography by Jacob Slaton. Courtesy of PCMA. **13.14.** © 2014. Courtesy of WSCC.

Chapter 14

14.1. © 2012. Courtesy of Gaylord Texan Resort & Convention Center, a Marriott Convention & Resort Network Hotel. **14.4.** © 2013. Photography by Jacob Slaton. Courtesy of PCMA. **14.5.** © 2014. Photography by Jacob Slaton. Courtesy of PCMA. **14.6.** © 2013. Courtesy of WSCC. **14.7.** © 2013. Photography by Jacob Slaton. Courtesy of PCMA. **14.8.** © 2014. AIGA. **14.9.** © 2014. Courtesy of PSAV. **14.10.** © 2014. Courtesy of PSAV.

Chapter 15

15.1. © 2013. Courtesy of Association Management Center. **15.2.** © 2014. Courtesy of PSAV. **15.6.** © 2014. Courtesy of PSAV. **15.7.** © 2013. Courtesy of the Pritzker Military Museum & Library. **15.8.** © 2010. Photography by David Hall. Courtesy of Orlando World Center Marriott, a Marriott Convention & Resort Network Hotel. **15.9.** © 2014. Courtesy of Lanyon. **15.10.** © 2014. Courtesy of PSAV. **15.12.** © 2010–2014 Kirkpatrick Partners, LLC.

Chapter 16

16.2. © 2014. Courtesy of Kendall College. **16.3.** © 2006. Courtesy of Gaylord Opryland Resort & Convention Center, a Marriott Convention & Resort Network Hotel. **16.5.** © 2013. Photography by Jacob Slaton. Courtesy of PCMA. **16.6.** © 2014. Photography by Jacob Slaton. Courtesy of PCMA. **16.8.** © 2013. Photography by Jacob Slaton. Courtesy of PCMA. **16.9.** © 2013. Photography by Jacob Slaton. Courtesy of PCMA.

Index

A

B

C

D

E

M

Q

R

S

Notes

Notes

Notes